Studies in Judaism

CANON AND CONNECTION

Intertextuality in Judaism

Jacob Neusner

UNIVERSITY
PRESS OF
AMERICA

LANHAM • NEW YORK • LONDON

Copyright © 1987 by

University Press of America,® Inc.

4720 Boston Way
Lanham, MD 20706

3 Henrietta Street
London WC2E 8LU England

British Cataloging in Publication Information Available

Library of Congress Cataloging in Publication Data

Neusner, Jacob, 1932-
   Canon and connection.

   (Studies in Judaism)
   Includes index.
   1. Rabbinical literature—History and criticism.
   2. Judaism—Sacred books. I. Title. II. Series.
   BM496.5.N478   1987   296.1'2   86-26798
   ISBN 0-8191-5796-1 (alk paper)
   ISBN 0-8191-5797-X (pbk. : alk. paper)

All University Press of America books are produced on acid-free
paper which exceeds the minimum standards set by the National
Historical Publication and Records Commission.

CANON AND CONNECTION

Intertextuality in Judaism

For

Brian Stock

and his daughter

Maxime

CONTENTS

Part Three
TAXONOMIC CONNECTION

Preface

Synoptic texts must always be studied synoptically, even if one text is 'later' than another.

Shaye J. D. Cohen

This system, composed of interlocking and re-interlocking parts possessed of an organic connection one to another, is never really divisible.

Lawrence H Schiffman

...all units are so closely interwoven and simultaneously present that none can be considered in separation from any other at any given moment; it is a world of 'intertextuality'...

...interpretation is not essentially separate from the text itself–an external act intruded upon it–but rather the extension of the text, the uncovering of the connective network of relations, a part of the continuous revelation of the text itself, at bottom, another aspect of the text.

Susan Handelman

In analyzing a very old literature, the canonical writings of Judaism, this book raises a peculiarly contemporary issue, that of intertextuality. The literature, the canon of Judaism as it took shape in late antiquity, comprises documents that relate both to a single common book, the Hebrew Scripture or Old Testament, and also to one another. Consequently the holy books of Judaism in its formative period provide an ideal example of the meanings and uses of the critical initiative represented by intertextuality. The urgency of the matter, however, derives not from the traits of old writings, but from current and acute interest in the use of those writings for consideration of today's issues. Specifically, the relevance of the category, intertextuality, derives from a broadly-held and widely circulated characterization of the writings of the Judaic sages of late antiquity. Literary critics familiar with the writings of the ancient rabbis propose – as we see in the quotations above, representative of widely held opinion – to treat as harmonious, uniform, and indivisible the whole canon of Judaism, formed in late antiquity and represented by the Mishnah, Tosefta, two Talmuds, and various compilations of scriptural exegesis called *midrashim* . That literary judgment further accords with theological convictions of faithful Jews, whether Orthodox or Reform, Conservative or Israeli or Reconstructionist.

So we see a curious concatenation of contemporary hermeneutics and received theology, both parties concurring on how we are to read the classical books of Judaism. Each for its own reason maintains that these writings form a primary arena for intertextual reading of texts, which, they clearly propose, means that we always are to understand everything in light of everything else. The received hermeneutic, long governing how the ancient texts are read, invokes all passages in the exposition of each, and each for all: intertextuality as the paramount hermeneutic, resting on theological principles. Contemporary expositions follow suit, so Handelman: "The rabbinic world is, to use a contemporary term, one of *intertextuality*. Texts echo, interact, and interpenetrate...."[1]

But is that really true? In this book I systematically and in detail pursue that question. Specifically, I now ask whether the received, theological hermeneutic accords with the *intrinsic* literary traits of the literature at hand, and whether, further, answering that question may contribute to the debate on intertextuality a set of useful *exemplia gratia*. It follows that I propose now to ask whether that characterization of the documents at hand as exemplary instances of intertextuality and occasions, therefore, for the nurture of that theory of literary connection and continuity constitutes a literary judgment, based on intrinsic traits of the writings. I wonder whether it may constitute only a social and (for the believers) a theological judgment, resting on *extrinsic* and imputed traits.

My method in particular is to construct two entirely different ways of uncovering *intrinsic* connections between and among the documents and to find out whether, as a matter of fact, because of intrinsic traits of literary connection, all passages must be read in the light of all others. This exercise serves the broader purpose of investigating the heuristic and hermeneutical pertinence of the concept of intertextuality, as just now defined, to a literature that, on the face of it, invites the application of that very concept. Since I supply two sizable samples of the documents under discussion, the reader is able to participate in the systematic exercise at hand. No special knowledge of the rabbinic writings serves as a prerequisite for joining the discussion. Here we can both listen to characterizations of the literature and also examine a significant sample of the same literature, so comparing the one to the other. I mean, therefore, to address a very wide world, one that wants to learn how to read one text in relationship to others. So while the literature at hand is ancient and does not circulate widely, the issue enjoys broad currency and urgently demands attention.

Proponents of the intertextualist approach to the canon of Judaism claim to discern deep connections between one document and the next, so that all documents impose meanings upon each, and each demands a reading solely in the setting of the whole literature. I propose to test that approach by asking what

---

[1]*The Slayers of Moses* (Albany, 1982: State University of New York Press), p. 47.

intrinsic traits of the entirety of the corpus of Judaism in late antiquity validate an intertextualist reading of that corpus. Of interest is not the well-known fact that one text relates to another. That truism will not have surprised anyone who has ever opened a single text, since all texts cite Scripture, or any passage of the Talmud, since the Talmud cites the Mishnah. The position at hand addresses the *entirety* of the writings of the ancient rabbis, all together, all at once, everywhere and all the time. Readers cannot imagine that I exaggerate the radical-intertextualist position on the Judaic canon: everything, everywhere, all at once. I do not impute to the proponents of the intertextualist theory of rabbinic writings positions they do not take: *"all units are so closely interwoven and simultaneously present that none can be considered in separation from any other at any given moment."* Nor do the figures cited at the outset stand for idiosyncratic positions, since the received and paramount hermeneutic of the rabbinic literature demands precisely the reading they advocate. So we take up a genuinely orthodox hermeneutic, today advocated by nearly everyone.

Now I shall demonstrate that that hermeneutical claim is not only not true as a matter of literary fact (as distinct from theological conviction or social construction), it is in fact the exact opposite of the truth as a matter of literary fact. Viewed from the angle of their intrinsic traits, the documents scarcely connect at all. Intertextuality constitutes a social construction, a theological conviction, not a literary dimension of the canon at hand, not an operative category for hermeneutics. We can read these texts one by one, we do well to consult points of intersection with other texts of the same canon where relevant, but we have no reason as a matter of a literary interpretation to invoke that invitation to chaos represented by the counsel: read everything in light of everything, everywhere, all at once.

While meant to be read on its own, as a closed systemic statement, this book forms the middle segment of a protracted three part research program concerning the autonomy of the texts of formative Judaism, their connections to one another, and, finally, the continuity that links them all into a single canon. The first stage took me fifteen years. In it I described principal documents of the canon of Judaism as it took shape in late antiquity. Some of the results are listed in the appendices, as I cite my translations and discussions of individual documents. In this second phase I ask in reference to the same texts I have now described about how one document relates to others, thus a community of texts. In the third phase I shall investigate the continuities among all documents, thus a textual community. But I find myself some distance away from that third stage in the work, and I am in no hurry to reach it. So I move from autonomy, through connection, to continuity, and here we make our way through the difficult, middle passage of the work. Let me now explain more fully.

The writings of the sages of Judaism in late antiquity form a vast literature, each document bearing its own integrity, connected to others, and also continuous with the entire canon of which it forms a part. It follows that if you pick up any book written by ancient Judaic sages, you rightly expect to read what that book says on its own, beginning, middle, and end. You also will want to know how that book relates to others of its setting. That is because each book bears points in common with others. These include citing a common Scripture and addressing a shared program of interests. And, finally, you will wish to see a book in its broader role as part of the canon of Judaism, that is, of the Torah. For no document of the Judaism under discussion, that which came to its original expression in the Mishnah, ca. A.D. 200, and reached its full statement, in late antiquity, in the Talmud of Babylonia, stands on its own. All documents reach us through the medium of the Judaic community, and all of them join together because of their authority in that community, their standing as statements of the Torah. In all, therefore, we discern three dimensions by which any document of that Judaism may be measured: autonomy, connection, continuity. To review: a book in the canon at hand stands by itself, within its own covers; it also relates to other books of the same canon through specific connections, indicated by intrinsic traits of rhetoric, topic, and logic or by shared materials, common to a number of documents. And it also forms part of an undifferentiated canon, that is, the Torah, or Judaism, through the dimension of complete continuity. Hence among those three dimensions, autonomy, connection, continuity, we address the second.

To clarify the perspective of this study, let me invoke the analogy of a library. (In Chapter Two I shall return to this same analogy.) Books brought together form a library. Each title addresses its own program and makes its own points. But books produced by a cogent community constitute not merely a library but a canon: a set of compositions each of which contributes to a statement that transcends its own pages. The books exhibit intrinsic traits that make of them all *a community of texts*. We should know on the basis of those characteristics that the texts form a community even if we knew nothing more than the texts themselves. In the Judaic system of the dual Torah, moreover, the documents at hand form a canon. All of them find a place in the Torah. But that is a fact we know only on the basis of information deriving from sources other than the texts at hand, which, on their own, do not link each to all and all to every line of each. Extrinsic traits, that is imputed ones, make of the discrete writings a single and continuous, uniform statement: one whole Torah in the mythic language of Judaism. The community of Judaism imputes those traits, sees commonalities, uniformities, deep harmonies: one Torah of one God. In secular language, that community expresses its system – its world view, its way of life, its sense of itself as a society – by these choices, and finds its definition in them. Hence, in the nature of things, the community of Judaism forms *a textual community*. That cogent community that forms a canon out of a selection of books therefore participates in the process of authorship, just as the books exist in at least two dimensions.

Let us turn to the problem of this book, the community of texts. Since the present angle of vision may prove fresh, let me unpack its terms. I just now pointed to two dimensions, *autonomy*, on the one side, and *connection*, on the second. That is to say, a book enjoys its own autonomous standing, but it also situates itself in relationship to other books of the same classification. Each book bears its own statement and purpose, and each relates to others of the same classification. The community of texts therefore encompasses individuals who (singly or collectively) comprise (for the authorships: compose) books. But there is a set of facts that indicate how a book does not stand in isolation. These facts fall into several categories. Books may go over the same ground or make use in some measure of the same materials. The linkages between and among them therefore connect them. In Part Two I review those sorts of connections, of a virtually material character. Traits of rhetoric, logic, and topic may place into a single classification a number of diverse writings. In Part Three I conduct an exercise in the taxonomic classification of writings, showing connections in the form of shared traits of a more theoretical character. Then, as I said, there is the larger consensus of members who see relationships between one book and another and so join them together on a list of authoritative writings. So, as is clear, a book exists in the dimensions formed of its own contents and covers, but it also takes its place in the second and third dimensions of relationship to other books.

For purposes of description, I present two sizable appendices of texts, so that readers can form their own judgments of my analyses and theses. Appendix I serves Part Two, and Appendix II, Part Three. In the former I take up a very specific theory as to the relationships – the connections – among documents that do relate. So I present a sample of four texts that stand in what some hold is a synoptic relationship. In the latter, I address a theory of the literature that encompasses all writings of all times. So I have constructed an appendix to deal with a theory as to the character of the literature as a whole, and not merely one type of writing within it. For a sample for my probe I take up nine principal documents. Others can serve just as well.

In time to come I shall take up the study of the textual community, the one that takes the measure of the third dimension of the books of a canon. But it presently eludes clear definition and demonstration. It is the dimension of continuity not between one book and the next but among all the books of the canon. That dimension – social, not literary, extrinsic and adventitious, not intrinsic and cogent and logical – addresses the whole, seen all together and all at once. It marks off the outer limits of the galaxy of writings that all together form the canon. Drawing upon the analogy of books in canonical relationship, we may say that the third dimension finds its perspective in the larger building that takes in all the books all together. It of course comprises the community that determines what falls within the canon and what does not.

Another analogy draws our attention to stars: all of them suns of their respective systems, but also parts of larger congeries, and these yet components of still larger ones: the sun, the milky way, the entirety of matter. Seen near at hand, our sun is the only star, so by day. But at night when we see the skies, we realize that ours is not the only sun, but a star like other stars. And, penetrating into deep space, we understand that the whole – our solar system, our galaxy – finds its place in a vast realm indeed. Hard as it is to come to grips with the whole, seen all at once, so difficult it is to reckon with the textual community.

Defining that community in time to come will require that I specify the type of community I believe stands behind the documents and forms them into a whole, a library, a canon. For while an individual or a small authorship may write a given book, and affines, two or more like books, an entire aggregate of books will come together only when people of one mind bring them together: a textual community. What force, what gravity and matter and anti-matter, holds the whole together? How to know the limits of the textual community, since these are not indicated by the covers of a book or even the sides of a book shelf? That question remains far in the future. I then shall move from having worked out [1] the description of texts, read one by one, to the present work, [2] the analysis of those same texts seen in relationship to one another, that is, to comparison and contrast among a set of documents, hence to connection, and, ultimately, will proceed [3] to the interpretation of texts under the aspect of continuity, that is to say, eternity.

The social dimension of the texts before us requires scarcely any demonstration: it is the given of the Judaic community. My argument here is that the shared conventions of rhetoric, topic, and logic moreover validate an approach to the texts that ignores all social dimensions, for intrinsic to the writings we discern entirely formal and intrinsic points of intersection and connection as well. These formalities characterize texts drawn from a broad variety of social settings and transcend them all, hence commanding attention to form as distinct from social meaning, the intrinsic as much as extrinsic context. But precisely how these connections emerge from those intrinsic traits, and, more important, what they mean for the theory of appropriate hermeneutics for the literature at hand – these matters will generate interesting debate.

Jacob Neusner

August 13, 1986
Program in Judaic Studies
Brown University
Providence, Rhode Island 02912-1826 U.S.A.

Part One
INTRODUCTION

Chapter One
How Documents Relate and Why It Matters

I. HOW DOCUMENTS RELATE

Documents – cogent compositions made up of a number of complete units of thought – by definition exist on their own. That is to say, by invoking as part of our definition the trait of cogency of individual units as well as of the entire composite, we complete a definition of what a document is and is not. A document is a cogent composite of cogent statements. But, also by definition, none of these statements is read all by itself. A document forms an artifact of a social culture, and that in diverse dimensions. Cogency depends on shared rhetoric, logic of intelligible discourse, topic and program – all of these traits of mind, of culture. Someone writes a document, someone buys it, an entire society sustains the labor of literature. Hence we place any document into its culture and society.

Each document therefore exists in both a textual and literary context, and also a social dimension of culture and even of politics. As to the former, documents may form a community whose limits are delineated by shared conventions of thought and expression. Those exhibiting distinctive, even definitive traits, fall within the community, those that do not, remain without. These direct the author to one mode of topic, logic, and rhetoric, and not to some other. So much for intrinsic traits. As to the extrinsic ones, readers bring to documents diverse instruments of intelligibility, knowledge of the grammar of not only language but also thought. That is why they can read one document and not some other. So one relationship derives from a literary culture, which forms the authorship of a document, and the other from a social culture. The literary bond links document to document, and the essentially social bond links reader to document – and also document (through the authorship, individual or collective) to reader. The one relationship is exhibited through intrinsic traits of language and style, logic, rhetoric, and topic, and the other through extrinsic traits of curiosity, acceptance and authority. While documents find their place in their own literary world and also in a larger social one, the two aspects have to remain distinct, the one textual, the other contextual.

It follows that relationships between and among documents also matter for two distinct reasons. The intrinsic relationships, which are formal, guide us to traits of intelligibility, teaching us through our encounter with one document how to read some other of its type or class. If we know how to read a document of one type, we may venture to read another of the same type, but not – without instruction – one of some other type altogether. The extrinsic relationships, which derive from context and are relative to community, direct us to how to understand a document as an artifact of culture and society. Traits not of documents but of doctrines affecting a broad range of documents come into play. The document, whatever its contents, therefore becomes an instrument of social culture, e.g., theology and politics, a community's public policy. A community then expresses itself through its choice of documents, the community's canon forming a principal mode of such self-definition. So, as I said, through intrinsic traits a document places itself within a larger community of texts. Extrinsic traits, imputed to a document by not its authorship but its audience, select the document as canonical and make of the document a mode of social definition. The community through its mode of defining itself by its canonical choices forms a textual community – a community expressed through the books it reads and values.

If I now may invoke the suggestive word, intertextuality,[1] we then treat the relationships in which a given document stands as one expressed in the prepositions *between* and *among*. That is to say, in its intellectual traits a document bears relationship, to begin with, to some other, hence we describe relationships between two documents. These constitute formal and intrinsic matters: traits of grammar, arrangements of words and resonances as to their local meaning, structures of syntax of expression and thought. But in its social setting a document finds bonds among three or more documents, with all of which it is joined in the imagination and mind of a community. These range widely and freely, bound by limits not of form and language, but of public policy in behavior and belief. Documents because of their traits of rhetoric, logic, and topic form a community of texts. Documents because of their audience and authority express the intellect of a textual community.

The principal issue worked out in establishing a community of texts is hermeneutical, the chief outcome of defining a textual community, social and cultural. The former teaches us how to read the texts on their own. The latter tells us how to interpret texts in context. When we define and classify the relationships between texts, we learn how to read the components – words, cogent thoughts formed of phrases, sentences, paragraphs – of those texts in the broader context defined by shared conventions of intellect: rhetoric, logic, topic. More concretely, hermeneutical principles tell me how, in light of like documents I have seen many times, to approach a document I have never before seen at all. Hermeneutics teaches me the grammar and syntax of thought.

Let me give one example of the role of hermeneutics in an inductive inquiry into form. Memorizing a passage of a complex text will teach me the rhythms of expression and thought, for instance, that make of the sounds of some other

---

[1]In the concluding chapter I shall define the matter at some length.

document an intelligible music. Not only so, but documents joined into a common classification may share specific contents, not only definitive traits of expression – meaning and not solely method. So when I know how to assess the relationships between documents, I also come to a better way of sorting out the effects of those relationships: the intersections, the repetitions.

The upshot of defining a textual community, by contrast, is quite other. It is not hermeneutical, since at issue is not the reading and interpretation of texts but their social utility, their status as cultural indicators. When I know the choices a community has made for its canon, I find my way deep into the shared viewpoint of that community, moving from the contents of the texts to the contexts in which those texts bear meaning. And that brings us back to the basic matter: a text exists in diverse contexts, on its own, among other texts, and as part of a much larger social canon, e.g., a library or a court of appeal for authoritative judgments such as proof-texts supply. It is important now to help us sort out the most basic matters for discussion.

So far I have framed matters as if I planned to present a treatise on rather abstract matters, e.g., the definition of intertextuality, without specific reference to a particular document, set of documents, or canon. But the reader knows the truth, which is the opposite, since this book addresses a very particular set of writings. My intent at the outset is to explain why the particularities before us exemplify much broader issues of literature and culture. In this way the writings that concern me may provide a set of valuable instances, *exempla gratia*, for broader and more public discourse. Let me then backtrack and specify how, in particular, the documents on which we concentrate provide an ideal case-study of the problem of intertextuality viewed both formally and socially. For as to the debate on reading documents all by themselves and only as statements of a social group, the writings at hand present unusually suggestive examples of an entirely concrete character. And I believe our task requires us to read them both as exercises of a sophisticated formal character, and also as documents of a social culture, once more, as both a community of texts and testimonies to a textual community.

The relationships among the documents produced by the sages of Judaism may take three forms: complete dependence, complete autonomy, intersection in diverse manner and measure. That second dimension provokes considerable debate and presents a remarkably unclear perspective. For while the dimensions of autonomy and continuity take the measure of acknowledged traits – books on their own, books standing in imputed, therefore socially verified, relationships – the matter of connection hardly enjoys the same clear definition. On the one side, intrinsic traits permit us to assess theories of connection. On the other, confusing theological and social judgments of continuities and literary and heuristic ones of connection, people present quite remarkable claims as to the relationships between and among documents, alleging, in fact, that the documents all have to be read as a single continuous document: the Torah. As we shall now see, some maintain that the connections between and among documents are such that each has to be read in the light of all others. So the documents assuredly do form a canon, and that is a position adopted not in some distant past or alien society but among contemporary participants to the cultural debate.

While I take up a community of texts and explore those intrinsic traits that link book to book, my inquiry rests on the premise that the books at issue derive from a textual community, one which, without reference to the intrinsic traits of the writings, deems the set of books as a group to constitute a canon. My question is simple but critical:

If in advance I did not know that the community of Judaism treats the writings before us (among others) as a canon, would the traits of the documents have told me that the writings at hand are related?

The inquiry is inductive, concerns intrinsic traits, and therefore pursues the matter of connection between document and document. In a later work I plan to ask questions about continuities among documents. Here I work within literary categories, later on within social ones. In order to clarify the task I have taken for myself, I have now to portray the state of opinion on the corpus of writings at hand. Only then will the reader appreciate not only what is at stake, but also why the issues transcend the boundaries of the documents before us.

II. WHAT IS AT STAKE

The results make a difference to both the writings under study and the theoretical debate to which I hope to contribute a set of interesting examples. We open with an account of what is under discussion.

Let us start back with a thumbnail sketch (amplified in the next chapter) of the literature that concerns us. It is a set of writings produced by sages of Judaism from about 200 to about 600 A.D. These writings rest on two base-documents, the Scriptures of ancient Israel (to Christianity, the Old Testament, to Judaism, the Written Torah), and the Mishnah (in Judaism, the first component of the Oral Torah ultimately encompassing all the literature at hand). All of the writings of Judaism in late antiquity copiously cite Scripture. Some of them serve (or are presented and organized) as commentaries on the former, others as amplifications of the latter. Since Judaism treats all of these writings as a single, seamless Torah, the one whole Torah revealed by God to Moses, our rabbi, at Mount Sinai, the received hermeneutic naturally does the same. All of the writings are read in light of all others, and words and phrases are treated as autonomous units of tradition, rather than as components of particular writings, e.g., paragraphs – units of discourse – and books – composite units of sustained and cogent thought.

The issue of connection therefore is legitimate to the data. But the outcome transcends these particular data. The stakes for public discourse about matters of general intelligibility are considerable, for when we can describe the relationships between two documents and among three or more, we shall know what a given group of editors or authorities contributed on its own, and also how that authorship restated or reworked what it received from a prior group. Determining that relationship further guides us to principles of exegesis of documents, allegations and formulations of ideas and rules. If a document depends on some other, prior one, then what we find in the later writing is to be read in light of the earlier (but, of course, never vice versa). If there is no clear evidence of dependence, then the later document demands a reading in essentially its own terms.

But what is at stake for the system in describing relationships transcends the matter of hermeneutics. Describing documents – the building blocks of the Judaism at hand – in their context forms the first step in tracing the history of the system as a whole. That work, now completed in considerable measure, allows us to limn distinct stages in the formation of the system. Determining the relationship of document to document forms the necessary second step. Finding out what changed and what remained the same in the unfolding of the system as a whole tells us the history of the system as its canonical writings contain that history. Later on, seeing the documents as a continuous and final statement, we shall understand the direction and goal of the history at hand and turn back to see how, from the viewpoint of the end, the system took shape: a history that emerges from a dialectical process of study and restudy. But for now, the history of the formation of Judaism comprises only these two steps: a stage, then a stage beyond, fully described in their sequential relationship: the given – the document – and how it changed. But we even now keep in mind the third dimension in the history of the system, besides the ones measured by each document in its own context and two or more documents in their sequential and even temporal relationships. That third dimension takes its perspective from a distance and encompasses all of the documents: the system as a whole. It sees the documents as continuous not from one to the next but all in all, all together, all at once. That, sum and substance is the scholarly program of which the present book forms a critical component.

The outcome for theoretical discourse is best determined by the parties to it. I believe that the framing of matters – a community of texts, spun out from within, as against a textual community, created from beyond the intellect of an authorship – may prove suggestive. For the conception of a community of texts forms the center of inquiry in this book. So before proceeding, let me make certain the conception is absolutely clear. Individual texts form a community when their internal traits indicate that they have been composed in relationship to one another. Such traits include a shared program of inquiry, e.g., into a single document; a common set of formal preferences; a single sort of substantive inquiries. That definition brings us to the particular writings of Judaism. To begin with the documents come to us as a group, that is, as important components of "the Oral Torah" of the Judaism of the dual Torah that took shape in late antiquity. But what if they had not come down bearing a single imprimatur, that of Judaism? Would we have imagined that these books form a community of interrelated documents? Only internal evidence allows us to form an answer to that question. Accordingly, I want to know how texts important in the canon of Judaism in its formative age form a community, that is to say, relate to one another not adventitiously or casually, by mere accidents of coincidence in a canon, but – let me say with due emphasis – *through deliberation of authorships to participate, in their work, in constituting a communion through documents, a community of texts.* And that matter seems to me to tell us something about literature: about how writers write.

I have in mind indications of a quite objective and material character, such as decisions of an authorship to refer to or not to refer to Scripture, to compose an intersecting set of agenda or to talk about essentially diverse things, to cite a prior text or not to cite one, to make ample use of materials common among a number of prior texts or to use only materials not earlier used, to imitate the rhetoric and redaction of earlier writings or to strike out in unexplored directions, and on and on. These matters of fact tell us whether, and how, autonomous documents connect with one another and so form a communion of authorships and give expression in textual form to a community. The connections include materials used in common, formal preferences dominant in two or more documents, substantive inquiries into topics interesting to two or more authorships, modes of intelligibility that characterize two or more sets of writers. In a word, we deal with rhetoric, topic, and logic. We take up such considerations as symmetrical or asymmetrical plans of logic and rhetoric, programs of topic and proposition about a given topic, sharing materials, not sharing materials, and other perfectly objective and factual criteria.

While we commonly hear about The Rabbinic Mind or intellect, or even about The Jewish Imagination, I doubt that these either naive or purely racist categories need detain us. I make no appeal to some inchoate "spirit" that I discern in two or more documents but not in one or five others, nor do I concede that by instinct we know something we cannot show through the application and testing of stated criteria of connection. Anyone who cares to can replicate my procedures and so test my results: matters of fact, not judgment, as to the intersection of texts and the sharing of premises among texts. In Part Two I have simply set up a grid for analysis, with indicators of likeness or difference, that is, clearly defined points of criteria, again and again applied to nine documents.

III. THREE THEORIES OF INTERTEXTUALITY
IN THE JUDAIC CANON

Let me now give a representative specimen of the prevailing hermeneutic, so that readers will not conclude I argue against a moribund position. Only then will the persistence, even today, of a wrong approach to these writings prove an urgent problem. For the argument addresses not the faithful, who cannot – by definition – care about what comes first and what happened then, and for whom anachronism nourishes true belief. It concerns those who here and now, in the world of the academy, claim to tell us how to read these texts and what they mean for the academy. When we give them their hearing, we listen to what is, in fact, the message of the Torah, speaking in its own categories: the hand is the hand of the academy, but the voice is the voice of Sinai: two media of a single Torah, timeless and eternal, everywhere harmonious and always cogent. Glorious faith, but dreadful history, the position at hand translates beliefs into facts. It moreover ignores the requirement to adduce in evidence traits of the documents themselves. Here is a single representative example of the position, as to hermeneutics and history, of both the received tradition of Judaism and also the contemporary intellectual avatars of that tradition in the academy (where they do not belong).

The way I frame the question before us will make sense only when we work our way through prevailing pictures of the literary character and therefore the appropriate hermeneutics of the rabbinic literature. For only when we sort out the prevailing theories of the one and the doctrines of the other shall we grasp the work of defining the correct questions and, it follows, the appropriate modes of answering those questions. Before proceeding, let me cite three statements that convey the flavor of the contemporary (not merely religious and received or "traditional") hermeneutic. All derive from younger scholars explaining why they read the corpus in one way rather than in some other. The brief citations at hand define the program of this book, with the first two dictating the issues of Part Two, and the third, Part Three.

> Synoptic texts must always be studied synoptically, even if one text is 'later' than another.
>
> Shaye J. D. Cohen

In Part Two we take up four texts that relate in a way some wish to call "synoptic," and ask what it means to study them "synoptically."

The second position introduces a somewhat different metaphor from the synoptic one.

> This system, composed of interlocking and re-interlocking parts possessed of an organic connection one to another, is never really divisible.
>
> Lawrence H. Schiffman[2]

---

[2]In his *Sectarian Law in the Dead Sea Scrolls* (Chico, 1983), p. 3.

This metaphor claims much more than the first. Now we are told that everything "interlocks" with everything else, and, in a hashing of the metaphor, we learn further that there is an "organic" connection, so that nothing is ever "really divisible" from anything else. Quite what that means in practice emerges from the third of the three spokesmen at hand.

It is Susan Handelman, who has provided the most ambitious theory of how rabbinic writings relate – and the least informed.[3] Her principal position, so far as the matter of connection and continuity is concerned (there is no room for the autonomy of documents in her reading of the literature), is stated as follows:

> ...all units are so closely interwoven and simultaneously present that none can be considered in separation from any other at any given moment; it is a world of 'intertextuality'...[4]

> ...interpretation is not essentially separate from the text itself–an external act intruded upon it–but rather the extension of the text, the uncovering of the connective network of relations, a part of the continuous revelation of the text itself, at bottom, another aspect of the text.[5]

This represents a far more extreme position than that of Cohen, who refers only to synoptic texts, and an even more radical statement of matters than that of Schiffman.

Handelman makes a variety of generalizations about the character of the rabbinic writings, e.g., "In Rabbinic thought...it is often the obverse–the

---

[3]Her discussion of "the development of the oral law," pp. 42-50, is breathtakingly uninformed. She grasps nothing of the scholarly issues and imperfectly understands the facts. What she does is merely recite in full gullibility the "Orthodox" doctrine, which itself has nothing to do with the diverse and interesting classical positions on the matter. She does not seem to realize, for example, that the heirs of the Mishnah took two conficting positions on the relationship of the laws of the Mishnah to Sinai. She reads the issue as a historical one, in terms of the origin of the law. But it was a question of *authority*, not origin -- a matter critical to the work of mine that she cites. Evidence of her imperfect grasp of issues is easy to adduce from her botched report of my work. I am given the opinion "that the oral law is not a product of organic historical development from the written text but an entirely autonomous coexistent body of thought correlative to but independent of the written scriptures...." *I have no position*, what I am doing is outlining positions I claim to discover in a variety of continuator-documents of the Mishnah, e.g., Avot as against Sifra and Sifré to Numbers. Handelman's larger theory of the literature in fact rests on unsound historical premises, and these historical premises are critical to her literary theory. But I choose here to ignore that fact and discuss the theory of the literature solely in relationship to the traits and characteristics of the literature, as exemplified in the sizable sample in the reader's hands. Then people can decide on the basis of the literature Handelman claims to discuss whether or not her description and consequent theory are right. But her amateur status, as contrasted to Cohen's and Schiffman's, should not be missed. They know the sources they discuss and she scarcely compares in knowledge to them.

[4]Susan A. Handelman, *The Slayers of Moses. The Emergence of Rabbinic Interpretation in Modern Literary Theory* (Albany, 1982: State University of New York Press), p.78.

[5]*Ibid.*, p. 39.

particular and concrete take precedence over the general and abstract." Her larger theory of hermeneutics is not at issue just now, only her characterization of the relationships among documents and her reading of intertextuality as that interesting conception applies to those documents. These characterizations of the rabbinic canon express broadly-held opinion. In Part Four we revert to these theories of intertextuality of Handelman's.

My purpose is to test that opinion, exemplified by Cohen, Schiffman, and Handelman, against the facts presented by the components of the canon. Specifically, how do documents of Judaism relate to one another? And, as to relationship, the specific issue here concerns connection of one document to the next and of all the documents together. We wonder whether, in Handelman's formulation, none can ever be considered in separation from any other, whether, in Schiffman's formulation, the documents cannot be read one by one because they are never really divisible, or, in Cohen's, whether (some of) the documents before us really do relate in a *synoptic* manner, a term to which we shall return, so that when the documents interrelate, each must be read in light of the other. Cohen and Schiffman raise the issue of texts that clearly interrelate, Cohen invoking the analogy of the synoptic relationships among Matthew, Mark, and Q in Gospels' research, Schiffman phrasing matters still more broadly. To investigate this claim we pursue the writings given in Appendix One. So much for Part Two. Handelman frames matters on a still broader basis, since she speaks of the *whole* of the literature and its governing hermeneutics: everything read in line of everything else. For that purpose we take up nine discrete documents, given in Appendix Two. That explains the program of Part Three.

As I said, I propose not to prove or disprove the allegations at hand, since, to begin with, those who make them present them as dogmas, not propositions awaiting analysis and argument. I take for granted that those who hold the cited views of the texts of late antique Judaism find ample reason for them in the character of the texts. I wish to locate that reason and to clarify the sense and meaning of relationship – connection – as dictated by the qualities and traits of the texts. Then we can say precisely how the documents form a community of texts, sorting out the facts in such a way as to define relationships: synoptic, interlocking, and so on and so forth.

IV. THE PUZZLE OF CONNECTION, THE MYSTERY OF INTERTEXTUALITY

In many ways we here take up the most difficult of the three dimensions, autonomy, connection, and continuity, because we ask a dubious question, the one concerning connection. As I shall explain, I find nothing self-evident in the conception that documents not by the same writer relate in some hermeneutically consequential way. For more is at stake than merely observing how a later document cites an earlier one, e.g., diverse Jewish writings cite or allude to Scripture. That, by itself, supplies a fact bearing no ineluctable implications of a hermeneutical character at all. Not what Scripture says, but how it serves the authorship of the later document, dictates our reading and interpretation of that later document. When Cohen, Schiffman, and Handelman take the positions that they do, in line with fifteen hundred years of a hermeneutic that dictated precisely the same way or reading the texts of the holy Torah, they do not think they state banalities, and neither do I. But determining that further range of hermeneutical meaning presents problems, since, as I said, I do not find manifest and obvious what distinctively *literary* issue is at stake.

In fact I marvel at the certainty of Handelman, Schiffman, and Cohen, and of the broadly-held consensus that they represent. Let me spell out what I find puzzling. It is, specifically, why in the world we should ever have wondered how – on the basis of *intrinsic* and not imputed traits – one document connects to others. Seeing each document on its own or viewing all documents all together by reason of a social consensus pose no special problems of logic or interpretation. The one perspective derives from the very definitive trait of a book or a document: its uniqueness. The other constitutes a social, not a textual issue: why do people see as one what in fact are several? The answer derives not from documents and their traits but from communities and their choices. Common sense tells us that a given document should undergo examination within its own framework, and it is equally reasonable to ask how a number of discrete documents preserved by a single community related to the interests expressed by that community.

But what makes the intermediate question urgent at all? It is hardly ineluctable, and perhaps may not even present an important issue at all. For when, in the middle, between autonomy and continuity, I ask the question of why one document should exhibit, on the basis of internal evidence and not social decision, connections to some others, I can appeal to no obvious basis for the inquiry. No common sense or logic requires that we approach matters from that perspective. Quite to the contrary, it is only a broadly held conviction, such as characterizes the views of Cohen, Schiffman, and Handleman, that all of the documents interrelate not through a social and political or theological decision but through internal traits of connectedness and connection, that necessitates writing this book. Many people, represented by those I have cited, maintain that all rabbinic documents relate synoptically to all others. Among the believers, whether Reform or Orthodox and all the more so Traditional, that view finds universal self-evidence. So I want to know whether the actual traits of the documents under discussion sustain that position or contradict it. Here I construct a systematic exercise to test the conviction at hand, which, for the moment, we must take to be a serious rational proposition susceptible of verification or falsification. It follows that, since I have already studied as single and individual documents nine principal texts of that Judaism, given through samples in the second Appendix, I now may ask whether and how these documents relate to one another, hence inquiring whether they form a *community of texts.*

True enough, the issue of connection presents a puzzle. It is not a dimension of a text that the text, seen as an autonomous statement, demands, But it *is* an issue that has proven its heuristic and hermeneutic centrality. For when we ask how documents relate to one another, we pursue a well-established exercise of comparison and contrast. Such questions as I ask present no new perspective. In scholarship on the Hebrew Scriptures, the comparison and contrast of Kings and Chronicles, of JE, P, and D, and, in parallel work on the New Testament, the comparison and contrast of the synoptic gospels among themselves as well as with Q and John provide solid precedent. Here the connections already established show us high stakes indeed, not for history or sociology or theology alone, but for the literary understanding and appreciation of the imaginative compositions of great writers, the Evangelists, for one example, the Chronicler(s), for another. So when I want to know how the Mishnah relates to the Tosefta, I pursue a perfectly familiar course. But when I continue the process to encompass disparate documents, with no formal or substantive relationship to one another, then I move in uncharted paths. And yet that is what we study when we deal with exemplary and important documents in the canon of Judaism in its formative stage and ask how they connect with one another.

Chapter Two
Connection

I. THE ISSUE OF CONNECTION AND THE CANON OF JUDAISM

A brief reprise of my generative metaphor for connection leads us directly to the data we shall now describe. A book exists in three dimensions: on its own, within its cover, thus, *autonomously*; then on the shelf of books, along with others of its classification, thus, *connected* to other books of the same type; and finally, within the larger collection, the library as a whole. The staff of a library – to continue the metaphor – forms the textual community, for it has chosen these books in particular – and no others – for its community of users. By decision of the library staff the book is *continuous* not only with other books on its shelf but with all the books in the same building. Let me now utilize the metaphor at hand in setting forth the character of the writings of the Judaic sages who in late antiquity created Judaism as it has flourished for nearly two millenia. The Judaism of the dual Torah comes to us in the extant literary sources, those that took shape from the Mishnah at the beginning, ca. A.D. 200, through the Bavli at the end, ca. A.D. 600. The documents of the formative period in the history of the Judaism at hand, the Judaism that rests on the premise that at Sinai God revealed the Torah in two media, written and oral, unfolded over a period of four hundred years or so.[1]

The first document beyond Scripture, the written Torah, was the Mishnah, represented later on as part of the Oral Torah, which drew together teachings of authorities of the period beginning in the first century, before 70, when the Temple was destroyed and autonomous government ended, and ending with the publication of the code in ca. 200. The last of the documents of the Oral Torah to reach written form in late antiquity was the Talmud of Babylonia (Bavli), which provided commentary on thirty-seven of the sixty-two tractates of the Mishnah as well as on substantial portions of the Hebrew Scriptures. In joining sustained discourse on the Scriptures, called, in the myth of the present system, the Written Torah, as well as on the Mishnah, held to be the Oral, or memorized

---

[1] No one, of course, can doubt that those same documents drew on materials from an indeterminate period before 200. We do not, however, have access to the materials prior to 200, and so far as they have survived, they reach us in the language and context imparted to them after that time. So to study the formation of Judaism, we work with what we have, the documents in hand, so our interest is in the documents in their initial form and subsequent history. For we want to know the character of the system that emerged, and that character stands fully exposed in the sources before us.

Torah, the Bavli's framers presented a summa, an encyclopaedia, of Judaism, to guide Israel, the Jewish people, for many centuries to come. In-between ca. 200, when autonomous government was well established again, and ca. 600 the continuous and ongoing movement of sages, holding positions of authority in the Jewish governments recognized by Rome and Iran, as political leaders of the Jewish communities of the Land of Israel (to just after 400) and Babylonia (to about 500), respectively, wrote two types of books. One sort extended, amplified, systematized, and harmonized components of the legal system laid forth in the Mishnah. The work of Mishnah-exegesis produced four principal documents as well as an apologia for the Mishnah.

This last – the rationale or apologia for the Mishnah – came first in time, about a generation or so beyond the publication of the Mishnah itself. It was tractate Abot, ca. 250 C.E., a collection of sayings attributed both to authorities whose names occur, also, in the Mishnah, as well as to some sages who flourished after the conclusion of the Mishnah. These later figures, who make no appearance in that document, stand at the end of the compilation. The other three continuators of the Mishnah were the [2] Tosefta, [3] the Talmud of the Land of Israel (the Yerushalmi), and [4] the Bavli. The Tosefta, containing a small proposition of materials contemporaneous with those presently in the Mishnah and a very sizable proportion secondary to, and dependent, even verbatim, on the Mishnah, reached conclusion some time after ca. 300 and before ca. 400. The Tosefta addresses the Mishnah; its name means "supplement," and its function was to supplement the rules of the original documents. The Yerushalmi mediates between the Tosefta and the Mishnah, commonly citing a paragraph of the Tosefta in juxtaposition with a paragraph of the Mishnah and commenting on both, or so arranging matters that the paragraph of the Tosefta serves, just as it should, to complement a paragraph of the Mishnah. The Bavli, following the Yerushalmi by about two centuries, pursues its own program, which, as I said, was to link the two Torahs and restate them as one. The Yerushalmi closed at ca. 400. The Bavli, as I said, was completed by ca. 600. All these dates, of course, are rough guesses, but the sequence in which the documents made their appearance is not. It is fixed at these stages: Mishnah, Avot, Tosefta, Yerushalmi, Bavli. In Appendix One I present one sequence of passages that stand in close relationship with one another through those four documents, excluding Avot, and in Appendix Two, a second.

The stream of exegesis of the Mishnah and exploration of its themes of law and philosophy flowed side by side with a second, much like the Mississippi and the Missouri where they meet at St. Louis, flowing side by side for miles beyond. This other river coursed up out of the deep wells of the written Scripture. But it surfaced only long after the work of Mishnah-exegesis was well underway and followed the course of that exegesis, now extended to Scripture. The exegesis of the Hebrew Scriptures, a convention of all systems of Judaism from before the conclusion of Scripture itself, obviously occupied sages from the very origins of their group. No one began anywhere but in the encounter with the Written Torah. But the writing down of exegeses of Scripture in a systematic way, signifying also the formulation of a program and a plan for the utilization of the Written Torah in the unfolding literature of the Judaism taking shape in the centuries at hand, developed in a quite distinct circumstance. In Appendix Two I present two exegetical treatments of Leviticus, Sifra and Leviticus Rabbah, as well as other exemplary selections of scriptural exegesis. Sifra represents one kind of exegesis of Scripture, Genesis Rabbah and Leviticus Rabbah, another.

Specifically, one aspect of the work of Mishnah-exegesis began with one ineluctable question. How does a rule of the Mishnah relate to, or rest upon, a rule of Scripture? That question demanded an answer, so that the status of the Mishnah's rules, and, right alongside, of the Mishnah itself, could find a clear definition. Standing by itself, the Mishnah bore no explanation of why Israel should obey its rules and accept its vision. Brought into relationship to Scriptures, in mythic language, viewed as part of the Torah, the Mishnah gained access to the source of authority by definition operative in Israel, the Jewish people. Accordingly, the work of relating the Mishnah's rules to those of Scripture got under way alongside the formation of the Mishnah's rules themselves. Collecting and arranging exegeses of Scripture as these related to passages of the Mishnah first reached literary form in the Sifra, to Leviticus, and in two books, both called Sifré, one to Numbers, the other Deuteronomy. All three compositions accomplished much else. For, even at that early stage, exegeses of passages of Scripture in their own context and not only for the sake of Mishnah-exegesis attracted attention. But a principal motif in all three books concerned the issue of Mishnah-Scripture relationships.

A second, still more fruitful path also emerged from the labor of Mishnah-exegesis. As the work of Mishnah-exegesis got under way, in the third century, exegetes of the Mishnah and others alongside undertook a parallel labor. It was to work through verses of Scripture in exactly the same way – word for word, phrase for phrase, line for line – in which, to begin with, the exegetes of the Mishnah pursued the interpretation and explanation of the Mishnah. To state matters simply, precisely the types of exegesis that dictated the way in which sages read the Mishnah now guided their reading of Scripture as well. And, as people began to collect and organize comments in accord with the order of sentences and paragraphs of the Mishnah, they found the stimulation to collect and organize comments on clauses and verses of Scripture. As I said, this kind of work got under way in the Sifra and the two Sifrés. It reached massive and magnificent fulfillment in Genesis Rabbah, which, as its name tells us, presents a line-for-line reading of the book of Genesis.

Beyond these two modes of exegesis and the organization of exegesis in books, first on the Mishnah, then on Scripture, lies yet a third. To understand it, we once more turn back to the Mishnah's great exegetes, represented to begin with in the Yerushalmi. While the original exegesis of the Mishnah in the Tosefta addressed the document under study through a line by line commentary, responding only in discrete and self-contained units of discourse, authors of units of discourse gathered in the next, the Yerushalmi, developed yet another mode of discourse entirely. They treated not phrases or sentences but principles and large-scale conceptual problems. They dealt not alone with a given topic, a subject and its rule, but with an encompassing problem, a principle and its implications for a number of topics and rules. This far more discursive and philosophical mode of thought produced for Mishnah-exegesis, in somewhat smaller volume but in much richer contents, sustained essays on principles cutting across specific rules. And for Scripture the work of sustained and broad-ranging discourse resulted in a second type of exegetical work, beyond that focused on words, phrases, and sentences.

Discursive exegesis is represented, to begin with, in Leviticus Rabbah, a document that reached closure, people generally suppose, sometime after Genesis Rabbah, thus in ca. 400-500, one might guess. Leviticus Rabbah presents not phrase-by-phrase systematic exegeses of verses in the book of Leviticus, but a set of thirty-seven topical essays. These essays, syllogistic in purpose, take the form of citations and comments on verses of Scripture to be sure. But the compositions range widely over the far reaches of the Hebrew Scriptures while focusing narrowly upon a given theme. They moreover make quite distinctive points about that theme. Their essays constitute compositions, not merely composites. Whether devoted to God's favor to the poor and humble or to the dangers of drunkenness, the essays, exegetical in form, discursive in character, correspond to the equivalent, legal essays, amply represented in the Yerushalmi.

In this other mode of Scripture-interpretation, too, the framers of the exegeses of Scripture accomplished in connection with Scripture what the Yerushalmi's exegetes of the Mishnah were doing in the same way at the same time. We move rapidly past yet a third mode of Scriptural exegesis, one in which the order of Scripture's verses is left far behind, and in which topics, not passages of Scripture, take over as the mode of organizing thought. Represented by Pesiqta deR. Kahana, Lamentations Rabbati, and some other collections conventionally assigned to the sixth and seventh centuries, these entirely discursive compositions move out in their own direction, only marginally relating in mode of discourse to any counterpart types of composition in the Yerushalmi (or in the Bavli).

Through a rather circuitous path we return to the final document, the Bavli. This is where the two streams – Mishnah-exegesis, Scripture-exegesis – intermingled and flowed in one vast river. As I said at the outset, at the end of the extraordinary creative age of Judaism, the authors of units of discourse collected in the Bavli drew together the two, up-to-then distinct, modes of organizing thought, either around the Mishnah or around Scripture. They treated both Torahs, oral and written, as equally available in the work of organizing large-scale exercises of sustained inquiry. So we find in the Bavli a systematic treatment of some tractates of the Mishnah. And within the same aggregates of discourse, we also find (in somewhat smaller proportion to be sure, roughly 60% to roughly 40% in the sample I made of three tractates) a second principle of organizing and redaction. That principle dictates that ideas be laid out in line with verses of Scripture, themselves dealt with in cogent sequence, one by one, just as the Mishnah's sentences and paragraphs come under analysis, in cogent order and one by one.

We may well ask who speaks through these documents, so defining the community, authority, and authorship represented by them. The answer is critical to framing a valid perspective on the whole. But a brief answer nonetheless serves. The entire literature derives from only a single type of Israelite, a type represented in a single, continuous movement, with ongoing personal and institutional relationships beginning long before the closure of the Mishnah and continuing long after the conclusion of the Bavli. This movement, with its traditions of learning, its continuities of institutions, leadership, and authority, its assured social position and substantial political power in the government of Israel, the Jewish people, in both centers of settlement in late antiquity, bears several titles. It is called "rabbinic," because of the title of honor accorded to some of its leaders, called rabbis. But "rabbi" meant simply "my lord," thus, in our context, not much than "sir," or (pro domo) "professor." The term of honor occurs, with slight variation, in Christian Syriac sources, e.g., Rabban, and therefore cannot connote a distinctively Jewish, let alone Judaic, meaning at all. Another title is "Talmudic," because of the principal document, the Talmud (meaning, the Bavli, the Talmud of Babylonia) produced at the end. Hence people quite properly speak of "Talmudic Judaism." Other, more theological titles circulate, for instance, "classical" or "normative," as in "classical Judaism" and "normative Judaism." Finally, within the system itself, the correct title would have to make use of the word "Torah," since the entire canonical literature forms "the one whole Torah of Moses, our rabbi," received from God at Mount Sinai. Accordingly, we could call the canon at hand the canon of the dual Torah, and the movement, the movement of Torah-sages.

From our perspective a single fact emerges from the multiplicity of titles. The literature at hand derives from a singular group of intellectuals, well-organized sages. These sages also formed a political class within Israel in the Land of Israel and in Babylonia. They further served as models for the nation at large, models of not merely virtue but piety and holiness. So when we review what the literature of Judaism in its formative age has to tell us, from whom and what do we hear? We listen to that singular, distinctive vision that derives from men of intellect.[2] And these facts further validate the hypothesis that the documents they produced exhibit important points of connection among

---

[2]Not a single woman of consequence, appears, early, middle, or late.

themselves, as well as the proposal that the canon as a whole constitutes a classic case of intertextuality: writings that intersect broadly and deeply, that speak in a single way to a common conversation. The literary issue rests upon deep social and political foundations. But before we proceed to the main point, we have to digress and take up a matter critical to the reading of the entire literature: the matter of authorship. For, as is clear, I treat documents as the creation of what I call authorships, meaning, an indeterminate number of people who select and arrange matters so as to give us as their statement the collage in our hands. The contrary stress focuses upon not authorships but authorities.

II. STATEMENTS ATTRIBUTED TO NAMED AUTHORITIES

Let me now explain the reason for my stress, in approaching the history of the formation of Judaism, on the order in which documents came to closure, which yields what I call the canonical history of ideas. There is a way not taken, and I have now to explain why I do not take it. It is the more familiar way of relying for the historical order in which ideas came to expression on the attributions of sayings to named authorities. The alternative for relying on the established order of documents therefore is presented by the simple fact that, within the documents, numbers of sayings are assigned to particular figures. We have a reasonably clear idea of when these authorities lived Tracing the history of ideas by assigning to a given point in time a saying attributed to an authority who lived at that time does represent an alternative. The reason for relying only on the relative order of documents is simple. We have no way of demonstrating that authorities to whom, in a given composition, statements are attributed really said what is assigned to them.

For one thing, the sayings of individual sages come down to us in collective compositions, so we cannot demonstrate that Rabbi X wrote a book in which his views are given, preserved by his immediate disciples for instance. We do not know that a given rabbi really said what is imputed to him at all, since there are no external witnesses to any attribution. All we have in hand is that the framers of document A have assigned diverse sayings to various names. For another thing, we have facts that make us wonder whether those assignments rest on the facts of a given figure's actual statements. First, the same saying may occur in more than a single name. What document A gives to Rabbi X, document B gives to Rabbi Y. Second, the actual wording of sayings assigned to individuals rarely bears distinctive traits and most commonly conforms to an overall pattern, imposed, in a given document, upon all sayings. These specific negative factors join a general one. In the picture we have of the formation of the documents and of the sayings in them, we cannot point to evidence of processes of individual writing, e.g., Rabbi X wrote book Y, or even to a program of preserving the very words of Rabbi X on the part of his disciples. The collective character of the writings before us testifies to a different purpose altogether from one which would preserve the particular views of a given individual.

The main consideration is simple and obvious. We have in hand something other than minutes of meetings, actual words spoken by particular authorities, results, for conditions pertaining in antiquity, of the counterpart of careful observations by trained reporters, with tape recorders or TV cameras. Whether or not in any writing other than that securely assigned to an individual author we have the actual words said by a specific authority remains to be seen. But in the writing of the ancient rabbis we do not. To assume that we know what any individual sage actually said, we have to impose upon the labor of factual description, analysis, and interpretation a crushing burden of faith – and that *a priori.* The sole fact in hand therefore is that the framers of a given document included in their book sayings imputed to named authorities. Are these dependable? Unlikely on the face of it. Since, as I said, the same sayings will be imputed to diverse authorities by different groups of editors, of different books, we stand on shaky ground indeed if we rely for chronology upon the framers' claims of who said what.

The notion, moreover, that we have in hand the exact words of a sage is groundless, since the documents at hand formalize whatever they use and impose their own rhetorical preferences on nearly everything in hand.

Some maintain that while we do not have in hand the actual words, we do have the gist of what someone said, that is, his opinion, if not his opinon as he framed it. But that carries us onto still more dubious ground. For attributions even of the gist of what is said by themselves cannot be shown to be reliable. We have no way of demonstrating that a given authority really maintained the views assigned to him – even not in the actual words attributed to him. There are no sources in which we can check what is attributed, e.g., a given authority's own writings, preserved by his disciples; diaries, notes, personal reflections of any kind. We have only the judgment and record provided by the collectivity of sages represented by a given authorship: that is, the document and that alone. *What we cannot show we do not know.* Lacking firm evidence, for example, in a sage's own, clearly assigned writings, or even in writings redacted by a sage's own disciples and handed on among them in the discipline of their own community, we have for chronology only a single fact.

It is that a document, reaching closure at a given time, contains the allegation that Rabbi X said statement Y. So we know as absolute fact that people at the time of the document reached closure took the view that Rabbi X said statement Y. The fact is that at a given moment an authorship thought that Rabbi X made statement Y – and that that statement was worth preserving and handing on. What follows is that, at the time of that authorship, that opinion (as it happens, assigned to an earlier figure, Rabbi X) was held, was accepted, was formulated for transmission to coming generations – so, in all, made a difference. And that forms an irreducible fact, on the foundations of which we may compose a history of ideas. We may then assign to statement Y a position, in the order of the sequence of sayings, defined by the location of the document in the order of the sequence of documents. The several documents' dates, as is clear, all constitute guesses. But the sequence Mishnah, Tosefta, Yerushalmi, Bavli for the exegetical writings on the Mishnah is absolutely firm and beyond doubt. The sequence for the exegetical collections on Scripture, Sifra, the two Sifrés, Genesis Rabbah, Leviticus Rabbah, the Pesiqtas and beyond is not entirely sure. Still the position of the Sifra and the two Sifrés at the head, followed by Genesis Rabbah, then Leviticus Rabbah, then Pesiqta deR. Kahana and Lamentations Rabbati and some related collections, seems likely. On the basis of the consensus presently in place concerning the relative order of documents, we shall recover whatever history – whether of literature or of ideas or of religion – we shall ever have. The specific, intrinsic traits of those documents then lay down the foundations of all else – the internal evidence at hand. Every proposition then is to be tested by reference to the traits of documents.

To summarize this somewhat lengthy explanation of why we do things in one way and not in some other: since the various compositions of the canon of formative Judaism derive not from named, individual authors but from collective decisions of schools or academies, we cannot take for granted attributions of sayings to individuals provide facts. We cannot show that if a given rabbi is alleged to have made a statement, he really did say what is assigned to him. We do not have a book or a letter he wrote such as we have, for example, for Paul or Augustine or other important Christian counterparts to the great rabbis of late antiquity. We also do not know that if a story was told, things really happened in the way the story-teller says, in some other way, or not at all. Accordingly, we cannot identify as historical in a narrow and exact sense anything that comes down to us in the canon of Judaism. What is absolutely firm and factual, by contrast, is that these books represent views held by the authorship behind them. At the point at which a document reached conclusion and redaction, views of a given group of people reached the form at that moment of closure in which we now have them (taking account of for variations of wording). That is why I do not allege we know what people were thinking prior to the point at which, it is generally assumed, a given document was redacted. Accordingly, if I wish to know the sequence in which views reached their current expression, I have recourse to the conventional order and rough dating assigned by modern scholarship to the several documents, from the Mishnah through the Bavli. All I allege as fact, therefore, is that the books belong in the order in which I survey them.[3] And, to move ahead, what I wish to know is how these documents, in their canonical order, relate to one another: autonomy, connection, continuity.

III. THE HISTORY OF THE FORMATION OF JUDAISM AND THE RELATIONSHIPS AMONG DOCUMENTS

This brings us to the critical importance of the relationships among documents and how that relationship imparts critical importance to the issue of this book, the *connections* among documents. We have now to ask what sort of history we may hope to gain. That history depends on the relationships between and among the documents, their connectedness, the connections among them. If documents appear essentially distinct from one another, then they may tell us about phases and sequences: history. We may attempt to relate context to contents and trace change from one document to the next. So if we read documents as autonomous of one another, then we have also to know *how* they interrelate. If, on the other hand, documents essentially repeat one another, then we cannot claim that the documents mark out phases in the unfolding of the system and its ideas. Standing by itself, the fact that one document comes before another tells us nothing about development and change – that is, history, the context of ideas, the comparison of context and content. So the historical stakes can be stated very simply:

Only when we know to what degree a document speaks for its authorship and to what degree it carries forward a received position can we come to an estimate of the character of that document's testimony to the unfolding of the system as a whole: [1] essentially its own and representative of the authorship of its stage in the unfolding of the canon, or [2] essentially continuous with what has gone before – or [3] somewhere in the middle.

Once we have established the degree to which documents speak for their respective authorships, we can begin to trace the order in which ideas make their appearance. So we may ask about the components in sequence ("history of

---

[3]In my *Foundations of Judaism. Method, Teleology, Doctrine* (Philadelphia, 1983-1985: Fortress) I-III, and *Vanquished Nation, Broken Spirit: The Virtues of the Heart in Formative Judaism* (Cambridge, 1986: Cambridge U. Press), I follow the same procedure in tracing the sequence in which a given set of ideas makes its appearance across the several components of the authoritative books of Judaism. This method of tracing "the canonical history," meaning, the history of ideas as the authoritative books lay forth those ideas, in the assumed order of those books, will guide future work in the formative history of Judaism. Specifically, in *Vanquished Nation* I have shown that the doctrine of affections remains constant and consistent in the unfolding canon of Judaism. But the same holy books, read in the same way, show that other critical matters produced evidence of striking shifts and changes. Specifically, hermeneutics, teleology, and central symbol all reveal a remarkable shift, always marked by the same document, the Yerushalmi. Other work of mine has already shown that emotions are not the only point of stability in the canon. Views of the city or metropolis retain their basic shape throughout the canon. So I must sketch a large picture and speculate more systematically on why what changes changes, and what status the same persists as well. This is in *Judaism in the Matrix of Christianity* (Philadelphia, 1986: Fortress).

Judaism") so far as we can trace the sequence. Then and only then shall we have access to issues of history, that is, of change and development. To spell this out: if a theme makes its appearance early on in one form, so one set of ideas predominates in a document that reached closure in the beginnings of the canon and then that theme drops out of public discourse or undergoes radical revision in writings in later stages of the canon, that fact may make considerable difference. Specifically, we may find it possible to speculate on where, and why a given approach proved urgent, and also on the reasons that that same approach receded from the center of interest.

Still more critical, in knowing the approximate sequence of documents and therefore the ideas in them (at least so far as the final point at which those ideas reached formal expression in the canon), a second possibility emerges. What if we find pretty much the same views, treated in the same proportion and for the same purpose, yielding the same message, early, middle, and late in the development of the canon? Then we shall have to ask why the literature remains so remarkably constant. Given the considerable shifts in the social and political condition of Israel in the land of Israel as well as in Babylonia over a period of more than four hundred years, that evident stability in the teachings for the affective life will constitute a considerable fact for analysis and interpretation. History thus produces two possibilities, both of them demanding sustained attention. Things change. Why? Things do not change. Why not? These questions now lie beyond the far horizon. The issue of connection between and among documents therefore carries a considerable freight for historical study. But up to this point I have not spelled out the particular matter before us: diverse ways by which we may imagine connection.

IV. METAPHORS OF CONNECTION: GENEALOGY THROUGH DIALECTIC VS. STRUCTURAL TAXONOMY

This brings us, at long last, to the matter at hand, connection. By connection I mean sharing like traits, including materials, and by the absence of connection I mean not sharing traits of plan and program. What is at issue is defining what we know as fact and avoiding what can come to us as mere impression. There are two appropriate metaphors, and we explore them both, genealogical and taxonomical. Genealogy serves for the relationships among texts some call synoptic in relationship, and I regard as dialectical in relationship. Taxonomy serves for all of the writings all together. The connections between and among the Mishnah, Tosefta, Yerushalmi, and Bavli are dialectical, in that each succeeding document takes up and responds to the problems and program of its predecessor, hence a moving, or dialectical, relationship and connection characterizes the whole. I shall spell this out in Part Two. The connections among all of the documents of the canon at hand, so far as they exhibit traits of connection at all, are taxonomic. If we see the documents all together and without differentiation, the metaphor of taxonomic relationship serves well. I maintain that, in light of the data we take up, it is only by classification – that is, by invoking the metaphor of taxonomy – that we determine relationship, specifically showing first the genus, then the species. This I explain in Part Three.

The taxonomic metaphor derives from natural history, and it sees things as connected when they fall into a single category, and as not connected when they do not. The notion of connection as an essentially taxonomic issue requires some explanation, since it is not the more familiar of the two connections. First to define the matter: the diverse species of a genus are connected by reason of their taxonomic traits, and two or more genera are not connected when they lack in common any taxonomic points. The metaphor that derives the sense of connection from taxonomy, that is, relationship of like and unlike traits, established through systematic classification, directs us to data that we can readily find for ourselves. Since the data prove congruent to the work, we invoke as our sole useful metaphor the taxonomic one: things are connected when they fall into a common classification, and taxonomic relationship – like, unlike – serves as the criterion for connection.   The analysis of the relationships., hence of the connections, between and among the principal documents of the Judaism of the dual Torah therefore pursues a program of comparison and contrast among those documents. The results of comparing and contrasting documents tell us how documents are or are not connected with one another.

Documents that fall into a single genus therefore may exhibit relationships, for instance points of rhetoric, logic, or topic, in common, and the speciation of those documents then tells us aspects in which they do not relate, that is, points not in common. Accordingly, by "community of texts" – within the metaphor deriving from taxonomy – I mean texts that coalesce, form a community and in that way establish connections with one another, thus texts that are connected are writings that fall within a single classification. The same traits exhibited by two or more texts will then indicate that the two texts form a single genus, falling into a shared category or classification – one defined by the traits they have in common. The connection, then, between one text and the next is established by shared traits of form or program or fixed relationship to a single document to which, in common, the texts relate. Such common characteristics therefore indicate that two or more texts connect with one another in a taxonomic framework, which seems to me the sole genuinely objective basis for establishing connection at all.

We may now turn to the more obvious metaphor, genealogical connection. The genealogical connection maintains the view that one thing is connected to some other because the one begat the other, a connection based on origin. One thing is not connected to another if there is no affinity based on genealogy. At issue, then, is how we may establish genealogy. It may derive from direct relationship or from indirect, and, in this chapter, we deal with the former, in the next, the latter. A direct relationship requires that document B not only draw upon document A but also take shape in response to the contents of document A. An indirect relationship involves document A as proximate ancestor for document B, C, and D, in that (necessarily) later writings draw upon an earlier source in common. An example of a direct relationship between documents comes from Kings and Chronicles, with the later drawing upon, and reworking, the former. An example of an indirect relationship, also of a genealogical character, would point to Genesis and Exodus, both of which draw heavily upon common materials, e.g., J, E, JE, and P, but neither of which draws upon the other. In either sort of relationship, we may establish a genealogical connection between two documents, direct or through a third document, as well as the same sort of connection among three or more documents, upon the same basis. The genealogical metaphor for connection invokes not taxonomic but human relationships, e.g., family, filiation, affinity, cousin, uncle, mother-in-law, and the like. In the anthropomorphic setting in which our thought goes forward, the conception of relationship invariably evokes the metaphor of family, surely a more "self-evidently" accessible category than mere classification.

The choice between the two metaphors for connections of the canon as a whole is governed by the character of our data, and our knowledge of the traits and history of the data. So we turn from the definition of the metaphors of connection to the data before us. When we sift the meanings of connection, sorting out the metaphors we may invoke for our study, we see that one available metaphor proves congruent to all of the data at our disposal, and the other does not in its simple form fit any of it. Specifically, taxonomy – by definition – serves all data. Genealogy fits the part of the data to which the synoptic issue is relevant – Mishnah, Tosefta, Yerushalmi, Bavli – but does not fit those data very well.

In order to utilize the metaphor of genealogy, we should have to know that document A has generated document B. While more commonsensical and therefore attractive, the metaphor for connection provided by family invokes considerations of history and precedence, generations and offspring, that, at this stage in our knowledge, we cannot take up. For how shall I determine affinities, filiations, and the like? What objective and factual data can I adduce in evidence of the claim that two or more texts form a family, hence stand in relationship as mother and daughter, or that one text stands in a filial relationship to some other? The metaphor, filiation, draws in its wake the issues of history in the sense of temporal sequence, the conception, for example, that A begat B, so B represents a generation of A. That represents a quite different statement of what we mean by relationship from the one I have offered. But, except for the Mishnah, we do not know that document A's framers came prior to document B's, and our dates for the documents and the order we assign to them, if not wholly arbitrary, do not rest upon firm foundations. Everything is at best approximate and derives from impressions and guesses.

More weighty still, except for the Mishnah, Tosefta, Yerushalmi, and Bavli, we do not know that the authorship of B had access to the work of A and as a matter of decision adopted the model of A. Evidence to prove filiation must encompass demonstrations of points of contact and intersection. That is to say, connection as a direct and concrete category requires that we make judgments of a historical order: this first, then that. But I cannot demonstrate such connection as would have one set of authors meet with and make use of the work of another's writings. So that kind of connection lies beyond demonstration, and a different metaphor of connection will prove more useful.

True, we can show that some small portion of the materials of document A occur also in document B. That fact provides some variant readings of modest interest. But what fact flows from the sharing of a unit of discourse in common? The shared use of some materials in common, and proves that two sets of authorships drew upon a common corpus of materials. The connection then is common access to a third authorship – that alone. We cannot then posit direct relationship between group A and group B, but only indirect and adventitious relationship. And that sort of relationship hardly tells us the two groups, that is, the two documents, stand in a relationship of connection that we can exploit, e.g., for hermeneutical or historical purposes. It tells us the opposite. These and similar problems of demonstrating the presence of relationships comparable to families, filiations, and the like require us to look elsewhere for our notion of relationship. In place of connection, I posit a metaphor that rests on no more than demonstrated points of similarity and difference.

Now that the metaphor and its rejected alternative have been fully exposed, let us turn to a clearer statement of connections between and among documents as I propose to investigate them. The genealogical metaphor, which compares connection, a rather abstract category, to genealogical affinity therefore rests on an essentially historical premise. One thing is connected to some other because the one begat the other, a connection based on origin. One thing is not connected to another if there is no affinity based on genealogy. But that metaphor, while self-evidently illuminating, cannot serve most of our documents here. The reason is that the premise of the metaphor of connection as genealogy within families demands data we do not have. We do not know that the Mishnah begat Leviticus Rabbah, or that the Sifra begat Genesis Rabbah, so if materials occur in both documents, we cannot claim that the one document is connected in a relationship of filiation to its predecessor. I have already explained why we do not know the relationships, as to history, of documents, though we can classify documents in relationship to common points of origin and focus, Mishnah and Scripture, respectively. On the other hand, as I have suggested, there are clear relationships among documents that stand in a straight line, the later ones commenting on the earlier ones. Those relationships demand analysis, and they are the ones characteristic of the Mishnah, Tosefta, and two Talmuds.

But for the literature as a whole we cannot show continuous unfolding out of a single, linear connection. The opposite is the case. Many of the documents stand quite independent of the generality of writings and intersect with the rest only casually and episodically. For the nine documents surveyed in Part Three, therefore, I have selected so utterly formal a mode of defining connection as the taxonomic one because of the facts we do have. So too, because of the absence of facts of a different order, I had to frame my question in other than historical terms, on the one side, and in terms of objective traits of composition, on the other. I required a metaphor that is ahistorical, rigorously structural and phenomenological, positing no temporal relationships among documents, except for one: placing the Mishnah at the head of the line, the Bavli at the end. The present mode, the taxonomic definition of connection, moreover, denies the need to specify that the authorship of text B knew and borrowed ideas from the authorship of text A – that is, attained connection in a more routine sense, rather in the sense of sharing and borrowing and influencing. My chosen metaphor does not entertain theses of borrowing and influence. Therefore to unpack the conception of relationship I have adopted relationship as a function of genus and species.

As we have seen, the theories of connection require us to deal with two different matters, one synoptic (Part Two), covering only the documents that (in the prevailing theory) exhibit synoptic relationships among one another, the other taking up the whole of the rabbinic canon – the *entirety* of the literature. Schiffman ("interlocking parts") and Handelman, representing nearly the entire world of scholarship on this literature, address the complete canonical corpus, beginning, middle, end. That is why both metaphors of connection will demand careful testing against a sample of the writings at hand. The genealogical model of connection (in its dialectical formulation) serves for only a small part of the whole, the part given in the appendix to Part Two, specifically, the Mishnah, Tosefta, Yerushalmi, and Bavli, the later of which not only intersect but also develop in response to the earlier one(s). Those particular writings form connections of filiation. The taxonomic model of connection serves – perforce, as I shall explain – to accommodate the entire literature, such as my sample in Part Three's appendix makes available.

Part Two

DIALECTICAL CONNECTION AND GENEALOGY

Chapter Three

Intertextuality and Textuality

[1]: Synoptic Texts and their Relationships

Synoptic texts must always be studied synoptically, even if one text is
'later' than another.

Shaye J. D. Cohen[1]

I. DEFINING SYNOPTIC TEXTS

Intertextuality takes place when two or more documents go over the same
materials, and the connection at hand derives from that intersection. Cohen
invokes, in this regard, the metaphor deriving from New Testament studies,
specifically, the synoptic theory on the relationships among Matthew, Mark,
Luke, and a prior source called Source, by its German word, Quelle, hence, Q.
The word "synoptic" in general means "taking a broad view," but, used in
relationship to connections between and among texts, not only derives from, but
is particular to, the connections among the New Testament Gospels of Matthew,
Mark, and Luke. These relate in two ways. First, they go over much the same
ground, and, second, they share sayings drawn from a prior source, called Q.

Now when Cohen invokes with respect to the relationships among rabbinic
documents the word "synoptic," quite what he means is not entirely clear. What
he ought to intend ("must always be studied synoptically") is to claim that
rabbinic documents relate as do the Synoptic Gospels, e.g., both to one another
and to a prior source, or Q. Otherwise all he accomplishes is to call attention to
the obvious fact that diverse documents, within the canon of Judaism, contain
some peripatetic materials. But that brings no news. We are then admonished
to pay attention to the variant readings supplied by the occurrence of the same
saying or story in two or more documents. But who thought otherwise? That is
to say, a handful of sayings and stories travel from one document to the next.
To call attention to that well-known fact we need hardly invoke the analogy of
Gospels' research, which is inappropriate. Assuming for the moment that when
people invoke the synoptic analogy, they mean to make an important point that
merely noticing the circulation of materials from document to document, we had

---

[1]Shaye J.D. Cohen, "Jacob Neusner, Mishnah, and Counter-Rabbinics," *Conservative Judaism*
1983, 37:48-63.

best begin with the assumption that Smith, Cohen, and others mean what they say.

The category of synoptic connections therefore provides a metaphor by which we are to understand the connections between and among (some) rabbinic writings. These of course require specification. Before proceeding to examine that theory of connection, however, let us exclude from consideration texts that in their connections are not synoptic. They do not exhibit the traits of, first, sharing a broad range of material, that, second, points toward a common source (or set of sources). I may add yet a third qualification, one that introduces a measure of taste and judgment. The discovery of Q vastly changed the understanding of Matthew and Mark and the ("broad") synoptic picture of the life and teachings of Jesus that emerged from the synoptic Gospels. Consequently, the fact that documents relate "synoptically" must make a difference, explaining, so to speak, why this, not that. The alternative position, as I said, merely is that synoptic connections yield variant readings of a given saying or story – and for that, we did not need to invoke so rich a metaphor as the synoptic one. If, for instance, Cohen means by "studying synoptic texts synoptically," merely that we should collect and arrange variant readings, he could have said so. His meaning has, therefore, to transcend the self-evident, which validates my insistence that the discovery of synoptic connections must make a difference beyond the known. Here therefore I present the three qualifications that follow in the wake of the synoptic metaphor of connection.

1. Texts that relate in that a later text cites and glosses an earlier one are not synoptic. Their connection is one of *commentary*, in that the second comments on the first. No one has alleged that commentaries do not relate to the base-text on which they comment. Nor can I locate in the literature the view that commentaries can be read without the text on which they comment, though, as we note, some hold that texts cannot be read without their commentaries. But that is a question not pertinent to synoptic connection.

2. Texts that relate in that two or more texts quote in common a prior third one by themselves do not relate synoptically. Such texts have in common a connection only to that third text, but not to one another. They connect only through that shared third source. They relate but they do not connect, or, to invoke a measure of gibberish, their connection is one of mere *relationship*, that is, to that third source. Since all rabbinic documents liberally quote verses of the Written Torah, by definition all of them connect through that third document. And, by itself, that fact yields no heuristic let alone hermeneutic point deriving from documents' connections among themselves.

3. Texts that contain verbatim or nearly so the same passage – e.g., a saying or story in common, on that basis alone do not stand in synoptic relationship. The mere fact that the same tale occurs in two or

more texts tells us only that the sources connect in that they use the same tale. There is no further connection to be imputed merely on the basis of that simple, formal fact. The connection therefore falls into the category of the merely *adventitious*.

The synoptic relationship among Matthew, Mark, Luke, and Q is not one of commentary, in that documents cite Q as an independent source and then comment on Q's materials. The evangelists make use of materials for their own purposes, integrating them into their larger system and structure, and that is hardly the counterpart to commentary. The synoptic connection derives not from mere citing of a common source, but presents important points of comparison and contrast as each of the documents related synoptically goes its own way with the shared materials. And, finally, the fact that the same sayings and stories occur among the synoptic Gospels and Q far transcends the merely adventitious, because the hermeneutics of the several documents take shape in response to the synoptic facts: one cannot read the texts by themselves, and one cannot read one text merely as a commentary on another. There is a parity, an equality of hermeneutical exposure, among the documents. So as soon as we invoke the synoptic metaphor, we call into play a set of factors that imparts to that metaphor enormous consequence.

These three exclusions seem to me matters of common sense. For the hermeneutical question is hardly addressed, let alone settled, by the fact that two texts quote a third, that two texts make use of an episodic third in common, or that two texts happen to relate in that one comments on the other. There is no hermeneutical consequence in the first fact. The second yields the obvious conclusion that several versions of the same saying or story may be compared and a single "original" version may be constructed (for whatever purpose). The relationship of the Synoptic Gospels differs from these connections. First, none constitutes a commentary on any other, or even on Q. Second, Matthew and Mark relate not merely in that they both cite Q, but in more extensive ways to one another as well. Third, the shared materials form an important component of the whole and join the several documents not adventitiously or episodically but at their core. So what we derive from Matthew, Mark, and Q is more than a repertoire of versions of the same saying or story, e.g., variant readings. And, above all, the paramount trait of the synoptic gospels is that they are synoptic, so that we cannot read the one without constant attention to the next. But none has demonstrated, though many have postulated, that parity in no way characterizes any rabbinic document. If we cannot read the Tosefta without the Mishnah, that is because of the traits of the Tosefta, not of the Tosefta and the Mishnah in common. The allegation that we cannot read the Mishnah without constant attention to the Bavli has yet to persuade any modern or contemporary scholar of the Mishnah. That claim presents an invitation to a rather innocent anachronism, and, while profoundly part of the received hermeneutic, it does not resist the test of fact: we can make ample sense of the Mishnah without attention to the Bavli, just as did the authorship of the Yerushalmi (!).

What Cohen demands when he asks us to "study synoptic texts synoptically" therefore is hardly clear. But the position he announces of course derives not from him but from Morton Smith, who first invoked, in the setting of the study of relationships among rabbinic documents, the analogy to the Synoptic Gospels. Let us therefore turn to the source and examine the specific metaphor of connection Smith proposes, namely, to the Synoptic Gospels.

II. "STUDYING SYNOPTIC TEXTS SYNOPTICALLY"[2]

In the classic work, *Tannaitic Parallels to the Gospels,* Morton Smith, Cohen's teacher, first made the observation that the relationship existing between books comes under analysis in the comparison of what he calls "Tannaite Literature" and the Gospels:

> Every literature consisting of several books – such as the Gospels or T[annaitic] L[iterature] – makes possible the discussion of the relationship which exists between the books, and in the comparison of literatures it is possible to compare the relationship which exists between the books of one literature with the relationship which exists between the books of a second literature [Smith, p. 142].

---

[2]References in this section are as follows:

Braude and Kapstein:

W.G. Braude and I.J. Kapstein, *Pesikta de Rab Kahana* (Philadelphia, 1975: Jewish Publication Society of America), pp. xlix-1.

Cohen:

Shaye J.D. Cohen, "Jacob Neusner, Mishnah, and Counter-Rabbinics," *Conservative Judaism* 1983, 37:48-63.

Herr:

Moshe David Herr, "Tosefta," *Encyclopaedia Judaica* (Jerusalem, 1971), 15:1283-5.

Melammed, 1943:

E.Z. Melammed, *Halachic Midrashim of the Tannain in the Talmud Babli* (Jerusalem, 1943). In Hebrew.

Melammed, 1967:

E.Z. Melamed [sic], *The Relationship between the Halakhic Midrashism [sic] and the Mishna and Tosefta. I. The Use of Mishna and Tosefta in the Halakhic Midrashim. II. Halakhic Midrashim in the Mishna and Tosefta* (Jerusalem, 1967). In Hebrew.

Melammed, 1973:

E.Z. Melammed, *An Introduction to Talmudic Literature* (Jerusalem, 1973). In Hebrew.

Neusner, 1974:

Jacob Neusner, *The Tosefta. Translated from the Hebrew. Sixth Division. Tohorot. The Order of Purities* (N.Y., 1974: Ktav), pp. ix-x.

Smith:

Morton Smith, *Tannaitic Parallels to the Gospels.* Philadelphia, 1951: Society of Biblical Literature. *Journal of Biblical Literature Monograph Series,* Volume VI.

Smith further observes that all four gospels are "very close to each other" and alleges that that is the case also in Tannaitic Literature:

> The striking fact is the large numbers of complete parallels to be found between its various books, especially between the Mishnah and Tosefta, Mekilta of R. Simon and Sifre on Deut., Sifre Zutta and Sifra, Mekilta and Sifre on Numbers. But apart from these pairs, there are to be found many passages common to all the midrashim [Smith, p. 142].

In his enthusiasm for the proposition at hand Smith goes on even to allege:

> I cannot recall even a word by any Jewish scholar remarking ... that the problem of the relationship between Tosefta and the Mishnah is similar to the synoptic problem, and this in spite of the fact that they are so similar as to be practically inseparable, and that any theory begun from a study of the one literature should have immediate application in the study of the other [Smith, p. 143].

Let us turn to Smith's allegation that the relationships between certain rabbinic compositions are such that a theory begun in the study of the Gospels should have immediate application in the study of any document of the rabbinic canon of late antiquity.

Clearly, that allegation, if it is true, imposes a very particular sort of connection on those documents to which it applies. While Smith refers to a variety of documents, we shall concentrate on the Mishnah and the Tosefta. For his meaning, I believe context makes clear, transcends the mere presence of shared materials, even though his statement, "there are to be found many passages common to all the midrashim," suggests that all he has in mind is the presence, in a variety of documents, of variations of a given saying or story. That rather trivial fact hardly requires Smith's conclusion that "the problem of the relationship between Tosefta and the Mishnah is similar to the synoptic problem, and this in spite of the fact that they are so similar as to be practically inseparable, and that any theory begun from a study of the one literature should have immediate application in the study of the other."

We rapidly review the premises of the metaphor deriving from the synoptic study of the gospels. These are, first, that the Gospels go over verbatim or nearly so the same materials, e.g., sharing the same sayings and stories, but, second and more important,, that some of the Gospels drew upon an available source of such sayings and stories ("Q"). The issue of a common Source is critical. What is claimed is that the shared materials in Matthew and Mark originate in a document like Matthew or Mark but independent of them – a document, not merely free-floating sayings from we know not where. So Q must enter English as Source, not merely sources in the sense of shared sayings or stories. Without that second fact, all we have is a rather inflated restatement of the simple fact that sayings and stories travel from document to document in the rabbinic corpus and sayings and stories make voyages, also, from one Gospel to the next. Smith himself goes further than the stated premises in claiming, in regard to all four Gospels:

As a matter of fact all of the four are very close to each other, and the more they are studied the more superficial their differences and the more important their similarities are seen to be [Smith, p. 142]. We may accordingly introduce a third premise in assessing the allegation of "parallels of parallelism" (in Smith's phrase). It is that given documents are "very close to each other," so differences among them are vastly outweighed by similarities.

Let us then summarize the indicators of the synoptic connection or relationship:

1. shared materials,

2. deriving from a common source, itself a Source,

3. and imparting their distinctive traits of doctrine or style to the several documents in which they occur.

Now the obvious strategy for examining the allegation at hand demands that we turn to compositions attributed to Tannaite authorship, since Smith makes explicit reference, in his catalogue, to those writings. But when Smith wrote, people took for granted that if a document's authors imputed sayings only to first and second century authorities ("Tannas"), then that document derived from, or formed part of, "Tannaitic Literature," of that period. In a formal sense, of course, that is so. In a concrete historical sense it is unlikely. The reason is that documents assigned to Tannaite authorship, e.g., Mekhilta, Sifra, Tosefta, now are known to have reached closure long after the second century. Since, in his treatment of the subject, Smith points toward Mishnah-Tosefta relationships, it is worth noting that I have demonstrated that most of the Tosefta stands as a secondary expansion and commentary to the Mishnah. So the Tosefta is not only not "Tannaitic" but probably fourth century or later [Herr]. The framers of the Tosefta, for instance, very often cite verbatim and then gloss or rework statements of the Mishnah. Matthew does not quote and gloss Mark in that (or any other) way. Much of the Tosefta is incomprehensible out of relationship to the Mishnah, but one can intelligibly read Matthew without reading Mark.

Accordingly, it is easy to show that the problem of the relationship between Tosefta and the Mishnah is in no way similar to the Synoptic problem. Why not? For the Synoptic Gospels to present us with a parallel to the actual relationship between the Mishnah and the Tosefta, Luke would have to be incomprehensible except in relationship (e.g., juxtaposition) to Mark, or Luke and Mark to "Q," just as vast tracts of the Tosefta prove incomprehensible except in juxtaposition to passages of the Mishnah.

That one exception is simple. It is the fact that, just as the Gospels share sayings and stories, the Mishnah and the Tosefta, among most rabbinic compositions, share sayings and stories. But very often when the Tosefta shares materials with the Mishnah, the Tosefta cites those materials briefly and not completely, and then expands upon the allusion. Where does an author of a Gospel cite another Gospel briefly, by way of allusion, and then expand upon what is clearly material quoted from another document? The answer is, no where. So the relationships in no way are parallel, even where materials are shared. In point of fact the relationship between the Mishnah and the Tosefta bears no parallel of any consequence but one to the relationship between two Gospels or among all four of them. The Tosefta cites and glosses passages of the Mishnah, treated as deriving from a text "out there," and commonly not fully cited but only subjected to rapid allusion. There is no parallel in any of the synoptic gospels to such a relationship. It is hardly much of a connection.

Let me state matters in somewhat more general terms by reverting to the matter of the saying or story that moves from one document to the next. We ask whether that simple fact that itinerant stories occur imparts to the rabbinic writings the character of synoptic documents, so that, as Smith claims, the problem of the relationship between Tosefta and the Mishnah is similar to the synoptic problem, and this in spite of the fact that they are so similar as to be practically inseparable, and that any theory begun from a study of the one literature should have immediate application in the study of the other." Just as Gospels, e.g., Luke and Matthew, know sayings and stories unknown to one or more of the others, so rabbinic writings, e.g., the two Talmuds (the one of the Land of Israel, ca. A.D. 400, the other of Babylonia, ca. A.D. 600) know sayings and stories unknown to other writings within the same canon. Stated in this way, the exception turns out to be trivial. Why so? The relationship among two or more documents based upon the appearance, in all of them, of the same sayings or stories turns out to be altogether general. What do we know (or, *what else* do we know) about those documents and the relationships among them because they share a given saying or story? In my judgment the answer is that we know only that they share a given saying or story. Beyond that fact everything remains as before. We do not grasp, solely out of the self-evident but trivial relationship of materials held in common, any further facts about the documents at hand. For example, we do not know about their common access to a prior source ("Q"), let alone the viewpoint and contents of that prior source, the disposition of the authors of the several documents of what they chose to utilize out of that prior source, and the like.

That is to say, the discovery of parallel relationships between the books of one canon and those of another canon can produce consequential results only when results of two types emerge.

First, if the parallel relationships point to a common source, then the growth of the materials in the synoptic documents, out of the common source, will present important insight into the character of the documents at hand.

Second, if the parallel relationships permit description of the contents of the common source, then the pre-history of the documents, that is, the intellectual history of the authors, becomes accessible. In my view one of the great achievements of Gospels' scholarship is the discovery of "Q." Knowing only that the Gospels go over shared materials, without the recognition of "Q," we should not have that great edifice of learning comprised by Gospels' scholarship in the past and present centuries. All we should have is the Diatesseron. So "Q" is at the center. To state matters more generally, the critical issue is the nature and character of the shared materials. Having set matters out in these general terms, let me now ask whether the Mishnah, Tosefta, Yerushalmi, and Bavli constitute synoptic texts, in that they connect with one another as the Synoptic Gospels relate. Or do they relate in some other way altogether? Then a different metaphor from that adopted from the Synoptic Gospels will serve.

III. SPECIFIC INDICATORS OF SYNOPTIC CONNECTIONS AMONG THE MISHNAH, TOSEFTA, YERUSHALMI, AND BAVLI

Smith's (and Cohen's) claim demands validation by criteria that require specification:

1. they must share materials – sayings or stories,

2. deriving from a common source, itself a Source,

3. and imparting their distinctive traits of doctrine or style to the several documents in which they occur.

There is a negative side to matters as well:

1. The connections between or among them may not fall into the classification of commentary, in that text B cites and glosses materials of text A.

2. The texts that occur in two or more of the documents may not simply derive from a shared third source. The relationship between the two documents must be affected by what they share. Merely citing a third source in common, e.g, the Scripture or Mishnah, does not by itself establish connection at all.

3. Presence by itself of a shared saying or story proves nothing about the connection between or among the documents, since the passage of a shared saying may mean no more than the appearance of a shared verse of Scripture. What is shared must partake of the traits of Q – that is to say, it must itself form part of a distinctive document on its own, with its definitive traits of form and doctrine or viewpoint.

IV. THE MISHNAH

Now to our sample, we turn to Appendix One, which contains Chapter Eight of Mishnah-tractate Berakhot and the materials of Tosefta, Yerushalmi, and

Bavli, that stand in a genealogical relationship to that chapter. My claim is that so far as the later documents take up the program of the Mishnah, it is as commentaries, moving from point to point in the unfolding of the documents. The Tosefta responds to the Mishnah, the Yerushalmi to the Tosefta and thence to the Mishnah, and the Bavli likewise. So the relationships are those of dialectical – moving – commentaries, one to the former. But as we review the data, we shall see in concrete terms why this conception of the connections fits the facts, and Smith's does not.

We begin with the Mishnah's connections to other writings. Except anachronistically – and anachronism cannot impose a hermeneutic! – there is none. The Mishnah bears no synoptic relationships with other documents known to us, and, as to other kinds of relationships, the Mishnah merely cites Scripture. The relationship constituted by citing documents hardly establishes connection in the present sense, because it is extrinsic. We may state quite simply that the chapter before us relates to no prior document known to us, except, of course, for Scripture. Yet that presents no important fact bearing hermeneutical consequence. For no one outside the circle of the faithful now contends that because a passage of the rabbinic canon cites Scripture, therefore Scripture and the later rabbinic writings form a single indivisible corpus. Nor does the Mishnah relate to any contemporary document known to us. That is to say, while materials that occur in the Tosefta respond to those in the Mishnah, none in the Mishnah has been demonstrated to respond to sentences now located outside of the Mishnah. That is because the Mishnah is not only the first document of its canon, it is the only document of its canon that took shape in its time and was closed when it was closed. So by definition, so far as Mark, Matthew, Luke, and Q derive from, let us say, the same fifty year period, from ca. 60 to ca. 110, there is no parallel. Merely because later authorships allude to the Mishnah and rework what they find there, we cannot maintain that those authorships and the Mishnah's authorship stand in a reciprocal relationship of any kind. They do not, unless today's Supreme Court communicates with the Court of John Jay – and the Court of John Jay answers back.

Let us proceed, nonetheless, to take seriously and at face value the allegations of those who have instructed us on issues of connection, Cohen and (as we shall see in the next chapter) Schiffman in particular. Cohen's statement, "Synoptic texts must always be studied synoptically, even if one text is 'later' than another," does not seem to me to pertain. For unless we can establish a synoptic relationship, we hardly have to "study texts synoptically" – whatever that may mean. Schiffman makes a broader claim. He says the documents connect in an "interlocking" fashion. For the sake of argument, let us accept his hypothesis on connection. If therefore we were to take the view that Scripture and the Mishnah constitute reciprocal readings of one another, so that they form, in Schiffman's words, "interlocking and re-interlocking parts possessed of an organic connection one to another...never really divisible," then which document must be read in light of the other? In fact, Scripture will require a rereading in light of the present chapter of the Mishnah, rather than vice versa. For while the Mishnah contains a rich corpus of assertions as to the law, none of these bears any relationship to rules known to legal texts in Scripture. At issue in our chapter are norms of behavior – saying a blessing over wine prior to the Sabbath, saying a blessing over the wine itself, washing hands, mixing the cup, not to mention considerations of cultic cleanness external to the Temple itself – of which the diverse law codes of Scripture know absolutely nothing. So the fact that the Mishnah and Scripture are supposed to be connected – interlocking, no less! – produces only hermeneutical chaos, with the later document imposing its facts upon the earlier one. The prevailing hermeneutic that all parts of the rabbinic corpus on the basis of intrinsic literary traits are to be read in light of all other parts, forming as they are supposed to an interlocking whole, for the Mishnah is simply wrong. In no way does the written component, whole or in its principal parts, of the Torah form an interlocking whole with the oral part, as represented by Mishnah-tractate Chapter Eight.

V. TOSEFTA

The relationship between the Tosefta's passage and the Mishnah's may be simply characterized. We proceed now to review both Tosefta-passages presented in the appendices. These show the Tosefta as the Mishnah's first commentary and secondary amplification. Nearly everything in hand depends on the Mishnah, either as a gloss of a passage cited from the Mishnah, or as an expansion of a statement of the Mishnah that can be understood wholly and completely only in relationship to the Mishnah's statement. There is a negligible amount of material completely autonomous of the Mishnah and also within its topical framework. Such material could be represented as correlative to that of the Mishnah and independent of, yet responsive to, the Mishnah. There is none before us. My survey of the entirety of the Tosefta yields too small a proportion to change our picture of an essentially uniform connection between the Tosefta and the Mishnah, one of propositional commentary and thematic augmentation.

1. Berakhot

The materials I present in the appendix to this part of the book show that the authorship of the Tosefta cites and glosses or otherwise amplifies the Mishnah-passage at hand. These have been selected to illustrate that fact, however, so it is only in our review of Tosefta to Sanhedrin that we can expand our inquiry.

If we review the comparison of M. 8:1ff. and T. 5:25ff., we see a quite fixed relationship, in which the framers of the Tosefta cite and then gloss the successive statements of the Mishnah. That establishes a relationship of commentary, in that the Tosefta, in the cited passage, serves as a commentary to the Mishnah. The authorship of the Tosefta expands the statements of the law given in the Mishnah; the Tosefta's formulations comment, amplify, add reasons, in other ways labor in complete dependency for meaning and sense. At some points one may argue that the Tosefta contains a different version of the law from that in the Mishnah. At others, e.g., M. 8:8 and T. 5:30 we can establish no clear relationship, other than a thematic intersection, between the two documents. At still further passages, e.g., M. 8:6 and T. 5:31, the two documents present separate and independent statements of substantially the same law. Yet even here we are able to find grounds for viewing the Toseftan version as an extension and expansion of the Mishnaic one. The connection consisting of citation and gloss hardly conforms to the picture of Mishnah-Tosefta relationships drawn by Smith.

2. Sanhedrin

Here the relationship of the Tosefta to the Mishnah proves diverse, because I have given the complete, corresponding chapter of the Tosefta, not merely the passages that clearly cite and amplify the Mishnah. T. San. 4:1 pursues the theme of the Mishnah and at several points cites the Mishnah. T. 4:2 falls into the same classification of Mishnah-citation and amplification, either as to theme or even as to problematic. T. 4:3 amplifies the theme. T. 4:4 continues the theme but pursues its own interest. T. 4:5 responds directly to the Mishnah's issues. T. 4:6 has its own problem on the established theme. T. 4:7 remains entirely within the Mishnah's orbit, even when it does not cite the Mishnah verbatim. T. 4:8A-C is independent of the Mishnah in theme and all the more so interest. T. 4:8D-I amplify the interest of the Mishnah in the king's having his own Torah-scroll, and T. 4:9 continues the same theme. T. 4:10-11 are independent of the interests of the Mishnah. So nearly the whole of the Tosefta to M. Sanhedrin Chapter Two serves not only the thematic program of the Mishnah-chapter but also the exploration of the particular interest of the Mishnah in the special rights and standings of the Israelite rulers. I see in proportion less than 10% of the whole as essentially independent in problematic, and if we look at T. 4:10-11 a second time, we realize that the passage amplifies the basic theme, the king, in essentially the spirit of the foregoing. So the Tosefta passage before us nearly completely intersects in theme and proposition and contains scarcely a line that the program of the Mishnah has not dictated. The Tosefta does not relate to the Mishnah as Mark relates to Matthew or as Mark and Matthew relate to Q. It is not a synoptic relationship. The connection here, as much as earlier, is one of text and commentary. These therefore are not synoptic texts.

VI. YERUSHALMI

The relationship between the materials collected and organized in the Yerushalmi and those in the Mishnah and Tosefta show points of connection and points of autonomy. Let us review each sort of entry and then characterize the whole.

1. The Yerushalmi Cites and Glosses the Mishnah and Tosefta

A. Berakhot

Y. Ber. 8:1: all components of this protracted discussion refer to the Mishnah or the Tosefta. Y. Ber. 8:2 follows suit, then broadening discussion to encompass secondary issues, e.g., the status of washing before and after a meal. The theme is the same as that of the Mishnah and Tosefta, but the issue shifts. What we then have is a repertoire of materials on hand-washing: the Mishnah's theme, but not the Mishnah's problematic and proposition. Y. Ber. 8:3 proceeds along the same pattern. First come citation of the Mishnah and amplification of its rule and the reasons, then the encomapssing principles, behind that rule. Y. Ber. 8:4 goes over the reasons behind the rulings of the Houses in the Mishnah. Only at Q do we come upon materials essentially distinct from those in the Mishnah. Y. 8:6A-E amplify the rule of the Mishnah. Y. Ber. 8:6F presents five rules on the coal, five on the flame, which closely pursue the Mishnah's basic interests. Y. 8:7 proceeds along the lines of the established pattern: first comes amplification of the Mishnah, specifically, reasons for the views of the Houses, then secondary facts important for the same matter. Y. 8:8 A-J adhere to the same pattern. Y. 8:4Q-LL append materials that in theme intersect with those of the Mishnah but in substance stand completely autonomous of the Mishnah's discussion. Y. 8:8K-S are appended because of their thematic relevance, but in fact the composition has been worked out in its own terms. To state the obvious with emphasis: *Citation and gloss do not characterize synoptic connections between documents.*

B. Sanhedrin

Y. 2:1I amplifies the Mishnah-passage. II, III, IV serve M. Hor. 3:1, added here because of the thematic relevance. V, carrying in its wake VI, VII, cites and comments on the Mishnah's rule. Y., 2:2I extends the rule of the Mishnah. II introduces a pertinent theme, leading to the citation of the Mishnah. III carries forward II. Y. 2:3I cites and glosses the Mishnah. The same is so of II, III, IV, V. The secondary expansion of V, of course, goes its own way, working out the theme introduced by the Mishnah. So the passage has been composed on its own terms, so V.Cff., but has been included because of the interest of Mishnah-amplification. Y. 2:4I amplifies the Mishnah. Y. 2:5I-II cite and gloss the Mishnah. Y. 2:6I cites and explains the Mishnah. Y. 2:6III, IV, cite and gloss the Mishnah or the Tosefta. So the plan of the Yerushalmi is systematically to amplify and expand the Mishnah's and the Tosefta's statements. In volume a rough guess would place the exegetical component of the Yerushalmi at a proportion of 75-80 per cent. These materials, in both tractates, connect as commentary and text, with the Yerushalmi citing the Mishnah as an independent document and then commenting on passages of that book.

2. The Yerushalmi Presents Materials Distinct from Those of the Mishnah and Tosefta

A. Berakhot

Everything in the Yerushalmi's treatment of the Mishnah and its associated Tosefta relates to the themes of the Mishnah, and nearly everything before us works out the issues of those themes as defined by the Mishnah. I see no editorial principle at hand other than that of commentary, which therefore defines the connection as well.

B. Sanhedrin

In this category falls Y. 2:3V, a systematic study of verses of Scripture introduced because of its thematic intersection with the Mishnah passage before us. Y. 2:4III presents a study of scriptural verses worked out on their own. Y. 2:5III-IV – a continuous unit – is tacked on because it carries forward the established theme, but it is completely independent of Mishnah-exegesis, concentrating instead on Scripture. Y. 2:6II is framed in exegesis of verses of Scripture. Y. 2:6V is inserted because it is relevant to the theme of the foregoing, but it is worked out as an independent story, entirely on its own. It focuses on sage-patriarch relationships. Y. 2:6VI is a story inserted because it carries forward a detail of the foregoing, that is, the allusion to Samaritan country. We can explain the selection and insertion of all of these materials: they serve to amplify a theme introduced by Mishnah or Tosefta exegesis. But, it is clear, the framers of the Yerushalmi have had access to materials formed on principles other than those that guide the authorship of Mishnah and Tosefta exegesis. The connections between the Yerushalmi and the Mishnah and the Tosefta in no way run parallel to the connections among the three synoptic Gospels. The Yerushalmi cites the Mishnah and the Tosefta, it does not go over, independently and autonomously, the same materials in splendid isolation from those available documents. The Yerushalmi responds to elements of the Mishnah and the Tosefta, and, so far as it is connected to them, it is a connection we may characterize as responsive, indeed dialectic. In following the program of the Mishnah and the Tosefta, the authors of the Yerushalmi consider questions and problems laid forth by the prior documents and take up the analysis of those matters. The connection is intellectual, exegetical, and articulated: extrinsic, dialectic. I see no parallel whatsoever between the Yerushalmi's connection with the Mishnah and the Tosefta and the relationships between or among Q, Matthew, Mark, and Luke.

VII. BAVLI

What we have seen in the connections between the Yerushalmi and the Mishnah and Tosefta recurs in our survey of the Bavli.

1. The Bavli Cites and Glosses the Mishnah and Tosefta

A. Berakhot

Following the outline given in the appendix to this part, we find the following: all of unit I, the Houses's disputes, cites and glosses the Mishnah and the Tosefta pertinent to the Mishnah. Unit II relates in the same way to the base passages of the Mishnah and the Tosefta. But materials assembled in unit II do more than cite and gloss the Mishnah and the Tosefta, since some of the compositions before us work on the same theme but raise distinct questions. Nonetheless, a single principle of aggregation governs: the theme and also the problematic of the Mishnah, specifically, saying a blessing over light, and, in particular, over light of a particular origin. Unit III may be classified in the same way. The theme is using the light, and a set of pertinent passages, assigned to the authority of Tannaim, then is cited and subjected to secondary amplification. Unit IV likewise works on the theme of the Mishnah and glosses the rulings of the Mishnah's authorities.

B. Sanhedrin

Bavli to M. 2:1-2 I, II, II, IIVI, V, VI,, VII, VIII, IX, X, XI, all cite and gloss the Mishnah or the Tosefta. XII is inserted because it proves a proposition important to XII, but it is formed on its own topic, involving exegesis of Scripture. The same is so of XIII. Bavli to M. 2:3I amplifies M. 2:3D-E, as cited. IV amplifies cited passages of the Mishnah and themes introduced by the citation. B. to M. 2:4A-DI-III, V amplify citations of the Mishnah. B. to M. 2:4E-I/I-II cite and clarify Mishnah's statements. B. to M. 2:4J-N/I-II, IV, V, and B. to M. 2:5/IX-XI amplify the statements or the themes of the Mishnah.

2. The Bavli Presents Materials Distinct from Those of the Mishnah and Tosefta

A. Berakhot

I see nothing in the Bavli to Mishnah-tractate Berakhot Chapter Eight that does not serve to gloss the Mishnah's or the Tosefta's statements or to amplify their themes. There is no independent editorial principle at hand. The Bavli does not connect to the Mishnah as synoptic documents relate.

B. Sanhedrin

The sizable corpus of materials that does not to begin with amplify the Mishnah or the Tosefta focuses on Scripture. The framers of Bavli Sanhedrin Chapter Two have drawn upon systematic treatments of sequences of verses of Scripture or of scriptural topics, e.g., David at Pas-Dammim for the former, Solomon for the latter, at B. to M. 2:4A-DIV. They have also had access to completed compositions on incidents in lives of sages or on sages' public addresses, exemplified by the sage-patriarch stories. As to specific passages that belong on this list: B. to M. 2:3/II, continued by III, clarifies a verse thematically relevant to I, but it is essentially worked out on its own terms B. to

M. 2:4E-I/III is attached because of the theme of the preceding discourse but is independent in its principle of composition, which derives from the cited passages of Scripture. B. to M. 2:4J-N/III works out the exegesis of two verses of Scripture and is inserted because of its relevant to the theme of the Mishnah. But the composition is independent of Mishnah-exegesis. The same is so of V. The single most interesting example of a sustained and completely independent composition is at B. to M. 2:5/I-VIII. This is a thematic essay on the divorce of the first wife, an essay worked out entirely in its own terms as the theme, not verses of Scripture let alone sentences of the Mishnah, dictates. This utterly independent and protracted composition typifies the possibilities. In our sample at hand, I estimate that not more than 20% of the volume, in all, falls into the present classification. In any event no one has alleged that the Bavli and the Mishnah stand in a synoptic relationship to Scripture or establish connection with one another through Scripture.

VIII. NOT SYNOPTIC BUT DIALECTIC RELATIONSHIPS

We now revert to the questions outlined above.

1. The Proportion of Shared Materials: Mishnah

A. Berakhot

The passage at hand stands completely separate from all other writings.

B. Sanhedrin

Apart from citing verses of Scripture, the Mishnah-passage intersects with no other document.

Tosefta:

A. Berakhot

The sample at hand completely depends on the Mishnah for program and structure. But I selected the passage for the purpose of showing how the Tosefta accomplishes that very task, and it is not a complete chapter.

B. Sanhedrin

The relationship of Tosefta to Mishnah finds more suitable amplification in this sample. Only T. 4:10-11 are essentially distinct from the Mishnah's program. The theme is shared, but the aspect of the theme and the pertinent issue are autonomous.

Yerushalmi:

A. Berakhot

We have to distinguish passages framed for exegesis of the Mishnah from those found after the fact useful in amplification of the themes of the Mishnah. The former have already been catalogued. As to the latter, I see the following: Y. 8:1: none; Y. 8:2: "Washing before the meal...," to the end of the treatment of M. 8:2 is fully developed on its own, not in response to the requirement of Mishnah-exegesis; Y. 8:3: none; Y. 8:4: none; Y. 8:5: Q-JJ: worked out entirely in its own terms; Y. 8:6: completely dependent on the Mishnah's passage, which it serves as amplification; Y. 8:6 from "They do not bless" A through DD is a composition on its own problem; Y. 8:7: solely Mishnah-exegesis; Y. 8:8 solely Mishnah-exegesis; Y. 8:9: K-S are composed on their own focus. The upshot is simple. Nearly the whole of the materials in the Yerushalmi focus directly on the exegesis of the Mishnah. Only a handful of compositions have been worked out other than for that one purpose, and even these have been inserted for the purpose of Mishnah-amplification if not exegesis. None of these passages establishes a connection from the document in which it occurs to the Mishnah – and that by definition.

B. Sanhedrin

If we give a rough estimate of the proportion of materials not devoted to Mishnah-exegesis, we count B. to M. 2:3/II-III, B. to M. 2:4E-I/III, B. to M. 2:4J-N/III, V, and, of importance, B. to M. 2:5/I-VIII. In all, I count 42 distinct units of discourse, of which, among those specified, 13 are essentially independent, not exercises in the exegesis of the language and themes of Mishnah-Tosefta, somewhat over a fourth of the whole. If we substract from that number the sustained unit of eight items and count that as a simple set, the disproportion is considerably more pronounced: six out of 34 or under 20%.

Bavli:

A. Berakhot

Unit I systematically explains the Mishnah and the Tosefta. There is no material in any way independent of those documents' propositions, not to mention their themes. Unit II works through the established themes. Some entries seem to me to move in directions not indicated by the Mishnah and the Tosefta, and these fall into the category of thematically dependent compositions, e.g., "...light which has rested on the Sabbath." It is possible, therefore, to identify some materials not written in response to the program and problematic of the Mishnah or the Tosefta, but these intersect in so extensive a way as to render those materials essentially one with the rest. Unit III for its part is no different from unit I. Unit IV is no different.

B. Sanhedrin

We have identified a number of compositions independent of the theme and all the more so of the problematic of the Mishnah and the Tosefta. These compositions ordinarily focus upon Scripture and subject a set of verses to the sort of exegesis that pertains, also to sentences of the Mishnah. A much smaller proportion of the whole comprises stories about sages.

2. The Function of Shared Materials in a Given Document:

Mishnah:

This category does not pertain.

Tosefta:

A. Berakhot

For Tosefta, what is "shared" in fact is cited from the Mishnah, and that set of materials supplies Tosefta with its purpose, plan, and program.

B. Sanhedrin

The same judgment applies here. What is shared is secondary and derivative: exegesis of a received text, not materials occurring independently in two or more texts.

Yerushalmi:

A. Berakhot

The materials that are shared verbatim are cited either from the Mishnah or from the Tosefta. Those that are shared in problem derive that problem from the prior documents. Those that are shared in theme are worked out along lines internal to themselves and inserted only because of their thematic intersection with the Mishnah-passage at hand. They serve for Mishnah-exegesis.

B. Sanhedrin

The same judgment applies without variation. What is shared derives not from a common third source but a received text, subjected by the later of the documents to a systematic exegesis.

Bavli:

A. Berakhot

The shared materials comprise citations of the Mishnah or the Tosefta followed by amplifications and secondary expansions of those same materials.

B. Sanhedrin

The same judgment pertains.

3. The Identity of the Shared Materials:

Shared materials are of two kinds: those cited from an existing document for purposes of exegesis, e.g., Mishnah or Tosefta or Genesis Rabbah, and those that occur in two or more documents but are not cited as a distinct and autonomous text, e. g., for purposes of exegesis. The former materials by definition constitute a distinct corpus, and we know what it is: Mishnah, Tosefta. Whether or not the materials not in Mishnah or Tosefta but marked TNY constitute yet another corpus remains to be demonstrated.

We now ask about the other materials that are shared among our documents and another one.

[A] Do shared materials constitute a distinct corpus in this document?

Mishnah: This category does not apply.

Tosefta:

A. Berakhot

The materials shared with a prior document of course form a distinct corpus: the Mishnah. I see no other point of pertinence, since the Mishnah is the only document that, according to the prevailing consensus, reached closure substantially before the redaction of Tosefta.

B. Sanhedrin

What is not unique to T. Sanhedrin derives from M. Sanhedrin, pure and simple.

Yerushalmi:

A. Berakhot

The shared materials constitute citations of the Mishnah or the Tosefta. They do form part of a distinct corpus, on that is identifiable and available. They do not form part of a corpus of materials upon which framers of diverse documents draw *ad lib.* Shared materials in fact constitute nothing other than citations of available documents. There are, to be sure, materials that share linguistic and formal conventions with the Mishnah and the Tosefta, those introduced by the signal-word, TNY and its variations. But these materials, attributed to Tannaite, that is, Mishnaic, authorities or, if not named, then at least, authority, in fact are autonomous of the Mishnah and the Tosefta. Nothing in the bits and pieces in our hands suggests that they form fragments of a third document originating in the period of the writing of the Mishnah.

B. Sanhedrin

Materials that occur in two or more documents seem to me discrete and not to give indication of deriving from a single, third document, that is, a Q.

Bavli:

A. Berakhot

What has been said about Yerushalmi Berakhot applies without significant variation to Bavli Berakhot. That composition depends for purpose and meaning on the Mishnah and the Tosefta, encompassing, also, some tertiary materials marked TNY (and similar signals) that also receive amplification. We can readily identify the shared materials that constitute nothing other than citations of antecedent writings. Whatever else is shared with other documents than those we can identify forms too small a proportion of the whole to permit analysis. We shall revert to this matter in a moment.

B. Sanhedrin

The cross-references supplied in the standard edition of the Bavli Sanhedrin to pp. 18a-22b direct our attention to, in addition to other passages of Scripture, the Mishnah, and the Tosefta, the Babylonian Talmud. For reasons already explained, we need not address ourselves to the first three sources. At issue then is what our pages of the Yerushalmi or the Bavli share with other pages of the Yerushalmi or the Bavli. We now turn to that question.

[B] Do Shared Materials Form a Distinct Corpus in the Entire Repertoire of Documents?

What we now wish to know is whether materials that occur in two or more passages exhibit traits in common such that we may assign those shared materials to a single point of origin.

Mishnah:

A. Berakhot: This question does not apply.

B. Sanhedrin: This question does not pertain.

Tosefta:

A. Berakhot

The answer is entirely affirmative. What is shared with a prior document derives from *the Mishnah* and, as such, forms part of that document in style and in literary convention. So far as we can now determine, there is no other "source" upon which Tosefta's authorship draws.

B. Sanhedrin

The fact for Tosefta Sanhedrin is as just now stated.

Yerushalmi and Bavli:

A. Berakhot

What has already been said need not be repeated. The greater part of what the Yerushalmi shares with another document derives from the Mishnah or the Tosefta. Whatever else in our passage occurs both in the Yerushalmi and some other document is too fragmentary in its representation in the Yerushalmi to permit speculation. It is not possible to demonstrate that a cogent collection originally contained the sherds and remnants of materials used here and elsewhere and not part of the Mishnah or the Tosefta or the exegetical corpus serving those documents. Of course the shared materials form a distinctive corpus, because they come from one in hand, as observed before. Whatever else is shared is miniscule in proportion and exhibits no clearcut and distinctive traits of its own.

Let us now conduct a very brief probe of materials that occur more than once or in more than a single document, that is, in both Bavli and Yerushalmi. We omit from our probe the obviously irrelevant items, that is, Mishnah, Tosefta, and proceed directly to passages that occur in both Talmuds. For that purpose, we deal with Sanhedrin in Yerushalmi and Bavli.[3] My purpose is simply to ask how the two Talmuds relate to one another when they deal with an identical topic: do they stand in a synoptic relationship or in some other? Our answer is that what they share is *only* scriptural proof-texts for the Mishnah's proposition. Here it is possible that a prior, third document presented a floreligium of conventional proof-texts for a sequence of propositions contained in the Mishnah.[4] That is not a rabbinic Q. Smith's statement of the possibilities becomes increasingly difficult to justify.

Yerushalmi Sanhedrin 2.6

A. **"He should not multiply wives to himself"** (Deut. 17:17) – only eighteen.

I.   A.   R. Kahana: "[The limitation to eighteen wives] is by reason of the following: *'And the sixth, Ithream, of Eglah, David's wife. These were born to David in Hebron'* (2 Sam. 3:5).   And what is stated further on? *'... I would add to you as much more ...'* (2 Sam. 12:8). [This indicates that there would be yet two more groups of six wives, eighteen in all.]"

B.   *"He should not multiply horses to himself"* (Deut. 17:16), only enough for his chariot (M. San. 2:6F).

C.   This is in line with the following: *"And David hamstrung all the chariot horses, but left enough for a hundred chariots"* (2 Sam. 8:4).

D.   *"Neither shall he greatly multiply to himself silver and gold"* (Deut. 17:17) – only enough to pay his army (M. San. 2:6G).

E.   R. Joshua b. Levi said, "But that provides solely for the wages for a given year alone [and not wages for several consecutive years]."

Bavli Sanhedrin 2:4E-I

II. A.   As to the number of eighteen [specified at M. 2:4E], what is the source for that number?

B.   It is from the following verse of Scripture: *"And unto David were sons born in Hebron, and his first-born son was Amnon, of Ahinoam the Jezreelites, the second, Chileab, of Abigail, the wife of Nabal the Carmelite, the third Absalom, son of Maacah; the fourth, Adonijah, son of Haggith; and the fifth, Shefatiah, son of Abital, and the sixth, Ithream, of Eglah, David's wife. These were born to David in Hebron "* (2 Sam. 3:2-5).

C.   And the prophet said to him, *"And if that were too little, then would I add to you the like of these and the like of these"* (2 Sam. 12:8).

D.   Each "like of these" means six more [since the referent is the original six], so eighteen in all.

---

[3]In my *Judaism. The Classical Statement. The Evidence of the Bavli* (Chicago, 1986: University of Chicago Press) I compare an entire chapter of Yerushalmi and Bavli Sukkah. The results are the same as those produced by the briefer survey here.

[4]In my *Aphrahat and Judaism* I review the interesting thesis that Gospels' authors drew upon a corpus of conventional proof-texts.

E. Rabina objected, "Might I say that 'Like of these' stands for twelve, and the second such reference means twenty-four [Shachter, *Sanhedrin* (London, 1948), p. 113, n. 3: He increased the number in geometrical progression, 6, 12, 24]?"

F. So it has been taught on Tannaite authority:

G. "*He should not multiply wives to himself*" (Deut. 17:17) – more than twenty-four.

H. In the view of him who interprets the "and," the number is forty-eight.

I. It has been taught on Tannaite authority along these very lines:

J. "*He should not multiply wives to himself*" (Deut. 17:17) – more than forty-eight.

K. And what is the reason for the view of the Tannaite authority who framed the Mishnah-passage at hand?

L. Said R. Kahana, "He draws an analogy between the first 'and the like' and the second 'and the like.' Just as the former refers to six, so the latter refers to the six."

M. But there was Michal [beyond the six wives who are listed]?

N. Rab said, "Eglah is Michal, and why was she called Eglah? Because she was as beloved of him as a calf [eglah] is of its mother.

O. "And so it is said, '*If you had not ploughed with my heifer*' (Jud. 14:18)."

P. But did Michal have children? And is it not written, "*And Michal, daughter of Saul, had no child to the day of her death*" (2 Sam. 6:23)?

Q. Said R. Hisda, "To the day of her death she had none, but on the day of her death she had one."

R. Now where, in point of fact, is the number of sons reckoned? It is in Hebron. But the case involving Michal took place in Jerusalem, for it is written, "*Michal, daughter of Saul, looked out at the window and saw King David leaping and dancing before the Lord, and she despised him in her heart*" (2 Sam. 6:16).

S. And R. Judah, and some say R. Joseph, said, "Michal took her due punishment, which was childlessness."

T. Rather, one might propose, prior to that event she had children, but afterward she had none.

U. [Referring to the issue of the number of eighteen specified in the Mishnah-paragraph], is it not stated, "*And David took concubines and wives out of Jerusalem*" (2 Sam. 5:13)?

V. It was to reach the number of eighteen [wives].

W. What is the difference between wives and concubines?

X. Said R. Judah said Rab, "Wives are with a marriage contract and a rite of betrothal, concubines are without a marriage contract and without a rite of betrothal."

Let us now ask how the two passages relate as to topic.

Y. San. 2:6	B. San. to 2:4E-I
I. Proof-texts, 2 Sam. 3:5, 2 Sam. 8:4	II. Proof-texts, 2 Sam. 3:23-5, 2 Sam. 12:18, plus extensive secondary expansion.

That, sum and substance, constitutes the relationship. The sole connection is through the shared proof-text.

What we derive from this rapid comparison affords slight comfort to the proponents of the synoptic theory of connection among the rabbinic documents. It is exceedingly difficult to see how these two documents relate as to a shared third source, Q, other than one that directs their attention to appropriate proof-texts for Mishnah propositions. But when Cohen states, "Synoptic texts must always be studied synoptically, even if one text is 'later' than another," that is not his intent. Can we concur with Smith that there are *many passages* common to all the documents? Yes and no. Scripture and the Mishnah clearly are common to all the later documents. But our sample does not yield many passages shared among the documents we surveyed, other than persistent citation of the Mishnah, considerably less attention to the Tosefta. But when Smith claims, "it is possible to compare the relationship which exists between the books of one literature with the relationship which exists between the books of a second literature," he will find very little satisfaction in the material before us. There is in fact no synoptic relationship. The Yerushalmi gives its proof-texts, the Bavli gives the same proofs. But beyond that point in common, there is no parallel, no synopsis, no connection but for two: to the Mishnah, to Scripture through the program of the Mishnah.

IX. CONNECTION AND DIALECTICS

Let us now conclude our consideration of the claim that the documents before us, the Mishnah and the Tosefta (in particular, as Smith has alleged) or those as well as the Yerushalmi and the Bavli, bear a synoptic relationship to one another. Going back over our criteria we find the following:

1. they must share materials – sayings or stories,

2. deriving from a common source, itself a Source,

3. and imparting their distinctive traits of doctrine or style to the several documents in which they occur.

The qualifications offered do not require restatement. The Tosefta cites the Mishnah, but nothing before us suggests that the what the Tosefta has in common with the Mishnah derives from a third source (Q), which has imparted through the shared materials distinctive traits of its own on the Mishnah and the Tosefta. The opposite is the case, as a review of the negative side indicates:

1. The connections between or among the documents may not fall into the classification of commentary, in that text B cites and glosses materials of text A. But the Tosefta cites the Mishnah, and the Yerushalmi and the Bavli cite the Mishnah and the Tosefta. And that is all: no Q here. What other synoptic relationship one might imagine I do not know.

2. The texts that occur in two or more of the documents may not simply derive from a shared third source. The relationship between the two

documents must be affected by what they share. Merely citing a third source in common, e.g, the Scripture or Mishnah, does not by itself establish connection at all. The shared third source that joins the Bavli to the Yerushalmi, other than Scripture and Mishnah, may possibly be a florigelium of proof-texts conventionally assigned to given Mishnah- and Tosefta-passages. But no one has remotely proposed the existence of such a source shared in common, and, in any event, it has not imposed on our two documents traits or details (other than the shared proof-texts) that we can identify.

3. Presence by itself of a shared saying or story proves nothing about the connection between or among the documents, since the passage of a shared saying may mean no more than the appearance of a shared verse of Scripture. What is shared must partake of the traits of Q – that is to say, it must itself form part of a distinctive document on its own, with its definitive traits of form and doctrine or viewpoint. What has just been observed about the Bavli's relationship to the Yerushalmi disposes of this matter as well.

We have now demonstrated that in no way does the synoptic analogy serve to characterize the relationship among the documents that do move from one to the next – Mishnah to Tosefta to Yerushalmi to Bavli – and that do share a single exegetical program, namely, Mishnah-exegesis. Each of the appropriate indicators proved a disappointment to Smith's and Cohens's position. How then does it appear that the four documents connect? The answer is simple. *They connect in a dialectical relationship, for one document sets the program of the next, and a movement in logic, rhetoric, and topic, from the first to the final document follows a singular dialectical path.* If the Mishnah gives a law, at the next remove, the Tosefta responds to that law, its contents, then its theme. The Yerushalmi, for its part, responds to the law of the Mishnah, proposition and theme, and also to the amplification in the Tosefta. It then goes its own way with the same theme – and that portion of the Yerushalmi stands in no way except one in a connection to the Mishnah or the Tosefta. That one connection is the shared theme. Because documents talk about the same topics, however, we cannot draw conclusions as to the appropriate hermeneutic to govern the reading of all of those documents. And that simple observation disposes of Handelman's thesis – and with it, the entire inherited hermeneutic that insists that we read all documents in light of all others, and none of them on its own.

Chapter Four

Textuality and Intertextuality

[2] Singular Texts and their Connections: The Case of Leviticus Rabbah

> This system, composed of interlocking and re-interlocking parts possessed of an organic connection one to another, is never really divisible.
>
> Lawrence H. Schiffman[1]

I. PARTS OF A WHOLE AND HOW TO TELL[2]

Having examined the relationships among synoptic texts, we move to a different type of text, namely, one that systematically and as a matter of program

---

[1] In his *Sectarian Law in the Dead Sea Scrolls* (Chico, 1983), p. 3

[2] The references in this chapter are as follows:

Braude and Kapstein
W.G. Braude and I.J. Kapstein, *Pesikta de Rab Kahana* (Philadelphia, 1975: Jewish Publication Society of America), pp. xlix-1.

Cohen
Shaye J.D. Cohen, "Jacob Neusner, Mishnah, and Counter-Rabbinics," *Conservative Judaism* 1983, 37:48-63.

Herr
Moshe David Herr, "Tosefta," *Encyclopaedia Judaica* (Jerusalem, 1971), 15:1283-5.

Melammed, 1943
E.Z. Melammed, *Halachic Midrashim of the Tannain in the Talmud Babli* (Jerusalem, 1943). In Hebrew.

Melammed, 1967
E.Z. Melamed [sic], *The Relationship between the Halakhic Midrashism [sic] and the Mishna and Tosefta. I. The Use of Mishna and Tosefta in the Halakhic Midrashim. II. Halakhic Midrashim in the Mishna and Tosefta* (Jerusalem, 1967). In Hebrew.

Melammed, 1973
E.Z. Melammed, *An Introduction to Talmudic Literature* (Jerusalem, 1973). In Hebrew.

Neusner, 1974
Jacob Neusner, *The Tosefta. Translated from the Hebrew. Sixth Division. Tohorot. The Order of Purities* (N.Y., 1974: Ktav), pp. ix-x.

Smith
Morton Smith, *Tannaitic Parallels to the Gospels.* Philadelphia, 1951: Society of Biblical Literature Journal of Biblical Literature Monograph Series, Volume VI.

intersects with not the Mishnah but Scripture. Since we have seen the ways in which the Tosefta, Yerushalmi, and Bavli stand in a dialectical relationship with the Mishnah, we immediately ask whether a text that amply cites Scripture and so appears to provide a commentary to Scripture stands in a dialectical relationship with Scripture. For the result we have already reached, namely, the thesis that some documents connect in a dialectical relationship with other, prior ones, now requires a test of comparison. Do all texts relate dialectically? If so, we may posit that the entire canon spins out from a single (or dual) original document. That accounts for the selection of a text that stands in relationship to Scripture as do the Tosefta, Yerushalmi, and Bavli do to the Mishnah. At the same time we create an occasion to take up Schiffman's description of the connections among rabbinic documents.

Schiffman's claim vastly exceeds Smith's and Cohen's. He alleges that the documents cannot be distinguished from one another, because they are made up of "interlocking and reinterlocking parts." That is why they are not divisible from one another and each one has always to be read in the light of all others. Is that really true? To answer that question we turn to a sizable document, Leviticus Rabbah, and examine its composition. We want to know whether it is made up of parts that are shared with many other documents, in which case Schiffman's characterization, as a matter of fact, is true. But if the document is not made up of large blocks of materials that occur in other writings, then Schiffman has falsely described the connections that link one document of the canon to the next. His further claim that the documents are not to be distinguished from one another, but that all are to be read in light of all others, also fails. The allegation of an "organic" connection is less easily tested, since what such an organic connection consists of, how we are able to find out whether that type of connection joins document to document, is not equivalently clear. So we remain within the limits of what we can grasp. But when we approach our test-case, we shall transcend the rather narrow definition of the problem supplied by Schiffman. We really ask about the integrity of our document, its autonomy, and not solely about the connections between this document and all others in the rabbinic canon.

Since no one now claims that that intersection in the case of Scripture imposes a connection of an "organic" character, in that we cannot read Scripture except in light of a rabbinic commentary, we reframe the question. Specifically, we take up the position, represented by Schiffman, that all documents in the rabbinic canon must be read in light of all others, because each is made up of "interlocking and reinterlocking" parts that connect organically. Let me ask the question very simply: is a document *really* "not divisible" from all others? Framing matters in a more analytical way, we ask about *the ways* in which the text of the type at hand connects with other documents. But, as I said, our interest in Leviticus Rabbah transcends the matter of mere connection. Our broader question is this: *does the document at hand stand on its own, or does it so substantially intersect with other documents as to lose all autonomous character?* For the position outlined by Schiffman in fact claims precisely that: no text enjoys an autonomous character, but all of them "interlock and reinterlock," as he says. We take up as our sample document Leviticus Rabbah, and in its regard I propose to demonstrate that a rabbinic document constitutes an autonomous document, a text, not merely a scrapbook or a random compilation of episodic materials that serve equally well in any number of other documents.

Since at the outset I resorted to the metaphor of a library, I invoke yet another one to show the possibilities at hand. Let me now define the issue just now introduced in terms of a different metaphor, namely, a text or a scrapbook. A text is a document with a purpose, one that exhibits the traits of the integrity of the parts to the whole and the fundamental autonomy of the whole from other texts. I shall show that the document at hand therefore falls into the classification of a cogent composition, put together with purpose and intended as a whole and in the aggregate on its own to bear a meaning and to state a message. I shall further compare the message I derive from one text and its formal preferences with that I derive from another text and its formal choices, so as to show that the points of stress, style and substance alike, constitute choices and therefore matter. Decisions in favor of saying one thing represent choices not to say some other. And we can explain why this, not that.

I shall therefore disprove the claim, for the case before us, that a rabbinic document serves merely as an anthology or miscellany or is to be compared only to a scrapbook, made up of this and that. Therefore one document is divisible from others, even though at specific points – words, phrases, and that by definition in a literature in one language, not some other, but also units of discourse, entire thoughts – occur elsewhere as well. In the present, exemplary instance I shall point to the improbability that a document has been brought together merely to join discrete and ready-made bits and pieces of episodic discourse. A document in the canon of Judaism thus does not merely define a context for the aggregation of such already completed and mutually distinct materials. Rather, I claim, a document constitutes a text. So in method at issue then is what makes a text a text, that is, the textuality of a document. At stake is how we may know when a document constitutes a text and when it is merely an anthology or a scrapbook. Once that question is settled, the further issue of a "synoptic" study of the particular text at hand will work itself out.

I choose for the test-case Leviticus Rabbah, because I already have made my own translation of it and have also completed certain studies of its rhetoric, modes of argument, and essential message. I could as well have chosen the Mishnah, the Tosefta, Sifra, the Yerushalmi, the Bavli, or other documents on which I have worked at length. Each of these, as well as every other document of the canon of Judaism completed in late antiquity, demands equivalent inquiry. Leviticus Rabbah forms no more promising, nor less promising, an arena for study than any other as to the synoptic side of rabbinic texts. Still, it is more difficult than the Mishnah, which is a far more cogent formal construction. It also appears to be less difficult (so I have the impression) than Genesis Rabbah, on the one side, and the Fathers according to Rabbi Nathan, on the other.[3] As an outsider to those texts, I do have the impression that they fall more readily into the category of scrapbooks or anthologies than cogent compositions. But only further study will tell. A long series of detailed analyses of each rabbinic composition of late antiquity therefore will flow from the present one. So, to conclude, I hope here to inaugurate a useful method of inquiry into a long-standing and much debated, if little-studied, question: whether and how rabbinic documents on their own constitute complete and autonomous statements, addresses exhibiting integrity and those traits of proportion and composition that we associate with well-crafted literature. Let me spell out the method I shall follow.

First, I have to prove that the document at hand rests upon clearcut choices of formal and rhetorical preference, so it is, from the viewpoint of form and mode of expression, cogent. If one taxonomy serves all and encompasses the bulk of the units of discourse at hand, I may fairly claim that Leviticus Rabbah does constitute a cogent formal structure, based upon patterns of rhetoric uniform and characteristic throughout.

Second, I isolate those passages in the document at hand that in fact are not unique to it but are shared with one or more other documents of the same larger canon. In this way I confront in a single test case (if an important one) Schiffman's theory of the character of the literature. These ("synoptic") passages will not only link one document to the next. As I said, they also will call into question the claim that any document stands essentially on its own, exhibiting an integrity that distinguishes that document from all others. What is shared and not unique by definition challenges any claim to integrity and autonomy. If, therefore, what is not particular proves to form an important component of the whole, or if it bears a substantial part of the burden of the message of the whole, then the document as a whole cannot be characterized as autonomous. It would appear, rather, that the document under study must constitute yet another, scarcely differentiated utensil for containing a message indifferent to its bearers. Then, as I said, one document cannot demand differentiation from others. The claim that a given document bears its own message and viewpoint and constitutes a statement of integrity will have to give way to the opposite one. We should then have to claim (with Judaic theologians) that all documents equally bear the message of the whole. Then any one of them indifferently may supply a context for the expression of what is common to them all. Hence,

---

[3]My present intent is to retranslate the Fathers According to Rabbi Nathan, because it seems to me the one rabbinic document that does systematically borrow from other writings and so serve as a kind of scrapbook. It would then provide an interesting contrast to the writings under study in this book.

documents will turn out to constitute not texts but merely contexts. So at issue in the analysis of what is shared is the critical claim at hand.

Third, I have to return to the materials unique to the document at hand and bring them into relationship with materials shared among two or more documents. The compositions particular to the document along with shared materials have to be reexamined and described. These now become the criteria: which sort of materials – unique or common – bear the main formal components of the formal construction of the whole? Are the unique or are the shared materials episodic? If materials unique to Leviticus Rabbah, those that conform to its recurrent literary structures, prove to form the principal parts, then we may say that we deal with a document made up by a distinct set of authors. This authorship has agreed on the formal and rhetorical preferences and has executed them consistently, time and again. If, again, the literary structures unique to the document as a whole cohere and present a cogent composition, then we may claim to know what is primary to the document, what expresses its topical and logical message. More than that, on formal grounds of rhetoric and pattern we again may allege that the document does present its own rhetorical and logical program. I have also to go back to the materials not particular to the document at hand and undertake to describe them. Do shared materials form a large or a negligible proportion? Do they cohere in formal or aesthetic or rhetorical ways? Or do they constitute a miscellany?

If they constitute a miscellany, one might wish to ask whether, in some documents other than the one at hand, the several shared items fit more suitably into an established formal and rhetorical setting than they do in the document under study. If it turns out that what is shared between the document under study and some other document exhibits the characteristic literary traits of that other document, on formal and rhetorical grounds one may claim that that other document, and not the one under study, bears the principal burden of the particular unit of discourse at hand. To state matters simply, it will turn out that in the case of shared items the document under study uses what is not native and natural to it. Rather, the document before us has borrowed from some other document, which then demands study on its terms and in its own analytical context.

It will follow that we can answer the question, for the document under study, of whether or not we deal with a text, exhibiting traits of composition, deliberation, proportion, and so delivering a message on its own. If we do not, then we shall turn out to affirm the now-broadly-held opinion that all of the documents in the canon of Judaism speak pretty much at random to a single common program. All contribute to Judaism equally and without differentiation. To describe Judaism – a theological or legal point – one may equally cite what is found in one document alongside what is located in some other. We then do not have to pay much attention to the locus of a given passage. We may ignore its relationship to what stands fore and aft. We may assume that all things are part of one thing, whether we call it "the one whole Torah of Moses, our rabbi," or merely "Judaism," "the halakhah," or "theology of Judaism" not making much difference. So, in all, the stakes are very high, and the work at hand will be protracted, so far as facts make a difference. In this way we ask whether the position enunciated by Schiffman, that all the documents constitute interlocking and reinterlocking, indivisible units, is correct. To state the result at the outset, Schiffman in the case of the document at hand, could not have made a more profound misstatement of the facts.

II. RECURRENT LITERARY STRUCTURES OF LEVITICUS RABBAH

A literary structure is a composition that adheres to conventions of expression, organization, or proportion, extrinsic to the message of the author. Such a structure conforms to rules that impose upon the individual writer a limited set of choices about how he will convey whatever message he has in mind. Or it will limit an editor or redactor to an equally circumscribed set of alternatives about how to arrange received materials. We obviously cannot allege on the basis of what merely appears to us to be patterned or needlessly formal that we have a structure in hand. Nor shall we benefit from bringing to the text at hand structures shown in other texts to define conventions for communicating ideas in those other texts. A text has to define its own structures for us. This its authors do simply by repeatedly resorting to a given set of literary conventions. It follows that the adjective "recurrent" constitutes a redundancy when joined to the noun "structure." That is to say, we cannot know that we have a structure if the text under analysis does not repeatedly resort to the presentation of its message through that disciplined structure.

Leviticus Rabbah comprises large-scale literary structures. How do we know that fact? It is because when we divide up the undifferentiated columns of words and sentences and point to the boundaries that separate one completed unit of thought or discourse from the next such completed composition, we produce rather sizable statements conforming to a single set of patterns. While in the Mishnah, for example, we can distinguish a few sentences as a paragraph, and a few paragraphs as a concluded statement, a completed unit of discourse, in Leviticus Rabbah we cannot. Rather, our divisions encompass many more sentences, a great many more words, than is the case in the Mishnah. On the other hand, in comparing the dimensions of completed units of discourse in Leviticus Rabbah to those in the Yerushalmi or the Bavli, we find in the former less sustained, less protracted discourse than in the latter. That is to say, a unit of thought or analysis in one of the two Talmuds in the average will be made up of a great many more subunits or components. On the other hand, these components of large-scale analytical units of discourse will appear autonomous of the larger composition in which they occur. They will not prove cogent within that composition. By contrast, units of discourse in Leviticus Rabbah tend not to run on as do those of the two Talmuds. But the components do prove more cogent with the larger discourse which they serve. In all, what I mean when I claim that Leviticus Rabbah is made up of large-scale literary structures is simple. When we divide a given parashah, or chapter, of Leviticus Rabbah into its sub-divisions, we find these sub-divisions sustained and on occasion protracted, but also stylistically cogent and well-composed.

What these facts mean is that, in Leviticus Rabbah, the repeated patterns follow protracted orbits, covering a sizable volume of material. The patterns are large in scale. We deal not with small-scale syntactic formalization, such as the Mishnah's authors use to good effect, for example three or five sentences made up of parts of the speech arranged in exactly the same way. But we do deal with a stylized mode of discourse, unlike the Tosefta's rather miscellaneous style in conveying its authors' ideas. Were we to be guided by either the Yerushalmi's or the Bavli's writers, further, we should look for rigid but abbreviated rhetorical patterns, signals conveyed by little more than parts of speech so set forth as to convey the purpose and sense of sizable discussion. We should be disappointed were we to ask the authors at hand in Leviticus Rabbah to demonstrate their equivalent skill at the use of rhetoric to lend structure and impart sense to otherwise unformed sentences. Where those authors excel, it is at holding in the balance a rather substantial composite of seemingly diverse materials, systematically and patiently working their way from point to apparently miscellaneous observation, and only at the end drawing the whole to an elegant and satisfying conclusion. So we look for large-scale patterns and point to such unusually sizable compositions as characteristic because they recur and define discourse, parashah by parashah. Indeed, as we shall now see, a given parashah is made up of a large-scale literary structure, which I shall define in a moment, followed by further, somewhat smaller, fairly formalized constructions.

How shall we proceed to identify the structures that define the document before us? It seems to me we had best move first to the analysis of a single parashah. We seek, within that parashah, to identify what holds the whole together. The second step then is to see whether we have identified something exemplary, or what is no example but in fact a phenomenon that occurs in fact only once or at random. For the first exercise, we take up Parashah Five. As we proceed, of course, we shall then provide statistics covering all thirty-seven of the parashiyyot and see the extent to which the patterns exhibited in one parashah in fact characterize the entire lot. The discussion that follows refers to Leviticus Rabbah Parashah 5, which is given in Appendix VIII.

III. TYPES OF UNITS OF DISCOURSE

Let us now turn to the classification of the units of discourse of which the parashah is composed. What we want to know is the structure of the parashah as a whole, where its largest subunits of thought begin and end and how they relate to one another. How shall we recognize a complete unit of thought? It will be marked off by the satisfactory resolution of a tension or problem introduced at the outset. A complete unit of thought may be made up of a number of subdivisions, many of them entirely spelled out on their own. But the composition of a complete unit of thought always will strike us as cogent, the work of a single conception on how a whole thought should be constructed and expressed. While that unitary conception drew upon already available materials, the main point is made by the composition as a whole, and not by any of its (ready-made) parts.

In the first classification we take up the single most striking recurrent literary structure of Leviticus Rabbah. It is what we may call the base-verse/intersecting-verse construction. In such a construction, a base-verse, drawn from the book of Leviticus, is juxtaposed to an intersecting-verse, drawn from any book other than a pentateuchal one. Then this intersecting-verse is subjected to systematic exegesis. On the surface the exegesis is out of all relationship with the base-verse. But in a stunning climax, all of the exegeses of the intersecting-verse are shown to relate to the main point the exegete wishes to make about the base-verse. What that means is that the composition as a whole is so conceived as to impose meaning and order on all of the parts, original or ready-made, of which the author of the whole has made use. For the one example in Parashah 5, the base-verse is Lev. 4:3 and the intersecting-verse Job 34:29-30. Here is the outline of the first three subdivisions of the parashah.

V:I.1.C-F	Lev. 4:3, Job 34:29-30 and the generation of the flood
V:I.2.A-C	Lev. 4:3, Job 34:29-30 and the generation of the flood
V:I.2.E-G	Lev. 4:3, Job 34:29-30 and the generation of the flood
V:I.3.A	Lev. 4:3, Job 34:29-30 and the generation of the flood
V:I.3.B-D	Job 21:11
V:I.4	Job 21:11
V:I.5.A-B	Generation of the flood
V:I.5.C-F	*Maaseh*
V:I.6.A-E	Job 34:29-30, Gen. 7:23. Relevance: Reference to God's hiding his face.
V:I.7.A-C	Job 34:29. Refers to Noah.
V:II.1	Job 34:29. Refers to Sodomites. First comes tranquility, then punishment. Job 28:7
V:II.2	Further exegesis of Job 28:7.
V:II.3	God hid his face from Sodomites (Job 34:29) and then punished them (Gen. 19:24).
V:III.1	Job 34:29. Refers to Ten Tribes, first tranquility, then punishment. Amos 6:1.
V:III.2	Further comment on Amos 6:1

V:III.3	Further comment on Amos 6:2
V:III.4	Amos 6:3
V:III.5	Amos 6:4
V:III.6	Amos 6:5
V:III.7	Amos 6:6
V:III.8	Amos 6:6
V:III.9	Amos 6:6, 7. All of the units on Amos simply comment on clauses of verses.
V.III.10	Job 34:29. How God hid his face from the Ten Tribes. Isaiah 36:1.
V:III.11	Isaiah 36:1
V:III.12	Job 34:29. Refers to Sennacherib (Joel 6) and Israel (Ez. 34:31).
V:III.13	Job 34:29 linked to Lev. 4:3-4. God exacts the same penalty from an individual or a community, so Job 34:29 and also Lev. 4:13-14.

As we saw when we followed the text in detail, the composition moves with striking cogency over its chosen examples: the Generation of the Flood, the Ten Tribes, Sennacherib and Israel. So three large-scale illustrations of Job 34:29-30 are laid out, and then the entire composition reverts to Lev. 4:3ff. to make a single point about all that has gone before.

Another form is the intersecting-verse/base-verse construction. Secondary in size and in exegetical complexity to the one just now surveyed, here the intersecting-verse is worked out, then comes the base-verse, given a simple exemplification. Just as in the first type, the exegete may assemble passages on that exemplificatory entry. We have two instances. The first example is V:V. Since Lev. 4:3 refers to the sin of an anointed priest, the exegete wishes to show us how an anointed priest may sin and so he invokes the name of Shebna. The rest follows.

V:V.2	Shebna (Is. 22:15-19)
V:V.3	Shebna (Is. 22:16-18)
V:V.4	Shebna and Joahaz

The second example is somewhat more subtle. Here we have a play on a word used in the base-verse. Then a whole series of verses will be adduced to make a point based on that play on words. These proof-texts cannot be called intersecting-verses in the way in which, in the earlier classification and in the first example of the present one, the cited verses intersect with, but take over discourse from, the base-verse. Quite to the contrary, the base-verse generates a point, which then is richly expanded by the cited verses. Nonetheless, I should regard the present example as a variation on the foregoing. The reason is that, in a strictly formal sense, the pattern remains what we have seen to this point: a set of illustrative verses that make the main point the exegete wishes to associate with or about the base-verse, given at the end.

V:VII.1-2   Lev. 4:13-15. Exegesis of the verse, with special attention to a word-play. The upshot is that Israel is distinguished from the nations. Then a long catalogue of such distinctions is appended.

A third classification derives from the clause-by-clause type of exegesis of the base-verse, with slight interest in intersecting-verses or in illustrative materials deriving from other books of the Scripture. The base-verse in this classification defines the entire frame of discourse, either because of its word-choices or because of its main point. Where verses of other passages are quoted, they serve not as the focus of discourse but only as proof-texts or illustrative-texts. They therefore function in a different way from the verses adduced in discourse in the first two classifications, for, in those former cases, the intersecting-verses form the center of interest. As we see at V:VI, we deal with the subject-matter of Lev. 4:3-4, on the one side, and we also explain the derivation of words used in the cited verse, on the other. These are distinct modes of exegesis – ideational, philological – but the difference is slight in determining the classification at hand. It is simply exegesis of verses of Leviticus, item by item. Here are examples of the exegetical type of unit of discourse.

V:VI.1   Lev. 4:3. Precedence in atonement rite.

V:VI.2   Lev. 4:3. How can an anointed priest sin?

V:VI.3   Lev. 4:3. Explanation of a word used in the cited verse.

V:VI.4   Lev. 4:3 and Shebna. Illustration.

V:VI.5   Lev. 4:4. Why bring the bell to the tent of meeting as Lev. 4:4 specifies.

The category of miscellanies and how they are joined now demands attention. By a "miscellany," I mean a construction that does not relate to any base-verse in Leviticus 4 or to the cited intersecting-verses; that does not address any theme or principle pertinent to the base-verse or to its larger context; and that appears to have been formed for purposes entirely distinct from the explanation or amplification of a passage of the book of Leviticus. One such example is at V:IV.1-4, at which, as we see, the general theme of Lev. 4:3 – the sacrifices of several officials, in order – triggers the inquiry into which offering comes first. But at issue is the principle that whoever sacrifices proportionately more in terms of his means is the one who gets the more credit. That notion is unrelated to Lev. 4:3. The passage is cogent. Here is the outline, which, as we see, deals with Prov. 18:16 and provides anthology of rather coherent materials for that verse.

V:IV.1	God recognizes the value of a gift to the cult, e.g., in accord with the donor's sacrifice. Deut. 12:19, 20; M. Hor. 3:6.
V:IV.2	"A man's gift makes room for him" (Prov. 18:16) and long illustrative story.
V:IV.3	Prov. 18:16
V:IV.4	Prov. 18:16

A second example, drawn from Parashah 5, serves Ps. 19:2-3, 13-14, and the reason for its inclusion with reference to Lev. 4 is not entirely clear.

| V:VIII.1 | Israel knows how to placate God. The point is joined to Ps. 19:23, 13-14. This construction does not belong to Lev. 4. |

We therefore discern three categories of units of discourse, illustrated by generally rather sizable subunits. These are, first, the (complex) base-verse/intersecting-verse construction (I); second, the (simple) intersecting-verse/base-verse construction (II); and, third, the clause-by-clause exegetical construction (III). We note, finally, the category of miscellanies (IV), always marked by the simple trait of irrelevance to the concrete context at hand.

Can we discern an order followed by the several types of units of discourse? I believe there is a quite fixed order of types of units of discourse.

1. Base-verse/intersecting-verse construction:

   V:I-III

2. Intersecting-verse/base-verse construction:

   V:V

   V:VII

3. Clause-by-clause exegetical construction:

   V:VI

4. Miscellanies:

   V:IV, V:VIII

The obvious problem is at V:V-VII. Can we account for the insertion of V:VI between V:V and V:VII? We certainly can. V:VI.1-4 form an appendix to V:V – pure and simple. The organizer of the whole had no choice but to insert his appendix behind the materials supplemented by his appendix. The same sort of reasoning then accounts for the insertion of miscellanies, e.g., V:IV after V:I-III. What V:IV does is simply carry forward the problem of which beast comes first when a number of beasts are awaiting offering for the purposes of atonement for various officials. That issue is very important to the author of V:III. So the first of the two cases in which we have miscellanies turns out to exemplify a rather careful mode of arranging materials. Where a major point carries in its wake exemplificatory materials, these will be inserted before the parashah moves on to new matters. There is no difficulty in explaining why the arranger of the whole has placed V:VIII at the end; what we do not know is why, to begin with, he selected that unit of discourse. But that issue need not detain us.

We emerge with two hypotheses, one firm, the other less so.

The first is the hypothesis that the units of discourse are framed in accord with conventions that define and distinguish three recurrent literary structures:

(1) base-verse/intersecting-verse construction

(2) intersecting-verse/base-verse construction

(3) clause-by-clause exegetical construction (invoking a broad range of intersecting-verses only for narrowly-illustrative purposes). We noted, in addition, a category we called "miscellaneous."

The second hypothesis is that the categories of units of discourse also explain the order of arrangement of types of units of discourse. First will come the (I) base-verse/intersecting-verse construction; then will come (II) intersecting-verse/base-verse construction; finally we shall have (III) clause-by-clause exegetical constructions. If we were to assign cardinal numbers to these types of constructions I, II, and III, we should also be able to use ordinal numbers, first, second, third. Why? Because in accord with the stated hypothesis, type I will come first, type II second, and type III third. Type IV encompasses miscellanies.

Let us now survey the whole. I count, in all of Leviticus Rabbah, 304 entries in four catalogues of types of units of discourse:

I.	38	12.5%
II.	84	27.6%
III.	94	30.9%
IV.	88	28.9%

The three defined taxa thus cover 71% of the whole. The two truly distinctive patterns, types I and II, cover a sizable part of the whole – 40%.

IV. ORDER OF TYPES OF UNITS OF DISCOURSE

Having classified the units of discourse of which our thirty-seven parashiyyot are composed, we now ask whether the types of units of discourse follow a single pattern, or whether a given type will appear in any sequence promiscuously, at the beginning, middle, or end of a given parashah. So from the taxonomy of the units of discourse, we proceed to the structure of the thirty-seven parashiyyot as a whole. We ask whether the editors exhibited preferences for a given type of unit of discourse when they faced the task in particular of beginning a parashah or of ending one. The facts may be stated through the summary that follows:

Type I comes in first position in the following parashiyyot:

I, II, III, IV, V, VI, VII, VIII, IX, X, XI, XII, XIV, XV, XVI, XVII, XVIII, XIX, XX, XXI, XXII, XXIII, XXIV, XXV, XXVI, XXVII, XXVIII.

Type II comes in first position in the following parashiyyot:

XII, XXXII, XXXIII, XXXIV, XXXV

Type III comes in first position in the following parashiyyot:

None.

Type IV comes in first position in the following parashiyyot:

XXXVI

Type I comes in second position in the following parashiyyot:

V, VI, IX, X, XI, XV, XVII, XXII, XXIII, XXVI, XXVII, XXVIII, XXXVII

Type II comes in second position in the following parashiyyot:

III, IV, VII, VIII, XIII, XIV, XVI, XVII, XVIII, XIX, XX, XXI, XXIV, XXV, XXIX, XXX, XXXI, XXXII, XXXIV, XXXV, XXXVI

Type III comes in second position in the following parashiyyot:

II

Type IV comes in second position in the following parashiyyot:

XII, XXXIII

Type I comes last in the following parashiyyot:

None.

Type II comes last in the following parashiyyot:

None.

Type III comes last in the following parashiyyot:

II, VIII, XV, XVI, XVII, XVIII, XIX, XX, XXI, XXIV, XXVI, XXVII, XXVIII, XXX, XXXI, XXXV

Type IV comes last in the following parashiyyot:

I, III, IV, V, VI, VII, IX, X, XI, XII, XIII, XIV, XXII, XXIII, XXV, XXIX, XXXII, XXXIII, XXXIV, XXXVI, XXXVII

We may compare the proportions as follows:

Type I comes in first position in	31/37	83.7%
Type II comes in first position in	5/37	13.5%
Type III comes in first position in	0/37	0.0%
Type IV comes in first position in	1/37	2.7%

Type I comes in second position in   13/37   35.1%

Type II comes in second position in   21/37   56.7%

Type III comes in second position in   1/37   2.7%

Type IV comes in second position in   2/37   5.4%

Type I comes in last position in   0/37   0.0%

Type II comes in last position in   0/37   0.0%

Type III comes in last position in   16/37   43.2%

Type IV comes in last position in   21/37   56.7%

I have probably overstated the instances in which type I comes in second position. Many of the entries of type I involve sustained and unitary compositions, in which a single intersecting-verse is worked out over a series of two or three subdivisions of a parashah. Otherwise the proportions conform to the impressions yielded by the catalogues just now presented.

To state the result very simply: the framer of a passage ordinarily began with a base-verse/intersecting-verse construction. He very commonly proceeded with an intersecting-verse/base-verse construction. Then he would provide such exegeses of pertinent verses of Leviticus as he had in hand. He would conclude either with type III or type IV constructions, somewhat more commonly the latter than the former. So the program of the authors is quite simple. They began with types I and II – 100% of the first and second position entries, proceeded with type III, and concluded with type III or IV. So, to conclude, Leviticus Rabbah consists of two main types of units of discourse, first in position, expositions of how verses of the book of Leviticus relate to verses of other books of the Hebrew Bible, second in position, exposition of verses of the book of Leviticus viewed on their own, and, varying in position but in any event very often concluding a construction, miscellaneous materials.

We now therefore know that units of discourse that fall into the classifications of types I, II, or III in their fixed order define that literary structure that imparts to Leviticus Rabbah the formal and stylistic unity exhibited by its principal components. So we may indeed speak of literary patterns – structures of completed discourse – that recur in Leviticus Rabbah. The recurrent traits prove to be both in formal character (for types I and II) and in conventional sequence (for all four types). Leviticus Rabbah, viewed whole and in its constitutive components, finds definition in a dominant literary structure and a recurrent mode of literary organization.

V. ALIKE AND NOT ALIKE: THE PROGRAM OF INQUIRY

Before we proceed to the next stage in our inquiry, let me outline the questions that now occupy us and explain their importance. We want to know whether and how Leviticus Rabbah is compared to other documents and to a prior but now unavailable document, a source (or: cogent sourses, Qs). To work out this matter, we consider systematic answers to a program of questions as follows:

1. The Proportion of Shared Materials: Do the authors of a document rely essentially on materials of which they alone make use, or do they make choices that fall into harmony with those made by other authorships? And does the document produced by one authorship exhibit essential autonomy of all other writings, before and at the same time, or does the document draw heavily upon materials that occur in more than a single compilation?

2. The Function of Shared Materials in a Given Document: Do materials that occur in two or more documents impart traits of topic, plan or program, rhetoric or logic, to the documents in which they occur? What role do shared materials play in the several documents, viewed singly?

3. The Identity of the Shared Materials: A further exercise requires the description and characterization of materials shared among two or more documents. Do these materials exhibit traits that permit us to differentiate the documents that present those materials in common from those that do not use them at all? We shall therefore have to characterize shared materials and ask two questions of them, one concerning the shared units of discourse, the other concerning the documents that share them:

[A] Do shared materials constitute a distinct corpus in this document? Do materials that occur in one document among themselves exhibit differentiating traits, that set aside what is shared from what is unique? In the setting of a single and autonomous document we view the shared materials collectively, as a whole, and ask whether shared materials constitute a distinct corpus.

[B] Do Shared Materials Form a Distinct Corpus in the Entire Repertoire of Documents? Do materials that occur in two or more documents share traits among themselves that differentiate the shared materials from the materials unique to the document in which they occur? Do materials that occur in one document among themselves exhibit differentiating traits, that set aside what is shared from what is unique? Here we raise the same question as at A, but now with the focus on the shared materials as a group, seen from the perspective of the nine documents at hand. Now to revert to the argument at hand.

It is not enough to know what units of discourse appear in two or more documents. We want also to specify what, in the documents under study, is unique, and how large a proportion of each document is formed of unique materials. This variable, of course, forms the reverse of the foregoing. But it bears its own testimony. For in characterizing what is unique, we differentiate one document from all others and so identify those documents that, at a fundamental level, defy classification altogether. A claim that a document made up essentially of unique materials stands in connection with other documents then demands considerable exposition, for the substance of the document on its own testifies otherwise. And that is essentially the point at which we began this work.

VI. NOT UNIQUE, NOT IMPORTANT

What proportion of a probe of three parashiyyot (7, 12, 18) is made up of shared materials – those occurring in another, earlier or contemporary document? For this purpose I count up the number of stichs encompassed by the materials at hand and also the number of stichs shared by Leviticus Rabbah and documents prior to its time or contemporaneous with it. A stich for this rough estimate is constituted by a lettered unit, whether that unit is made up of one sentence or several.

	Stichs Particular to Leviticus Rabbah		Shared Stichs (in 7, 12, 18)
Parashah 7	103	96.2%	4
Parashah 12	172	97.7%	4
Parashah 18	152	92.8%	12

The analysis for Parashah 18 omits reference to items that occur also in the Mishnah, on the one side, or the Bavli, on the other. If we add these to the totals, we have another 13 stichs, thus 85.8% are particular to Leviticus Rabbah. In all, the results are one-sided. While rough, they confirm the impression of the essential autonomy of Leviticus Rabbah. How so? Nearly everything, that is, something like 95% of all stichs, in our probe of the composition, from the viewpoint of the extant canon in hand prior to the redaction of, or contemporary with, Leviticus Rabbah, is unique.

When we ask about the integrity of the document as a whole, we take up the encompassing traits, the definitive literary and redactional characteristics. Accordingly, we ask whether Leviticus Rabbah is an anthology or a sustained composition. On formal grounds we conclude that it constitutes a text with its own integrity, not merely a collection of this and that. When we examine a sample of the smallest components of the document, brief sayings of various kinds, we find two facts. First of all, a probe of three parashiyyot yields an astonishingly small proportion of materials that are not unique. We may conclude that, in the context of the whole document, what is not unique takes up a very minor place and contributes episodic and unsustained supplements.

Second, much of that shared component turns out to be formally diverse. Little indicates that the items shared with other documents fit well into Leviticus

Rabbah. Why not? Within Leviticus Rabbah, the shared items do not conform to the formal preferences, as to the construction of large-scale discourse, dominant in the document as a whole. Accordingly, our probe leaves no doubt that a catalogue of phrases and sentences or even groups of sentences – from two to ten stichs – that occur in both Leviticus Rabbah and another document of its own time or earlier would list little more than editorial detritus. Such a catalogue of all of the passages shared with documents other than Scripture and the Mishnah, at the beginning, through to the Yerushalmi and other contemporary writings, at the end, would prove a random collection of this and that. That is to say, all we should turn up is lists of items shared by Leviticus Rabbah and, e.g., Sifra, the two Sifres, the Yerushalmi, and the like. If our now-completed probe is suggestive, such lists by themselves would not tell us anything we wish to know. Leviticus Rabbah does not stand "very close" to any other document so as to present a synoptic problem. It scarcely intersects with any other document of its day. (As to its relationship with Pesiqta deR. Kahana, we take up that matter in a moment.)

VII. MISCELLANIES OR A SOURCE: IN SEARCH OF "Q" AND THE SYNOPTIC PROBLEM

Since in our earlier probe, in Chapter Three, we took up the question of a rabbinic Q, we have now to ask the same question. For while the dialectical relationship between the Mishnah and its successor-documents may preclude utilization of some other, dialectically-independent source of the law, in the case of Leviticus Rabbah (and its friends), serving Scripture, matters may prove otherwise. Specifically, we now entertain the possibility of a florilegium of sources serving up proof-texts for Mishnah-propositions. Perhaps diverse documents circulated, in which collections of exegeses of Scripture for a variety of purposes, were worked out. Then, drawn upon by two or more documents prepared later on, these circulating – but no unavailable – compilations or compositions will have left their imprint on the documents in hand. That would form a significant relationship and a substantial connection between document and document. It would give us a basis on which to affirm the position Schiffman proposes, not to mention that originally presented by Smith about how a theory begun in one literature applies to the other. So we now turn to an analysis of the repertoire of materials shared between Leviticus Rabbah and other documents of its own day or succession. We raise two simple questions, one cursorily, the other at length.

First, we return to the program of questions introduced in the preceding section and now ask: do the shared materials exhibit literary traits in common? Then we may posit the theory that the shared materials testify to a now-unknown document on which the compilations that share the materials have drawn. Second, do the shared materials conform to the literary preferences of Leviticus Rabbah? The importance of the former of the two questions can be briefly explained. (The latter is the focus of part X.) If the materials that occur in two or more compilations follow a single pattern of literary formulation and construction, then we may postulate that those materials derive from a cogent source and so constitute part of a larger, itself autonomous, document. By such a postulate, that autonomous and distinct source will then have made its contribution here and there, to the Yerushalmi, to Leviticus Rabbah, to Genesis Rabbah, not to mention to Pesiqta deR. Kahana and even to the Bavli. Enjoying its own definition, organized around its own lines, exhibiting its own distinctive formal traits, one must call this otherwise unknown source by the German name for source, that is, *Quelle*, or merely RQ for *rabbinische Quelle*.

We turn to the following questions: on the basis of the surveyed population, may such a source indeed be reconstructed? That is, out of a broad range of existing compilations and even compositions of rabbinic writings, are we able to collect and restore those bits and pieces of an antecedent rabbinic source (or set of sources) that have circulated on their own and also exhibit distinctive traits in common? And will these collected pieces then allow us to see part of that original source, the one from which they broke off? At stake in asking whether the materials common to two or more compilations and compositions is a considerable possibility. The answer is negative at all points: no Q, no source at all, merely itinerant and peripatetic sayings, rushing this way and that, scarcely meeting: electrons in an atom.

A mere glance at the materials catalogued below suggests that the quest for the unknown rabbinic source leads nowhere. Why so? Because materials common to two or more documents turn out to be everything and its opposite: long and short; exegetical statements on verses of Scripture; autonomous statements of individual authorities; protracted stories; brief stories. In short, those shared materials may be anything at all. However we classify the traits of a given snippet, we find among other passages the opposite traits. Among themselves items that occur in more than a single composition, that is, in our case, Leviticus Rabbah and some other compilation, share no distinctive traits. That is to say, these same shared sources draw upon a broad variety of authorities' names or lack any identified authority. They focus upon a vast range of topics but coalesce around none in particular. They exhibit every sort of literary pattern. Some fit neatly into the literary structures of Leviticus Rabbah, which I have demonstrated to be subject to definition. Others exhibit traits or structures evidently characteristic of Genesis Rabbah (thus: similar to those of Leviticus Rabbah) on the one side, Yerushalmi's episodic sayings, on the second, the Pesiqta's protracted constructions (again: similar to those of Leviticus Rabbah), on the third. But still others share traits with none of the foregoing, on the fourth. And there are yet other sides and aspects too.

To avoid repeating the obvious through each of the appropriate criteria for definition of a single and uniform composition – whether formal, topical, or even merely logical – I state one simple fact. The shared sources share only one trait. It is that they appear in more than a single composition. We have therefore to dismiss the notion that sizable compositions, circulating from document to document, in fact originated in a single composition, one marked off by its definitive and distinctive traits. That judgment pertains not only to sizable compositions, entire units of discourse or more, such as are shared between Leviticus Rabbah and Genesis Rabbah and Pesiqta deR. Kahana. It applies also to brief sayings, such as pop up hither and yon, for example, in the Yerushalmi, Leviticus Rabbah and Genesis Rabbah (not to mention numerous other, still later compositions and compilations).

Let me spell out what I mean. We note that there are two types of shared sources, long and brief. The long ones clearly conform to a variety of patterns. In no way do these long sayings suggest that they originate in a single, uniform, and now-lost, document. But what about the brief lemmas? These short sayings may make an appearance in a well-composed and sizable unit of discourse, e.g., a piece of a passage of Leviticus Rabbah, but also in a quite different, and also well-composed and sizable unit of discourse, e.g., a piece of a passage in the Yerushalmi. Clearly, these brief lemmas did circulate broadly. No one can doubt that. But if we draw together all of those lemmas that appear in two or more documents, do they exhibit distinctive traits in common? And if we compare all such sayings to equivalently brief lemmas that appear in only one document, do the latter exhibit traits of formulation and formation into larger compositions different from the former? These two questions govern. For we must establish dual criteria, one group of criteria to exclude, the other group of definitive traits to include. If then we attempt to include all the circulating brief sayings, those that appear in two or more compositions, by reference to shared and distinctive traits, and if we then propose to exclude all one-time brief sayings, the ones appearing in only one document, by reference to the absence of the shared and distinctive traits of the circulating sayings, we come up with nothing.

I lay down that judgment flatly and without proof. Why not? Because we should have to compose long lists of traits not distinctive to one set of sayings as against the other and demonstrate that said traits occur at random among either of the two sets of sayings. But a mere glance at the context of any brief saying shared among two or more documents provides adequate information. That is, brief sayings that occur in Leviticus Rabbah ordinarily share the traits of other sayings of Leviticus Rabbah and unique to that document, among which they occur, fore and aft. These same sayings, however, appear just as randomly and comfortably but episodically in, e.g., Genesis Rabbah or the Yerushalmi. So the simple fact is that brief sayings, consisting of a line or two, rarely conform to those distinctive formal traits that allow us to distinguish, in a given compilation or composition, between one unit of discourse and another unit of discourse.

Only at a larger scale than the brief sayings, viewed one by one, do the processes of literary definition and differentiation begin to make sense in analyzing our documents. (As we shall see below, large-scale constructions prove miscellaneous too and rarely exhibit traits distinctive to Leviticus Rabbah.) Accordingly, brief sayings clearly serve numerous, that is, two or more, contexts. The reason brief sayings prove serviceable hither and yon is simple. By themselves they do not exhibit distinctive traits, so they present no formal problems to the compositors, or authors, of larger discussions. They are neutral, whether viewed formally or construed substantively. Brief sayings constitute available building blocks. Shared or unique, they are bricks all of a single dimension. Only in context, e.g., large examples of a single pattern of syntax or structure, do these brief sayings form discernible compositions.

Since that is the fact, we must wonder not at how many, but at how few, such shared brief sayings have come to our attention. Our original result, showing in a rough way that something in the range of 95% of the stichs of three parashiyyot of Leviticus Rabbah appear to be particular to that composition, now returns to mind. Given the formal consistency and the absence of what seem to me to be highly patterned and distinctive formulary character of brief sayings (so often: X says, plus a standard or entirely commonplace and therefore random syntactic pattern), we should have expected a different result. We ought to have had sound reason to expect a far broader portion than we have found, a pattern in which a given composition is composed of sayings shared with two or more other compositions.

It would carry us far afield to speculate on the reason for the near-uniqueness of the document at hand. But the issue in its proper context demands considerable reflection. A suitable answer cannot be merely that, in a given document, one set of subjects, rather than some other set of subjects, required one set of sayings, rather than some other. Or, to put it simply, no one can imagine that we can explain the near-uniqueness of the bulk of the contents of a given composition, in this case, Leviticus Rabbah, by reference to the near-uniqueness either of the overall topical program or of the concrete sentiments and values to be expressed. Such a thesis would contradict what, to the naked eye, constitutes the definitive trait of all of the documents of the canon of Judaism. That is, that they are canonical. The document's authors therefore wish in many different ways to say some one thing.

VIII. DIFFERENTIATING AMONG SHARED SOURCES IN THE SETTING OF LEVITICUS RABBAH IN PARTICULAR

We now ask whether the materials shared by Leviticus Rabbah with some other composition of the same age conform to the distinctive literary patterns of Leviticus Rabbah, on the one side, and organize materials in the same sequence of types of units of discourse as Leviticus Rabbah, on the other. What we shall see in a catalogue of details is that nearly all units of tradition – brief and long alike – shared by Leviticus Rabbah with some other composition of composition or compilation prove miscellaneous. These shared miscellaneous materials both testify against use by these authors of a RQ and also attest to the integrity of Leviticus Rabbah.

First, they point to the distinctiveness of the literary patterns of Leviticus Rabbah as well as to the uniqueness of the organization of types of units of discourse by the compositors of Leviticus Rabbah. So on the face of it the compositors of our document have given us a composition that conforms to a clearcut plan, distinctive to their group, for both organization and expression of ideas. Second, beyond the miscellaneous character of the shared materials is the simple fact of the slight and inconsequential place taken up by those shared materials in Leviticus Rabbah. What that means is that the compositors have made their document mainly of materials particular to their interests. They expressed their own literary and redactional preferences and only tangentially and randomly included bits and pieces of materials serviceable for purposes other than those of Leviticus Rabbah.

The upshot is simple. Leviticus Rabbah is no scrapbook, no random collection of this and that. It is an orderly, proportioned, well-considered composition. Leviticus Rabbah exhibits integrity. It enjoys autonomy. It is not made up of "interlocking and reinterlocking" parts, but of parts that conform to the pattern of the document at hand – and not to that of any other document. The parts that are shared with other writings not only do not reinterlock, they do not even interlock. They are random, isolated, episodic, alone. Schiffman's theory of the connections among documents in no way conforms to the reality of this particular document. Readily distinguished from other writings and not at all "indivisible," from them, Leviticus Rabbah is quite distinct. As to its connections with other collections or compositions of its age, even though it shares with them a small and miscellaneous corpus of brief sayings and even protracted discussions, it is essentially unconnected in its redactional formal repertoire and in its substantive program. Let us now catalogue these shared materials in two taxa, first, brief, then, protracted, and, in both cases, among four classifications, namely, the four types of units of discourse I identified above. We now classify the two varieties of shared materials – brief, then protracted – in accord with the four taxa yielded by the several units of discourse of Leviticus Rabbah: I. Base-verse/intersecting verse, II. Intersecting verse/base-verse, III. Exegesis of verse, IV. Miscellany. We deal only with the shared materials occurring in Genesis Rabbah and the Yerushalmi. My sample is now a population, covering the bulk of the document.

1. The classification of *brief* sayings

I. Base-verse/intersecting verse

(Y. + Gen. R.)

None

II. Intersecting verse/base-verse

(Y. + Gen. R.)

None

III. Exegesis of a verse

(Y. + Gen. R.)

III:III   Lev. 2:1,8

IV. Miscellanies

(Y. + Gen. R.)

VII:I	2N	Mishnah-citation
VII:V	1D-E	Yerushalmi-Tanna-saying
VII:VI	1D	Said x
XII:I	9C	X said
XII:II	2A	Said x
XII:IV	4A	X said
	3B	Mishnah-citation
XVIII:I	1C-H	Mishnah-citation + exegesis
XVIII:I	10A-B	X said ... he said to him
	12G	X + Y + saying
	12J	Mishnah-citation
III:II	1B	X, Y + saying

2. The classification of *protracted* sayings

I. Base-verse/intersecting verse

(Y. + Gen. R.)

V:I	1-7	Gen. 9:18/Job 34:29, Lev. 4:3/Job 34:29
X:I	1	Gen. 18:25/Ps. 45:7-8, Lev. 8:1-3/Ps. 45:7

II. Intersecting verse/base-verse

(Y. + Gen. R.)

None

III. Exegesis of a verse
(Y. + Gen. R.)

XVIII:I	4A-G	Qoh. 12:3 + phrase by phrase exegesis. N.B. Qoh. 12:3 is part of the intersecting-verse construction here.
XVIII:II	1C-F	Ps. 139:5. Proposition followed by proof-text.
XVIII:III	2H	Ex. 32:16 + read not. Proposition + proof-text.
IX:VI	1	X said, Y said + proof-texts on proposition.
XVI:VIII	2	Exegesis of Deut. 7:15
XIX:V	6	Exegesis of Lev. 15:25
XXXIII:V	1-2	Exegesis of 2 Chr. 13:17, etc.
XXXIV:XIV	1-5	Exegesis of Is. 58:7 + story.
XXXVII:I	1	Exegesis of Qoh. 5:5
X:IX:	3-8	Gen. 1:9 + exegetical observation
XXXIV:IX	1-2	Deut. 28:13 + clarifications, + other verses clarified.
XXVI:I	2	Gen. 7:2, 11:4, etc., explained.

IV. Miscellanies
(Y. + Gen. R.)

III:III	1B-C	Said x.
V:IV	2-4	Verse + extended stories.
V:VI	2	Said x + story.
IX:IX	1	Long story.
X:VI	1	Proposition + proof-texts (not exegetical).
X:VIII	1	As above.
XXI:X	1	As above.
XXII:IX	1	As above.
XXV:I	4	As above.
XXXII:VII	1-3	Thematic essay.
XXXVI:VI	1	Propositions + proof-texts.
XXXVII:III	1	Story
IX:IX	3-4	X said + sayings + proof-text.
XVII:V	3	Proposition + proof-text.
XIX:II	6	As above.

XXIII:IX	3	As above.
XXV:VI	1-3	Argument a portion + proof-text + various propositions.
XXXVI:I	1	Proposition + proof-texts.
XXXVII:IV	1-5	Proper petitionary language + proof-texts.

IX. SHARED SOURCES AND THE LITERARY STRUCTURES OF LEVITICUS RABBAH: GENESIS RABBAH AND THE YERUSHALMI

To state in a few sentences the results of the preceding classification, we note that the shared sources, whether brief or protracted, fall into two categories, exegesis of a cited verse of Scripture (III) and miscellanies (IV). As to the brief sayings shared between Leviticus Rabbah and the two documents with which it most commonly intersects, Genesis Rabbah and the Yerushalmi, only one falls into category III, 12 into category IV. So when we deal with brief sayings that float from one document to another, in the case of the Yerushalmi and Genesis Rabbah, such sayings, when they occur in Leviticus Rabbah, very rarely will conform to the literary structures of Leviticus Rabbah. That is hardly a surprising result, since the literary structures distinctive to Leviticus Rabbah and its classification of literature – types I and II – are by definition protracted and exhaustively worked out.

But when we come to the classification of protracted sayings, we find the same result. That is another matter indeed. Now we have two entries in category I as against 13 in category III and 19 in category IV. So once more we must conclude that what is shared among two or more compilations of materials will not exhibit traits distinctive to Leviticus Rabbah (or any one of those compilations). What this means is very simple. When Leviticus Rabbah shares materials with other documents, those shared materials will not ordinarily take on or exhibit the literary traits definitive of Leviticus Rabbah.

The shared materials prove simply miscellaneous and casual. They are miscellaneous in that they exhibit no traits both uniform and also particular to themselves. As I said at the outset, all that marks shared materials in common is the fact that they occur in more than one compilation. By themselves, the shared materials common to Leviticus Rabbah and Genesis Rabbah or the Yerushalmi exhibit no single formal pattern. They express no distinctive viewpoint. They pursue no uniform program of inquiry. No "Q" here. If we study this allegedly synoptic text, part of a synoptic canon, synoptically, we learn nothing in particular either about the text or about the canon ("the tradition") of which it forms a component. Not only is there no "RQ," there also is no "synoptic problem." The burden of proof now shifts onto the shoulders of those who argue that the components of a text constitute interlocking and reinterlocking parts. The opposite seems to be the case. For the text at hand, the components appear mostly unique to that text, and the proportion of shared materials proves inconsequential. The character of the materials that occur in more than a single document (within the probe at hand) moreover does not show that – to repeat – they are interlocking, let alone reinterlocking. There is for our sample-document one substantial exception to that rule. To that we now turn.

X. THE FIVE PARASHIYYOT SHARED WITH PESIQTA DER. KAHANA

When we come to materials shared between Leviticus Rabbah and Pesiqta deR. Kahana, we deal with a quite different problem. Now, the shared materials cover a sizable portion of both documents, 5 out of 37 complete Parashiyyot (13.5%) of Leviticus Rabbah, 5 out of 28 pisqaot (17.9%) of Pesiqta deR. Kahana, according to the count of Braude and Kapstein. The correspondences are word for word, with minor exception, in the parashah/pisqa I examined in detail. The question before us is not whether or not the shared parashiyyot "belong" or prove "particular to" Leviticus Rabbah as against their place, primary or secondary, original or borrowed, in Pesiqta deR. Kahana. The sole issue is whether these enormous constructions – I repeat, entire parashiyyot – exhibit traits characteristic of Leviticus Rabbah. They certainly do. How do we know it? Because in a survey of the shared parashiyyot/pisqaot, they conform to exactly those literary structures I have shown to characterize Leviticus Rabbah. The order of the types of units of discourse is the same – I, II, III, with IV interspersed according to rules we can discern – as the order of types of units of discourse I have shown to characterize the remainder of Leviticus Rabbah.

It follows that where entire parashiyyot of Leviticus Rabbah are shared with some other composition, these parashiyyot prove integral to Leviticus Rabbah. Since they conform to the literary patterns and redactional program of the remainder of Leviticus Rabbah, they give ample evidence that Leviticus Rabbah, as a whole, is a document that exhibits integrity. Its definitive traits of literary composition – form, pattern, redaction alike – mark the document as autonomous at the very point at which the document intersects in a truly substantial and extensive way with some other document. As to the integrity or miscellaneous character of Pesiqta deR. Kahana, that is a question to be asked in its own framework, the systematic analysis of that document. That has yet to be undertaken; the translator(s) did not do it.

XI. MISCELLANIES OR INTERLOCKING PARTS?

The materials shared by Leviticus Rabbah with other compositions of the same period or shortly afterward, Genesis Rabbah, the Yerushalmi, and Pesiqta deR. Kahana, as is now clear, exhibit in common only the trait that they occur in one or more documents of the age. They otherwise follow no uniform pattern or patterns. They reveal no cogent program of topics. They express no single viewpoint. The shared materials prove miscellaneous by every objective criterion of form and order we can devise. In no way can we demonstrate that two or more documents drew upon a single, prior composition. All we know is that two or more documents drew upon miscellaneous materials, circulating hither and yon, coming we know not whence, deriving from whatever circles or schools made up materials of the type at hand. That is to say, about the shared materials, miscellanies, we know nothing of consequence. There was no autonomous source, now represented only by the bits and pieces, uniform and cogent among themselves, scattered among the four documents with which we have dealt. Excluding the five parashiyyot shared by Leviticus Rabbah with Pesiqta deR. Kahana, the shared sources, whether long or short, prove random. Of them we cannot reconstruct a single cogent source, "Q." We may state flatly that the evidence at hand in no way suggests the existence of a rabbinic "Q." So supposedly-synoptic sources, represented by those at hand, cannot ever be read synoptically; only odds and ends compare and intersect. And then there is little basis for comparison, because they are nearly identical. All we get out of the comparison of versions of a shared item is alternative wordings of a single text, raw materials not for the history of ideas (or of religious groups) but only for the apparatus of a critical text.

If, then, we may return to the point at which we began, we may simply declare that shared sources do not derive from a single source, "Q." The shared materials, to be sure, ordinarily ignore the literary patterns of Leviticus Rabbah. But what is common on two or more documents turns out to be itself diverse and to exhibit random formal and formulary traits. On that basis we look in vain for "Q." How so? We search hopelessly for some large-scale and ubiquitous body of floating materials, fully formed, exhibiting characteristic literary traits, and entirely composed, available for use by any authorship for any given purpose. True, we may imagine that such a vast corpus of floating materials did circulate. But, lacking evidence as to its character, contents, viewpoint(s), and purpose(s), we can say nothing about it. Appeal to origin in such a shared an common "tradition" therefore tells us nothing that we did not know without the postulate that such a "tradition" circulated among the various rabbinic authorships. So if such a "Q" was there, we cannot define it or demonstrate what it contained and did not contain, how authors used it or did not use it, why people would have reshaped one of its sayings for one set of purposes rather than for some other set of purposes. We cannot pursue any of those questions that make the postulate of "Q" suggestive and fructifying in other fields of inquiry into anonymous and collective authorships, parallel to the authorships at hand. So apart from the possibility of "Q," there is nothing at stake in the hypothesis of a floating "tradition."

What must follow? It is that if we cannot show there was such a source common to two or more documents but can demonstrate only that random sayings circulated hither and yon, we also cannot invoke the perspective of analysis that demands systematic and synoptic reading of what otherwise constitute discrete documents. That is to say, we cannot link document to document as a common synoptic exercise and present the result as a shared position ("Judaism"). We also cannot show how the authors of document X have used shared materials in a way distinctive from the way in which the authors of document Y have used those same shared materials. Why not? There is no fixed point, no shared source that permits comparison. And without a common point for comparison, information on what is like, and what is unlike, document X in document Y, lacks context, perspective, therefore also meaning. So, as I said, I see nothing at stake in the postulate of a shared source, short of the discovery of "Q," and a rabbinic source behind two or more documents. We cannot show and so do not know that there was a "Q," that is, a single harmonious rabbinic "tradition."

XII. LEVITICUS RABBAH IN PARTICULAR

This discussion has carried us far from our specific purpose, which is to ask whether or not Leviticus Rabbah exhibits the traits of integrity, therefore autonomy. Lest we lose touch with the purpose for the assembly of the facts at hand, we have now carefully to restate our purpose.

Let us begin with the restatement of the facts at hand.

1. Leviticus Rabbah conforms to distinctive literary patterns. There are three readily defined classifications to which we may assign approximately 70% of the units of discourse of which the document is composed. In the exposition of ideas of a complete parashah, moreover, discourse conform to a fixed order, I, II, III. The other 30% of the document fall into the category of miscellany.

2. Leviticus Rabbah includes passages shared with other documents of its day. These are of two types, short and long. They turn out to be miscellaneous by all available criteria.

What we wish to ask, having described the simple literary traits of the document and investigated the passages of the document shared with other compositions or compilations, has to do only with Leviticus Rabbah. It is whether and to what extent Leviticus Rabbah exhibits integrity and so constitutes an autonomous and distinctive composition. It is, further, whether and to what extent Leviticus Rabbah constitutes a scrapbook, a collection of materials in no way formed into a single, formally disciplined, sustained and harmonious statement: a text.

The ultimate purpose of asking whether Leviticus Rabbah constitutes an autonomous composition or a scrapbook, whether it exhibits the trait of integrity or the trait of miscellany, is to deal in a concrete documentary context with the claim framed by Smith and others. They hold that rabbinic documents are "always" to be studied synoptically and not (as I claim) both in isolation from one another as well as in relationship to one another. So the heart of the matter is represented by the conception of "Q."

To conclude this part of the larger study, let me review the arguments and facts adduced here as these relate to the issue of "Q," that is, the claim that rabbinic documents (here represented by Leviticus Rabbah) constitute components of an essentially synoptic system (or, in Judaic theological language, of a "tradition" or "one whole Torah"). What we have done is to ask whether on the basis of common materials we discover that "parallel of parallelism" to which Smith points. That is to say, do we really find the relationships which exist between the books of one canon (or some of those books) parallel to the relationships which exist between the books of the other canon? Can a theory begun in the study of the Gospels – e.g., "studying synoptic texts synoptically" – immediately apply to the study of two or more documents of the rabbinic canon of late antiquity? Specifically, do documents of the latter canon go over the same materials, and do the materials shared among the documents point toward a common source, upon which the several compositions at hand have drawn? Are the documents "very close" to one another? If these points prove to characterize two or more documents of the rabbinic cannon, then Smith's fundamental observation will prove sound and define further research.

The three questions at hand required that we focus, to begin with, on one document, only then to work our way to examine others with which it intersects. Why so?

1. We established the extent to which a given document stands on its own, and the extent to which it shares materials – phrases, sentences, paragraphs, whole units of discourse – with some other. For the proportion, not only the character, of the materials shared among the Gospels defines the relationships among them, as Smith alleges at the very outset ("all the four are very close to each other"). We found that the proportion of shared materials in a given composition proved negligible. So, to begin with, any allegation of parallel relationships proves false on a merely quantitative basis.

2. A single document, moreover, supplied a logical place from which to go off in search of parallels in other and related documents. Why so? The canon of Judaism in late antiquity is sizable. Compiling lists of parallels among a vast variety of compositions thus far has yielded collections merely of variant readings [for example, Melamed, 1943, 1967, 1973]. So it seemed best to work from a well-defined point of reference and collect parallels relevant to that one point. So we required a base-document that intersects in substantial ways with more than a single composition.

3. The one document I chose for an appropriate probe of the results to be expected from studying synoptic texts synoptically is Leviticus Rabbah. The reason is simple. That document intersects with two others of the period in which it came to closure, Genesis Rabbah and the Yerushalmi (the Talmud of the Land of Israel). Conventional dates for the Yerushalmi, Genesis Rabbah, and Leviticus Rabbah, tend to come together around the end of the fourth century and

the beginning of the fifth. These documents in time stand far closer to one another than do those in Smith's catalogue of "Tannaitic literature." They share materials of various kinds, all deriving from the same geographical area and (people generally suppose) the same schools. Accordingly, if we are going to uncover relationships to begin with relevant to comparison with the relationships among the Gospels, we do well to begin with that family of writings circumscribed by the same place and time represented by the three documents at hand.

Leviticus Rabbah intersects, moreover, with yet another, somewhat later document, Pesiqta deR. Kahana. Here we found the condition met that the documents be "very close," since Pesiqta deR. Kahana and Leviticus Rabbah share nearly verbatim no fewer than five complete and really protracted compositions or chapters. Accordingly, we were able to frame questions about the character of the source of shared materials ("Q") not at random and on a small scale but in a systematic way and upon a large scale. And, it goes without saying, that curious claim that "synoptic texts must always be studied synoptically" has now come up to the light of day, for we can see precisely what it means to do exactly that. So we may now ask whether the results are such as to require "always" doing so.

4. The answer is that the intersecting materials among the documents (excluding Pesiqta deR. Kahana) took up too slight a portion of Leviticus Rabbah to sustain the allegation that the only way to study the allegedly-synoptic documents, Genesis Rabbah and Leviticus Rabbah, or the Yerushalmi and Leviticus Rabbah, was synoptically. To state the simple truth, if we were to study those documents "always," but also only, synoptically, we should end up ignoring most of the materials in those documents. Why so? Because much that is shared proves episodic and random. Little that is shared plays a significant role in those components of a large-scale composition in Leviticus Rabbah.

So far as the data we have examined indicate, Smith simply is wrong to allege there is any sort of "parallel of parallelism." The opposite is the case. Cohen's contribution, of course, turns out a still more extreme error and makes me wonder whether I have accurately understood what he wishes to claim. In any event, to conclude, for Genesis Rabbah, Leviticus Rabbah, and the Yerushalmi, there is no "Q." As to the shared compositions of Leviticus Rabbah and Pesiqta deR. Kahana, these prove integral to Leviticus Rabbah (whatever role they play in the other composition).[4] The shared materials only

---

[4]To find out the character of the shared materials as they affect and define the Pesiqta, we should have to establish the repertoire of redactional and formal preferences characteristic of the Pesiqta and to see to what extent the shared materials conform to the conventions otherwise paramount in that document. Braude and Kapstein have done no analysis at all of that text.

reenforce the claim that the document is autonomous and exhibits a profound integrity of both literary pattern and redactional policy.

XIII. THE PARTICULARITY OF AUTONOMOUS DOCUMENTS: SIFRE TO NUMBERS COMPARED TO GENESIS RABBAH

Now to return to the position that the literature at hand is made up of interlocking segments, which are indivisible, we have to address another question: What about the *message* of a document, as distinct from its literary, redactional, and other rhetorical and logical traits? When Schiffman and others speak of an organic unity, they may mean not as to topic, rhetoric, and logic, but as to substance. So we wonder whether we can say that one document says pretty much the same as what some other document says, even though it may use different formal and rhetorical means to say it. There is one way in which to show that what is striking in Leviticus Rabbah also forms a message particular to that document, and that is by comparing one document to some other of its classification as to formal repertoire and substantive message of that formal program. For that purpose I need not consider another document concerning the book of Leviticus. The reader has in hand Sifra, which treats the same biblical book. I need hardly point out, therefore, that the message of Sifra and that of Leviticus Rabbah have nothing whatsoever in common. The two documents ask different questions and answer them, each in its own distinctive way. They are different in rhetoric, logic, *and also topic,* that is to say, the substantive program.

Let me turn to another two documents, therefore, ones that treat different biblical books, and compare their message to one another. I deal with Sifré to Numbers and Genesis Rabbah. That comparison permits us to ask whether what is striking in our text also is particular to that text. I turn to Sifré to Numbers, because I have worked on that document and given an account of what I think the framers wished to emphasize. Then I take up Genesis Rabbah because I have already completed a systematic characterization of the message and method of that document as well. Let me rapidly describes its formal traits and its substantive message and then compare both to the counterparts in Genesis Rabbah, reverting at the end to the comparison already briefly made between Leviticus Rabbah and Sifra. On this way we shall deal with four documents, and the issue of their divisibility or indivisibility will be settled.

The Forms of Sifré to Numbers: Let us first of all review the forms of Sifré to Numbers, highlighting their main traits.

1. Extrinsic exegetical form: The form consists of the citation of an opening verse, followed by an issue stated in terms extrinsic to the cited verse. The formal traits: [1] citation of a base verse from Numbers, [2] a generalization ignoring clauses or words in the base verse, [3] a further observation without clear interest in the verse at hand. The form yields a syllogism proved by a list of facts beyond all doubt.

2. Intrinsic exegetical form: The verse itself is clarified. The focus is on the base verse and not on a broader issue. There are diverse versions of this exercise, some consisting only of a verse or a clause and a statement articulating the sense of the matter, others rather elaborate. But the upshot is always the same.

3. Dialectical Exegesis: Intrinsic: A sequence of arguments about the meaning of a passage, in which the focus is upon the base verse focuses upon the meaning of the base verse. This is the internal-exegetical counterpart to the on-going argument on whether logic works. Now logic pursues the sense of a verse, but the results of logic are tested, forthwith and one by one, against the language at hand, e.g., why is this stated? Or, you say it means X but why not Y? Or, if X, then what about Y? If Y, then what about Z? All of these rather nicely articulated exegetical programs imposes a scriptural test upon the proposals of logic.

4. Dialectical Exegesis: Extrinsic. The Fallacy of Logic Uncorrected by Exegesis of Scripture: The formal indicator is the presence of the question, in one of several versions: is it not a matter of logic? The exegesis of the verse at hand plays no substantial role.

5. Scriptural Basis for a Passage of the Mishnah: What we have is simply a citation of the verse plus a law in prior writing (Mishnah, Tosefta) which the verse is supposed to sustain. The Mishnah's or the Tosefta's rule then cannot stand as originally set forth, that is, absent any exegetical foundation. On the contrary, the rule, verbatim, rests on a verse of Scripture, given with slight secondary articulation: verse, then Mishnah-sentence. That suffices, the point is made.

6. Miscellanies: All three formally miscellaneous items turn out to have a single characteristic. They involve stories about sages.

Let us now characterize the formal traits of Sifré to Numbers as a commentary. These we may reduce to two completely objective classifications, based on the point of origin of the verses that are catalogued or subjected to exegesis: exegesis of a verse in the book of Numbers in terms of the theme or problems of that verse, hence, *intrinsic* exegesis; exegesis of a verse in Numbers in terms of a theme or polemic not particular to that verse, hence, *extrinsic* exegesis.

The forms of extrinsic exegesis: The implicit message of the external category proves simple to define, since the several extrinsic classifications turn out to form a cogent polemic. Let me state the recurrent polemic of external exegesis.

[1] The Syllogistic Composition: Scripture supplies hard facts, which, properly classified, generate syllogisms. By collecting and classifying facts of Scripture, therefore, we may produce firm laws of history, society, and Israel's everyday life. The diverse compositions in which verses from various books of the Scriptures are compiled in a list of evidence for a given proposition – whatever the character or purpose of that proposition – make that one point. And given their power and cogency, they make the point stick.

[2] The Fallibility of Reason Unguided by Scriptural Exegesis: Scripture alone supplies reliable basis for speculation. Laws cannot be generated by reason or logic unguided by Scripture. Efforts at classification and contrastive-analogical exegesis, in which Scripture does not supply the solution to all problems, prove few and far between (and always in Ishmael's name, for whatever that is worth). This polemic forms the obverse of the point above.

So when extrinsic issues intervene in the exegetical process, they coalesce to make a single point. Let me state with appropriate emphasis the recurrent and implicit message of the forms of external exegesis:

Scripture stands paramount, logic, reason, analytical processes of classification and differentiation, secondary. Reason not built on scriptural foundations yields uncertain results. The Mishnah itself demands scriptural bases.

The forms of intrinsic exegesis: What about the polemic present in the intrinsic exegetical exercises? This clearly does not allow for ready characterization. As we saw, at least three intrinsic exegetical exercises focus on the use of logic, specifically, the logic of classification, comparison and contrast of species of a genus, in the explanation of the meaning of verses of the book of Numbers. The internal dialectical mode, moving from point to point as logic dictates, underlines the main point already stated: logic produces possibilities, Scripture chooses among them. Again, the question, why is this passage stated? commonly produces an answer generated by further verses of Scripture, e.g., this matter is stated here to clarify what otherwise would be confusion left in the wake of other verses. So Scripture produces problems of confusion and duplication, and Scripture – and not logic, not differentiation, not classification – solves those problems.

To state matters simply: Scripture is complete, harmonious, perfect. Logic not only does not generate truth beyond the limits of Scripture but also plays no important role in the harmonization of difficulties yielded by what appear to be duplications or disharmonies. These forms of internal exegesis then make the same point that the extrinsic ones do. In so stating, of course, we cover all but the single most profuse category of exegesis, which we have treated as simple and undifferentiated:

[1] verse of Scripture or a clause, followed by

[2] a brief statement of the meaning at hand. Here I see no unifying polemic in favor of, or against, a given proposition. The most common form also proves the least pointed: X bears this meaning, Y bears that meaning, or, as

we have seen, citation of verse X, followed by, [what this means is].... Whether simple or elaborate, the upshot is the same.

What can be at issue when no polemic expressed in the formal traits of syntax and logic finds its way to the surface? What do I do when I merely clarify a phrase? Or, to frame the question more logically: what premises must validate my *intervention*, that is, my willingness to undertake to explain the meaning of a verse of Scripture? These seem to me propositions that must serve to justify the labor of intrinsic exegesis as we have seen its results here:

[1] My independent judgment bears weight and produces meaning. I – that is, my mind – therefore may join in the process.

[2] God's revelation to Moses at Sinai requires my intervention. I have the role, and the right, to say what that revelation means.

[3] What validates my entry into the process of revelation is the correspondence between the logic of my mind and the logic of the document.

Why do I think so? Only if I think in accord with the logic of the revealed Torah can my thought-processes join issue in clarifying what is at hand: the unfolding of God's will in the Torah. To state matters more accessibly: if the Torah does not make statements in accord with a syntax and a grammar that I know, I cannot so understand the Torah as to explain its meaning. But if I can join in the discourse of the Torah, it is because I speak the same language of thought: syntax and grammar at the deepest levels of my intellect.

[4] Then to state matters affirmatively and finally: Since a shared logic of syntax and grammar joins my mind to the mind of God as revealed in the Torah, I can say what a sentence of the Torah means. So I too can amplify, clarify, expand, revise, rework: that is to say, create a commentary.

It follows that the intrinsic exegetical forms stand for a single proposition:

While Scripture stands paramount, logic, reason, analytical processes of classification and differentiation, secondary, nonetheless, man's mind joins God's mind when man receives and sets forth the Torah.

The Purpose of the Authorship of Sifré to Numbers: Can we then state in a few words and in simple language what the formal rules of the document tell us about the purpose of Sifré to Numbers? Beyond all concrete propositions, the document as a whole through its fixed and recurrent formal preferences or literary structures makes two complementary points.

[1] Reason unaided by Scripture produces uncertain propositions.

[2] Reason operating within the limits of Scripture produces truth.

To whom do these moderate and balanced propositions matter? Sages in particular, I think. The polemic addresses arguments internal to their circles. How do we know, and how may we be certain? If we contrast the polemic of our document about the balance between revelation and reason, Torah and logic, with the polemic of another canonical document about some other topic altogether, the contrast will tell. Then and only then shall we see the choices people faced. In that way we shall appreciate the particular choice the authorship at hand has made. With the perspective provided by an exercise of comparison, we shall see how truly remarkable a document we have in Sifré to Numbers. By itself the book supplies facts. Seen in context, the book makes points. So we require a context of comparison.

The Contrast of Sifré to Numbers with Genesis Rabbah: Having characterized the generative propositional position, based on the formal rhetoric, of Sifré to Numbers, we wonder whether that document is particular or part of a larger, general approach, e.g., to Scripture. To find out, we turn to Genesis Rabbah. The authorship of Genesis Rabbah focuses its discourse on the proposition that the book of Genesis speaks to the life and historical condition of Israel, the Jewish people. The entire narrative of Genesis is so formed as to point toward the sacred history of Israel, the Jewish people: its slavery and redemption; its coming Temple in Jerusalem; its exile and salvation at the end of time. The powerful message of Genesis in the pages of Genesis Rabbah proclaims that the world's creation commenced a single, straight line of events, leading in the end to the salvation of Israel and through Israel all humanity. Therefore a given story will bear a deeper message about what it means to be Israel, on the one side, and what in the end of days will happen to Israel, on the other. If I had to point to the single most important proposition of Genesis Rabbah, it is that, in the story of the beginnings of creation, humanity, and Israel, we find the message of the meaning and end of the life of the Jewish people. The deeds of the founders supply signals for the children about what is going to come in the future. So the biography of Abraham, Isaac, and Jacob also constitutes the history of Israel later on. If the sages could announce a single syllogism and argue it systematically, that is the proposition on which they would insist. The sages understood that stories about the progenitors, presented in the book of Genesis, define the human condition and proper conduct for their children, Israel in time to come. Accordingly, they systematically asked Scripture to tell them how they were supposed to conduct themselves at the critical turnings of life. In a few words let me restate the conviction of the framers of Genesis Rabbah about the message and meaning of the book of Genesis:

> We now know what will be in the future. How do we know it? Just as Jacob had told his sons what would happen in time to come, just as Moses told the tribes their future, so we may understand the laws of history if we study the Torah. And in the Torah, we turn to beginnings: the rules as they were laid out at the very start of human history. These we find in the book of Genesis, the story of the origins of the world and of Israel.
>
> The Torah tells us not only what happened but why. The Torah permits us to discover the laws of history. Once we know those laws, we may also peer into the future and come to an assessment of what is going to

happen to us – and, especially, of how we shall be saved from our present existence. Because everything exists under the aspect of a timeless will, God's will, and all things express one thing, God's program and plan, in the Torah we uncover the workings of God's will. Our task as Israel is to accept, endure, submit, and celebrate.

We now ask ourselves a simple question: is the message of Sifré to Numbers the same as that of Genesis Rabbah? The answer is obvious. No, these are different books. They make different points in answering different questions. In plan and in program they yield more contrasts than comparisons. Why does that fact matter to my argument? Since these *are* different books, which *do* use different forms to deliver different messages, it must follow that there is nothing routine or given or to be predicted about the point that the authorship of Sifré to Numbers wishes to make. Why not? Because it is not a point that is simply "there to be made." It is a striking and original point. How, again, do we know it? The reason is that, when the sages who produced Genesis Rabbah read Genesis, they made a different point from the one at hand. So contrasting the one composition with the other shows us that each composition bears its own distinctive traits – traits of mind, traits of plan, traits of program. The upshot is simple. Once we characterize the persistent polemic of Sifré to Numbers and then compare that polemic to the characteristic point of argument of Genesis Rabbah (and, as it happens, Leviticus Rabbah as well),[5] we see that our document has chosen forms to advance its own distinctive, substantive argument. Its exegetical program points, explicitly in extrinsic exegesis, implicitly in intrinsic exegesis, to a single point, and that point is made on every page.

XIV. SIFRE TO NUMBERS, GENESIS RABBAH, LEVITICUS RABBAH, AND SIFRA: INDIVISIBLE PARTS OF AN INTERLOCKING WHOLE, OR INDIVIDUAL AND AUTONOMOUS DOCUMENTS

Let me conclude by answering two broad questions. [1] Does the document at hand deliver a particular message and viewpoint or does it merely serve as a repository for diverse, received materials? [2] Does the authorship deliver its message, its choices as to form and meaning, or merely transmit someone else's? To broaden the question by reverting to our original formulation of the present issue of connection: do we have a cogent statement or a mere scrapbook? Let me review what I said at the beginning of this chapter. A document may serve solely as a convenient repository of prior sayings and stories, available materials that will have served equally well (or poorly) wherever they took up their final

---

[5]My comparison of Genesis Rabbah and Leviticus Rabbah, in *Comparative Midrash: The Plan and Program of Genesis Rabbah and Leviticus Rabbah* (Atlanta, 1986: Scholars Press for Brown Judaic Studies), underscores this result.

location. A composition may exhibit a viewpoint, a purpose of authorship distinctive to its framers or collectors and arrangers. Such a characteristic literary purpose would be so powerfully particular to one authorship that nearly everything at hand can be shown to have been (re)shaped for the ultimate purpose of the authorship at hand. These then are collectors and arrangers who demand the title of authors. Context and circumstance form the prior condition of inquiry, the result, in exegetical terms, the contingent one. I believe that the second of the two propositions finds ample support here.

If we ask about the textuality of a document – is it a composition or a scrap book? – we wish to know whether the materials unique to a document also cohere, or whether they prove merely miscellaneous. In form and in polemic, in plan and in program, the materials assembled in Sifré to Numbers do cohere. Not only so, but the program – the framing of a position on the role of logic and reason in the mind of sages – and the plan – the defining of recurrent rhetorical forms and patterns – join into a single statement. And since they do cohere, we may conclude that the framers of the document indeed have followed a single plan and a program. That justifies my claim that the framers of Sifré to Numbers have carried out a labor not only of conglomeration, arrangement and selection, but also of genuine authorship or composition in the narrow and strict sense of the word. Sifré to Numbers emerges from authors, not merely arrangers and compositors.

It remains to observe that just as Genesis Rabbah bears formal and substantive affinity to Leviticus Rabbah; the plan and program of both documents present an essential congruity, so too in plan and in program Sifra and Sifré to Numbers form a community. The forms and polemic of Sifra and Sifré to Numbers cohere, with the forms so designed as to implicitly state and so to reenforce the substantive argument of both books. And, I am inclined to think, further study will suggest the same for the forms of Genesis Rabbah and Leviticus Rabbah.

If, then, I may end with a point worth further study: we may then classify Sifra (serving Leviticus) and Sifré to Numbers as inner-directed, facing within, toward issues of the interior life of the community vis à vis revelation and the sanctification of the life of the nation, and, intellectually, as centered on issues urgent to sages themselves. For to whom are the debates about the relationship between Torah and logic, reason and revelation, going to make a difference, if not to the intellectuals of the textual community at hand? Within the same classification-scheme, Genesis Rabbah and Leviticus Rabbah appear outer-directed, addressing issues of history and salvation, taking up critical concerns of the public life of the nation vis a vis history and the world beyond. Sifra and Sifré to Numbers address sanctification, Genesis Rabbah and Leviticus Rabbah, salvation.

The four documents respectively do not merely assemble this and that, forming a hodgepodge of things people happen to have said. In the case of each document we can answer the question: Why this, not that? The four are not compilations but compositions; seen as a group, therefore, (to state matters negatively) they are not essentially the same, lacking all viewpoint, serving a single undifferentiated task of collecting and arranging whatever was at hand. Quite to the contrary, these documents of the Oral Torah's exegesis of the written Torah emerge as rich in differences from one another and sharply defined each through its distinctive viewpoints and particular polemics, on the one side, and formal and aesthetic qualities, on the other. We deal with a canon, yes, but with a canon made up of highly individual documents. But that, after all, is what a canon is: a mode of classification that takes a library and turns it into a cogent if composite statement. A canon comprises separate books that all together make a single statement. In terms of the Judaism of the dual Torah, the canon is what takes scriptures of various kinds and diverse points of origin and turns scriptures into Torah, and commentaries on those scriptures into Torah as well, making them all into the one whole Torah – of Moses, our rabbi. And at that point, the claim that we deal with "interlocking and reinterlocking" documents from a theological viewpoint is absolutely sound – but only at that point.

Part Three

TAXONOMIC CONNECTION

Chapter Five

Connection and a Community of Texts

Criteria of Analysis

...all units are so closely interwoven and simultaneously present that none can be considered in separation from any other at any given moment; it is a world of 'intertextuality'...[1]

....interpretation is not essentially separate from the text itself an external act intruded upon it–but rather the extension of the text, the uncovering of the connective network of relations, a part of the continuous revelation of the text itself, at bottom, another aspect of the text.[2]

Susan Handelman

I. CRITERIA FOR ANALYSIS OF CONNECTION: COMPARISON AND CONTRAST THROUGH FIXED POINTS OF DIFFERENTIATION AMONG DOCUMENTS

Handelman certainly expresses the consensus of the masters of the Torah, and that view now demands attention. Is it the case that all documents have to be read in light of all others all the time? Can none be considered in separation from any other at any given moment? Is interpretation not essentially separate from the text itself? We may readily dispose of these propositions. The third, for instance, will have astonished the authorship of the Tosefta, which carefully distinguished the citation of the language of the Mishnah from the commentary or amplification that that authorship proposed to contribute. The reworking of the Mishnah rarely is accomplished through paraphrase, commonly is achieved through citation and gloss. That the authors of the units of discourse of the Bavli and Yerushalmi worked in the same way is self-evident. Similarly, we could without difficulty find one exception to the (loosely-framed) rule that "none can (ever) be considered in separation from any other at any given moment." But I think a sustained exercise in analyzing the relationships between and among documents will provide a more persuasive response than

---

[1]Susan A. Handelman, *The Slayers of Moses. The Emergence of Rabbinic Interpretation in Modern Literary Theory* (Albany, 1982: State Universty of New York Press), p.78.

[2]*Ibid.*, p. 39.

mere dismissal of the obvious absurdities at hand. For that purpose I propose to develop a theory of connection that will permit us to test Handelman's picture of the character of the literature she purports to discuss. Then, through systematic description, we may respond to her account, just as we have to Cohen and Schiffman.

The connection among documents invoked by the metaphor of genealogy and described by the comparison to the synoptic relationships among Matthew, Mark, and Luke, no longer serves. For the claim before us now encompasses still broader ground than Schiffman's version of the received theory of connection. To make certain the proposition before us is clear, let me repeat it yet again: "all units are so closely interwoven and simultaneously present that none can be considered in separation from any other at any given moment." Handelman speaks of the entire literature, "all units." So we have to develop a theory of connection encompassing the entire literature – *all the time, all at once.* Genealogy connects document to document, hence, not everything, everywhere, all the time, all at once. So we require a new criterion of connection, one pertinent to the thesis before us.

We have therefore to reconsider the meaning of connection and to consider a different approach altogether. We start not with connection, but with that broader genus of which connection constitutes only a species. I mean, specifically, *relationship.* To frame the question of this part of the book, if we wish to ask about *connection*, we have to know what we mean by that sub-category of the classification, *relationship*, and we must also define the evidence we deem appropriate to guide us to assign to that category of relationship, that is, connection, two or more documents. What evidence will lead us to see two or more documents as "connected," thus in a relationship of connection? My answer, for purposes of experiment, derives from an exercise of taxonomy. Two or more documents attain connection through the sharing of definitive traits and do not connect when they do not share indicative characteristics.

It follows that, for the present purposes, by connection I mean a species of relationship: close, distant, non-existent. Documents that share traits of plan and program relate *through those shared traits* and in that sense stand in connection with one another. Those that do not share traits are not related, not connec:ed. So I use *relationship* and *connection* as near-synonyms, even though we may readily distinguish the one from the other. Relationships not of connection, after all, are ready at hand, e.g., relationship of parallel lines, of symmetry, and the like. To conclude these definitions and proceed to the experiments: by relationship, therefore, I mean that two or more documents share traits in common, so relate through those traits; or do not share traits in common, so do not stand in a relationship of taxonomic connection at all.

Our principal problem is to define indicators of an objective character. To begin with, therefore, I stress external and objective traits of form and program, that is, rhetoric and topic, rather than proposition, so as to invoke as evidence only facts of a most extrinsic and hence objective sort. I can think of no better way to establish how documents relate than by looking for shared traits of plan and program, cataloguing traits common to two or more compositions, sizing up fixed relationships of dependence or independence between two or more documents and a third document to which all refer. These constitute matters of fact and description, not mere impression, and anyone can replicate my experiments and test my results. A less systematic analysis, for instance comparing documents not by a fixed set of criteria but by salient traits particular to two documents,[3] seems to me to yield nothing more than episodic if not subjective results. Appeal to shared values or opinions all the more so leads us into guesswork and an exchange of opinions of self-evident – therefore unarguable – facticity. A quite separate exercise of topical description, rigorous inquiry into propositions yielded by document A and not known to the authorship of document B will ultimately allow making judgments on matters of proposition, rather than mere literary convention. That is why I invoke the criteria, as to classification for purposes of assessing relationship, of literary convention: rhetoric, topic, logic, fixed relationship. Only when we cover a broad sample of the documents of the canon shall we gain a measure of certainty about how, over all, rules of interrelationship govern the connection of document to document.

I frame a set of questions to apply uniformly and rigorously to the nine documents under consideration here, samples of which are given in Appendix Two. By the categories formed through the questions at hand, I describe the documents in accord with a uniform scheme. These same categories of description for purposes of comparison and contrast applied throughout will then yield descriptive rules on how documents relate. That is to say, uniform description will indicate how documents connect to one another, hence, the connections between and among them. The discovery of uniform patterns of relationship (if there are such) then requires demonstrating that documents relate by conforming, in their composition, to a single plan and program, hence fall into a single classification; or do not relate because they do not exhibit traits in common. Let me spell out the uniform questions I propose to ask, and then begin the logical construction of appropriate points of analysis of the traits of documents.

What I want to know in describing and analyzing relationships is [1] whether one document essentially continues the discourse of precedessors and copies one or more of them, making minor improvements, or whether a document stands essentially independent of its precedessors and goes its own way. If I find replication, then I can define one sort of relationship of connection, and if I find essentially fresh discourse, then I define a different

---

[3]I refer to my *Comparative Midrash. The Plan and Program of Genesis Rabbah and Leviticus Rabbah* (Atlanta, 1986: Scholars Press for Brown Judaic Studies). That work is particular to only two texts.

relationship of connection between two documents or among more than two. I ask, further, not only about the traits of documents each viewed on its own in relationship to others, that is moving from a description of one autonomous document to the comparison of two or more documents, also viewed whole.

I want to know [2] about materials that surface in two or more (autonomous) documents and, in particular, with reference to shared materials, whether and how these materials link the two or more documents in which they occur. That is to say, what difference, if any, does the fact make that a unit of discourse finds its way into more than a single document.

This brings us to [3] the issue of connection: how connected, really, are the documents? Do they exhibit "affinities" of a substantial order, or do they merely intersect here and there (and which documents do the one, which the other)? If the overall pattern is adventitious intersection, then the viability of the notion of documentary connection has to be called into question. To revert to the original metaphor, were there bookshelves at all, or just a library building?

For it is not self-evident that documents relate at all, even though, in the context in which they are preserved, people say that they do. For what happens beyond the pages of a book has no bearing on what is in the book, how the authors of a book made their book, or even how we should read that book. That *extrinsic* dimension of meaning testifies to how the book is received and used, not to what is in the book and the relationship of the authorship of the book to other authorships. And that simple observation leads us to the distinction that serves as premise of this inquiry. It is between relationships *imputed* or inferred from without and relationships *implied* from within.

An imputed relationship is imposed on a document by the community that receives and reveres that document, hence testifies to the presence of a textual community, and an implied relationship is one to which the contents and structure of a book bear witness, testifying on their own through objective traits of plan and program. An implied relationship testifies to the community of texts. The one is extrinsic, the other intrinsic. In terms of the three dimensions introduced earlier, the imputed relationship testifies to the traits of the community that infers from a book propositions external to the book – the library building, in my original metaphor. An implied relationship derives from the book itself, not from the social context in which the book finds its afterlife – even from the bookshelf. Since at issue are documents' interrelationships, we have to deal with implied, not inferred relationships. So we define those properties of texts that lead us to recognize that a document belongs into a classification shared by some other – hence interrelationships between two texts or among three or more texts.

That brings us to the critical issue: What properties provide adequate evidence to generate propositions on that matter, what traits do not? Let me now list those that prove self-evident, external and obvious. We may invoke only facts visible to the naked eye, deal only with matters of concrete and material reality. We permit only a single unproved premise: all documents of the Judaism at hand must situate themselves in relationship to Scripture. Scripture forms the distant horizon, the fixed stars, the constant against which all perspective is formed, all navigation takes place. That constitutes the sole fact I posit without proof.

II. SCRIPTURE

Starting from the given, Scripture, we want to know how diverse documents relate to Scripture in plan, program, and proposition. The primacy of the relationship to Scripture derives from a simple fact. All documents of the canon of the dual Torah make reference to the written part of "the one whole Torah of our rabbi, Moses." So the relationship to Scripture forms the one sure constant, uniting all documents and making possible comparison and contrast on a single plane, and against a fixed horizon. So it is that constant against which we may discern variables. We have then to specify the variables in such a way as to allow for maximum objectivity, minimum subjectivity. Our estimate of matters must play a minimal role in judgment, simple facts deriving from objective traits, the maximal one. Let me spell out the questions.

1. Proportion of Units of Discourse in which Verses of Scripture Play a Role

A document may make frequent reference to Scripture, or seldom resort to Scripture. That variable is a matter of fact, not impression. Documents that refer frequently to verses of Scripture then form one classification, those that do not form another.

2. Redaction

A second formal variable derives from the redational plan of documents. A document requires a trellis on which to hang its vines and leaves. Some depend upon Scripture for the plan for their overall arrangement of units of discourse, others draw upon the program of the Mishnah, still others do neither. The variable is a matter of fact: documents that depend on passages of Scripture for their organizing element fall into one classification, documents that depend on the Mishnah into a second, documents that depend on neither into a third.

3. Citation of a Verse of Scripture: Probative or Propositional

Here we come to a somewhat more subtle variable, but one accessible of a purely factual analysis. Some units of discourse draw upon verses of Scripture to supply the proof for propositions framed on grounds independent of the program of Scripture. These units make use of such verses as proof-texts or even as pretexts. (For our purposes the distinction makes no difference.) Other units of discourse focus upon the sense and propositions of verses of Scripture.

In such compositions the role of Scripture is different, since it is the allegation of Scripture that defines the problem at hand. Documents in which the former use of verses of Scripture predominate in units of discourse fall into one category, those in which the latter use proves paramount fall into another.

4. The Propositions of Scripture

Some compositions are made up of units of discourse that take up propositions of Scripture and focus discourse on those propositions, thus centering upon the points that Scripture wishes to make. That interest in the contents of Scripture may be discerned even though a particular verse or set of verses is not cited. Other compositions ignore the substantive interests particular to Scripture and pursue different propositions from those supplied by Scripture. The units of discourse of these compositions simply go their own way and rarely if at all intersect with a topical point of Scripture.

Let me now expand on these categories and generalize on their meaning. The several classifications produce answers to a single basic question: does a document adopt from Scripture its mode of organizing topics and the manner of linking thought to thought to form a cogent state? That is, do the *topoi* and *logoi* of a document form a symmetry with those of a passage of Scripture? We know that they do when we find a correspondence between the sense and proposition of Scripture and those of the unit of discourse at hand, and, in our context, a document will fall into the topcial and logical classification of Scripture when in the aggregate its units of discourse place it into that classification.

We proceed to the next possibility in line: does discourse proceed on other topics than Scriptures, through other modes of cogent and intelligible discourse than those of Scripture? Here we have a striking and objective point of likeness or difference, which permits the differentiation of document from document and the identification of a genus and, consequently, also of its species. So we ask whether the ideas of a passage of Scripture dominate in a given document, or whether the document pursues not only its own selection of topics, but also its own inquiry about those topics. Does what a document wants to know about a topic conform to what Scripture wants to say about that same topic, or does a document take up in an essentialy fresh and original way a topic that occurs in Scripture too? Finally, we address the issue of proposition. Does a document wish to say in its own way what Scripture says, or does it make an essentially autonomous point of its own. These questions find their answers in perfectly factual ways and do not demand the exercise of taste and judgment.

III. LOGICAL AND RHETORICAL PLAN: FORMAL TRAITS OF INTELLIGIBLE DISCOURSE

I see numerous ways in which a unit of discourse may take shape as a logical proposition. That is to say, there are diverse modes by which intelligible statements come forth, points are made, and a cogent statement given form. I name three that operate in the literature before us:

1. **The Syllogistic List:** A document may make its point by composing lists of examples that reveal, in traits in common, proof of a given proposition. Through the underlying principle contained in the several examples a list may generate an encompassing rule.

2. **The Commentary:** A document may express a cogent proposition not through autonomous discourse, but through commenting on points made by a base-document, hence a document may comprise a commentary to a text supplied by another document. A commentary falls into a different classification from an independent propositional exercise in syllogistic discourse such as a list.

3. **The Tradental List:** A document may take form through listing authorities, cited in a given order, e.g., Rabbi X said Rabbi Y said. What is attributed to those authorities will not contribute to the cogency of the document. The list of names supplies whatever structure the unit of discourse possesses. No principle of cogency other than such names imparts to the list of names a general intelligibiliy. But then, to the framers, association of diverse sayings with a single authority constitutes an adequate principle of intelligible discourse.

IV. TOPICAL AND PROPOSITIONAL PROGRAM: THE SUBSTANCE OF INTELLIGIBLE DISCOURSE

The matter of topic yields diverse meanings. Reduced to its simplest component, however, the topic encompasses two matters: subject-matter and problematic. To ask the question simply: what subject does the text take up? And what does the authorship wish to know *about* that subject? The purpose may involve merely laying out information about a given subject. But very commonly, an authorship wishes to inquire, as to a given subject, about a particular problem or aspect. The topic may produce a range of pieces of information. An authorship brings to that topic a very particular problem, which dictates to that authorship the things it wishes to know about the topic, hence, as I said, the problematic addressed to the topic. So in the present classification we raise these questions: exactly what does a document wish to say, and how does the message – the topical program – of a document relate to that of some other?

The problem is to compare and contrast topics, and that means, *types* of topics. Here, of course, the sources before us present us with a number of choices, e.g., Scripture as against non-Scripture, law as against lore, norms of theology as against norms of behavior. The classification of the propositional program by definition bears as many categories as there are documents, so the taxonomy of propositions does not present the same self-evident choices as does the taxonomy of modes of forming intelligible statements. A further problem derives from the difficulty in identifying inductive evidence suitable for classification, other than the statements of a given document. The evidence from without, e.g., the distinction between law and lore, norm of behavior and norm of belief, yields distinctions that, within the literature, make remarkably little difference.

Still, if we stipulate that the entire canon unfolds in relationship to two base-documents, Scripture and the Mishnah, then the topical programs of two or more documents may be compared and brought into relationship with one another. Using the topics made available in Scripture as our base, we may compare the topical programs of two or more compositions that focus on Scripture and ask what, in Scripture, each document chooses to treat, and how it does so. So too we may ask how a given document has selected for amplification the tractates of the Mishnah.

1. **Scripture and its Topical Program**: Here we compare two or more documents that focus on Scripture and ask whether the authorships have chosen the same themes or different ones. By "theme" I mean both the concrete narrative of Scripture at a given passage and also a broader frame of interest. For example, while the Mishnah does not introduce themes of history and its interpretation, Scripture does, so two or more documents may fall into the same classification, in regard to Scripture and its topical program, if they take up issues of the meaning of history.

2. **The Mishnah and its Topical Program**: On the other hand, the Mishnah presents a rather sizable and cogent set of topics, and here too two or more authorships may intersect in their choices of what, within that set, they choose to take up and amplify and explain.

V. THE SAMPLE

In the appendix I give a sample of nine documents, and in the shank of the chapters of this part of the book I repeatedly probe the traits of those nine documents, as represented by that sample. The reason that a sample of a meaningful proportion of the whole serves is simple. Each of the documents not only exhibits distinctive literary and topical traits, but all of them preserve an internal cogency and uniformity to those distinctive traits. The nine documents thus differ among themselves but, individually, present us with ample evidence of remarkable internal consistency. The study of connections focuses, as I shall explain, on the presence or absence of objective traits, e.g., of rhetoric, logic, and types of topic. When, therefore, I allege that rhetorical or logical or topical trait X characterizes document A and not document B, the basis of a given sample more than suffices, because the sample of a text represents and exemplifies a text that is, in rhetoric, logic, and topic (as defined above) uniform within and distinctive in comparison to the other documents of the canon of Judaism. Readers have in hand exactly the data on which I perform my surveys and probes, but, since I have translated all of the documents under study, they can turn for the examination of my results to a far broader sample of the whole.

The texts I take up cover the two received categories, *halakhah* and *aggadah*, law and lore respectively, so that we may test various propositions that rest on the distinction between these two types of documents. The former type of discourse, on norms of behavior, predominates in the Mishnah, Tosefta, Yerushalmi, and Bavli, as well as Sifra and Sifré to Numbers. The latter, on norms of belief, is paramount in Avot, Genesis Rabbah, and Leviticus Rabbah. I of course have taken up both types of discourse in all of my prior research, as the materials at hand required. But the issue of connection requires reconsideration of the matter, since, it has been alleged, the one – *aggadah* – forms the premise of the other – *halakhah*. Whether or not that is so depends upon what people mean when they speak of implicit premises.[4] If they mean that one document takes for granted conceptions found in some other document, then I can understand and deal with that allegation by asking whether, in fact, we can find evidence that that is true.

If they mean that all documents rest upon premises expressed in none of them, or that an indeterminate body of *aggadic* thought forms the basis for an indeterminate corpus of *halakhic* rules, then I am at a loss to comprehend precisely what proposition I am asked to entertain. I can grasp the claim that a premise derives from document A and serves as the foundation for document B. Then I can go in search of evidence that a statement in logic becomes possible only on the stated premise – or that that premise would contradict such a statement of an explicit character. So the proposition proves subject to testing. But if, as I said, that simple logic does not form the allegation before us, then no intelligible statement is at hand. For how am I supposed to know whether a premise or a presupposition is before me, if I have no evidence of that fact, and, further, no way of testing whether I am right or wrong in declaring implicit something not visible to the naked eye.

That brings me to the matter of *halakhah* (law) and *aggadah* (lore). The categories do not derive from the character of documents, most of which contain, in varying measure, materials of both types. The categories in my judgment stand in an asymmetrical relationship with the components of the literature that forms our sole source for the Judaism of the dual Torah. But since the question of the *aggadic* premise of a *halakhic* book comes to the fore, as diverse scholars insist we have to read into one document convictions important in some other, we shall attempt to find out what we can about the premises of documents. That is, once more in the sole formulation I can imagine, *the*

---

[4]See for example Haim Maccoby in *Midstream* (September, 1986).

connections among documents. If those who posit unstated premises and implicit propositions appeal to something other than documentary evidence, e.g., to a "Judaism" that is prior to all documents and expressed through each of them, then I shall have to resume the dialogue with them when I reach the problem of continuity. But that is some way off.

VI. CONCLUSION

The task before us presents striking impediments. For, as I explained in the opening part of this book, the matter of connection between and among documents hardly rests on self-evident traits of documents. We may demonstrate that a document stands on its own. We also may recognize that, through the actions of a community, documents may relate to one another. But why take for granted that there are intrinsic traits that connect document to document? We therefore take up a set of essentially contradictory propositions:

[1] texts stand autonomous of one another and can and should be described individually and on their own,

[2] or texts connect with one another and are to be read in a broader context than that supplied by their own statements alone.

On the one hand I have spent fifteen years trying to show that diverse documents in the canon of Judaism bear each its own integrity, its own message, its own voice, mode of presenting its ideas, communicating them through logical discourse made up of intelligible statements. Each document I have characterized on its own as to topic and logic, rhetoric and proposition. Now I reverse ground and insist that documents not only stand on their own but intersect, interrelate, connect with one another in intrinsic aspects and traits. Now were we to speak of extrinsic connection, we should not address the two contradictory propositions I have taken up in this book. For within that other proposition, we infer on the basis only of extrinsic traits merely that documents form a continuity. Since that continuity, of course, derives in the end from the consensus of the community that sees the documents not as a library but as a canon, we should not find ourselves confounded by the conflict of the two propositions pertinent to the internal data alone: data distinct from other data, data connected with other data. So were I to leap from the long-argued and now proved proposition of the autonomy of documents directly to the issues of continuity, I should not establish for myself the contradictory propositions with which I am trying to cope. Yet I believe this middle range of relationships – connection, established through intersection, genealogy, or even abstract taxonomy – demands attention. For here is where we take the writings seriously in their own terms, with focus on their own intrinsic traits. We do not wish to relinquish the study of these writings to wholly social, let alone entirely theological, inquiry, nor to concede at the outset that the sole appropriate hermeneutic derives from sociology and history on the one side, or theology on the other. We wish to allow literature to be literature: to be read on its own, therefore to establish its connections in its own terms, aesthetic, structural, linguistic, for example, and not only on terms imputed by others.

It follows that in positing an intermediate dimension of relationship, one midway between entire autonomy and complete continuity, one validated by the intrinsic, specific and particular traits of a document, the other by the extrinsic decisions of a community that reveres texts whatever their particular traits, I create my own problem.[5] It is, as I said, the contradictory assertions I have offered that documents both form autonomous units, each with its own integrity, and also interrelate in ways that count. Obviously, that middle ground demands exploration solely in the search for the intrinsic facts of our sample: what sort of connections – defined taxonomically, as I have said – do we actually uncover? We now turn from the general and the theoretical to those details in which alone the truth endures.

---

[5]True enough, it is a problem that derives from propositions of a theological, not a literary character, and it is one that all students of the canon of Judaism must recognize.

Chapter Six

Scripture

I. PROLOGUE

All documents in the rabbinic canon – the Oral Torah – relate to Scripture, the Written Torah. That is not merely by definition imputed from without. It is the simple fact that all documents in the Judaic canon cite verses of Scripture, if not all of the time, then at least not uncommonly. What connects all of the documents of the Oral Torah to one another, then, is that every one of them cites verses of Scripture and otherwise resorts to the themes and program and even propositions of Scripture. If, on the surface, all documents form connections *to* Scripture, we nonetheless have to pursue our inquiry. For when we want to know whether the documents connect not only to a common source but also *to one another*, these connections to Scripture turn out to supply important points of differentiation among the documents themselves. That is to say, the character of the scriptural connection of one document differs from that of another. So on the surface the documents do join one another in their common interest in Scripture – the written Torah. But that vertical line, upward to Scripture, hardly runs parallel for all documents.

Quite to the contrary, the documents relate to Scripture in different ways, and the lines that connect them to Scripture do not run along the same course. The connections between the nine documents and Scripture divide into a number of distinct taxonomic categories. That means that the scriptural connection is too diverse and varied to sustain the claim that, on the basis at hand, the nine documents fall into a single classification – the one deriving from relationship to Scripture – and so constitute documents related through the connection demonstrated by taxonomy. Quite to the contrary, the closer we view the connections to Scripture exhibited by the nine documents, the more clearly we see the lack of connection between one document and the next. Despite the shared trait of citing verses of Scripture, common to all documents, our present classificatory taxonomy distinguishes and differentiates document from document rather than uniting and connecting the documents to one another. Let us begin with a review of our classifications.

1. Proportion of Units of Discourse in which Verses of Scripture Play a Role

A document may make frequent reference to Scripture, or seldom resort to Scripture. Documents that refer frequently to verses of Scripture form a classification, those that do not form another.

2. Redaction

Some documents depend upon Scripture for the plan for their overall arrangement of units of discourse, others draw upon the program of the Mishnah, still others do neither.

3. Citation of a Verse of Scripture: Probative or Propositional

Some units of discourse draw upon verses of Scripture to supply proof for propositions framed on grounds independent of the program of Scripture. These units make use of such verses as proof-texts or even as pretexts. Other units of discourse focus upon the sense and propositions of verses of Scripture.

4. The Propositions of Scripture

This exercise flows from the foregoing. Some compositions are made up of units of discourse that take up propositions of Scripture – whether or not these propositions are given in the exact wording of a verse of Scripture – and focus discourse on those propositions, thus centering upon points that Scripture wishes to make. Other compositions ignore the substantive interests particular to Scripture and pursue different propositions from those supplied by Scripture.

II. THE MISHNAH

We take up the Mishnah-passage in Appendix One because it is essentially different from that in Appendix Two. The former is completely unaffected by Scripture, citing no proof-texts and addressing issues of law unknown to Scripture. The Mishnah-passage before us in Appendix Two, by contrast, alludes to Scriptural laws and works its way through scriptural themes. It further explicitly cites a passage of Scripture. We do well, therefore, to treat both sorts of Mishnah-chapter, even though the former is far more commonplace than the latter.

1. Proportion of Units of Discourse in which Verses of Scripture Play a Role

Berakhot

This chapter does not contain a citation or allusion to Scripture.

Sanhedrin

Direct citation of a verse of Scripture occurs at M. 2:1J, proof-text; M. 2:2J, proof-text; M. 2:3D, proof-text, M. 2:4F, proof-text, with the same text worked over at M. 2:4G-I, M. 2:4J-L, M. 2:5C. In point of fact, therefore, all of the distinct pericopes before us contain citations of Scripture. That trait happens to set the present Mishnah-chapter apart from the generality of the document, which uncommonly cites verses of Scripture.

2. Redaction

Berakhot

The category does not apply.

Sanhedrin

Some tractates in the Mishnah selection do follow the plan and program of Scripture, tractate Yoma, for example, and Pesahim as well. Most do not. The one at hand follows its own plan, though a portion of the passage shows a systematic adherence to the topical plan of a verse of Scripture. Scripture does not supply the order of topics. The program of the pericope derives from its own topical interests, M. 2:1, and does not depend upon the cited verses, e.g., Deut. 25:7-9, even though those verses do provide an important component of the topical plan before us. When proof-texts are cited, e.g., Lev. 21;12, 2 Sam. 12:8, they in no way dictate the order or redactional plan of the pericope. The way in which a verse of Scripture can impose its order and plan on a Mishnah-pericope emerges at M. 2:4E-N, which systematically cites Deut. 17:16 and then goes over its clauses. But that passage, even here, hardly imparts its program on the whole, and, in the broader setting of the Mishnah, forms an exception.

3. Citation of a Verse of Scripture: Probative or Propositional

Berakhot

The issue does not pertain.

Sanhedrin

Most of the citations of verses of Scripture provide proofs for propositions at hand. Only Deut. 17:16 supplies the propositions on which the passage rests. So that component of the larger composition shows us what the Mishnah would have looked like, had it worked out its propositions in response to the redactional and substantive program of Scripture.

4. The Propositions of Scripture

Berakhot

The matter is irrelevant.

Sanhedrin

What Scripture wishes to say at the cited passage, with special reference to Deut. 17:16f., provides the Mishnah-passage with its program. But that is only a small proportion of the composition as a whole. This result complements the foregoing.

III. TRACTATE AVOT

1. Proportion of Units of Discourse in which Verses of Scripture Play a Role

Our sample of tractate Avot cites proof-texts only episodically, M. 1:18, 2:9, 13. There is no systematic interest in assigning to sayings scriptural proof; the contrary seems the plan, to allow most sayings to stand on their own. Scripture plays a decidedly subordinated role in our sample.

2. Redaction

The passage makes no reference to a scriptural composition, and in stringing together sayings assigned to named authorities, it adopts a redactional plan of its own – neither topical, as in the Mishnah, nor scriptural, as in reference to Deut. 17:16ff.

3. Citation of a Verse of Scripture: Probative or Propositional

The verses that are cited do serve as proof-texts, but the propositions they serve to prove do not derive from a scriptural program. M. 1:18 speaks of three things on which the world stands, but while those things occur in the cited verse, the verse does not make that point. M. 2:19 falls into the same category in its use of Ps. 37:21. I do not see a close relationship between Joel 2:13 and the proposition of M. 2:13.

4. The Propositions of Scripture

The propositions of M. Avot 1-2 derive from the program of the framers, not from Scripture; there is scarcely pretense at appeal to Scripture – or, as a matter of fact, even reference to Scripture.

IV. THE TOSEFTA

1. Proportion of Units of Discourse in which Verses of Scripture Play a Role

Berakhot

The comparison of M. Ber. 8:1ff. and T. Ber. 5:25ff. shows no difference between the one and the other. Tosefta's authorship does not find pertinent proof-texts for the Mishnah-passages which it supplements, even though the focus of interest is on amplifying reasons for the Mishnah's rules. We do not further deal with T. Berakhot, there being no reason to do so.

Sanhedrin

We may generalize with some certainty on the basis of our passage, that the authorship of the Tosefta did not concur with that of the Mishnah that propositions of law may go forth naked or proof-texts. For that authorship did its best to clothe in a cloak of Scripture propositions that, for the Mishnah's authorship, did not require that protection. For the fact before us is simple and one-sided. Where the Mishnah lacks proof-texts, the Tosefta may supply them, as at T. 4:2K. A variation is for the Tosefta's framers to present a different proof-text, as at T. 4:1K. Further and more interesting is the interest in the conflict of proof-texts, as at T. 4:1M-O. Even though our particular passage of the Mishnah presents an unusually rich repertoire of proof-texts, the Tosefta's passage provides a still more ample selection of scriptural texts and discourse, so that, in the aggregate, the Tosefta's counterpart to our Mishnah-passage focuses on scriptural cases and precedents and proofs for propositions important both to the Mishnah and also to the Tosefta. In all, the single most common word in our passage is "as it is said."

2. Redaction

Sanhedrin

The program of the Tosefta derives from two sources, that of the Mishnah, as signified, but also that of various passages of Scripture. The sustained discussion of passages of Ezra, the still more striking recourse to scriptural themes – these give the Tosefta's counterpart the appearance of a sustained exegesis of selected passages of Scripture. If we survey the passage as a whole, we see that the first part – T. 4:1-5J – follows the program of the Mishnah and amplifies its individual statements. The second part – T. 4:5K-4:7 K – follows suit, though it introduces thematically relevant, but substantively fresh materials. Then at the final part – T. 4:7L-4:11 – we leave the Mishnah's pericope behind and move out in a completely new direction. And that movement is toward Scripture and its themes. These themes do not intersect with those of the Mishnah-chapter, dealing, as we see, with Ezra's giving of the Torah, the Aramaic language, the writing of the Torah, the king in the model of Moses as Joshua was in the model of Moses, and other rules about the kingship in general. In all of this we may say that the Tosefta has exhibited a tendency to move from the Mishnah's materials, viewed verbatim, then in general, to its themes. The introduction of these themes draws attention to the pertinent passages of Scripture, read on their own. But has Scripture dictated the redactional structure of the Tosefta-passage? In no way.

3. Citation of a Verse of Scripture: Probative or Propositional

The Tosefta's authors' interest in verses of Scripture is not only in proof-texts. The propositions of Scripture take over to define the formation of components of the passage as a whole, for example, at T. 4:7Lff., 4:8. Scriptural provides probative examples for the Mishnah's propositions, e.g., at T. 4:7I-J, L-P. The cited verses are not mere pretexts but form an integral part of the argument.

4. The Propositions of Scripture

The proposition that everyone should have his own Torah-scroll yields a sustained interest in Joshua. Cases of scriptural history, moreover, serve to prove propositions of the law, as at T. 4:11, though here the building frame derives from the proposition of the framers, not a theme of Scripture. In the balance, however, I judge that, while scriptural proofs prove propositions, laying the factual foundation for laws of society and history, the propositions at hand derive, in the end, from the larger interests of the framers – hence, from the Mishnah – in both theme and content. I see no point at which a scriptural theme, on its own, has provided the frame of discourse. To state matters affirmatively, every topic covered by the Tosefta-passage comes directly or derivatively from the interests of the Mishnah.

V. THE YERUSHALMI

1. Proportion of Units of Discourse in which Verses of Scripture Play a Role

At Y. Sanhedrin 2:1III we have an inserted exegesis, invoking proof-texts pertinent to the proposition at hand. Y. 2:3/IA presents a proof-text, so too IIA, B, IVA. Y. 2:3V provides a systematic exegesis pertinent to Rispah, Abigail, and Bath Sheba. This passage rests on the cited verses. Y. 2:4III is of the same sort. Y. 2:5IIB cites a proof-text. Y. 2:5III-IV works its way through 1 Chr. 11:13-14/2 Sam. 2311f. Y. 2:6/I, II fall into the same classification. Y. 2:6III, IV invoke a number of proof-texts, but focus on their own themes and topics. If we may divide the matter into its classifications, we point for compositions in which scriptural interests predominate to Y. 2:3V, 2:4III, and 2:5III-IV. The discourse otherwise proves remarkably focused on the program of the Mishnah. Scripture does not supply Yerushalmi's authorship with a rich corpus of themes or topics; the Mishnah does.

2. Redaction

The redactional structure of Y. Sanhedrin 2A:3V, 2:4III,Y. 2:5III-IV, 2:6I-II, derives from the order or thematic program of verses of Scripture. Everything else comes from the Mishnah. This result conforms to the foregoing.

3. Citation of a Verse of Scripture: Probative or Propositional

Proof-texts serve Sanhedrin throughout, in varying measure. Propositions of Scripture take over at the passages in which Scripture, not the Mishnah, defines the redactional structure as well. There we identify the center of interest with the stories of Scripture. These I find at Y. Sanhedrin 2:3IV, 2:4III,2:5III, IV, 2:6II. In volume and sustained interest, the passages make a stronger impression than this brief catalogue would suggest.

4. The Propositions of Scripture

What has just been said answers the question at hand. The specified compositions work out Scripture's propositions – stories, in particular – and the other compositions ignore those propositions. To state the matter more generally, where the authorship of the Yerushalmi as an autonomous exercise pursues the exegesis of verses of Scripture, it is when a story of Scripture provides the center of interest. Where we find scriptural verses serving as proof-texts, it is when the discourse focuses upon the passage of the Mishnah. The bulk of the Yerushalmi overall is of the latter character.

VI. SIFRA

1. Proportion of Units of Discourse in which Verses of Scripture Play a Role

For the authorship of Sifra the book of Leviticus serves as the center of interest, beginning, middle, and end. Therefore verses of Scripture and not sentences of the Mishnah comprise the structure of the whole, and, it goes without saying, all units of discourse bear their freight of verses of Scripture.

2. Redaction

All units of discourse also are built around the cited verses of Scripture.

3. Citation of a Verse of Scripture: Probative or Propositional

While verses of Scripture occasionally serve merely to prove points introduced from elsewhere, the focus overall is upon the propositions of Scripture. Where a passage of the Mishnah intervenes, these scriptural propositions come first. That is because the purpose of the redactors is to prove that all of the propositions of the Mishnah relevant to the cited passage of Scripture depend for authority on the passage of Scripture, not on the working of practical reason unguided by Scripture.

4. The Propositions of Scripture

What has been said answers this question. We may say that Mishnah is to the Yerushalmi as Scripture is to Sifra. In the one document Scripture serves to prove the propositions of the Mishnah, Scripture is subordinate and Mishnah definitive of structure and topic, and in the other, matters are the opposite.

VII. SIFRE TO NUMBERS

1. Proportion of Units of Discourse in which Verses of Scripture Play a Role

Every unit of discourse in Sifré to Numbers contains citations of verses of Scripture.

2. Redaction

Scripture provides the structure of redaction for every unit of discourse. When the Mishnah is cited, it is for the purpose of showing that on the basis of reason the Mishnah's laws can (or cannot) have been discovered.

3. Citation of a Verse of Scripture: Probative or Propositional

Verses of Scripture are cited both as proof-texts and as the foundation for discourse. Those that stand at the head of units of discourse serve the latter purpose, those in the middle or at the end, the former. But in the aggregate Scripture serves to provide all the important propositions under discussion.

4. The Propositions of Scripture

What has just been said answers this question. We may take note that, as to the criteria of use of Scripture, Sifra and Sifré to Numbers fall into a single classification.

VIII. GENESIS RABBAH

1. Proportion of Units of Discourse in which Verses of Scripture Play a Role

Verses of Scripture make an appearance in every unit of discourse, and, ordinarily, they appear at the head of each unit.

2. Redaction

The redactional structure of Genesis Rabbah rests on systematic citation of verses of Scripture, ordinarily in sequence, beginning to end of a given pericope of Scripture.

3. Citation of a Verse of Scripture: Probative or Propositional

Verses of Scripture serve both purposes. At I:I.1 the verse of Scripture provides information, specifically, a word that requires amplification, and this leads to a broader point, imputed to several verses of Scripture. So the base-verse is hardly propositional. I:V likewise rests on a basically syllogistic, not exegetical structure. The verses of Scripture in no way are propositional, and their probative force is limited to illustration. So the impression of an exegesis belies the reality, which is that Scripture serves a subordinated function, and the main point is to offer propositions illustrated or even proved by Scripture, but not deriving – in the hands of the compositors themselves – from Scripture. The contrast to the propositions concerning David, given in the Yerushalmi's sample, shows the different character of what is before us in this sample. At I:VI, by contrast, the purpose is to explain words of Scripture, but here too the end purpose is not exegesis in any narrow sense, but propositional. Genesis Rabbah in this criterion hardly falls into the same classification as Sifra and Sifré to Numbers.

4. The Propositions of Scripture

In no way have propositions of Scripture provided the compositors with their main focus and theme, other than the very general one of Creation. Once we have absorbed that theme, however, the specific propositions of Scripture on that theme move to the background, and a set of cosmological issues takes over. So in the aggregate Genesis Rabbah does not compare to Sifra and Sifré to Numbers, for the latter pursue the propositions of the passages of Scripture at hand, while the former has its own program of inquiry, thematically relevant to, but substantively autonomous of, Scripture.

IX. LEVITICUS RABBAH

1. Proportion of Units of Discourse in which Verses of Scripture Play a Role

Every unit of discourse is dominated by citations of verses of Scripture.

2. Redaction

The citation of a verse of Leviticus opens each unit of discourse. But unlike the situation at Sifra and Sifré to Numbers, the verses do not follow one after the other in accord with Scripture's order. Rather, they are cited in no clear pattern of relationship to Scripture and serve as a kind of pretext for discussion of a theme. So it is the theme, not the redaction of Scripture, that dictates the redactional plan at hand. In this trait Leviticus Rabbah seems to me to differ from Genesis Rabbah, as well as from Sifra and Sifré to Numbers.

3. Citation of a Verse of Scripture: Probative or Propositional

The theme of each unit of discourse derives not from a verse of Scripture but from the result of juxtaposing two or more verses of Scripture. What that means is that Scriptures serve narrowly probative purposes, rather than broadly propositional ones. The verses of Scripture are chosen to develop the selected theme, and it is that theme that imposes on the cited verses their probative task: prove this, not that.

4. The Propositions of Scripture

What has been said applies here as well. The basic propositions here do not derive from Scripture in particular, although, as is to be expected, once the proposition comes into view Scripture provides its share of relevant data. But the theme, e.g., sin and expiation, is not Scripture's in particular, in that the verse of Leviticus that purports to provide the redactional framework for the whole, Lev. 4:3-4, on the sin of the anointed priest, hardly directs our attention to the broad and encompassing propositions at hand. So, over all, Scripture's themes play a large role, but the proposition before us is not particular to Scripture, and, in the base at hand, is not Scripture's at all.

X. THE BAVLI

1. Proportion of Units of Discourse in which Verses of Scripture Play a Role

Verses of Scripture are cited for various purposes in most, though by no means all, of the units of discourse. Taking a rapid probe of Sanhedrin 2:1-2, we find, among the thirteen complete units of discourse, that eight contain verses of Scripture, and five do not. But among the eight, only three pursue the interests of Scripture in a sustained way, and in the other five the appearance of a verse of Scripture makes no profound mark on discourse.

2. Redaction

In the probe before us only a few units of discourse draw upon a sequence of verses as a redactional framework, at Sanhedrin 2:1-2 these being XI-XIII.

3. Citation of a Verse of Scripture: Probative or Propositional

The distinction just now made on redactional grounds serves once more. Where a verse of Scripture appears as part of a discussion autonomous of Scripture, there it is a proof-text or a pretext. Where the redactional framework derives from a sequence of verses of a scriptural topic or proposition, there the citation is for propositional purposes. In the sample before us B. Sanhedrin 2:1-2 XI-XIII fall into the latter category.

4. The Propositions of Scripture

What has been said just now answers this question too.

XI. CLASSIFICATION OF DOCUMENTS OF THE SAMPLE: TAXONOMIC CONNECTION

Our nine texts viewed by the differentiating criterion of the role and use of Scripture fall into three categories. When we ask whether Scripture provides the redactional framework, on the one side, and a source of proof-texts or propositions, on the other, on the surface the Mishnah, Tosefta, Yerushalmi, and Bavli differ from Sifra, Sifré to Numbers, and the two Rabbah-compilations. Avot stands all by itself, in its nearly total disinterest in Scripture not only for propositions but even for proof-texts.

Let us begin by classifying our texts in the conventional way, then turning to the taxonomy supplied by scriptural relationships. On first glance, our sample of canonical texts falls into three categories:

I	II	III
Law	**Lore**	**Sagacity**
Mishnah	Sifra	Avot
Tosefta	Sifré to Numbers	
Yerushalmi	Genesis Rabbah	
Bavli	Leviticus Rabbah	

Now to deal with the fresh classification devised by me. We want to know whether or not the received taxonomy stands up. The answer is that it does not.

The authorship of the Mishnah tractates Berakhot and Sanhedrin clearly follows its own program in its own language and by its own plan. In Berakhot the authorship displays no concern whatsoever for Scripture, even as a source of proof-texts. In Sanhedrin it has no sustained interest in Scripture and its propositions, and when measured against the Tosefta's plan of proof-texts, sparingly inserts proof-texts. The Mishnah's authorship in Sanhedrin rarely resorts to Scripture for a redactional structure or for a sustained set of propositions. These two traits of the Mishnah emerge with great force through the comparison to the Tosefta. The Mishnah stands by itself by the criterion of resort to Scripture. But by that same criterion I do not see important differences between the Tosefta, on the one side, and the two Talmuds, on the other. The latter indeed appear undifferentiable. Both employ full corps of proof-texts, but neither resorts to Scripture for sustained and important redactional structures or propositional compositions.

This brings us to the four compositions I classify as "lore." By that I mean simply that the compositions address themes or topics not of a normative order but of a speculative character. By the criterion at hand we have to divide, as to lore, between Sifra and Sifré to Numbers on the one side, and the two Rabbah-compilations, on the other. Once viewed by simple and standard criteria, the former and latter pairs really exhibit few taxonomic traits in common. The former set work their way through Scripture's propositions and rely upon Scripture's order of verses, which they follow more or less routinely. The latter do not comment on Scripture's verses one by one, but rather adduce as their topical program the themes of a passage of Scripture (Genesis Rabbah) or themes provoked by, but not necessarily explicit in, a passage of Scripture (Leviticus Rabbah).

The upshot is that our original division proves inadequately differentiated, and we have to make the further division as follows:

I	II	III	IV	V
Mishnah	Tosefta	Sifra	Genesis Rabbah	Avot
	Yerushalmi	Sifré to Numbers	Leviticus Rabbah	
	Bavli			

In point of fact we shall have ample reason to differentiate from other documents the items in the column of legal texts – but not on the basis of the criterion of Scripture. By that criterion we distinguish the Mishnah from the other three documents. But we have already found ample reason, on the foundations of the differentiating criterion provided by Scripture, not only to group the nine documents into five categories, but to find substantial differences even within those categories. Genesis Rabbah and Leviticus Rabbah in particular exhibit important points of difference, and a closer examination of Tosefta, Yerushalmi, and Bavli would show us that Scripture serves Bavli more amply and in more ways than it does Yerushalmi, all the more so Tosefta. But the point, for our purposes, hardly demands sustained attention. I have in any case spelled it out in my *Judaism. The Classic Statement. The Evidence of the Bavli* (Chicago, 1986: University of Chicago Press), where I have demonstrated that the Yerushalmi's authorship rarely resorts to Scripture, rather than the Mishnah, for a redactional framework to impart cogency to a sustained discourse. The Bavli's authorship commonly does so. The proportion, in my sample, was close to half. That is to say, in the Bavli approximately 40% of all sustained sequences of units of discourse were organized around sequences of verses of Scripture, as against 60% around sequences of paragraphs of the Mishnah or the Tosefta. In the Yerushalmi the proportion of Scriptural-structured sequences of units of discourse was negligible, in my sample well under 10%.

When we want to find out the taxonomic categories dictated by the differentiating criterion of the role of Scripture, what we learn about connection in particular is simple, but decisive. We cannot establish a relationship among the nine documents by the criterion of a taxonomy of their relationships to Scripture. The pattern is too diverse to yield taxonomic connection. On the contrary, by the present criterion of differentiation, our nine documents seem to fall into nine distinct categories. The claim that the documents of the Judaic canon form a continuously-connected corpus of writings does not stand. May we say that the entire literature forms a taxonomic collectivity in the relationship to Scripture? No, the opposite is the case. Our sample breaks down into taxonomic units. So by the criterion at hand, the "interlocking and reinterlocking units" do not respond to a single key, and the use of Scripture does not open all locks all the time and equally well. Let me state the result with appropriate emphasis: *The nine documents in a rather general way do form connections to Scripture, but although all relate to Scripture, on that basis – through Scripture, its uses and functions – they do not form relationships between one another, let alone uniformly among themselves all together.*

Chapter Seven

Logic and Rhetoric

I. PROLOGUE

Our search for the taxonomic masterkey to unlock our "interlocking and reinterlocking" units brings us to the inner logic of discourse that, one might anticipate, infuses the whole. For after all readers reviewing our two protracted appendices will discern a certain sameness of discourse, a certain pervasive logic and sense that transcends the parts but infuses them all. So that shared logic that permits mutual comprehension, therefore communication, that forms of words, sentences, and, of sentences, cogent paragraphs of meaning – that is what should validate the claim of "interlocking and reinterlocking" parts, the allegation that, after all, we have to read everything in light of everything everywhere and all at once.

In fact, I should argue that basic claim of a shared and pervasive logic of cogent discourse finds considerable support. In point of fact, all intelligible discourse in the canon of Judaism attains cogency and intelligibility through the formation of lists. The logic of the canon of Judaism in its formative age is the, by then age-old, logic of *Listenwissenschaft*. That is so of the two logically monumental compositions before us, the Mishnah and Leviticus Rabbah.[1] It is, by definition, true of the three continuators of the Mishnah, Tosefta, Yerushalmi, and Bavli. I have not demonstrated that that is the case also for the other compilations of exegeses of Scripture, e.g., Genesis Rabbah, Sifra, Sifré to Numbers. The forebearing reader will have to stipulate that fact, which awaits sustained inquiry. For the present argument it will not impede us.

Lists put together like-data and yield a rule that covers data not on the lists themselves – hence a list constitutes a syntactic statement of logic. The list moreover produces a rule for unlike data, contrary to those collected on the list, and that rule will be the opposite of the one that applies. So the list forms a powerful instrument of science and communication of the results of science. The list itself imposes its category on otherwise chaotic data – both on one type of data and upon the opposite, hence on everything. Hence the making of lists guides us to the logic (and, by the way, the rhetoric, a byproduct of logic) of a document. Stated more broadly, category-formation forms the key to logical

---

[1]That is the argument of my *Judaism and Scripture. The Evidence of Leviticus Rabbah* (Chicago, 1986: University of Chicago Press).

discourse, that is, to the principles of intelligible interchange of thought. Data derive significance – hence, cogency – from those processes of selection and arrangement that produce out of data intelligible statements. Before proceeding, let me expand on this point, which forms the central issue of the matter of intelligible discourse attained through the logic by which sentences form paragraphs, or, in broader terms, data are composed into meaningful propositions.

Categories dictate the intellectual processes of learning and so determine understanding: what we choose to learn, how we proceed to explain and make sense of it. Our category – in terms of this chapter, our list – tells us what we want to know, and, once we have selected our data for that list, we find out also what we wish to know about it. But the category we select will guide us to data appropriate to that category. Categories take form in the context not of the unconstrained mind but of the social intellect: the imagination formed, made plausible, by society, culture, politics – that is to say, context and circumstance. What we want to know society tells us we should find out. How we shall find out what we want to know culture explains. And beyond the two lies the social compact that imparts sense and acceptance to the facts we think we know and to the categories that legislate the rules of comprehension and collective understanding. These are common sense and self-evidence. They in the end form the criteria for description. Description lends order and meaning to discrete pieces and bits of information, so forming the beginning of comprehension, of knowledge. So what we want to know, that is, the categories of knowledge, and how we find it out, namely, through selecting appropriate data and analyzing them, come to us as the gifts and the givens of our social world. Our context, provides the technology of finding things out, identifying sources we want to study and determining how to read them, also specifying sources we ignore and explaining why they contain only gibberish. All these, when brought to the surface and examined, testify to the formation of the categories of our minds, the structure and construction of all knowledge. So category-formation forms the critical component of consciousness and defines the structure of understanding.

How a document's authorship joins sentences into paragraphs of cogent thought, propositions bearing meaning beyond the specific, atomic fact-statement of a single sentence, proves diverse. But all cogent discourse in all the documents of our sample (and, I speculate, of the canon represented by the sample) rests on list-making, and the cogency of all cogent documents – those made up of statements of meaning that transcend individual sentences and so constitute syllogisms of various kinds – derives from the single principle of list-making, which is classification and speciation. But there are diverse types of lists, and the cogency of each may be distinguished from that of another. Rhetorical preferences conform to the larger task of logical cogency, so these require analysis only in the present context. Let me review the principal categories outlined earlier.

1. The Syllogistic List: A document may make its point by composing lists of examples that reveal, in traits in common, proof of a given proposition. Through the underlying principle contained in the several examples a list may generate an encompassing rule. That is the simplest and most obvious principle of *Listenwissenschaft*.

2. The Commentary: A document may make its point not through autonomous discourse, but through commenting on points made by a base-document, hence a document may comprise a commentary to a text supplied by another document. A commentary falls into a different classification from an independent propositional exercise in syllogistic discourse such as a list. But commentaries ordinarily serve to make points, and that is accomplished by a recurrent pattern of inquiry: into this, not that. The sustained message therefore emerges in the character of the commentary, specifically, its repeated points of emphasis, its recurrent questions, addressed to diverse materials in such a way as to frame and impose a cogent viewpoint on the whole. We have already noticed how some commentaries are so formed as to establish sustained and well-argued propositions.

3. The Tradental List: A document may take form through listing authorities, cited in a given order, e.g., Rabbi X said Rabbi Y said. What is attributed to those authorities will not contribute to the cogency of the document. The list of names supplies whatever structure the unit of discourse possesses. No principle of cogency other than such names imparts to the list of names a general intelligibility. Yet that does not mean the text lacks a message. The names will bear the main message, and, it may also be the case, the substance of what is expressed, though not cogent, may harp on a single value or theme in such a way as to make a coherent statement.

We should not miss the simple point that all three logical-rhetorical choices comprise a single principle, which is list-making, for the tradental list, self-evidently, is simply another type of list. The commentary rests on a list composed of entries of yet a third type: a fixed external document is broken up into subunits, then these units are formed into a list that gains cogency from the fact that they originate in that single external document. Whatever is joined within the commentary in fact forms a coherent list of entries, with the principle of list-making deriving from the cogency of the original, external document.

II. THE MISHNAH

1. The Syllogistic List

The Mishnah rests on the ancient logic of *Listenwissenschaft*, that is, classification of data by shared traits, highlighting of the larger meaning of those shared traits. Lists in the Mishnah ordinarily exhibit a common syntactic structure, which shifts when a new proposition or syllogism comes to the fore. The rhetoric therefore requires resort to recurrent syntactic patterns, which underline and express the commonalities among the discrete entries into the list, and, in form, point our gaze at the substantive uniformities of deep proposition contained and conveyed at the surface by discrete facts: the rule of A is X, the rule of B is Y, the rule of C is Z. What A, B, C have in common then stands behind the rules, X, Y, and Z, and the (ordinarily unstated) encompassing principle that explains X, Y, Z will then constitute the (rarely spelled out) syllogism at hand. Very often these lists of discrete facts joined in form in a common rhetorical structure are made up of entries of three or five examples, or multiples of those numbers, presumably because of the mnemonic ease which those multiples contribute. That, sum and substance, constitutes the logic of intelligible discourse by which the Mishnah's authorship makes the statements they wish to make.

Berakhkot

I could not offer a finer, more simple and self-evident example of *Listenwissenschaft* than this sample. But it would take considerable exposition, not pertinent here, to spell out the propositions both proved and also powerfully presented by our list.[2] The premise of our chapter is the list: *the differences between...*, and the list's rhetorical character underlines its substantive trait of intelligible discourse. The heavily-mnemonic rhetoric, with its shift in the order of words meant to convey the deeper proposition, e.g., *day vs. wine* or *wine vs. day*, with its resort even to shifts in a single letter to make the point, e.g., HZR vs. ZKR, testifies to the tight framing of the whole. The larger issue – principles of uncleanness and other rules applying to the Sabbath meal – permits the exposition of differences of an abstract character. But these are not made explicit, so the effect of *Listenwissenschaft* in the present character is to require a further document, which will spell out the reasoning behind the position. That, of course, describes the Tosefta's service to the Mishnah-chapter. And Tosefta's materials themselves require substantial reshaping into abstract generalizations. For without exposition of the reasoning imputed by Tosefta's authorship to the Mishnah's Houses' propositions, we do not gain that level of abstraction that permits the original list to make its point. So the Yerushalmi and the Bavli take up the larger task of exposition of a logic implicit (so it is assumed) in the original list. It would be difficult to point to a better example of dialectical unfolding of propositions from list of instances to general principles of a wholly abstract character. When, therefore, we designate as an example of *Listenwissenschaft* the Mishnah-chapter before us in M. Berakhot Chapter Eight, we open more questions concerning logical cogency of public discourse than we close.

Sanhedrin

The application of *Listenwissenschaft* in our brief sample makes its appearance time and again. Wherever we see a recurrent syntactic construction,

---

[2] I do so in my *Invitation to the Talmud*, second edition (San Francisco, 1985: Harper & Row).

our attention is drawn to the commonalities of the entries that resort to that uniform rhetoric. M. 2:1, for example, has the X does and Y do it to him, M. 2:1A, B, C. The pattern then shifts into miscellaneous formations, M. 2:1D, others do, but he does not, because, with a sequence of other miscellanies. So we start the sustained pericope with a rigorously applied List-form, three entries, and, of course, the point is that in some ways the king or the high priest (as will be the joint theme of M. 2:1-2) are subject to the same rules as others, in some not. M. 2:2 starts with the same rhetoric, now quintupled: M. 2:2A, the king does not and does not, B, does not and do not, C, does not and do not, D, does not and do not, G, do not. M. 2:3 seems to me rhetorically miscellaneous, and, as a matter of fact, it does not encompass a formal list. But M. 2:3 presents lists of rules on what happens when a king suffers a death in his family, M. 2:3A, F. And that list carries forward the theme of M. 2:2, so should be regarded as a modest complement joined by theme, not by form. M. 2:4A, B give simple rules, the king does...may open a road, the people plunder and lay before him and he....These statements of subject, active verb and complement again exhibit no clear pattern except that: subject, verb, complement. But contrasted to what sets fore and aft – M. 2:3, [if the king] suffers a death, he does not...And when they provide him, all the people do A while he does B, then M. 2:4E-N, citation of a verse plus a comment – M. 2:4A-D's declarative sentences stand out as patterned as much as the more striking rhetorical devices of M. 2:1-2. The syllogism at hand of course is so obvious as scarcely to require specification: the king and the high priest are subject to rules that in some ways are not the same as those to which every one else is subject. Or to put the syllogism most simply: the king and high priest form a distinct category, and the king is in a category different from that of the high priest, thus, three syllogisms of ineffable self-evidence. And that expresses the power of the syllogistic list: to state its proposition is to say the obvious. But since no one has said the obvious, the authorship has enjoyed complete success in its rhetoric and logic: it has through specific and very concrete, repeated examples established a category and also made explicit the classificatory rules that apply to that category, the apex of *Listenwissenschaft*.

Any number of other chapters of the Mishnah will upon analysis yield identical results. While the Mishnah's framers made use, also, of two other principles of logical discourse, namely, the tradental (e.g., M. Kelim Chapter Twenty-four, nearly the whole of Mishnah-tractate Eduyyot) and the commentary (e.g., M. Sotah Chapters Seven through Nine), these constitute exceptions of no consequence.

2. The Commentary

Rare in the Mishnah, but represented in our brief sample in Sanhedrin, is the rhetoric that consists in the citation of a base-passage, one exclusive of the composition at hand, in our case, a verse of Scripture, followed by a comment on that verse of Scripture. The rhetoric is simple: cited passage + simple declarative sentence of the meaning of message of that passage. The cogency of the passage as a whole derives not from a proposition, such as is conveyed by the artfully organized list, but from the base-passage and only from there. When we look at M. 2:4E-N, we see the result, sytematic citation of clauses of the base-passage, Deut. 17:16-17, followed by what seem to me episodic observations, with six entries – that is, cited clauses of the base passage – in all, M. 2:4E, J, L, N, and M. 2:5C. The citations are not followed by uniform syntax. Do they create a message that transcends the entries, a sum that exceeds the parts? Indeed they do, and it is expressed at M. 2:5: "reverence for him will be upon you." The king is subject to rules, and the effect of these rules is to set the king into a classification subject to its own rules. The king is *sui generis*. And that is precisely the message of the list of M. 2:1-4D.

3. The Tradental List

The Mishnah does resort to the tradental list, e.g., M. Kelim Chapter Twenty-Four, a marvelous example, not to mention the whole of tractate Eduyyot, but not in our selection of Berakhot and Sanhedrin. In such a list, items are joined not by topic, let alone proposition, and also not by a common rhetoric, but only by a formally-dictated selection of names, e.g., Rabbi X, Rabbi Y, Rabbi Z and only those names, or, still more commonly, only Rabbi X, followed by a topically-diverse selection of Rabbi X's rulings, none of them expressive of a common proposition or syllogism. I see no such pattern in our selection. In M. Ber. 8:1-5, dealt with below, by contrast, we do have a tradental composition, in which a variety of themes are joined by a rigidly narrow selection of authorities.

III. TRACTATE AVOT

1. The Syllogistic List

Tractate Avot contains no syllogistic compositions of any kind, and our sample conveys the character of the document as a whole. In my commentary to Avot,[3] I found it exceedingly difficult to identify among sequences of sayings a propositional list of any kind. The sayings seemed to me discrete, joined only by the convention (if it was a convention) constituted by a tradental list.

2. The Commentary

While tractate Avot does present examples of citation of a verse followed by a comment, these do not cohere into a coherent composition, i.e., of two or more such examples. Consequently, this mode of logical discourse does not make an appearance.

---

[3]*Torah from Our Sages. Pirke Avot* (Chappaqua, 1984: Rossel).

3. The Tradental List

Tractate Avot, in the present sample, resorts only to the tradental list as a means of making its points. The result is that the tradental list bears the syllogism of the document as we have it before us. The list of names of M. 1:1-15 leads from the Mishnah's authorities backward to Sinai, and the point of the sample is that the authority of the Mishnah's principal figures derives from Moses at Sinai. Chapter Two's tradental list – Yohanan and his disciples – makes its own point, on the superiority and priority of Eleazar b. Arakh. It bears a powerful rhetoric as well, in maintaining that in one virtue, many virtues are subsumed. Not surprisingly, the tradental point matches the substantive one: just as many virtues are subsumed in one, so many disciples' merits come to expression in one disciple. I would not propose that all of the materials of tractate Avot exhibit the same remarkable cogency of logic and rhetoric. But so far as the discrete components – the sentences – of tractate Avot coalesce into a single cogent statement, that is to say, exhibit a logic of discourse joined to an appropriate rhetoric of persuasion, all of them conform to the single logic of the tradental list.

IV. THE TOSEFTA

1. The Syllogistic List

In the main, the Tosefta's framers in tractate Sanhedrin present materials meant to complement or supplement the Mishnah. Therefore, in the nature of things, they follow the principles of logical discourse and rhetorical preference exhibited in the Mishnah. The Tosefta relates to the Mishnah in three ways. First, some of its compositions cite and amplify corresponding passages of the Mishnah. Second, other passages depend for full meaning on the corresponding passage of the Mishnah, but do not cite and gloss the Mishnah verbatim. Third, a few passages stand in complete isolation from the Mishnah. These may exhibit the traits of rigid formalization of rhetoric and careful exposition of logic through the composition of lists that we observe in the Mishnah itself. Materials of this third type on a logical and rhetorical basis cannot be readily distinguished from those in the Mishnah. The first type of materials in the Tosefta belongs in the second of our three divisions of rhetoric and logic. The second and third may fit into the present rubric.

The syllogistic lists overall do not conform so rigidly to singular patterns. In the sample before us, I see as appropriate items for classification as syllogistic lists T. 4:1, T. 4:2. These items follow the plan and program of the Mishnah. T. 4:3 in concrete syllogism is independent of the Mishnah, but in substance simply restates the Mishnah's list's main point: the king is in a class by himself. What this item introduces to complement the Mishnah is the statement that the patriarch falls into the classification of the king, an issue not raised by the Mishnah. T. 4:4 is an example of a set of sentences that cohere but do not form a clearly identifiable list. The proof-texts before us, T. 4:4D, E-F, do not seem to me to change the picture.

2. The Commentary

The Tosefta presents us with two varieties of logical discourse effected through commentary, first, citation of the Mishnah, e.g., T. 4:2G-J, second, citation of Scripture, e.g., T. 4:5-8. TR. 4:5 typifies the commentary-form in Tosefta as it pertains to Scripture: statement of proposition, followed by citation of verse, which then serves as a proof-text.

3. The Tradental List

I see no examples of this logical-rhetorical possibility. One might make a case for viewing T. Berakhot 5:25ff. as tradental in formation, but it seems to me that the Mishnah-chapter that forms the substrate of the Tosefta passage rests on propositional, not solely tradental, foundations.

If we now ask which of the three logical-rhetorical choices predominates in the Tosefta Sanhedrin sample before us, we may point to the commentary as primary, the syllogistic list as subordinated. In the passage before us, cogent discourse emerges through commentary on an external text at T. 4:1, 2 (citation of Mishnah plus gloss or amplification), T. 4:5-11, citation of Scripture or of Mishnah with gloss or amplification or use of the base-text as a proof-text.

V. THE YERUSHALMI

The Yerushalmi and the Bavli take the form of a commentary to the Mishnah. That form imparts to both Talmuds that overall large scale cogency that both documents exhibit. When we turn to the units of discourse of which the documents are made up, however, the matter proves less one-sided. We have therefore to classify the units of discourse of the two Talmuds as to the logical-rhetorical characteristics predominant and characteristic. On that basis we shall be able to determine the definitive traits of the documents as a whole, hence determine their connections viewed taxonomically.

1. The Syllogistic List

I see in our sample no clearcut instances in which the logic of discourse rests entirely on the spelling out, through examples, of a syllogism, or of any other sort of syllogistic discourse.

2. The Commentary

Virtually the whole of our sample of the Yerushalmi consists of commentary to texts external to the Yerushalmi, mainly the Mishnah, secondarily, Scripture. For example all of the Yerushalmi to M. 2:1, that is, units I, IV-VII, serves as an explicit citation and commentary of the Mishnah, and units II, III pursue the topics of the Mishnah and amplify them in a complementary way. As I classify the entries, all of Y. 2:2, 3, 4, 5, and most of 6 are made up solely of citations and glosses, of one sort or another, of the Mishnah or of Scripture.

3. The Tradental List

Our sample presents no examples of this mode of logical-rhetorical cogency.

The Yerushalmi turns out to find logical cogency in appealing to a text outside of itself, ordinarily the Mishnah, secondarily, Scripture. This result recapitulates that of my sustained study, *The Talmud of the Land of Israel* (Chicago, 1984: University of Chicago Press) 35. *Introduction. Taxonomy.*

VI. SIFRA

1. The Syllogistic List

No examples of this mode of establishing the logical cogency of discourse occur in our sample (or in Sifra in general).

2. The Commentary

All examples in our sample are composed of this simple rhetorical form: citation of a verse, then proposition attached to that citation.

3. The Tradental List

Sifra contains no tradental lists.

One important polemic of the document is that exegesis, not reason alone, serves to establish reliable principles. For that purpose the commentary serves exceptionally well. Not all units of discourse before us, or in Sifra as a whole, make that polemical point – but all of them implicitly express it. A further exercise in Sifra is to cite a passage of the Mishnah in the setting of exegesis, indicating that the Mishnah's rule derives from Scripture.

VII. SIFRE TO NUMBERS

1. The Syllogistic List

The syllogistic list in its familiar, Mishnaic version does not occur in our sample or in the document as a whole. But the document contains numerous syllogistic compositions, in which a basic general rule is demonstrated through a list of probative examples. Here the difference from the Mishnah is clear. The examples will be not cases drawn from the rules governing everyday life but rather verses of Scripture that provide a different set of facts. But the facts are equally factual, so to speak, at Sifré to Numbers I:III.1, where we have two syllogisms, Judah b. Beterah's "The effect of a commandment serves...," and Simeon b. Yohai, "the purpose is only to...." In both cases the syllogism is critical, the list of evidence then central to sustained, cogent discourse. Neither of these cases can be called a commentary in any sense. So, unlike the Sifra's materials, a portion of those in the Sifré to Numbers falls into the category of logical discourse through syllogistic *Listenwissenschaft* such as we find in the Mishnah. In this respect Sifré to Numbers combines traits logical and rhetorical cogency of the Mishnah with those of commentary on Scripture in a way in which the Yerushalmi sample before us does not.

2. The Commentary

The mode of logical cogency derives from the citation of a base verse, followed by an exegesis of the themes or issues of that verse. But the exegesis itself is no more random than it is in Sifra. A number of concrete propositions recur, some having to do with overall principles of exegesis of Scripture for the purpose of clarifying the law, some to prove that logic by itself may not (Aqiba) or may (Ishmael) serve for finding out the correct rule.

3. The Tradental List

There are no tradental lists in Sifré to Numbers.

VIII. GENESIS RABBAH

1. The Syllogistic List

Genesis Rabbah's compositors worked out propositional arguments, making their points by adducing illustrations and facts drawn from a variety of scriptural bases. Accordingly, the basic picture of Sifré to Numbers repeats itself, but on an incomparably broader scale. We see this fact at I:I, which wishes to make the case for the syllogism that God looked into the Torah for instructions on how to create the world, so that the Torah contains the design of creation. This proposition is argued at I:I.1-2 on a philological basis, then is illustrated by I:V, IV. A further proposition has to do with the polemic against those who say there is more than one god; then I:II, God alone is god, and the nations have nothing, I:III, God alone can have made things as they are, and so on and so forth. In all these systematic statements, therefore, the point the framers wish to make clearly and articulately emerges. The materials that are assembled to make the various points differ radically from those assembled in the Mishnah's lists. Specifically, sages in Genesis Rabbah drew together finished units of discourse, themselves ordinarily of a syllogistic character, and then assembled these completed units into lists to demonstrate through example a syllogism. A further difference from the Mishnah is that the syllogism always is made explicit, ordinarily at the end of the composition. Occasionally, as at I:IV, the syllogism will be announced at the outset: Six things came before creation, and then the assemblage of proofs – facts supplied by Scripture – follows in rather tight and disciplined rhetorical style.

2. The Commentary

The one thing our sample of Genesis Rabbah does *not* present is a commentary pure and simple. That is, the structure and organization of our sample rests upon syllogistic propositions. The form – citation of verses in the sequence in which they occur in Scripture – does not change the picture. The only thing that follows a form we would call "commentary" consists in the citation of the verses of Genesis, one by one. And yet even that point demands qualification, since we do not have a systematic phrase by phrase and verse by verse commentary at all. The base-text – that is, the book of Genesis – does not dictate in an orderly way the exposition of the topics. The topics come first, the base-verse serves only as a redactional pretext. So Genesis Rabbah in no way falls into the category of a commentary.

3. The Tradental List

Genesis Rabbah contains no materials organized around a single name or a set of recurrent names.

IX. LEVITICUS RABBAH

1. The Syllogistic List

Everything we noted with regard to Genesis Rabbah applies here as well. But Leviticus Rabbah follows an incomparably more disciplined and powerful rhetorical plan. It contains three types of materials. First, it presents a base-verse, drawn from Leviticus, contrasted with an intersecting verse. Then it systematically spells out the latter, ignoring the former. A variety of themes will pass in review. At the end, however, a theme will emerge which draws us back to the base-verse and says, in respect to that base-verse, what the framers wish to say: the proposition important to the theme at hand. The effect of this sustained discourse on something that does not matter, ending with the point that does make a difference, is to broaden the range of thematic review and turn the syllogism into a statement of how, overall in a variety of circumstances of contexts, things must be worked out. The second variety of materials will comment on verses in Leviticus itself. But this type also serves the interests of the broader syllogism. So the list as worked out in Leviticus Rabbah is made up of diverse materials, some of them clearly autonomous and selected after the fact, some of them made up to serve the interests of the document at hand. In our example, V:I-III lead to the syllogism: God exacts the same penalty from an individual and from a community. I:IV is thematically continuous with the foregoing. I:VII (+ I:VIII) presents its own syllogism, beautifully constructed, that Israel is essentially different from the nations of the world. While falling into the same classifications, Israel in fact is *sui generis*.

2. The Commentary

Leviticus Rabbah in no way constitutes a commentary to the book of Leviticus. Even the pretense that the overall structure serves as a commentary to a biblical text plays no redactional role whatsoever. For the framers choose phrases or a whole verse only at random and not systematically. Only the general order of the book, from beginning to end, is followed. But within the *parashiyyot* of Leviticus Rabbah as much as of Genesis Rabbah, the theme takes over. Leviticus Rabbah in this respect takes a still more rigorous position on the centrality of syllogistic argument. Each *parashah* takes up a theme and makes its point about that theme, and no *parashah* introduces materials essentially irrelevant to the theme and the prevailing syllogism. The syllogism governs the *parashah* in ways in which in Genesis Rabbah it does not; that is to say, in Genesis Rabbah we find a variety of syllogisms within a given *parashah*, while in Leviticus Rabbah a single theme and a single syllogism, proved through examples strung out as lists, predominate. Nonetheless, the *parashah* does contain exegetical material, e.g., I:V.

3. The Tradental List

There is no tradental dimension whatsoever.

X. THE BAVLI

1. The Syllogistic List

I find a syllogism followed by a list of scriptural proofs at B. Sanhedrin 2:5 III-VIII, which systematically state and work out a series of propositions independent of the Mishnah and in no way constituting commentary to Scripture. These propositions, moreover, cohere among themselves: III, Whoever divorces his first wife – even the altar weeps tears on that account; IV, on the death of a wife; V, on making matches; VI, on not being able to replace one's first wife; VII, first wife; VIII, a woman makes a covenant only with the man who deflowers her. The entire composite is thematically cogent, and, furthermore, makes a series of syllogistic points of some interest. The whole was formed on its own and then inserted whole after 2:5II: "They permitted David to be alone with the woman but did not permit him to divorce one of his other wives." That triggers the insertion of III.A, Whoever divorces his first wife, which brings in its wake the large and cogent discourse on the first wife. What makes this composition especially interesting is that, in our sample, it is the only one that does not constitute a commentary on either the Mishnah's rule or a passage of Scripture (pertinent to the Mishnah's rule or theme).

2. The Commentary

Like the Yerushalmi, the Bavli overall takes shape as a commentary to the Mishnah, read paragraph by paragraph, then clause by clause, in a systematic and orderly way. I see all of the units of discourse serving 2:1-2, 3, 4A-D, C-I, J-N, and most of those serving 23:5 – I, II, and IX-XI – as nothing more than commentaries to cited passages, or amplifications of those commentaries.

3. The Tradental List

While in the Bavli we may isolate passages that find cogency in the name of a given tradent, in our sample there is none.

XI. CLASSIFICATION OF DOCUMENTS OF THE SAMPLE: TAXONOMIC CONNECTION

Let us now classify the connections among our documents as the taxonomic traits of rhetoric and logic reveal them. We distinguish documents by the logic that forms their units of discourse into cogent statements, as explained in the prologue.

Syllogistic Lists	Commentaries	Tradental Lists
Mishnah	Sifra	Avot
Genesis Rabbah	Sifré to Numbers	
Leviticus Rabbah	Yerushalmi	
	Tosefta	
	Bavli	

These results yield interesting taxonomic connections between documents, but not among them all. We can show profound logical affinities between otherwise quite different documents, the Mishnah and Leviticus Rabbah, Tosefta and Bavli. We see once more the taxonomic oddity of Avot, not only in relationship to the Mishnah, but in comparison with everything else in the literature. Other points of notice present themselves. But the pursuit of a taxonomic order and regularity encompassing the entire canon – "the one whole Torah of Moses our rabbi" – finds no treasure here. Logic of cogent discourse provides no master key to unlock the doors of every document.

Moreover, more disheartening still, there is no correlation between what is before us and the results of the prior taxonomies. By the criterion of logic we see connections among documents that by other taxonomic criteria are not connected at all. The upshot is to call into question the theory that the documents of the canon exhibit uniform traits to justify a theory of connection between or among the writings as a whole. In terms of principles of logical discourse and intelligibility, the nine documents connect in one way, in terms of relationship to Scripture, in another. As we shall now see, by the criterion of topic, yet a third pattern emerges.

Chapter Eight

Topic and Proposition

I. CRITERIA OF TAXONOMIC DISTINCTION

Documents take form in three dimensions, rhetoric, logic and topic. Classifying topical traits of a document involves recourse to a variety of extrinsic distinctions of a purely formal character. One is between law and norms of behavior as against lore and norms of belief, a distinction to which we have already resorted. Another is between Scripture and the Mishnah. Let us begin with these simple points of differentiation and comparison.

Law, norms of behavior	Lore, norms of belief
Mishnah	Avot
Tosefta	Genesis Rabbah
Sifra	Leviticus Rabbah
Sifré to Numbers	(Yerushalmi)
Yerushalmi	(Bavli)
Bavli	

The point of distinction does not seem to me to make much of a difference. We cannot classify the two Talmuds either as principally devoted to law or as mainly focused upon lore; certainly the Bavli exhibits nearly equal interest in each. Genesis Rabbah, for its part, lays forth a theology of history, with important dimensions affecting behavior, and Leviticus Rabbah provides an equivalent topical program, with further interest in ethical rules governing not only belief but also behavior. So the distinction between behavior and belief bears no promise for criteria of differentiation by topic. Let us proceed to another set of criteria.

II. SCRIPTURE AND ITS TOPICAL PROGRAM

Here we compare two or more documents that focus on Scripture and ask whether the authorships have chosen the same themes or different ones. By "theme" I mean not so much the concrete narrative of Scripture at a given passage as a broader frame of interest. For example, while the Mishnah does not introduce themes of history and its interpretation, Scripture does, so two or more documents may fall into the same classification, in regard to Scripture and its topical program, if they take up issues of the meaning of history. More to the point, both Sifra and Leviticus Rabbah treat the book of Leviticus, so they share a common text. Yet it would be difficult to imagine two more different compositions. The topical plan of the one bears nothing in common with the topical plan of the other – to which, in fact, the book of Leviticus serves at best as an ancillary matter: pretext, not even proof-text. So if we take up the differentiation of those compilations that focus on Scripture, we realize that a labor of comparison and contrast is at hand.

Let us take up one possible point of differentiation. Our completed comparisons have drawn our attention to one topical-programmatic classification, the recurrent polemic, concerning the priority of exegesis over reason, and to yet another mode of argument, how the facts of history prove syllogisms concerning the social laws that govern Israel. The result follows of a comparison:

	Social Laws Proved by
Exegesis over Reason	Facts of Scripture
Sifra	Genesis Rabbah
Sifré to Numbers	Leviticus Rabbah

Now we see how a broad-based topical (propositional) distinction does serve – but only in a rather general way. We see that documents may relate to one another. But we also see that they do not establish connections encompassing a variety of scripturally-focused writings. So, in all, we may distinguish one compilation of exegeses from another by reference to the encompassing topical and propositional program of a document. But when we do so, we find ourselves comparing incomparables. Topical connections based on shared interest in Scripture do not emerge. As to shared propositions, our remarks on the programmatic relationships among Genesis Rabbah, Leviticus Rabbah, Sifra, and Sifré to Numbers, require no repetition. Each document makes the points its authorship wished to make, and these have no bearing on those another authorship, in a different document – even one based on the same book of Scripture – planned to establish.

III. THE MISHNAH AND ITS TOPICAL PROGRAM

On the other hand, the Mishnah presents a rather sizable and cogent set of topics, and here too two or more authorships may intersect in their choices of what, within that set, they choose to take up and amplify and explain. Our brief excursion into taxonomy of topics and propositions requires us to move beyond the limits of our sample. But the facts on which our taxonomy rests are self-evidently and broadly available. What we wish to know is how the documents subsequent to the Mishnah treat the topical program of the Mishnah.

Three classifications must serve, all in relationship to that program. In the first type of document, the Mishnah's program of topics is completely ignored. In the second, the entire plan of topics is systematically covered, beginning to end. In the third, the framers pick and choose the topics they wish to treat.

I	II	III
All Ignored	All Covered	Selected Passages Treated
Avot	Tosefta	Sifra
Genesis Rabbah		Sifré to Numbers
Leviticus Rabbah		Yerushalmi
		Bavli

The third division alone attracts our attention. We may forthwith explain why for the two scriptural-exegetical compilations, on Leviticus and Numbers, respectively, one thing – one passage of the Mishnah – is included and not another. The polemic of the framers accounts for the passages of the Mishnah that will be selected. But both documents deal with verses on the theme or program of which the Mishnah contains no law whatsoever, and this is blatant at Sifré to Numbers in particular. There are simply no Mishnah-tractates on the subjects important in a number of important, legal passages in the book of Numbers. So the intent of the authorship of both scriptural-exegetical compilations is systematically and sequentially to cover all of the verses of *their* chosen scriptural passages, and therefore, as a matter of fact, it is only incidental to that purpose that their compositions intersect with passages of the Mishnah. The criterion of topical connections yields relationships only between the two Talmuds.

Since the two Talmuds formulate their compositions as commentaries to the Mishnah, on the surface both of them fall into a single classification as to topic, namely, the Mishnah's larger topical program, connects the one to the other. But as a matter of fact, a topical criterion distinguishes the one from the other, and that is for a simple and well-known reason. Only partially intersecting at three of the Mishnah's six divisions – Appointed Times, Women, and Damages, one Talmud covers one set of Mishnah-topics, the other a different set. The Yerushalmi treats Agriculture but not Holy Things, the Bavli Holy Things but not Agriculture, and neither treats Purities. There are also tractates within the various divisions treated in one Talmud and not the other, for instance, all of Niddah is supplied with Talmud in the Bavli, but only a few chapters in the Yerushalmi, but that fact may testify only to the vagaries of survival of manuscript-evidence. For its part, as we see, Tosefta covers all six divisions.

So, in all, there is no formal topic that joins the eight post-Mishnaic writings. These remarks bring us to our sample in particular.

IV. TRACTATE AVOT

1. Scripture and its Topical Program

Verses of Scripture serve as proof-texts. There is no pretense at opening Scripture to discover appropriate topics for discussion.

2. The Mishnah and its Topical Program

Our sample of tractate Avot does not recognize a single topic that occurs in the Mishnah (apart from the present tractate).

V. THE TOSEFTA

1. Scripture and its Topical Program

Where the Tosefta takes up scriptural topics, they have reached the Tosefta via the Mishnah. Not only does the Tosefta cover everything in the Mishnah, it also addresses scriptural themes only when the Mishnah directly or implicit introduces those themes. So the dependence on the topical program of the Mishnah is complete.

2. The Mishnah and its Topical Program

The Tosefta's topical program derives directly from the Mishnah's, pure and simple.

VI. THE YERUSHALMI

1. Scripture and its Topical Program

What we have said about the Tosefta Sanhedrin applies here at Yerushalmi Sanhedrin as well. Where our sample of the Tosefta takes up a scriptural topic, it is because the Mishnah's discussion has called attention to that topic. One example is at 2:3VBff., once we refer the cited verse to Rispah, Abigail, and Bath Sheba, then the framers absorb a systematic discussion of the topics introduced by those figures. But the intrusion of that discussion can be explained only on grounds that the Mishnah has drawn attention to it. The same is to be said for 2:4III. I would be inclined to the same view of 2:5III-IV, although this sizable passage seems only loosely connected to the Mishnah and its amplification, 2:5I-II. Nonetheless, the reference of 2:5II to David invites the insertion of the enormous composition on David and his wars.

2. The Mishnah and its Topical Program

The topical program of the Mishnah predominates, beginning, middle and end.

VII. SIFRA

1. Scripture and its Topical Program

Sifra in our sample works its way through the Scripture's program and introduces passages of the Mishnah as Scripture invites our attention to them. So we deal with the opposite of the foregoing. Here the topical program of Scripture predominates.

2. The Mishnah and its Topical Program

The introduction of a passage of the Mishnah is on account of the interests of Scripture, which, at that point, intersect with the Mishnah's discussion. I see no pretense at an interest in the Mishnah on its own terms, that is, in the present case, a systematic discussion of Mishnah-tractate Negaim. The contrary is the case. What *in* Mishnah-tractate Negaim and its colleague Tosefta-tractate Negaim interests the framers of Sifra is only one thing: passages amenable to proof on the foundation of Scripture and that alone. The sizable component contributed by the Mishnah does not change the picture. Mishnah contributes proof-texts to the authorship of Sifra, much as Scripture provides proof-texts to the authorship of the Mishnah.

VIII. SIFRE TO NUMBERS

1. Scripture and its Topical Program

A verse of Scripture will be systematically expounded, clause by clause. So it is Scripture's program that defines the topical plan of our sample of Sifré to Numbers.

2. The Mishnah and its Topical Program

I see no systematic interest in the Mishnah's discourse on the topics of the scriptural passage that occur, also, in the Mishnah. The introduction of a Mishnah-passage will serve the polemic identified earlier: exegesis, not reason, provides reliable guidance to the law. The Mishnah plays a substantially smaller part in the topical program of our sample of Sifré to Numbers than it does in Sifra.

IX. GENESIS RABBAH

1. Scripture and its Topical Program

The topical program of Scripture predominates, beginning, middle, and end. But we should not miss the highly selective character of the choice of passages requiring exegesis. In fact the topics of Scripture are shaped to broader agenda, specifically, propositions concerning the character of the creator and creation. Only in a rather general sense can we say that the exegetical program of Genesis Rabbah corresponds to the topical program of Scripture. Once we move from topic to proposition, we see the appropriate classification.

2. The Mishnah and its Topical Program

The Mishnah plays no role whatsoever in our sample.

X. LEVITICUS RABBAH

1. Scripture and its Topical Program

Here I see little evidence that Scripture's topical program has predominated, even though, on the surface, what we have is a systematic play on various verses of Scripture. The fundamental proposition guides us to the topic of Scripture, and that proposition is distinct from Scripture. For instance, V:I-III wishes to say that God will eventually punish people, even though for a time they may think they are safe. So they are given tranquillity for a while but then they suffer their punishment. Scripture may prove that point, but Scripture – Lev. 4:3 in particular – has not contributed that proposition, and Scripture also has not defined that topic. So I am struck by the fresh and independent topical program of Leviticus Rabbah, not by the dependence upon Scripture of the framers of the topical program.

2. The Mishnah and its Topical Program

I see no interest whatsoever in the topical program of the Mishnah, with which Leviticus Rabbah never intersects. In a general way we may say that while the Mishnah is interested in giving the laws of everyday life, Leviticus Rabbah contributes the laws of history and society. In theological terms, the one speaks of sanctification, the other of salvation. In any event the Mishnah makes no impact whatsoever upon our sample.

XI. THE BAVLI

1. Scripture and its Topical Program

One point matters. Does the Bavli to tractate Sanhedrin treat topics of Scripture not introduced by the Mishnah, or does the Bavli fall into the same classification as the Yerushalmi in taking up only those scriptural topics that the Mishnah's theme and program suggest? 2:1-2XII, 2:4A-DIV, 2:4J-NV, and

2:5II, what is the story of Abishag, seem to me compositions that have taken shape wholly outside of the interests and themes of Scripture as mediated by the Mishnah (inclusive of the Tosefta). (2:5III-VIII work out their own thematic interests, resorting to verses of Scripture only as proof-texts, so we cannot list this section as a working out of the topical program of Scripture.) That is a considerable corpus of material and tells us that the framers of the Bavli included systematic treatments of scriptural themes even when the requirements of Mishnah-exegesis did not dictate it. So in this regard the Bavli does not fall into the same classification as the Yerushalmi.

2. The Mishnah and its Topical Program

The topical program of the Mishnah dictates to the framers of the Bavli the subjects they will treat.

XII. CLASSIFICATION OF DOCUMENTS OF THE SAMPLE: TAXONOMIC CONNECTION

The result of our detailed sorting out of the classifications of our samples of the eight documents (excluding the Mishnah) corresponds to our original hypothesis.

1. Scripture and its Topical Program

The topical program of Scripture proves less paramount than we should have expected. It plays no independent role in some of the documents, and only a limited one in others, predominating in only a few.

Topical Identity	Topical Selectivity	Topical Indifference
Sifra	Bavli	Avot
Sifré to Numbers	Genesis Rabbah	Tosefta
		Yerushalmi
		Leviticus Rabbah

The documents that form strong connections on one basis form equally strong ties on another. That we see, in particular, with the first of the three entries.

2. The Mishnah and its Topical Program

Let us turn at the end to the taxonomy afforded by diverse approaches to the Mishnah's topical program. The documents fall into the these possible classifications: wholly dominated by the Mishnah's themes, wholly dominated by the Scripture's topics, dominated by neither, dominated by both. Avot ignores the Mishnah's program, so too do Genesis Rabbah and Leviticus Rabbah. Tosefta adheres to the Mishnah's program. Sifra, Sifré to Numbers, the Yerushalmi, and the Bavli select passages to be treated. So we find taxonomic connections among the Tosefta, Yerushalmi, and Bavli. We find taxonomic ties, also, between Sifra and Sifré to Numbers, in their shared polemic concerning the Mishnah's appropriate foundations, and between Genesis Rabbah and Leviticus Rabbah in their shared indifference to the Mishnah. The eight documents then break into these divisions:

Topical Identity	Topical Selectivity	Topical Indifference
Tosefta	Sifra	Avot
Yerushalmi	Sifré to Numbers	Genesis Rabbah
Bavli		Leviticus Rabbah

Once more we see that Sifra and Sifré to Numbers form a tightly connected corpus, as do Genesis Rabbah and Leviticus Rabbah. The relationships among Tosefta, Yerushalmi, and Bavli are somewhat more complex. The upshot of our taxonomic distinction is to find in the topical criterion grounds for identifying connections among some of our documents, but discerning substantial points of disconnectedness among others.

The experiment undertaken in this part proves a complete failure. On a taxonomic basis we not only cannot establish connections among *all* of the documents of the canon, we cannot even find grounds for connecting any two documents with one another, except for Sifra and Sifré to Numbers, on the one side, and Genesis Rabbah and Leviticus Rabbah on the other. And even here the taxonomic connections prove not uniform but episodic. The claims of those represented by Handelman completely contradict the traits of the documents about which those claims are made. To conclude where we began this part:

> ...all units are so closely interwoven and simultaneously present that none can be considered in separation from any other at any given moment; it is a world of 'intertextuality'...[1]

> ....interpretation is not essentially separate from the text itself—an external act intruded upon it—but rather the extension of the text, the uncovering of the connective network of relations, a part of the continuous revelation of the text itself, at bottom, another aspect of the text.[2]

---

[1]Susan A. Handelman, *The Slayers of Moses. The Emergence of Rabbinic Interpretation in Modern Literary Theory* (Albany, 1982: State Universty of New York Press), p.78.

[2]*Ibid.*, p. 39.

Handelman's position finds no support whatsoever in the taxonomic theory of connection – the loosest, most encompassing theory I could imagine. Units meaning documents not only are not closely interwoven, but they rarely intersect at all. Handelman may mean not document but unit of discourse, so let us proceed to that, much easier matter. If we do, then Handelman finds slight support, since units of discourse in the sample(s) we have surveyed rarely go over the same ground as other such units of discourse. How we can consider the bulk of the units in relationship to other such units I do not know, if they do not intersect. How, then, Handelman explains the intersections – connections – of Yerushalmi and Sifré to Numbers, of Leviticus Rabbah and Sifra (other than through the common base-text, Leviticus!) – I cannot say, since these documents contain virtually nothing in common. In my view the facts require the following descriptive statement: *all units are so rarely interwoven and simultaneously present that a negligible proportion can be considered in relation to any other at any given moment.* The uncovering of the connective network of relations is in fact not possible, for there is none.

Handelman (and Schiffman with her) may fairly claim that there is a profound topical cogency that unites the entire canon – and that wholly on the basis of intrinsic qualities. What demonstrates that the whole is a set of interlocking and reinterlocking parts (S) to be read everywhere, all together, all at once (H) is the recurrence of basic beliefs and convictions, e.g., concerning God, the Torah, Israel, and on and on. Since every passage makes the same (set of) point(s), the profoundly pervasive uniform program of topicality validates on a purely factual basis the position that the dimension of intertextuality describes the documents before us. They may fairly argue that I have read the matter of topicality in too narrow and material a framework. To move a step forward, a convention of contemporary scholarship maintains that within both law and lore a single set of convictions prevails, reaching expression, here through concrete deed ("action symbol"), there through story, in a third passage through exegesis of Scripture, and on and on. Under the aspect of eternity – that is, from God's perspective (a matter to which we return in Chapter Nine) – Handelman is assuredly on firm ground. But as a matter of description of literature, two obstacles have to be overcome. First, alleging topical cogency and proving it are not the same thing. Second, the kind of topical cogency that seems to me alleged is not literary in character, appealing as it does to inchoate ideas or principles, but essentially theological. Efforts to demonstrate the underlying unities within diverse writings (the master key for the reinterlocking parts?) have to date produced no scholarly consensus. And the reason is that that profound unity, like all beauty, probably is in the eye of the beholder. So while, as a matter of theory, we may treat with considerable sympathy the claim that documents connect through the things that they say, we shall have for the moment to declare a simple fact: sometime, but, so far as we can now tell, not all the time, everywhere, and all at once. At least, not yet.

And yet, with Handelman, I maintain that the conception of intertextuality does illuminate what is, in fact, a community of texts. But it is because of social, not literary, facts. We have communities of texts, formed into a community of text by a textual community. In terms of my original metaphor, the library is there before the shelves, and the librarians decide what to put on the shelves. To the redefinition of that dimension of the documents, the reading of the community of texts as an aspect of the working of the textual community, we have now to turn.

Part Four

CANON AND CONNECTION

Chapter Nine

Intertextuality and the Canon of Judaism

I. WHAT IS AT STAKE: A REPRISE

We have now to ask what is at stake in the issue of connection. It is the appropriate heuristic framework for the interpretation of the documents at hand, the correct hermeneutic for reading them one by one. So, I contend, the stakes are very high. Claims as to the character of the literature of Judaism entail judgments on the correct hermeneutics, down to the interpretation of words and phrases. We can read everything only in light of everything else, fore and aft. That is how today nearly everyone interested in these writings claims to read them. Or we can read each item on its own, a document as an autonomous statement, a unit of discourse as a complete and whole composition, entire unto itself, taking account, to be sure, of how, in the larger context imposed from without, meanings change(d). That is how I maintain any writing must be read: in its own context, entirely on its own, not only in the one imposed by the audience and community that preserved it. For whatever happens to thought, in the mind of the thinker ideas come to birth cogent, whole, complete – and on their own. Extrinsic considerations of context and circumstance play their role, but logic, cogent discourse, rhetoric – these enjoy an existence, an integrity, too. If sentences bear meaning on their own, then to insist that sentences bear meaning only in line with friends, companions, partners in meaning contradicts the inner logic of syntax that, on its own, imparts sense to sentences. These are the choices: everything imputed, as against an inner integrity of logic and syntax.[1] But there is no compromise between what I shall argue is the theologically grounded hermeneutic, taken as a given by believers represented in our own time by Cohen, Schiffman, and Handelman, and the descriptive and historical, utterly secular hermeneutic, presented by me.

The literature commonly finds representation as wholly continuous, so that everything always testifies to the meaning of everything else, and, moreover, no book demands or sustains a reading on its own. As a theological judgment, that view enjoys self-evidence, since, after all, "Judaism" is "a religion," and it

---

[1] No one can maintain that the meanings of words and phrases, the uses of syntax, bear meanings wholly integral to discrete occasions. Syntax works because it joins mind to mind, and no mind invents language. But that begs the question and may be dismissed as impertinent, since the contrary view claims far more than the social foundation of the language.

presents its doctrines and dogmas, rules and regulations. So every document contributes to that one and encompassing system, that Judaism. But a system, a religion, makes its judgments at the end, *post facto*, while the authorships at hand worked at the outset, *de novo*. So reading what they wrote – a problem of textual analysis and interpretation – undergoes distortion if we impose, to begin with, the interpretation of the audience that received the writing. We err if we confuse social with literary categories, and the religious system at the end constitutes a social, not a literary, classification. Hermeneutics begins within the text and cannot sustain definition on the basis of the (later, extrinsic) disposition of the text. Nor should we miss the gross anachronism represented by the view that the way things came out all together at the end imposes its meaning and character upon the way things started out, one by one. Reading the Mishnah, ca. 200, as the framers of the two Talmuds read it two hundred, then four hundred years later, vastly distorts the original document in its own setting and meaning – and that by definition. A mark of the primitive character of discourse[2] in the field at hand derives from the need to point to self-evident anachronism in the prevailing hermeneutics.

Much is at stake. For I see irreconcilable choices. On the one side I identify a heuristic system, with a hermeneutic built out of theology and anachronism, yielding a chaotic and capricious reading of everything in light of everything else, all together, all at once. In such a situation no test of sense limits the free range of erudition, and erudition transforms discourse into political contest: who can make his judgment prevail against whom. Against that I offer an orderly and systematic reading of the documents, one by one, then in their second order connections, so far as they intersect, finally, as a cogent whole – thus a genuinely secular reading of documents, one by one, in connection with others, as part of a continuous whole, each in its several contexts, immediate and historical, synchronic and diachronic.

II. A COMMUNITY OF TEXTS? COHEN, SCHIFFMAN, AND HANDELMAN REVISITED

Viewing the documents from the angle of their intrinsic traits, we find no single community of texts. That position claims too much and finds no substantiation in the data. I see not only an absence of a collectivity, but a failure even of sustained imitation of later texts by earlier ones. Indeed I am struck by the independence of mind and the originality of authorships that pretend to receive and transmit, but in fact imagine and invent. True, individual texts do relate to other individual texts, either in a sustained dialectical relationship, as in the case of Mishnah and its continuator-exegeses, or in a taxonomic relationship of connection, as in the case of Sifra and Sifré to Numbers and of Genesis Rabbah and Leviticus Rabbah, or in an episodic and

---

[2]We note that Shaye Cohen is explicit about indifference to priority of documents.

anecdotal relationship, as in the case of documents that make use of sayings or stories in common. (The connection between these sayings or stories that occur in two or more documents scarcely requires analysis in the present context; what we have is simply diverse versions of given units of discourse.) But the received position, outlined today by Cohen, Schiffman, and Handelman, maintains far more than that and will not find satisfaction in the modest points of intersection and overlap that we have noted. In fact, overall, there is no community of texts existence of which is proven by intrinsic traits. We conclude at the point at which we began, with three theories of how the documents and their units of discourse relate.

To review, we turn to Cohen and Schiffman. Shaye Cohen states, "Synoptic texts must always be studied synoptically, even if one text is 'later' than another." Lawrence H. Schiffman says, "This system, composed of interlocking and re-interlocking parts possessed of an organic connection one to another, is never really divisible." Cohen is certainly right that we must take account of diverse versions of a given saying or story as these may occur in two or more documents in sequence. But if that is all he means, then he has not told us something anyone doubted. Since he borrows language from Gospels' research, he clearly intends something more than the admonition that we not ignore parallel versions of a single story or saying. He errs, specifically, in invoking the metaphor of the Synoptic Gospels, or of synoptic relationships among some of the Gospels and Q. The metaphor does not pertain.

Schiffman is right that sayings and stories do recur in two or more documents. He is wrong to maintain that, on that account, documents are not divisible (as he says), and what he further may mean by "possessed of an organic connection to one another" I cannot say. The formulation, so far as it pertains to literary and redactional traits, is murky, the sense unclear. My best guess is that Schiffman, like Cohen, refers to the mere fact that we have some sayings and stories occur in more than a single document. Cohen's and Schiffman's formulation of the issue of connection leads nowhere. My sense is that, in their rather portentous framing of matters, there is less than meets the eye.

Handelman presents a weightier claim, but her mastery of the texts, conspicuously less than that of Cohen and Schiffman, leads to some infelicities of thought and argument. By Handelman, we are told, "...all units are so closely interwoven and simultaneously present that none can be considered in separation from any other at any given moment; it is a world of 'intertextuality'...." And, she further states, "...interpretation is not essentially separate from the text itself–an external act intruded upon it–but rather the extension of the text, the uncovering of the connective network of relations, a part of the continuous revelation of the text itself, at bottom, another aspect of the text." The "connective network of relations," in Handelman's formulation, would correspond to that dimension of "continuity" in mine. For it is an extrinsic, not an intrinsic, aspect of the document to which, in the nature of things, we speak when we ask about relations. People impute meanings to texts, and that too forms a dimension of interpretation. But we commit anachronism and so misinterpret a text if we find in a text of the second century issues otherwise first attested in the seventh. When we treat as indivisible the text and its later interpretation, what we describe is not the text and its author's meaning, but the community and its enduring values. These relate, but they are not one and the same thing.

The importance of Handelman's formulation of matters lies in her explicit invocation of the matter of interpretation. When, however, she says that no document or unit of discourse can be considered on its own, she lays down a claim that she does not – and cannot – make stick. Once more, if all she means is that when a unit of discourse occurs in more than a single document, we cannot consider one version in isolation from another, then she has found a remarkably extreme way in which to express a perfectly routine fact of everyday observation. If she means more than that, I cannot say what she wishes to propose. My guess is that she wants to say we have to read everything in light of everything else. Indeed we do, when we propose to describe, analyze, and interpret a system whole and complete, in light of all its literature. But if we ignore the lines of structure and order that separate one text from another and that account for the sequence in which the textual canon unfolds, we invite chaos. Then how to sort things out and find the rules of order? That is the challenge to learning, which in time to come all parties to the debate will have to undertake. But Handelman's contribution is not only to set the terms for debate. She introduces the issue of intertextuality. That many-splendored jewel seems to refract whatever light people cast on it. We turn to two settings of the gem, those derived from materials cogent to our task.

III. CRITERIA OF INTERTEXTUALITY: MORGAN ON GENETTE AND HANDELMAN ON SAID

In her article, "Is There an Intertext in This Text? Literary and Interdisciplinary Approaches to Intertextuality" (*American Journal of Semiotics* 1985: 3), Thais E. Morgan provides a clear account of basic issues of intertextuality.[3] She surveys, in particular, major proponents of intertextuality. Her guidance allows us to compare our results to those among the theorists of intertextuality whom Morgan renders accessible. In general, I find in theories of intertextuality somewhat less than meets the eye, because definitions of terms turn out to be few, applications of theory episodic and anecdotal, criteria for validation or invalidation pretty much absent. But we do gain from Morgan's excellent reprise of the subject access to one theory that comes to clear expression and proposes interesting criteria of inquiry.

---

[3]She was kind enough to send me a pre-publication copy of her excellent paper. I thank her most cordially, as well as my colleague Robert Scholes who drew my attention to her work.

Among the diverse theories at hand, the one of greatest relevance[4] is that of Genette, who defines the matter as "a relation of co-presence between two or more texts, that is to say,...the demonstrable presence of one text in another...." Obviously, Scripture penetrates everything. But that does not establish a dimension of intertextuality that yields important hermeneutic, let alone heuristic, consequences. In fact, it is a merely formal fact, bearing no meaning at all. For it does not tell us how to interpret a text that, not knowing that banality, we did not know how to read. There are then these subcategories: quotation, which is explicit, allusion, implicit, and plagiarism, falling between the two. By that definition, of course, we correctly invoke the category of intertextuality. All components of the rabbinic canon quote from Scripture, and some of them quote from the Mishnah, or the Tosefta. Allusion is another matter; I am inclined to think allusion always bears a material mark, e.g., a brief indication of a few words to direct attention to another passage. As to plagiarism, that seems to me to address the appearance of a single story or saying in two or more documents. Then either one has borrowed from the other, or both from a third authorship.

None of these observations seems to me to open any important doors. They all pertain to our canon, but they present no astounding insights into its hermeneutics. If on that basis we are supposed, as Handelman demands, to read everything in terms of everything else, then we accept an invitation to either chaos or banality. For the fact that millions of diverse pieces of stationery in New York City all cite the New York City phone book does not bear profound consequences for the reading of mail that I receive from diverse sources in New York City. Scripture is inert and malleable, serving many purposes for many parties, determining meaning for none – except after the fact. Everyone finds in it pretty much anything he wants. Intertextuality meaning merely the propensity to cite a common corpus of proof-texts presents us in wonderful new garb with what is in fact entirely familiar, a not very interesting triviality. It is hardly even a fact of literature.

A further point of relevance is Genette's notion of metatextuality, by which he means, "the relation of 'commentary,' which unites one text to another text about which the former speaks, without necessarily citing it." This relationship presents difficulties. It is one thing to identify a text on which another depends. We may even demonstrate that fact, e.g., Tosefta contains numerous passages that without actually citing them in fact comment on Mishnah-passages. Quoting, paraphrasing, commenting – these are not mysterious matters but

---

[4]Or, at any rate, the only one I could understand. The others did not seem to me pertinent to the issues at hand. That is to state as a simple fact, theories of intertextuality do not illuminate that sizable corpus of documents that form a single canon, rich in reciprocal allusion and citation, of Judaism. My suspicion is that the fault lies with a theory not much tested against cogent data. Or, to state matters more boldly, the emperor looks naked. But, then, most emperors do.

subject to demonstration and exposition. The task of the exegete is to sort out precisely these matters. Where we have difficulty is demonstrating that sort of inchoate metatextual-intertextuality in texts in which there is no clear paraphrase, citation, or commentary. Search as we may, we find it exceedingly difficult to specify concrete criteria to tell us where we do, and do not, deal with that sort of interpenetration of texts. How shall we know the difference between the presence of an allusion and our imputation of the presence of an allusion? Criteria, to be sure, can be defined – that is the work of sustained and rigorous scholarship. Surely these criteria will give slight satisfaction to those who concur with Handelman's wild claim that "all units are so closely interwoven and simultaneously present that none can be considered in separation from any other at any given moment." Surely she lays down a claim that demands more than the mere citation of texts, directly or palimpsestually – or even allusion. But in a moment we shall see what misled Handelman to her extreme position, which far transcends the sense of intertextuality before us.

Morgan cites the following: "Each literary or aesthetic text produces a palimpsest, superimposing several other texts which are never completely hidden, but always hinted it." The literary palimpsest hovers between originality and imitation, she explains. But, she judges, "The idea that the other texts can be seen transparently through the centering text is highly dubious." The conception of imitation as against originality stimulates us to see things in a fresh way. If we ask which documents in our entire corpus, as represented by the two Appendices, imitate any other, the answer is: only one. The Bavli in important ways imitates the Yerushalmi. To state the negative: the authorship of the Tosefta does not imitate the Mishnah; that of Leviticus Rabbah does not imitate that of the Sifra; and on and on. There are paramount and definitive points of originality in *every* document, including the Bavli. In fact, we now realize, a criterion for an adequate theory of the intrinsic connections among the documents ("locking and reinterlocking parts" indeed!) of the rabbinic canon must derive from the issue of not originality but imitation. Let us see where and how the diverse components of the canon imitate one another – and where and how they do not. When we rapidly survey the texts in the two appendices, we see few marks of imitation, and a vast corpus of indications of total originality. Our difficulty in discerning connections between and among documents underlines that simple fact. Genette through Morgan opens our eyes to a potential inquiry by asking whether text imitates text. For as we survey our appendices and see that one authorship establishes a stance of independence from others of its own and earlier times, we recognize facts we should otherwise have missed. If I had to specify a single aesthetic tension confronting any of our authorships, it is *to establish a claim of continuity while doing pretty much anything someone wanted to do.* The Mishnah's authorship rejected that matter altogether, ignoring the inherited conventions of language as Scripture dictated the characteristics of Hebrew, ignoring the topical program of Scripture's legal codes for its own program (absorbing the received one to be sure), ignoring the entire structure of authority based on pseudepigraphic authorship characteristic of Scripture ("Moses" as author of Deuteronomy, for instance). No imitation here! Nor any in Tosefta. And even the Bavli at the end yielded a fundamental structure utterly original, independent of that of the Yerushalmi, as I have shown elsewhere.[5]

But the criterion of imitation as against originality does lead us toward relationship imputed extrinsically, that is, socially, specifically to the concept of the textual community. What is of special interest is Genette's judgment: "I see the relation between the text and its reader as more socialized, more openly contractual, as the result of a conscious and organized practice." That view places us squarely into the category of the textual community, to which we turn in conclusion. The appeal is to extrinsic, not intrinsic, traits of the documents – continuity not connection. But no one has ever doubted that the rabbinic corpus constitutes a socially-constructed canon – and that by definition. The perspective of intertextuality teaches lessons of literature in society, writings received and read. The more we labor to uncover the inner traits of system and order among diverse documents, the less we yield, beyond banality. For citation, allusion, reference to something else and other – these are just other forms of words, things the author uses to say whatever he or she wishes to say. Art comes from color, but also from collage, and references, allusions, citations – these form, in writing, the counterpart to the raw materials of collage.

A further approach to intertextuality derives from Susan Handelman's exposition of Edward Said's definition of the matter.[6] I have already cited part of Handelman's use of Said's theory. Let me now go over her exposition of the two points of particular interest:

> The fourth convention, *finality*, is the assumption that each portion of the text is a discrete unit, firmly established in its place, precluding consideration of what precedes and follows it at any given moment. This convention obviously never applied to Rabbinic interpretation. There, not only is contextual reading and exegetical principle, but all units are so closely interwoven and simultaneously present that none can be considered in separation from any other at any given moment; it is a world of 'intertextuality,' to use a contemporary literary term.
>
> Said's fifth category, *finality*, is the maintenance of the unit of the text through genealogical connections, such as author-text, beginning-middle-end, text-meaning, and reader-interpretation. These distinctions are blurred in rabbinic thought: the text has a divine author, but is continuously created by its readers-interpreters.

---

[5]*Judaism: The Classic Statement. The Evidence of the Bavli* (Chicago, 1986: University of Chicago Press), and compare*The Talmud of the Land of Israel. 35. Introduction. Taxonomy* (Chicago, 1984: University of Chicago Press).

[6]*Slayers of Moses*, pp. 77-79.

We have labored long and hard to discover grounds for maintaining, as Handelman proposes, that "all units are so closely interwoven...that none can be considered in separation from ay other at any given moment." That theory of intertextuality, however, applies only occasionally, which is to say, that theory is only part true and therefore wholly false.

As to genealogical connections, here it seems to me Handelman grossly confuses quite distinct categories. Specifically, in order to provide a literary theory on the heuristic and hermeneutic requirements of a text (or a set of texts), she has drawn upon a theological conception, namely God's giving of the one whole Torah, oral and written, to Moses at Sinai. It is true that the faithful impute the authorship to God. But I do not think literary scholarship of a descriptive and interpretive character has to invoke that fact of faith as a fact of literature. So Handelman seems to me guilty of confusing categories best kept apart. If we do not acknowledge as a matter of descriptive fact that "the text has a divine author" – thus One Authorship, Creator of not only this text, but, as it happens, heaven and earth, the fish in the sea, the birds in the sky, and you and me and all in all – then genealogical connections have, as a matter of fact, to emerge on their own. We have worked hard at showing the simplest genealogical connections. We have found some, between one document and another, but none among all the documents.

The distinctions between author and text, beginning, middle, and end, text and meaning, reader and interpretation, Handelman says are blurred in "Rabbinic thought." But the category "Rabbinic thought" itself blurs distinctions among and between documents, so the blurring derives not from the data but from the category. If I knew to what court of facts and judgments she here appeals in speaking of "Rabbinic thought," I could propose modes of analyzing and evaluating her thesis as to that sort of genealogical connections that she wishes to evoke in showing "the unity of the text." Our inquiry into connections has sorted out a variety of possibilities. None serves to validate applying to the literature at hand the conception of "intertextuality" as defined by Handelman in her reading of Said. I find a measure of pathos in Handelman's reading, because she has made every effort to master a theoretical literature in the service of a received and holy canon which, as a matter of fact, she seems to know only imperfectly. The work derives from piety, reverence for the received canon, as the imputation of the single authorship of God suggests. Certainly the givens of her thought, like those of Cohen and Schiffman, accord more comfortably with Orthodox Judaic than with secular literary or historical canons of inquiry. But good will and faith do not substitute for the hard work of learning, including mastery of not only the texts but the scholarly debates that do, after all, circulate today. My sense is that Handelman's (to me) impressive mastery of contemporary critical thought finds no match in her (to me) rather limited knowledge of contemporary debates on the canon of Judaism in its formative age, which I doubt she has fully sorted out for herself. Joined to convictions of a profoundly theological character treated as matters of literary fact, these imbalances in learning produce propositions that prove somewhat awry.

The upshot is that so far as definitions and theories of intertextuality serve at all, intrinsic traits of the canonical writings indicate that those theories form a faulty fit, proving asymmetrical to the data at hand. I should expect that other versions of the category of intertextuality will provide more substantial guidance in tracing lines of connection from one document to the next These have offered none.

IV. CRITERIA OF CONTINUITY: THE PROGRAM OF BRIAN STOCK

The upshot is that intertextuality as a literary category of interpretation draws us forward to that third and final dimension introduced at the outset, the one of continuity – a dimension I defined to begin with a social and extrinsic, not literary and intrinsic. We can identify communities of texts, but no community of texts. But future work will, I believe, demonstrate that we can identify one textual community – which forms of communities of texts a single canon – and that as a matter of social fact. So from the inquiry into intrinsic connection we turn to one into social connection of literature, and, forthwith, seek guidance from one profound statement of the matter, that of Brian Stock:

> Where there are texts, there are also presumably groups to study them. The process of learning and reflection inevitably influences the members: how individuals behave towards each other and how the group, if it is not transitory, behaves towards the outside world, will bear some relation to attitudes formed during the educational experience. From reading, dialogue, and the absorption of texts, therefore, it is a short step to 'textual communities,' that is, to groups of people whose social activities are centered around texts, or, more precisely, around a literate interpreter of them....the group's members must associate voluntarily; their interaction must take place around an agreed meaning for the text. Above all, they must make the hermeneutic leap from what the text says to what they think it means; the common understanding provides the foundation for changing thought and behavior.[7]

Let me now translate the matter into the terms of this book. When we move from the intrinsic traits of texts to those extrinsic qualities, imputed from without, we view the documents no longer as a community of texts, but as texts that have *been formed* into a community. So we leave behind the books, set one by one, then gathered on shelves of the library and turn to examine the building that houses the books on their shelves. The building is built by a community and serves the interests of that community – and that by definition. So we want to know how to describe, then analyze and interpret, that community, the one

---

[7]*The Implications of Literacy,* p. 522.

represented by the library (in terms of our analogy), or by the canon (in terms of our sources, viewed whole and all at once).

Our initial inquiry finds guidance in a theory of the textual community laid out by Brian Stock in his *The Implications of Literacy. Written Language and Models of Interpretation in the Eleventh and Twelfth Centuries* (Princeton, 1983: Princeton University Press).[8] Stock's main point, relevant to this work, is that texts emerge "as a reference system both for everyday activities and for giving shape to many larger vehicles of explanation." In terms of the literature at hand, as the several authorships describe everyday life, they portray a world that makes constant reference to a circumscribed set of writings, that finds guidance in all matters in what is found in those writings, and that attains cogency as a social entity in the recurrent citation of that set of words and no other. A textual community then is a community that takes shape by reference to a set of documents – which, as a matter of fact, that community in its system has identified for itself in a reciprocal process of social self-definition, on the one side, and canonization of individual candidates for the canon, on the other.

Stock's focus of interest hardly corresponds to mine. He lays stress on the presence of a written text: "An importance consequence of literacy in any human community arises from the area of social organization. Relationships between the individual and the family, the group, or the wider community are all influenced by the degree to which society acknowledges written principles of operation. Literacy also affects the way people conceptualize such relations, and these patterns of thought inevitably feed back into the network of real interdependencies." My concern does not begin with the distinction between the oral and the written, but with the identification of a given set of writings (whether formulated and transmitted orally, as was the Mishnah, or in writing, as seems to have been the case for most of the documents as we now have them). Rather, my concern is with the description of a community that reaches its social formulation in the identification of a canon, that is, in the (extrinsic) social foundations for the continuity of documents. I want to know how Judaism became Judaism, that is, "the one whole Torah or Moses, our rabbi." For if the documents as an entirety do not exhibit pervasive connections among themselves over all, still, the documents, as we know full well, viewed by Judaism do form a continuity in the social and intellectual conventions imputed to them as Torah, that is, as a Judaism. They state in writing whatever there is to be said in words for "Judaism." They speak God's will for Israel: "Judaism" or the Torah. So Stock's interest and my use of his basic ideas do not entirely match.

---

[8]William Scott Green originally directed my attention to Stock and the importance of his ideas, for which I am grateful. I then had the pleasure of hearing Stock and meeting him, and I find him still more stimulating and interesting in person than I do in writing. I am fortunate indeed to do my work in such an age as this, with such friends and teachers as these.

But I invoke without modification Stock's use of the term "textual community," which bears considerable precision. He means a group that makes use of texts "both to structure the internal behavior of the groups' members and provide solidarity against the outside world...The outside world was looked upon as a universe beyond the revelatory text." Now when we turn from the documents to that world that preserved and valued the documents, we find in hand testimonies to the existence of a community that has made of diverse and (viewed over all) discrete documents into a single document, one which, as we have seen, people may confidently describe as "indivisible," made up of "interlocking and reinterlocking parts," and the like. True, these judgments mark imputed, not intrinsic, traits. But that fact focuses our attention on precisely the correct issue: defining through intertextuality the society that defined the system which, as a matter of fact, comes to written expression in the documents. They are these, not those, these and no others, hence, in the documentary canon, we call them all at once and all together "the Torah," or "Judaism."

V. FROM CONNECTION TO CONTINUITY

The community frames the system, the system infuses the writings, the writings then, whether read all together or one by one, say everything everywhere all at once. The writings speak, in particular, to those who can hear, that is, to the members of the community, who, on account of that perspicacity of hearing, constitute a textual community. The textual community is that social group the system of which is recapitulated by its selected canon. The textual community then imposes continuity and unity on whatever is in its canon – and the intrinsic traits constitute adventitious and trivial aspects of the matter. The appropriate hermeneutic, therefore, derives only from theology, and never from literature or philology or history. Texts may form community when they exhibit traits in common, or when they stand in a genealogical relationship with one another, fore and aft. A textual community imparts continuity to discrete or related texts (it makes no difference) because that community chooses to give expression to its larger system in part through these documents: these, not those.

The texts recapitulate the system. The system does not recapitulate the texts. The system comes before the texts and defines the canon. No universally shared traits or characteristics, topical, logical, rhetorical, within the diverse texts can account by themselves for the selection of those texts for places in the canon. Cohen, Schiffman, and Handelman correctly express the consequences of theology – that is, of canon – in their incorrect literary judgments. This they do when they confuse theology with literary criticism, finding traits dictated by theological conviction in documents that, as a matter of fact, only occasionally exhibit the allegedly paramount traits. They therefore commit equivalent of creationism, confusing propositions of the faith with properties of the world out there. Creationism maintains that, since Scripture says God created the world this way, not that, therefore geology must be rejected. For hermeneutics the equivalent error is to maintain that, since the system joins the texts, therefore the texts are indivisible and have to be read each in the light of all, always all together and all at once. But the correct theological conviction has misled the faithful into insisting that, because everything is Torah, and Torah is everywhere, therefore, in hermeneutical terms, nothing may be read in its own setting. We could not demonstrate the presence of those connections that would as a matter of fact validate theological convictions. So, as hermeneutic, they do not apply. But when Handelman, speaking for ages of faithful Judaists, says, "...interpretation is not essentially separate from the text itself–an external act intruded upon it–but rather the extension of the text, the uncovering of the connective network of relations, a part of the continuous revelation of the text itself, at bottom, another aspect of the text," as a matter of theology she speaks with accuracy. But it is solely from the aspect of theology, that is, of the canon. It is therefore a social judgment, extrinsic to the traits of the texts and intruded upon them. Once canonical texts then do participate in that common discourse, each contributing its component of the single, continuous discussion.

Let me account for the enormous error of Cohen, Schiffman, and Handelman, as well, as a matter of fact, as all the faithful past and present for whom they speak:

We err when we seek to demonstrate that a system recapitulates its texts.

That is what leads us to impute to texts intrinsic traits of order, cogency, and unity. It is, further, what provokes us to postulate connection, rather than demonstrating it. The source of error flows from treating as literary facts what are, in fact, judgments of theology, that is, the reification of faith, the transformation of convictions of culture into facts of literature and – it must follow – a theory of hermeneutics. The fact is that the system not only does not recapitulate its texts, it selects and orders them, imputes to them as a whole cogency that their original authorships have not expressed in and through the parts, expresses through them its deepest logic, and – quite by the way – also dictates for them the appropriate and operative hermeneutics. The canon (so to speak) does not just happen after the fact, in the aftermath of the texts that make it up. *The canon is the event that creates of documents holy texts before the fact: the canon is the fact.*

Since we could not demonstrate connection, we must draw conclusions of a heuristic and hermeneutical character. These are readily stated. The simple rule may be laid down both negatively and positively. The documents do not (naturally, as a matter of fact) *coalesce* into a canon. They (supernaturally, as a gesture of faith) are *constructed* into a canon. The canon emerges not through recognition of mere facts, pre-existing unities, but of made up and imputed ones. The canon comes into being through a process not of post facto aggregation of like documents or connected ones drawn by a kind of unnatural magnetism to others of their kind, but of selection, choice, deliberation.

The system does not recapitulate the canon. The canon recapitulates the system. In the beginning are not words of inner and intrinsic affinity, but the word: the system, all together, all at once, complete, whole, finished – the word awaiting only that labor of exposition and articulation that the faithful, for centuries to come, will lavish at the altar of the faith.

Appendix to Part Two

Mishnah, Tosefta, Yerushalmi, and Bavli to Berakhot VIII

I. MISHNAH-TRACTATE BERAKHOT CHAPTER EIGHT

I

8:1. A. These are the things which are between the House of Shammai and the House of Hillel in [regard to] the meal:

B. The House of Shammai say, "One blesses over the day, and afterward one blesses over the wine."

And the House of Hillel say, "One blesses over the wine, and afterward one blesses over the day."

8:2. A. The House of Shammai say, "They wash the hands and afterward mix the cup."

And the House of Hillel say, "They mix the cup and afterward wash the hands."

8:3. A. The House of Shammai say, "He dries his hands on the cloth and lays it on the table."

And the House of Hillel say, "On the pillow."

8:4. A. The House of Shammai say, "They clean the house, and afterward they wash the hands."

And the House of Hillel say, "They wash the hands, and afterward they clean the house."

8:5. A. The House of Shammai say, "Light, and food, and spices, and *Havdalah.*"

And the House of Hillel say, "Light, and spices, and food, and *Havdalah.*"

B. The House of Shammai say, "'Who created the light of the fire.'"

And the House of Hillel say, "'Who creates the lights of the fire.'"

II

8:6. A. They do not bless over the light or the spices of gentiles, nor the light or the spices of the dead, nor the light or the spices which are before an idol.

B. And they do not bless over the light until they make use of its illumination.

III

8:7. A. He who ate and forgot and did not bless [say Grace] —

B. The House of Shammai say, "He should go back to his place and bless."

And the House of Hillel say, "He should bless in the place in which he remembered."

C. Until when does he bless? Until the food has been digested in his bowels.

8:8. A. Wine came to them after the meal, and there is there only that cup —

B. The House of Shammai say, "He blesses the wine, and afterward he blesses the food."

And the House of Hillel say, "He blesses the food, and afterward he blesses the wine."

C. They respond *Amen* after an Israelite who blesses, and they do not respond *Amen* after a Samaritan who blesses, until hearing the entire blessing.

II. TOSEFTA TO MISHNAH BERAKHOT CHAPTER EIGHT

5:21 (Lieberman, p. 28, Is. 41-2).

They answer *Amen* after a gentile who says a blessing with the divine name. They do not answer *Amen* after a Samaritan who says a blessing with the divine name until they have heard the entire blessing.

5.25 (Lieberman, p. 29, Is. 53-57).

A. [The] things which are between the House of Shammai and the House of Hillel in [regard to] the meal:

B. The House of Shammai say, "One blesses over the day, and afterward he blesses over the wine, for the day causes the wine to come, and the day is already sanctified, but the wine has not yet come."

C. And the House of Hillel say, "One blesses over the wine, and afterward he blesses over the day, for the wine causes the Sanctification of the day to be said.

"Another explanation: The blessing over the wine is regular [= always required when wine is used], and the blessing over the day is not continual [but is said only on certain days]."

D. And the law is according to the words of the House of Hillel.

5:26 (Lieberman, pp. 29-30, Is. 57-61).

A. The House of Shammai say, "They wash the hands and afterward mix the cup, lest the liquids which are on the outer surface of the cup be made unclean on account of the hands, and in turn make the cup unclean."

B. The House of Hillel say, "The outer surfaces of the cup are always deemed unclean.

"Another explanation: The washing of the hands must always take place immediately before the meal.

C. "They mix the cup and afterward wash the hands."

5:27 (Lieberman, p. 30, Is. 61-65).

A. The House of House of Shammai say, "He dries his hand on the napkin and leaves it on the table, lest the liquids which are in the napkin be made unclean on account of the cushion, and then go and make the hands unclean."

B. And the House of Hillel say, "A doubt in regard to the condition of liquids so far as the hands are concerned is resolved as clean."

C. "Another explanation: Washing the hands does not pertain to unconsecrated food.

D. "But he dries his hands on the napkin and leaves it on the cushion, lest the liquids which are in the napkin be made unclean on account of the table, and they go and render the food unclean."

5:28 (Lieberman, p. 30, Is. 65-68).

A. The House of Shammai say, "They clean the house, on account of the waste of food, and afterward they wash the hands."

B. The House of Hillel say, "If the waiter was a disciple of a sage, he gathers the scraps which contain as much as an olive's bulk.

C. "And they wash the hands and afterward clean the house."

5:29 (Lieberman, p. 30, Is. 68-72).

A. The House of Shammai say, "He holds the cup of wine in his right hand and spiced oil in his left hand."
He blesses over the wine and afterward blesses over the oil.

B. And the House of Hillel say, "He holds the sweet oil in his right hand and the cup of wine in his left hand."

C. He blesses over the oil and smears it on the head of the waiter. If the waiter was a disciple of a sage, he [the diner] smears it on the wall, because it is not praiseworthy for a disciple of a sage to go forth perfumed.

5:30 (Lieberman, pp. 30-31, Is. 72-75).

A. R. Judah said, "The House of Shammai and the House of Hillel did not dispute concerning the blessing of the food, that it is first, or concerning the Havdalah, that it is at the end.
"Concerning what did they dispute?
"Concerning the light and the spices, for —
"The House of Shammai say, 'Light and afterward spices.'
"And the House of Hillel say, 'Spices and afterward light.'"

5:30 (Lieberman, p. 31, Is. 75-77).

B. He who enters his home at the end of the Sabbath blesses the wine, the light, the spices, and then says Havdalah.

C. And if he has only one cup [of wine] he leaves it for after the meal and then says all [the liturgies] in order after [reciting the blessing for] it.

5:31 (Lieberman, p. 31, Is. 81-85).

A. If a person has a light covered in the folds of his garment or in a lamp, and sees the flame but does not use its light, or uses its light but does not see its flame, he does not bless [that light]. [He says a blessing over the light only] when he both sees the flame and uses its light.

As to a lantern — even though he had not extinguished it (that is, it has been burning throughout the Sabbath), he recites a blessing over it.

B.   They do not bless over the light of gentiles. One may bless over [the flame of] an Israelite kindled from a gentile, or a gentile who kindled from an Israelite.

5:32 (Lieberman, p. 31, Is. 80-81).

In the house of study —
The House of Shammai say, "One [person] blesses for all of them."
And the House of Hillel say,"Each one blesses for himself."

III. THE TOSEFTA AND THE MISHNAH COMPARED

Mishnah	Tosefta
M. 8:1. A. These are the things which are between the House of Shammai and the House of Hillel in [regard to] the meal:	Tos. 5:25. [The] things which are between the House of Shammai and the House of Hillel [as regards] the meal:
B. The House of Shammai say, "One blesses the day, and afterward one blesses over the wine."	The House of Shammai say, "One blesses the day, and afterward one blesses over the wine, *for the day causes the wine to come, and the day is already sanctified, but the wine has not yet come.*"
And the House of Hillel say, "One blesses the wine, and afterward one blesses over the day."	And the House of Hillel say, "One blesses over the wine, and afterward one blesses the day, *for the wine causes the Sanctification of the day to be said.*"
	"Another matter: The blessing of the wine is continual, and the blessing of the day is not continual."
	And the law is according to the words of the House of Hillel.
M. 8:2.A. The House of Shammai say, "They wash the hands and afterward mix the cup."	Tos. 5:26. The House of Shammai say, "They wash the hands and afterward mix the cup, *lest the liquids which are on the outer surfaces of the cup may be made unclean on account of the hands, and they may go back and make the cup unclean.*"
And the House of Hillel say, "They mix the cup and afterward wash the hands."	The House of Hillel say, *"The outer surfaces of the cup are perpetually unclean.*
	"Another matter: The washing of the hands is only [done] near [at the outset of] the meal."

"They mix the cup and afterward wash the hands."

8:3.A. The House of Shammai say, "He dries his hands on the napkin and lays it on the table." And the House of Hillel say, "On the cushion."

5:27. The House of Shammai say, "He dries his hand on the napkin and lays it on the table, *lest the liquids which are in the napkin may be made unclean on account of the pillow, and they may go and make the hands unclean.*

The House of Hillel say, A doubt in regard to the condition of liquids so far as the hands are concerned is clean.

"Another matter: Washing the hands does not pertain to unconsecrated food. But he dries his hands on the napkin and leaves it on the cushion lest the liquids which are in the pillow may be made unclean on account of the table, and they may go and render the food unclean."

M. 8:4.A. The House of Shammai say, "They clean the house and afterward wash the hands." And the House of Hillel say, "They wash the hands and afterward clean the house."

Tos. 5:28. The House of Shammai say, "They clean the house *on account of the waste of food* and afterward wash the hands."

The House of Hillel say, *"If the waiter was a disciple of a sage, he gathers the scraps which contain as much as on olive's bulk.*

"They wash the hands and afterward clean the house."

8:5.A. The House of Shammai say, "Light, and food and spices, and *Havdalah.*" And the House of Hillel say, "Light, and spices, and food, and *Havdalah.*"

5:30. R. Judah said, *"The House of Shammai and the House of Hillel did not dispute concerning the blessing of the food, that it is first, and concerning the* Havdalah *that it is the end. Concerning what did they dispute? Concerning the light and the spices, for the* House of Shammai say, 'Light and *afterward* spices,' and the House of Hillel say, 'Spices and *afterward* light.'"

B. The House of Shammai say, "'Who created the light of the fire.'" And the House of Hillel say, "'Who creates the lights of the fire.'" M. 8:8.A. Wine came to them after the meal, and there is there only that cup —

[No equivalent.]

Tos. 5:30 (Lieberman, p. 31, ls. 75-77). A. *He who enters his home at the end of the Sabbath*

B. The House of Shammai say, "He blesses over the wine and afterward he blesses over the food."

And the House of Hillel say, "He blesses over the food and afterward he blesses over the wine."

[If wine came to them after the meal and] there is there only that cup House of Shammai say, "He blesses the wine and then the food."

(House of Hillel say, "He blesses the food and then the wine.")

M. 8:6.A. They do not bless the light or the spices of gentiles, nor the light or the spices of the dead, nor the light or the spices which are before an idol.

B. And they do not bless the light until they make use of its illumination.

M. 8:8.C. They respond *Amen* after an Israelite who blesses, and they do not respond *Amen* after a Samaritan who blesses, until one hears the entire blessing.

blesses over the wine, the light, the spices, and then says Havdalah.

B. *And if he has only one cup* [of wine], *he leaves it for after the meal and then says them all in order after* [blessing] *it.* If he has only one cup [of wine] [he leaves if for after the meal and then says them all in order, thus:] Wine, then food.

Tos. 5:31.B. They do not bless the light of gentiles. *An Israelite who kindled* [a flame] *from a gentile, or a gentile who kindled from an Israelite — one may bless* [such a flame].

Tos. 5:31 (Lieberman, p. 31, Is. 81-85). A. *If a person has a light covered in the folds of his garment or in a lamp, and he sees the flame but does not use its light, or uses its light but does not see its flame, he does not bless.* [He blesses only] *when he both sees the flame and uses its light.*

Tos. 5:21 (Lieberman, p. 28, Is.41-2). *They answer "Amen" after a blessing with the divine name recited by a gentile.*

They do not answer *Amen* after a Samaritan who blesses *with the divine name* until they hear the entire blessing.

IV. YERUSHALMI TO MISHNAH BERAKHOT CHAPTER EIGHT

8:1. The House of Shammai say, "One blesses the day and afterward one blesses over the wine."

And the House of Hillel say, "One blesses over the wine and afterward one blesses the day."

I.   A.   *What is the reason of the House of Shammai?*

The Sanctification of the day causes the wine to be brought, and the man is already liable for the Sanctification of the day before the wine comes.

What is the reason of the House of Hillel?

The wine causes the Sanctification of the day to be said.

Another matter: Wine is perpetual, and the Sanctification is not perpetual. [What is always required takes precedence over what is required only occasionally.]

B.   R. Yosé said, "[It follows] from the opinions of them both that with respect to wine and *Havdalah*, wine comes first."

"*It is not the reason of the House of Shammai* that the Sanctification of the day causes the wine to be brought, and here, since *Havdalah* does not cause wine to be brought, the wine takes precedence?"

"*Is it not the reason of the House of Hillel that* the wine is perpetual and the Sanctification is not perpetual, and since the wine is perpetual, and the *Havdalah* is not perpetual, the wine comes first?"

C.   R. Mana said, "From the opinions of both of them [it follows] that with respect to wine and Havdalah, *Havdalah* comes first."

"*Is it not the reason of the House of Shammai that* one is already obligated [to say] the Sanctification of the day before the wine comes, and here, since he is already obligated for *Havdalah* before the wine comes, *Havdalah* comes first?"

Is it not the reason of the House of Hillel that the wine causes the Sanctification of the Day to be said, and here, since the wine does not cause the *Havdalah* to be said, *Havdalah* comes first?"

D.   R. Zeira said, "From the opinions of both of them [it follows] that they say *Havdalah* without wine, but they say the Sanctification only with wine."

E.   *This is the opinion of R. Zeira, for* R. Zeira said, They may say *Havdalah* over beer, *but they go from place to place* [in search of wine] *for the Sanctification."*

II.   A.   R. Yosé b. Rabbi said, "They are accustomed there [in Babylonia], where there is no wine, for the prayerleader to go before the ark and say one blessing which is a summary of the seven, and complete it with, 'Who sanctifies Israel and the Sabbath Day.'"

B.   *And thus the following poses a difficulty for the opinion of the House of Shammai: How should one act on the evenings of the Sabbath?*

He *who was sitting and eating on the evening of the Sabbath,* and it grew dark and became Sabbath evening, and there was there only that one cup — [The House of Shammai say, "Wine, then food," and the House of Hillel say, "Food, then wine," so Mishnah 8:8].

Do you say he should leave it for the end of the meal and say all of them [the blessings] on it?

What do you prefer?

Should he [first] bless the day? The food takes precedence.

Should he bless the food? The wine takes precedence.

Should he bless the wine? The day takes precedence.

C.   *We may infer* [the answer] *from this:*

If wine came to them after the meal, and there is there only that cup — R. Ba said, "Because it [the wine's] is a brief blessing, [he says it first, for] perhaps he may forget and drink [the wine]. But here, since he says them all over the cup, he will not forget [to say a blessing over the wine in the cup]."

D.   What, then, should he do according to the opinion of the House of Shammai?

Let him bless the food first, then bless the day, and then bless the wine.

E. *And this poses difficulty for the opinion of the House of Hillel: How should one act at the end of the Sabbath?*
If he was sitting and eating on the Sabbath and it grew dark and the Sabbath came to an end, and there is there only that cup —
Do you say he should leave it [the wine] for after the meal and say them all on it?
What do you prefer?
Should he bless the wine? The food comes first.
Should he bless the food? The light comes first.
Should be bless the light? The *Havdalah* comes first.

F. *We may infer* [the solution to the impasse] *from this:* R. Judah said, "The House of Shammai and the House of Hillel did not differ concerning the blessing of the food, that it comes first, nor concerning *Havdalah,* that it comes at the end.
"Concerning what did they differ?
"Concerning the light and the spices, for:
"The House of Shammai say, 'The spices and afterward the light.'
"And the House of Hillel say, 'The light and afterward the spices.'"

[G. R. Ba and R. Judah in the name of Rav (said), "The law is according to him who says, 'Spices and afterward light.'"]

H. What should he do according to the opinion of the House of Hillel?
Let him bless the food, afterward bless the wine, and afterward bless the light.

III. A. As to [the beginning of the] festival day which coincides with the end of the Sabbath —
R. Yohanan said, "[The order of prayer is] wine, Sanctification, light, *Havdalah.*"
Hanin bar Ba said in the name of Rav, "Wine, Sanctification, light, *Havdalah, Sukkah,* and season."
And did not Samuel rule according to this teaching of R. Hanina.

B. R. Aha said in the name of R. Joshua b. Levi, "When a king goes out and the governor comes in, they accompany the king and afterward bring in the governor."

C. Levi said, "Wine, *Havdalah,* light, Sanctification."

IV. A. R. Zeira asked before R. Yosé, "How shall we do it in practice?"
He said to him, "According to Rav, and according to R. Yohanan."
And so too did the rule come out in practice — according to Rav and according to R. Yohanan.

B. *And when R. Abbahu went south, he would act in accord with R. Hanina, but when he went down to Tiberias, he would act in accord with R. Yohanan, for one does not differ from a man* ['s ruling] *in his own place* [out of courtesy].

C. *According to the opinion of R. Hanina this poses no problem.*

D. *But it poses a problem to the opinion of R. Yohanan:* In the rest of the days of the year does he not bless the light, lest it go out [because of a draft, and he lose the opportunity to say the blessing]? And here too he should bless the light before it goes out!

E. *What did R. Yohanan do in this connection?* [How did he explain this difficulty?]

F. Since he has wine [in hand], his light will not go out [for it is protected].

G. Then let him bless the light at the end?

H. So as not to upset the order [of prayer; lit.: time of the coming Sabbaths, [he does not do so].

8:2. The **House of Shammai say, "They wash the hands and afterward mix the cup." And the House of Hillel say, "They mix the cup first and afterward wash the hands."**

I. A. *What is the reason of the House of Shammai?*
So that the liquids which are on the outer side of the cup may not be made unclean by his hands and go and make the cup unclean.
What is the reason of the House of Hillel?
The outer side of the cup is always unclean [so there is no reason to protect it from the hands' uncleanness].
Another matter: One should wash the hands immediately before saying the blessing.

B. *R. Biban in the name of R. Yohanan* [said], *"The opinion of the House of Shammai is in accord with R. Yosé and that of the House of Hillel with R. Meir, as we have learned there* [Mishnah Kelim 25:7-8]:
"[In all vessels an outer part and an inner part are distinguished, and also a part by which they are held.]"
"R. Meir says, 'For hands which are unclean and clean.'"
"R. Yosé said,'This applies only to clean hands alone.'"

C. R. Yosé in the name of R. Shabbetai, and R. Hiyya in the name of R. Simeon b. Laqish [said], "For *Hallah* [Dough-offering] and for washing the hands, a man goes four miles [to find water]."
R. Abbahu in the name of R. Yosé b. R. Hanina said, "This is what he said, '[If the water is] before him [that is, on his way, in his vicinity, or near at hand, he must proceed to it and wash]. But if it is behind him [that is, not on his way], they do not trouble him [to obtain it and wash].'"

D. Regarding those who guard gardens and orchards [and who cannot leave their posts], what do you do for them as to the insides and the outer sides [of a cup]? [How do we rule in their case? Do we judge them to be in the status of those for whom the water is] on their way, or in the status of those who would have to backtrack?
Let us infer the answer from this [Mishnah Hallah 2:3]:
The woman sits and cuts off her Dough-offering *[Hallah]* while she is naked, because she can cover herself up, but a man cannot.
Now does not a woman sit in the house, yet you say they do not bother her? So too here they do not bother him.

II. A. *It has been taught:*
Washing before the meal is a matter of choice, but afterward it is a matter of obligation.
But in respect to the first washing, he washes and interrupts, and in the case of the second washing, he washes and does not interrupt.

B. What is the meaning of "He 'washes and interrupts'?"

R. Jacob b. Aha said, "He washes and then repeats the washing."

R. Samuel bar Isaac said, *"If he is required* to repeat the washing, *how do you claim it is a matter of choice?*

["Or if you want, I may point out you require one to go four miles (in search of water], *so how do you claim* it is a matter of choice!"

C.   R. Jacob bar Idi said, "On account of the first [washing of hands], a pig's flesh was eaten; on account of the second [washing of hands], a woman left her house.

"And some say, three souls were killed on her account. [It is not a matter of choice at all.]"

III.   A.   *Samuel went up to visit Rav. He saw him eating with* [his hands covered by] *a napkin. He said to him, "How so?* [Did you not wash your hands?]"

He said to him, "I am sensitive."

B.   *When R. Zeira came up here* [to Palestine], *he saw the priests eating with a napkin. He said to them, "Lo, this is in accord with the story of Rav and Samuel."*

C.   R. Yosé bar Kahana came [and said] *in the name of Samuel,* "One washes the hands for Heave-offering, not for unconsecrated food."

D.   R. Yosé says, "For Heave-offering and for unconsecrated food."

E.   R. Yosah in the name of R. Hiyya bar Ashi, and R. Jonah and R. Hiyya bar Ashi in the name of Rav [said], "They wash the hands for Heave-offering up to the wrist, and for unconsecrated food up to he knuckles."

F.   *Measha the son of the son of R. Joshua b. Levi said, "If one was eating with my grandfather and did not wash his hands up to the wrist, grandfather would not eat with him."*

G.   R. Huna said, "Washing the hands applies only for bread."

H.   R. Hoshia taught, "Whatever is unclean on account of liquid [is protected by washing the hands]."

I.   R. Zeira said, *"Even for cutting beets, he would wash his hands."*

IV.   A.   Rav said, "He who washed his hands in the morning is not required to do so in the afternoon."

B.   *R. Abina ordered his wine-steward, "Whenever you find sufficient water, wash your hands and rely on this washing all day long."*

C.   *R. Zeira went up to R. Abbahu in Caesarea. He found him saying,* "I shall go to eat."

D.   *He gave him a chunk of bread to cut. He* [Abbahu] *said to him* [Zeira], *"Begin, bless."*

E.   *He* [Zeira] *said to him* [Abbahu], *"The host knows the value of his loaf."* [You should bless.]

F.   *When they had eaten, he* [Abbahu] *said to him* [Zeira], *"Let the elder bless."*

G.   *He said to him, "Rabbi, does the rabbi* [you] *know R. Huna, a great man, who would say, 'He who opens* [blesses first] *must close* [and say Grace after Meals]'?"

H.   *A Tannaitic teaching differs from R. Huna, as it has been taught:*

I.   The order of washing the hands in this: With up to five people present, they begin with the greatest. [If] more than this [are present], they begin with the least. In the middle of the meal, they begin with the eldest. After the meal they begin with the one who blesses.

J.   Is it not [done] so that he may prepare himself for the blessing? [So he did *not* bless at the beginning!

K.   *If you say* the one who opens is the one who closes, he is already prepared [having opened the meal].

L.   *R. Isaac said, "Explain it in regard to those who come in one by one and did not know which one had blessed* [at the outset]."

8:3. **The House of Shammai say, "He dries his hands on the napkin and puts it on the table."**

And the House of Hillel say, "On the cushion."

I.   A.   The Mishnah deals with either a table of marble [which is not susceptible to uncleanness] or a table that can be taken apart and is not susceptible to becoming unclean.

B.   *What is the reason of the House of Shammai?*

So that the liquids which are on the napkin may not become unclean from the cushion and go and render his hands unclean.

And what is the reason of the House of Hillel?

The condition of doubt[ful uncleanness] with respect to the hands is always regarded as clean.

Another reason: The [question of the cleanness of] hands does not apply to unconsecrated food [which in any case is not made unclean by unclean hands which are unclean in the second remove].

C.   *And according to the House of Shammai,* does [the question of the cleanness of] hands [indeed] apply to unconsecrated food?

D.   *You may interpret* [the tradition] either in accord with R. Simeon b. Eleazar or in accord with R. Eleazar b. R. Saddoq.

According to R. Simeon b. Eleazar, as it has been taught:

R. Simeon b. Eleazar says in the name of R. Meir, "Hands unclean in the first remove of uncleanness can affect [even] unconsecrated food, and in the second remove of uncleanness can affect [only] Heave-offering."

E.   Or according to R. Eleazar b. R. Saddoq, *as we have learned there:*

F.   Unconsecrated food which has been prepared along with consecrated [food] is like unconsecrated food [and subject to the same, less strict cleanness rules].

G.   R. Eleazar b. R. Saddoq says, "Lo, it is like Heave-offering, capable of becoming unclean from [something unclean in the] second remove of uncleanness and being rendered unfit from [something unclean in] still a further remove of uncleanness."

H.   *There we have learned:*

I.   He who anoints himself with a clean oil and is made unclean and goes down and bathes [in ritual pool] —

J.   The House of Shammai say, "Even though he drips [with oil], [the oil] is clean."

K.   And the House of Hillel say, "It is unclean [so long as there remains enough to anoint a small member]."

L.   And if the oil was unclean in the first place —

M.   The House of Shammai say, "[It remains unclean, even after he has immersed himself, so long as there remains] sufficient for anointing a small limb."

N.   And the House of Hillel say, "[So long as it remains] a dripping liquid."

O.   R. Judah says in the name of the House of Hillel, "So long as it is dripping so as to moisten something else."

P.   *The principle of the House of Hillel has been turned around.*

Q.   *There* [in the just-cited law] *they say it is* unclean. *And here* [in our Mishnah] *they say it is* clean.

R.   *There* it is present. *But here* it is absorbed in the napkin.

8:4. The House of Shammai say, "They clean the house and afterward wash the hands."   And the House of Hillel say, "They wash the hands and afterward clean the house."

I.   A.   *What is the reason of the House of Shammai?*

      B.   Because of the waste of food.

      C.   *And what is the reason of the House of Hillel?*

      D.   If the servant is clever, he removes the crumbs which are less than an olive's bulk, and they wash their hands and afterward they clean the house.

8:5. The House of Shammai say, "Light, and food, and spices, and *Havdalah.*"   And the House of Hillel say, "Light, and spices, and food, and *Havdalah.*"   The House of Shammai say, "'Who created the light of the fire.'"   And the House of Hillel say, "'Who creates the lights of the fire.'"

I.   A.   It was taught:

      B.   R. Judah said, "The House of Shammai and the House of Hillel did not differ concerning the [blessing for] the mean, that it comes at the beginning, or concerning *Havdalah,* that it comes at the end. And concerning what did they differ? Concerning the light and spices, for the House of Shammai say, 'Spices and light.' And the House of Hillel say, 'Light and spices.'"

      C.   R. Ba and R. Judah in the name of Rav [said], "The law is in accord with him who says, 'Spices and afterward light.' [That is, Judah's House of Shammai.]"

      D.   The House of Shammai say, "The cup [should be] in his right hand, and the sweet oil in his left hand. He says [the blessing for] the cup and afterward says the blessing for the sweet oil."

      E.   The House of Hillel say, "The sweet oil [should be] in his right hand and the cup in his left hand, and he says [the blessing for] the sweet oil and rubs it in the head of the servant. If the servant is a disciple of a sage, he rubs it on the wall, for it is not fitting for a disciple of a sage to go forth scented in public."

      F.   *Abba bar bar Hanna and R. Huna were sitting and eating, and R. Zeira was standing and serving them. He went and bore both of them* [oil and cup] *in one hand.*

      G.   *Abba bar bar Hanna said to him, "Is one of your hands cut off?" And his* [Abba's] *father was angry at him.*

      H.   *He* [the father] *said to him* [Abba], *"Is it not enough for you that you are sitting and he is standing and serving? And furthermore, he is a priest, and Samuel said,* 'He who makes [secular] use of the priesthood has committed sacrilege.' *You make light of him.*

I.   *"I decree for him to sit and you to stand and serve in his place."*

J.   How do we know that he who makes use of the priesthood has committed sacrilege?

K.   R. Aha in the name of Samuel said, "'And I said to them, You are holy to the Lord and the vessels are holy' [Ezra 8:28]. Just as one who makes use of the vessels commits sacrilege, so he who makes use of the priests commits sacrilege."

L.   [The House of Shammai say, "'Who created ...'"]

M.   According to the opinion of the House of Shammai, [one should say as the blessing for wine], "Who created the fruit of the vine" [instead of "who creates ...," as actually is said].

N.   According to the opinion of the House of Hillel, [one should say,] "Who creates the fruit of the vine" [as is indeed the case].

O.   [The Shammaite reply:]

P.   The wine is newly created every year, but the fire is not newly created every hour.

Q.   The fire and the mule, even though they were not created in the six days of creation, were thought of [entered the Creator's mind] in the six days of creation.

R.   Proof of the mule: "These are the sons of Zibeon: Aiah and Anah; he is the Anah who found the hot springs (HYYMYM) in the wilderness [as he pastured the asses of Zibeon his father (Genesis 36:24]."

S.   *What is the meaning of* hot springs (HYYMYM)?

T.   R. Judah b. Simeon says, "Mule." [Greek: *hemiovos.]*

U.   *And the rabbis say,* "Half-a-horse [Greek: *hemi-hippos]*, half was a horse, half an ass."

V.   And what are the marks [to know whether the father was a horse, the mother an ass, or vice versa]?

W.   R. Judah said, "If the ears are small, the mother was a horse and the father an ass. If they are big, the mother was an ass and the father a horse."

X.   *R. Mana instructed the members of the Patriarchate, "If you want to buy a mule, buy those whose ears are small,* for the mother was a horse and the father an ass."

Y.   What did Zibeon and Anah do? They brought a female ass and mated her with a male horse, and they produced a mule.

Z.   The Holy One, blessed be He, said to them, "You have brought into the world something which is destructive. So I too shall bring upon that man [you] something which is destructive."

AA.   What did the Holy One, blessed be He, do?

BB.   He brought a snake and mated it with a lizard and it produced a *havarbar*-lizard.

CC.   A man should never say to you that a *havarbar*-lizard bit him and he lived, or a mad dog nipped him and he lived, or a she-mule butted him and he lived. We speak only of a white she-mule.

DD.   As to the fire:

EE.   R. Levi in the name of R. Nezira [said], "Thirty-six hours that light which was created on the first day served [the world]. Twelve on the eve of the Sabbath [Friday], twelve on the night of the Sabbath, and twelve on the Sabbath.

FF. "And the First Man [Adam] looked at it from one end of the world to the other. When the light did not cease [from shining], the whole world began to sing, as it is said, 'Under the whole heaven, he lets [his voice] go, and his light to the corners of the earth' [Job 37:3].

GG. "When the Sabbath ended, it began to get dark. Man became frightened, saying, 'This is the one concerning whom it is written,"He will bruise your head, and you shall bruise his heel" [Genesis 3:15].

HH. "'Perhaps this one has come to bite me.' And he said, 'Let only darkness cover me'" [Psalm 139:11].

II. R. Levi said, "At that moment the Holy One, blessed be He, prepared two flints and struck them against each other, and the light came forth from them. This is the meaning of that which Scripture says, 'And the night around me be light' [Psalm 139:11].

JJ. "And he [man] blessed it, 'Who creates the lights of the fire.'"

KK. Samuel said, "Therefore they bless the fire at the end of the Sabbath, for that is when it was first created."

LL. R. Huna in the name of R. Abbahu in the name of R. Yohanan [said], "Also at the end of the Day of Atonement one blesses it, for the light has rested that entire day."

8:6. They do not bless the light or spices of gentiles, nor the light or spices of the dead, nor the light or spices which are before an idol. They do not bless the light until they make use of its illumination.

I. A. R. Jacob taught before R. Jeremiah, "They do bless the spices of gentiles."

B. *What is the difference* [between this view and the Mishnah's]?

C. *We explain that the latter refers to the* gentile's deeds before his own store [while the Mishnah refers to a banquet].

D. Even though it has not gone out [but burned the entire Sabbath], they may bless [the light of] a lantern [because no prohibited work has been done by its light].

E. As regards a flame in the folds of one's garment, in a lamp, or in a mirror, if one sees the flame but does not make use of its light, or makes use of its light but not see the flame, one may not bless it. [One may bless] only when one may see the flame and makes use of the light.

F. Five things were said in regard to the burning coal, and five with regard to the flame.

1. A coal of the sanctuary is subject to the law of sacrilege, but a flame is neither used for pleasure nor subject to the law of sacrilege.

2. A burning coal used for idolatry is prohibited, but a flame is permitted.

3. He who vows not to have enjoyment from his fellow may not use his burning coal, but may use his flame.

4. He who brings a coal out to the public way [on the Sabbath] is liable, but if he brings a flame, he is not liable.

5. They bless the flame, but not the burning coal.

G.   R. Hiyya bar Ashi in the name of Rav said, "If the coals were glowing, they may bless them."

H.   R. Yohanan of Kerasion in the name of R. Nahum bar Simai [said], "On condition that it was cut off." [That is, the flame was shooting up from the coal.]

I.   *It was taught:*

J.   Now the [light of] a gentile who kindled [a light from the flame of] an Israelite, and an Israelite who kindled [a light from the flame of a gentile] — *this poses no problems.*

K.   But [the light of] a gentile who kindled [a light from the flame of] an Israelite [may be blessed]. If so, even [the flame of] a gentile who kindled from a gentile [should be allowed].

L.   *It is indeed taught:* They do *not* bless [a light kindled by] a gentile from a gentile.

M.   R. Abbahu in the name of R. Yohanan [said,] "As to an alleyway which is populated entirely by gentiles with a single Israelite living in its midst — if the light comes from there, they may bless it on account of that one Israelite who lives there."

N.   R. Abbahu in the name of R. Yohanan [said], "They do not bless either the spices on Sabbath evenings in Tiberias or the spices on Saturday nights in Sepphoris, or the light or the spices on Friday mornings in Sepphoris, for these all are prepared only for another purpose [cleaning clothes]."

O.   **Nor over the light or spices of the dead.**

P.   R. Hezekiah and R. Jacob b. Aha in the name of R. Yose b. R. Hanina [said], "This refers to the following case: 'When they are placed over the bed of the dead. But if they are placed before the bed of the dead, they may be blessed [that is, a blessing may be recited over them].'"

Q.   "[For] I say, they are prepared for the purposes of the living."

R.   **Nor the light nor the spices of idolatry.**

S.   But is not that of gentiles the same as that of idolatry? [Why repeat the same rule?]

T.   Interpret it as applying to an Israelite idol.

They do not bless the light until they make use of its illumination.

I.   A.   R. Zeira, son of R. Abbahu expounded, "'And God saw the light, that it was good' [Genesis 1:4]. And afterward,'And God divided the light from the darkness'" [Genesis 1:5]. [That is, first it was seen and used, then comes the *Havdalah.]*

B.   R. Berekiah said, "Thus the two great men of the world [age], R. Yohanan and R. Simeon b. Laqish, expounded: 'And God divided — a certain division.'" [That is, he did so literally.]

C.   R. Judah b. R. Simon said, "They divided for Him."

D.   And the rabbis say, "They divided for the righteous who were destined to come into the world.

E.   "They drew a parable: To what is the matter to be likened? To a king who has two generals. This one says, 'I shall serve by day,' and this one says, 'I shall serve by night.'

F.   "He calls the first and says to him, 'So-and-so, the day will be your division.'

G. "He calls the second and says to him, 'So-and-so, the night will be your division.'

H. "That is the meaning of what is written, 'And God called the light day, and the darkness he called night.'

I. "To the light he said, 'The day will be your province.' And to the darkness he said, 'The night will be your province.'"

J. R. Yohanan said, "This is what the Holy One, blessed be He, said to Job [Job 38:12], 'Have you commanded the morning since your days began, and caused the dawn to know its place?'

K. "What is the place of the light of the six days of creation — where was it hidden?"

L. R. Tanhuma said, "I give the reason: 'Who creates light and makes darkness, and makes peace' [Isaiah 45:7]. When he went forth, he made peace between them."

M. **They do not bless the light until they make use of its illumination.**

N. Rav said, "They use [spelled with an 'alef]."

O. And Samuel said, "They enjoy [spelled with an 'ayin]."

P. He who said "they use" [may draw support from the following]:

Q. "Only on this condition will we consent to you" [Genesis 34:15].

R. He who said "enjoy" [may draw support from the following:

S. "How to sustain with a word him that is weary" [Isaiah 50:4].

T. There we have learned: "How do they extend (M'BR) the Sabbath limits of cities?"

U. Rav said, "Add" ['alef].

V. And Samuel said, "Increase" ['ayin].

W. He who said it is with an 'alef means they add a limb to it.

X. He who said it with an 'ayin means it is [increased] like a pregnant woman.

Y. There we learned, "Before the festivals ('YD) of gentiles."

Z. Rav said, "Testimonies" ['ayin].

AA. And Samuel said, "Festivals" ['alef].

BB. He who said it is with an 'alef [may cite this verse], "For near is the day of their calamity ['YD]" [Deuteronomy 32:35].

CC. He who said it is with an 'ayin [may cite], "Their testimonies neither see nor know, they they may be put to shame" [Isaiah 44:9].

DD. How does Samuel deal with the reason of Rav? [He may say,] "And their testimonies are destined to shame those who keep them on the day of judgment."

EE. **They do not bless the light until they have made use of its illumination.** [How much illumination must there be?]

FF. R. Judah in the name of Samuel said, "So that women may spin by its light."

GG. R. Yohanan said, "So that one's eye can see what is in the cup and what is in the saucer."

HH. R. Hanina said, "So that one may know how to distinguish one coin from another."

II. R. Oshaia taught, "Even [if the flame is in] a hall ten-by-ten, they may say the blessing."

JJ. *R. Zeira drew near the lamp. His disciples said to him, "Rabbi, why do you rule so stringently for us? Lo, R. Oshaia taught, "One may bless even in a hall ten-by-ten."*

8:7 **He who ate and forgot and did not bless —**

The House of Shammai say, "He should go back to his place and bless."

And the House of Hillel say, "He may bless in the place in which he remembered."

"Until when may he say the blessing? Until the food has been digested in his bowels."

I. A. *R. Yusta b. Shunam said,* "[There are] *two authorities. One gives the reason of the House of Shammai and the other the reason of the House of Hillel."*

B. *"The one who gives the reason of the House of Shammai* [says], 'If he had forgotten a purse of precious stones and pearls there, would he not go back and take his purse? *So too* let him go back to his place and bless.'

C. *"The one who gave the reason of the House of Hillel* [states], 'If he were a worker on the top of the palm or down in a pit, would you trouble him to go back to his place and bless? *But he should bless in the place where he remembers* [to do so]. *Here too* let him bless in the place where he remembers.'"

D. **Until when does he recite the blessing?**

E. R. Hiyya in the name of Samuel says, "Until the food has been digested in his bowels."

F. And the sages say, "So long as he is thirsty on account of that meal."

G. R. Yohanan says, "Until he becomes hungry again."

8:8. **If wine came to them after the food, and there is there only one cup —**

The House of Shammai say, "He blesses the wine and afterward blesses the food."

And the House of Hillel say, "He blesses the food and afterward blesses the wine."

They answer *Amen* after an Israelite who blesses, and they do not answer *Amen* after a Samaritan who blesses until the entire blessing has been heard.

I. A. R. Ba said, "Because it is a brief blessing, he may forget and drink the wine. But because it is joined to the [blessings for] cup, he will not forget."

B. **After an Israelite they answer *Amen*,** even though he has not heard [the Grace]. Has it not been taught, "If he heard [the Grace] and did not answer, he has carried out his obligation [to say Grace]. If he answered *[Amen]* and did not hear [the Grace], he has not carried out his obligation."

C. Hiyya the son of Rav said, "The Mishnah speaks of him who] did not eat with them as much as an olive's bulk."

D. *So too it has been taught:* If he heard and did not answer, he has carried out his obligation. If he answered and did not hear, he has not carried out his obligation.

E. Rav in the name of Abba bar Hanna [said], *and some say Abba bar Hanna in the name of Rav* [said], "And this applies to a case in which he answered at the chapter [paragraph] headings."

F. *R. Zeira asked, "What are these chapter headings?"*

G. "Praise the Lord, praise the servants of the Lord, praise the name of the Lord" [Psalm 113:1].

H. *They asked before R. Hiyya b. Abba, "How do we know that, if one heard and did not answer [Amen], he has carried out his obligation?"*

I. *He said, "From what we have seen the great rabbis doing, so they do in public, for they say this:* 'Blessed is he that comes.' *And the others say,* 'In the name of the Lord.' *And both groups thus complete their obligation."*

J. R. Oshaia taught, "A man responds *Amen*, even though he has not eaten, and he does not say, 'Let us bless him of whose bounty we have eaten,' unless he actually ate."

K. *It has been taught,* They do not respond with an orphaned *Amen*, a cut-off *Amen*, or a hasty *Amen*.

L. Ben Azzai says, "If one answers an orphaned *Amen*, his sons will be orphans. A cut-off one — his years will be cut off. A hasty one — his soul will be cut down. A long one — his days and years will be lengthened with goodness."

M. What is an orphaned *Amen?*

N. R. Huna said, *"This refers to a person who sat down to bless,* and he answered, but did not know to what [prayer] he answered *[Amen]."*

O. It was taught: If a gentile who blessed the divine name, they answer *Amen* after him.

P. R. Tanhum said, "If a gentile blesses you, answer after him *Amen, as it is written,* 'Blessed will you be by all the peoples'" [Deuteronomy 7:14].

Q. A gentile met R. Ishmael and blessed him. He said to him, *"You have already been answered."*

R. *Another met him* and cursed him. He said to him, *"You have already been answered."*

S. His disciple said to him, *"Rabbi, how could you say the same to both?"* He said to them, "Thus it is written in Scripture: 'Those that curse you will be cursed, and those that bless you will be blessed'" [Genesis 27:29].

V. BAVLI

I

THE HOUSES' DISPUTES

[51b] *Gemara: Our rabbis have taught:*

The things which are between the House of Shammai and the House of Hillel in [regard to] a meal:

The House of Shammai say, "One blesses over the day and afterward blesses over the wine, for the day causes the wine to come, and the day has already been sanctified, while the wine has not yet come."

And the House of Hillel say, "He blesses over the wine and afterward blesses over the day, for the wine causes the Sanctification to be said.

"Another matter: The blessing over the wine is perpetual, and the blessing over the day is not perpetual.   Between that which is perpetual and that which is not perpetual, that which is perpetual takes precedence."

And the law is in accordance with the words of the House of Hillel.

What is the purpose of "another matter"?

If you should say that there [in regard to the opinion of the House of Shammai] *two* [reasons are given] *and here* [in regard to the opinion of the House of Hillel] *one, here too* [in respect to the House of Hillel], *there are two* [reasons, the second being]: "The blessing of the wine is perpetual and the blessing of the day is not perpetual. That which is perpetual takes precedence over that which is not perpetual."

And the law is in accord with the opinion of the House of Hillel.

This is obvious [that the law is in accord with the House of Hillel], *for the echo has gone forth* [and pronounced from heaven the decision that the law follows the opinion of the House of Hillel].

If you like, I can argue that [this was stated] before the echo.

And if you like, I can argue that it was after the echo, and [the passage is formulated in accord with the [opinion of [52a] R. Joshua, who stated, "They do not pay attention to an echo [from heaven]."

And is it the reasoning of the House of Shammai that the blessing of the day is more important?

But has a Tanna not taught: "He who enters his house at the close of the Sabbath blesses over the wine and the light and the spices and afterward he says *Havdalah.* And if he has only one cup, he leaves it for after the food and then says the other blessings in order after it." [*Havdalah* is the blessing of the day, yet comes last!]

But lo, on what account [do you say] *this is the view of the House of Shammai? Perhaps it is the House of Hillel*['s opinion]?

Let [such a thought] *not enter your mind, for the Tanna teaches:* "Light and afterward spices." *And of whom have you heard who holds this opinion?* The House of Shammai, *as a Tanna has taught:*

R. Judah said, "The House of Shammai and the House of Hillel did not differ concerning the [blessing of the] food, that it is at first, and the *Havdalah,* that it is at the end.

"Concerning what did they dispute? Concerning the light and the spices.

"For the House of Shammai say, 'Light and afterward spices.'

"And the House of Hillel say, 'Spices and afterward the light.'"

And on what account [do you suppose that] *it is the House of Shammai as* [interpreted by] *R. Judah? Perhaps it is [a teaching in accord with] the House of Hillel* [as interpreted by] *R. Meir?*

Do not let such a thing enter your mind, for lo, a Tanna teaches here in our Mishnah: House of Shammai say, "Light and food and spices and *Havdalah.*"

And the House of Hillel say, "Light and spices, food and *Havdalah.*"

But there, in the "baraita," *lo he has taught:* "If he has only one cup, he leaves it for after the food and then says the other blessings in order after it."

From this it is to be inferred that it is the House of Shammai's teaching, according to the [interpretation] *of R. Judah.*

In any event there is a problem [for the House of Shammai now give precedence to reciting a blessing for the wine over blessing the day].

The House of Shammai suppose that the coming of the holy day is to be distinguished from its leaving. As to the coming of the [holy] *day, the earlier one may bring it in, the better. As to the leaving of the festival day, the later one may take leave of it, the better, so that it should not seem to us as a burden.*

And do the House of Shammai hold the opinion that Grace requires a cup [of wine]? *And lo, we have learned:* [If] wine came to them after the food, and there is there only that cup, the House of Shammai say, "He blesses over the wine and afterward blesses over the food." [So Grace is said *without* the cup.]

Does this not mean that he blesses it and drinks [it]?

No. He blesses it and leaves it.

But has not a master said, "He that blesses must [also] taste [it]."

He does taste it.

And has not a master said, "Tasting it is spoiling it."

He tastes it with his hand [finger].

And has not a master said, "The cup of blessing requires a [fixed] measure."

And lo, he diminishes it from its fixed measure.

[We speak of a situation in which] *he has more than the fixed measure.*

But lo, has it not been taught: If there is there *only* that cup ... [so he has not more].

There is not enough for two, but more than enough for one.

And has not R. Hiyya taught: House of Shammai say, "He blesses over the wine and drinks it, and afterward he says Grace."

Then we have two Tannas' [traditions] in respect to the opinion of the House of Shammai.

The House of Shammai say, ["They wash the hands and afterward mix the cup]...

Our Rabbis have taught:

The House of Shammai say, "They wash the hands and afterwards mix the cup, for if you say they mix the cup first, [against this view is] a [precautionary] decree to prevent the liquids on the outer sides of the cup, which are unclean by reason of his hands' [touching them], from going back and making the cup unclean."

But will not the hands make the cup itself unclean [without reference to the liquids]?

The hands are in the second remove of uncleanness, and the [object unclean in] the second remove of uncleanness cannot [then] render [another object unclean] in the third [remove] in respect to profane foods, [but only to Heave-offering]. But [this happens] only by means of liquids [unclean in the first remove].

And the House of Hillel say, "They mix the cup and afterward wash the hands, for if you say they wash the hands first, [against this view is] a [precautionary] decree lest the liquids which are [already] on the hands become unclean on account of the cup and go and render the hands unclean."

But will not the cup [itself] *make the hands unclean?*

A vessel cannot render a man unclean.

But will they [the hands] *not render the liquids which are in it* [the cup] *unclean?*

Here we are dealing with a vessel the outer part of which has been made unclean by liquid. The inner part is clean but the outer part is unclean. *Thus we have learned:*

[If] a vessel is made unclean on the outside by liquid, the outside is unclean, [52b] but its inside and its rim, handle, and haft are clean. If, however, the inside is unclean, the whole [cup] is unclean.

What, then, do they [the Houses] *dispute?*

The House of Shammai hold that it is prohibited to make use of a vessel whose outer parts are unclean by liquids, as a decree on account of the drippings. [There is] *no* [reason] *to decree* lest the liquids on the hands be made unclean by the cup.

And the House of Hillel reckon that it is permitted to make use of a vessel whose outer part is made unclean by liquids, *for drippings are unusual. But there is reason to take care* lest the liquids which are on the hands may be made unclean by the cup.

Another matter: [So that] immediately upon the washing of the hands [may come] the meal [itself].

What is the reason for this additional explanation?

This is what the House of Hillel said to the House of Shammai: "According to your reasoning, in saying that it is prohibited to make use of a cup whose outer parts are unclean, *we decree on account of the drippings. But even so,* [our opinion] *is better, for* immediately upon the washing of the hands [should come] the meal."

The House of Shammai say, "He dries his hand on the napkin..."

Our rabbis have taught:

The House of Shammai say, "He wipes his hands with the napkin and lays it on the table, for if you say, 'on the cushion,' [that view is wrong, for it is a precautionary] decree lest the liquids which are on the napkin become unclean on account of the cushion and go back and render the hands unclean."

And will not the cushion [itself] *render the napkin unclean?*

A vessel cannot make a vessel unclean.

And will not the cushion [itself] *make the man unclean?*

A vessel cannot make a man unclean.

And the House of Hillel say,"'On the cushion,' for if you say, 'on the table,' [that opinion is wrong, for it is a] decree lest the liquids become unclean on account of the table and go and render the food unclean."

But will not the table render the food which is on it unclean?

We here deal with a table which is unclean in the second remove, and something unclean in the second remove does not render something unclean in the third remove in respect to unconsecrated food, except by means of liquids [which are always unclean in the first remove].

What [principle] *do they dispute?*

The House of Shammai reckon that it is prohibited to make use of a table unclean in the second remove, as a decree on account of those who eat Heave-offering [which is rendered unfit by an object unclean in the second remove].

And the House of Hillel reckon that it is permitted to make use of table unclean in the second remove, for those who eat Heave-offering [the priests] are careful.

Another matter: There is no Scriptural requirement to wash the hands before eating unconsecrated food.

What is the purpose of "another explanation"?

This is what the House of Hillel said to the House of Shammai: If you ask what is the difference in respect to food, concerning which we take care, and in respect to the hands, concerning which we do not take care — even in this regard [our opinion] *is preferable,* for there is no Scriptural requirement concerning the washing of the hands before eating unconsecrated food.

It is better that the hands should be made unclean, *for there is no Scriptural basis for* [washing] *them, and let not the food be made unclean, concerning which there is a Scriptural basis* [for concern about its uncleanness].

The House of Shammai say, "They clean house and afterward wash the hands ..."

Our rabbis have taught:

The House of Shammai say, "They clean the house and afterward wash the hands, for if you say, 'They wash the hands first,' it turns out that you spoil the food."

But the House of Shammai do not reckon that one washes the hands first.

What is the reason?

On account of the crumbs.

And the House of Hillel say, "If the servant is a disciple of a sage, he takes the crumbs which are as large a an olive [in bulk] and leaves the crumbs which are not so much as an olive [in bulk]."

(This view supports the opinion of R. Yohanan, for R. Yohanan said, "Crumbs which are not an olive in bulk may be deliberately destroyed.")

In what do they differ?

The House of Hillel reckon that it is prohibited to employ a servant who is an ignorant man, *and the House of Shammai reckon that* it is permitted to employ a servant who is an ignorant man.

R. Yosé bar Hanina said in the name of R. Huna, "In our entire chapter the law is in accord with the House of Hillel, excepting this matter, in which the law is in accord with the House of Shammai."

And R. Oshaia taught the matter contrariwise. And in this matter too the law is in accord with the House of Hillel.

The House of Shammai say, "Light and food ..."

R. Huna bar Judah happened by the house of Rava. He saw that Rava blessed the spices first.

He said to him, "Now the House of Shammai and the House of Hillel did not dispute concerning the light, [it should come first].

"For it was taught: The House of Shammai say, 'Light, and food, spices, and *Havdalah,'* and the House of Hillel say, 'Light, and spices, and food, and *Havdalah.'*

Rava answered him, "This is the opinion [=version] *of R. Meir, but R. Judah says,* 'The House of Shammai and the House of Hillel did not differ concerning the food, that it comes first, and concerning the *Havdalah,* that it is at the end.

"'Concerning what did they differ?"

"'Concerning the light and the spices.'

"For the House of Shammai say, 'The light and afterward the spices.'

"And the House of Hillel say, 'The spices and afterward the light.'"

And R. Yohanan said, "The people were accustomed to act in accord with the House of Hillel *as presented by* R. Judah."

The House of Shammai say, "Who created ..."

Rava said, *"Concerning the word* 'bara' [created] *everyone agrees that* 'bara' *implies* [the past tense]. *They differ concerning* 'boré' [creates]. *The House of Shammai reckon that* 'boré' *means, 'Who will create in the future.'* And the House of Hillel reckon that 'boré' also means what was created* [in the past]."

R. Joseph objected, "'Who forms light and creates darkness' [Isaiah 45:7], 'Creates mountains and forms the wind' [Amos 4:13], "Who creates the heavens and spreads them out'" [Isaiah 42:5].

"But," R. Joseph said, *"Concerning* 'bara' *and* 'boré' *everyone agrees that* [the words] *refer to the past. They differ as to whether one should say 'light' or 'lights.'*

"The House of Shammai reckon there is one light in the fire.

"And the House of Hillel reckon that there are many lights in the fire."

We have a Tannaitic teaching along the same lines:

The House of Hillel said to the House of Shammai, "There are many illuminations in the light."

II
THE LIGHT AND THE SPICES

A blessing is not said ...

Certainly, [in the case of] *the light* [of idolators, one should not say a blessing] *because it did not rest on the Sabbath. But what is the reason that for spices* [one may not say the blessing]?

R. Judah said in the name of Rav, *"We here deal with a banquet held by idolators,* because the run-of-the-mill banquet held by idolators is for the sake of idolatry."

But since it has been taught at the end of the clause, "Or over the light or spices of idolatry," *we must infer that the beginning of the clause does not deal with idolatry.*

R. Hanina from Sura said, "What is the reason is what it explains, namely, what is the reason that they do not bless the light or spices of idolators? Because the run-of-the-mill banquet held by idolators is for the sake of idolatry."

Our rabbis have taught:
One may bless a light which has rested on the Sabbath, but one may not bless a light which has not rested on the Sabbath.

And what is the meaning of "which has not rested on the Sabbath"?

[53a] *Shall we say* it has not rested on the Sabbath on account of the work [which has been done with it, including] even work which is permitted?

And has it not been taught: They do bless the light [kindled on the Sabbath for] a woman in confinement or a sick person.

R. Nahman bar Isaac said, *"What is the meaning of* 'which enjoyed Sabbath-rest'? Which enjoyed Sabbath-rest on account of work, the doing of which is a transgression [on the Sabbath]."

We have learned likewise in a baraita:
They may bless a lamp which has been burning throughout the day to the conclusion of the Sabbath.

Our rabbis have taught:
They bless [a light] kindled by a gentile from an Israelite, or by an Israelite from a gentile, but they do not bless [a light] kindled by a gentile from a gentile.

What is the reason one does not do so [from a light kindled by] a gentile from a gentile?

Because it did not enjoy Sabbath-rest.

If so, lo, [a light kindled by] *an Israelite from a gentile also has not enjoyed Sabbath-rest.*

And if you say this prohibited [light] *has vanished, and the one* [in hand] *is another and was born in the hand of the Israelite,* [how will you deal] *with this teaching?*

He who brings out a flame to the public way [on the Sabbath] is liable [for violating the Sabbath rule against carrying from private to public property].

Now why should he be liable? What he raised up he did not put down, and what he put down he did not raise up.

But [we must conclude] *that the prohibited* [flame], *is present, but when he blesses, it is over the additional* [flame], *which is permitted, that he blesses.*

If so, a gentile['s flame kindled] *from a gentile*['s flame] *also* [should be permitted].

That is true, but [it is prohibited by] *decree, on account of the original gentile and the original flame* [of light kindled on the Sabbath by the gentile].

Our rabbis have taught:
[If] one was walking outside of the village and saw a light, if the majority [of the inhabitants of the village] are gentiles, he does not bless it. If the majority are Israelites, he blesses it.

Lo, the statement is self-contradictory. You have said, "If the majority are gentiles, he does not bless it." *Then if they were evenly divided, he may bless it.*

But then it teaches, "If the majority are Israelites, he may bless." *Then if they are evenly divided, he may not bless it.*

Strictly speaking, even if they are evenly divided, he may bless. But since in the opening clause [the language is], "The majority are gentiles," *in the concluding clause,* [the same language is used:] "A majority are Israelites."

Our rabbis have taught:
[If] a man was walking outside of a village and saw a child with a torch in his hand, he makes inquiries about him. If he is an Israelite, he may bless [the light]. If he is a gentile, he may not bless.
Why do we speak of a child? Even an adult also [would be subject to the same rule].
Rav Judah said in the name of Rav, "In this case we are dealing with [a time] *near sunset. As to a gentile, it will be perfectly clear that he certainly is a gentile* [for an Israelite would not use the light immediately after sunset]. *If it is a child, I might say it is an Israelite child who happened to take up* [the torch]."

Our rabbis have taught:
[If] one was walking outside of a village and saw a light, if it was as thick as the opening of a furnace, he may bless it, and if not, he may not bless it.
One Tanna [authority] [says], "They may bless the light of a furnace," *and another Tanna* [says], "They may not bless it."
There is no difficulty. The first speaks at the beginning [of the fire], *the other at the end.*
One authority says, "They may bless the light of an oven or a stove, " *and another authority says,* "They may not bless it."
There is no problem. The former speaks of the beginning, the latter of the end.
One authority says, "They may bless the light of the synagogue and the schoolhouse," *and another authority says,* "They may not bless it."
There is no problem. The former speaks [of a case in which] an important man *is present, the latter* [of a case in which] an important man *is not present.*
And if you want, I shall explain both teachings as applying to a case in which an important man *is present. There still is not difficulty. The former* [teaching speaks of a case in which] *there is a beadle* [who eats in the synagogue], *the latter in which there is none.*
And if you want, I shall explain both teachings as applying to a case in which a beadle *is present. There still is no difficulty. The former teaching* [speaks of a case in which] *there is moonlight, the latter in which there is no moonlight.*

Our rabbis have taught:
[If] they were sitting in the schoolhouse, and light was brought before them—
The House of Shammai say, "Each one blesses for himself."
And the House of Hillel say, "One blesses for all of them, as it is said, 'In the multitude of people is the King's glory'" [Proverbs 14:28].
Certainly [we can understand the position of the House of Hillel because] *the House of Hillel explain their reason.*
But what is the reason of the House of Shammai?

They reckon [it as they do] *on account of* [avoiding] *interruption in* [Torah study] *in the schoolhouse.*

We have a further Tannaitic tradition to the same effect:

The members of the house of Rabban Gamaliel did not say [the blessing] "Good health" [after a sneeze] in the schoolhouse on account of the interruption [of study] in the schoolhouse.

They say a blessing neither on the light nor on the spices of the dead ...

What is the reason?

The light is made for the honor [of the deceased], *the spices to remove the bad smell.*

Rav Judah in the name of Rav said, ["Light made for] whoever [is of such importance that] they take out [a light] before him both by day and by night is not blessed. [and light made for] whoever [is not important, so that] they take out [a light] before him only by night, is blessed."

R. Huna said, "They do not bless spices of the privy and oil made to remove the grease."

Does this saying imply that wherever [spice] *is not used for smell, they do not bless over it? It may be objected:*

He who enters the stall of a spice dealer and smells the odor, even though he sat there all day long, blesses only one time. He who enters and goes out repeatedly blesses each time.

And lo, here is a case in which it is not used for the scent, and still he blesses.

Yes, but it also is used for the odor — so that people will smell and come and purchase it.

Our rabbis have taught:

If one is walking outside of a village and smelled a scent, if most of the inhabitants are idolators, he does not bless it. If most are Israelites, he blesses it.

R. Yose says, "Even if most are Israelites, he *still* may not bless, because Israelite women use incense for witchcraft."

But do they "all" burn incense for witchcraft!

A small part is for witchcraft, and a small part is also for scenting garments, which yields a larger part not used for scent, and wherever the majority [of the incense] *is not used for scent, one does not bless it.*

R. Hiyya bar Abba said in the name of R. Yohanan, "He who walks on the eve of the Sabbath in Tiberias and at the end of the Sabbath in Sepphoris and smells an odor does not bless it, because it is presumed to have been made only to perfume garments."

Our rabbis taught: If one was walking in the gentiles' market and was pleased to scent the spices, he is a sinner.

III
USING THE LIGHT

[53b] **They do not recite a blessing over the light until it has been used ...**

Rav Judah said in the name of Rav, "Not that he has actually used it, but if anyone stood near enough so that he might use the light, even at some distance, [he may say the blessing]."

So too R. Ashi said, "We have learned this teaching even [concerning] those at some distance."

It was objected [on the basis of the following teaching]: If one had a light hidden in the folds of his cloak or in a lamp, or saw the flame but did not make use of its light, or made use of the light but did not [actually] see the flame, he may not say the blessing. [He may say the blessing only when] he [both] sees the flame and uses its light.

Certainly one finds cases in which one may use the light and not see the flame. *This may be when the light is in a corner.*

But where do you find a case in which one may see the flame and not make use of its light? *It is not when he is at a distance?*

No, it is when the flame keeps on flickering.

Our rabbis have taught:
They may say a blessing over glowing coals, but not over dying coals (*'omemot*).

What is meant by glowing coals?

R. Hisda said, "If one puts a chip into them and it kindles on its own, [these are] all [glowing coals]."

It was asked: Is the word 'omemot ['alef] *or* 'omemot ['ayin]?

Come and hear, for R. Hisda b. Abdimi said, "'The cedars in the garden of God could not darken [*'amamuhu*] it'" [Ezekiel 31:8].

And Rava said, "He must make actual use of it."

And how [near must one be]?

Ulla said, "So that he may make out the difference between an *issar* and a *pundion* [two small coins]."

Hezekiah said, "So that he may make out the difference between a *meluzma* [a weight] of Tiberias and one of Sepphoris."

Rav Judah would say the blessing [for the light of the] *house of Adda the waiter* [which as nearby].

Rava would say the blessing [for the light of the] *house of Guria bar Hama.*

Abbaye would say the blessing [for the light of the] *house of Bar Abbahu.*

R. Judah said in the name of Rav, "They do not go looking for the light in the way they go looking for [means to carry out other] commandments."

R. Zera said, "At the outset, I used to go looking [for light]. Now that I have heard this teaching of R. Judah in the name of Rav, I too will not go searching, but if one comes my way, I shall say the blessing over it."

IV
FORGETTING GRACE, AMEN.

He who ate [and did not say Grace] ...

R. Zevid, and some say R. Dimi bar Abba, said, "The dispute [between the Houses] applies to a case of forgetfulness, but in a case in which a person deliberately [omitted Grace], all agree that he should return to his place and say the blessing."

This is perfectly obvious. It is [explicitly] *taught,* "And he forgot."

What might you have said? That is the rule even where it was intentional, but the reason that the Tanna taught, "And he forgot," *is to tell you how far the House of Shammai were willing to go* [in requiring the man to go back to where he ate. They did so even if a man accidentally forgot.] *Thus we are taught* [the contrary. Even if one forgot, unintentionally, he must go back].

It was taught:

The House of Hillel said to the House of Shammai, "According to your opinion, someone who ate on the top of the Temple Mount and forgot and went down without saying Grace should go back to the top of the Mount and say the blessing."

The House of Shammai said to the House of Hillel, "According to your opinion, someone who forgot a purse on the top of the Temple Mount would not go back and retrieve it.

"For his own sake, he [assuredly] will go back. For the sake of Heaven [should he] not all the more so [go back]?"

There were these two disciples. One did it [forgot Grace] *accidentally, and, following the rule of the House of Shammai,* [went back to bless], *and found a purse of gold. And one did it deliberately* [omitted Grace], *and following the rule of the House of Hillel* [did not go back to say it], *and a lion ate him.*

Rabbah bar bar Hanna was traveling in a caravan. He ate and was sated but [forgot and] *did not say Grace.*

He said, "What shall I do? If I tell the men [of the caravan with me] *that I forgot to bless, they will say to me, 'Bless here. Wherever you say the blessing, you are saying the blessing to the Merciful* [God].' *It is better that I tell them I have forgotten a golden dove."*

So he said to them, "Wait for me, for I have forgotten a golden dove."

He went back and blessed and found a golden dove.

And why was a dove so important?

Because the community of Israel is compared to a dove, as it is written, "The wings of the dove are covered with silver, and her pinions with the shimmer of gold" [Psalm 68:14]. Just as the dove is saved only by her wings, so Israel is saved only by the commandments.

Until when can he say the Grace? Until the food is digested in his bowels ...

How long does it take to digest the food?

R. Yohanan said, "As long as one is no longer hungry."

Resh Laqish said, "As long as one [still] is thirsty on account of his meal."

R. Yemar bar Shelamia said to Mar Zutra — and some say, Rav Yemar bar Shizbi said to Mar Zutra — "Did Resh Laqish really say this? And did not R. Ammi say in the name of Resh Laqish, 'How long does it take to digest a meal? The time it takes to go four miles.'"

There is no problem: Here [we speak of] a big meal, there [we speak of] a small meal.

If wine came to them ...

This implies that in the case of an Israelite['s saying Grace], *even though one has not heard the entire blessing, he responds [Amen].*

But if he has not heard [the whole Grace], *how can he have performed his duty by doing so* [assuming he has eaten also? For he has to hear the entire Grace to carry out his obligation to say Grace.]

Hiyya bar Rav said, "[We speak of a case] in which he did not eat with them."

So too did R. Nahman say in the name of Rabbah bar Abbahu, "[We speak of a case] in which he did not eat with them."

Rav said to Hiyya his son, "My son, seize [the cup] and bless."

So did R. Huna say to Rabbah his son, "Seize and bless."

This implies that he who says the blessing is better than he who answers Amen. *But has it not been taught:*

R. Yosé says, "The one who answers *Amen* is greater than the one who says the blessing."

R. Nehorai said to him, "By heaven! It is so. You should know it, for behold, common soldiers go ahead and open the battle, but the heroes go in and win it."

It is a matter of dispute between Tannaim, as it has been taught:

Both the one who says the blessing and the one who answers *Amen* are implied [in the Scripture (Nehemiah 9:5)]. But the one who says the blessing is more quickly [answered] than he who answers *Amen*.

Samuel asked Rav, "Should one answer *[Amen]* after [the blessings of] children in the schoolhouse?"

He said to him, "They answer *Amen* after everyone except children in the schoolhouse, since they are [saying blessings solely] for the sake of learning."

And this applies when it is not the time for them to say the "Haftarah," *but in the time to say* "Haftarah," *they do respond [Amen].*

Our rabbis have taught:

"The absence of oil holds up the blessing [Grace]," the words of Rabbi Zilai.

R. Zivai says, "It does not hold it up."

R. Aha says, "[The absence of] good oil holds it up."

R. Zuhamai says, "Just as a dirty person *[mezuham]* is unfit for the Temple service, so dirty hands are unfit for the blessing."

R. Nahman Bar Isaac said, "I know neither Zilai nor Zivai nor Zuhamai. But I know a teaching which R. Judah said in the name of Rav, and some say it was taught as a 'baraita':

"'And be you holy' [Leviticus 20:7] — this refers to washing the hands before the meal.

"'And you shall be holy' — this refers to the washing after the meal.

"'For holy' — this refers to the oil.

"'Am I the Lord your God' — this refers to the blessing [Grace]."

Appendix to Part Three

Sample of Documents that Form a Community of Texts

Let me now review the documents, seen as autonomous, we shall analyze in this exercise. I supply the bibliography on the basis of which my description of the volumes one by one rests. Scriptural verses are given in italics. When we have citations of Mishnaic and Toseftan passages in the context of some other document than theirs, e.g., in the body of the Yerushalmi or of the Bavli, I give the passage in boldface type.

1. THE MISHNAH

Editor: *The Modern Study of the Mishnah.* Leiden, 1973: Brill.

A History of the Mishnaic Law of Purities. Leiden, 1974-1977: Brill. I-XXII.

I. *Kelim. Chapters One through Eleven.* 1974.

II. *Kelim. Chapters Twelve through Thirty.* 1974.

III. *Kelim. Literary and Historical Problems.* 1974.

IV. *Ohalot. Commentary.* 1975.

V. *Ohalot. Literary and Historical Problems.* 1975.

VI. *Negaim. Mishnah-Tosefta.* 1975.

VII. *Negaim. Sifra.* 1975.

VIII. *Negaim. Literary and Historical Problems.* 1975.

IX. *Parah. Commentary.* 1976.

X. *Parah. Literary and Historical Problems.* 1976.

XI. *Tohorot. Commentary,* 1976.

XII. *Tohorot. Literary and Historical Problems.* 1976.

XIII. *Miqvaot. Commentary.* 1976.

XIV. *Miqvaot. Literary and Historical Problems.* 1976.

XV. *Niddah. Commentary.* 1976.

XVI. *Niddah. Literary and Historical Problems.* 1976.

XVII. *Makhshirin.* 1977.

XVIII. *Zabim.* 1977.

XIX.   *Tebul Yom. Yadayim.* 1977.

XX.   *Uqsin. Cumulative Index, Parts I-XX.* 1977.

A History of the Mishnaic Law of Holy Things. Leiden, Brill: 1979. I-VI.

I.   *Zebahim. Translation and Explanation.*

II.   *Menahot. Translation and Explanation.*

III.   *Hullin, Bekhorot. Translation and Explanation.*

IV.   *Arakhin, Temurah. Translation and Explanation.*

V.   *Keritot, Meilah, Tamid, Middot, Qinnim. Translation and Explanation.*

Form Analysis and Exegesis: A Fresh Approach to the Interpretation of Mishnah. Minneapolis, 1980: University of Minnesota Press.

A History of the Mishnaic Law of Women. Leiden, Brill: 1979-1980. I-V.

I.   *Yebamot. Translation and Explanation.*

II.   *Ketubot. Translation and Explanation.*

III.   *Nedarim, Nazir. Translation and Explanation.*

IV.   *Sotah, Gittin, Qiddushin. Translation and Explanation.*

A History of the Mishnaic Law of Appointed Times. Leiden, Brill: 1981-1983. I-V.

I.   *Shabbat. Translation and Explanation.*

II.   *Erubin, Pesahim. Translation and Explanation.*

III.   *Sheqalim, Yoma, Sukkah. Translation and Explanation.*

IV.   *Besah, Rosh Hashshanah, Taanit, Megillah, Moed Qatan, Hagigah. Translation and Explanation.*

A History of the Mishnaic Law of Damages. Leiden, Brill: 1983-1985. I-V.

I.   *Baba Qamma. Translation and Explanation.*

II.   *Baba Mesia. Translation and Explanation.*

III.   *Baba Batra, Sanhedrin, Makkot. Translation and Explanation.*

IV.   *Shebuot, Eduyyot, Abodah Zarah, Abot, Horayyot. Translation and Explanation.*

The Mishnah. A New Translation. New Haven and London, 1986: Yale University Press.

A History of the Mishnaic Law of Purities. Leiden, 1977: Brill.

XXI.   *The Redaction and Formulation of the Order of Purities in the Mishnah and Tosefta.*

XXII.   *The Mishnaic System of Uncleanness. Its Context and History.*

A History of the Mishnaic Law of Holy Things. Leiden, 1979: Brill.

VI.   *The Mishnaic System of Sacrifice and Sanctuary.*

A History of the Mishnaic Law of Women. Leiden, 1980: Brill.

    V.   *The Mishnaic System of Women.*

A History of the Mishnaic Law of Appointed Times. Leiden, 1981: Brill.

    V.   *The Mishnaic System of Appointed Times.*

A History of the Mishnaic Law of Damages. Leiden, 1985: Brill.

    V.   *The Mishnaic System of Damages*

The Mishnah and the Tosefta. Formal and Redactional Relationships. Hoboken, 1987: Ktav.

Judaism. The Evidence of the Mishnah. Chicago, 1981: University of Chicago Press. Paperback edition: 1984. *Choice,* "Outstanding Academic Book List" 1982-3. Second printing, 1985. Hebrew translation: Tel Aviv, 1986: Sifriat Poalim. Italian translation: Casale Monferrato, 1987: Editrice Marietti.

Ancient Israel after Catastrophe. The Religious World-View of the Mishnah. The Richard Lectures for 1982 . Charlottesville, 1983: The University Press of Virginia.

From Mishnah to Scripture. The Problem of the Unattributed Saying. Chico, 1984: Scholars Press for Brown Judaic Studies. Reprise and reworking of materials in *A History of the Mishnaic Law of Purities.*

In Search of Talmudic Biography. The Problem of the Attributed Saying. Chico, 1984: Scholars Press for Brown Judaic Studies. Reprise and reworking of materials in *Eliezer ben Hyrcanus. The Tradition and the Man.*

The Memorized Torah. The Mnemonic System of the Mishnah. Chico, 1985: Scholars Press for Brown Judaic Studies. Reprise and reworking of materials in *Rabbinic Traditions about the Pharisees before 70* I and III, and *A History of the Mishnaic Law of Purities* XXI.

Judaism: The First Two Centuries. Abbreviated version of *Judaism: The Evidence of the Mishnah.* Chicago, 1987: University of Chicago Press.

M. Sanhedrin 2:1-2

  A. A high priest judges, and [others] judge him;

  B. gives testimony, and [others] give testimony about him;

  C. performs the rite of removing the shoe [Deut. 25:7-9], and [others] perform the rite of removing the shoe with his wife.

  D. [Others] enter levirate marriage with his wife, but he does not enter into levirate marriage,

  E. because he is prohibited to marry a widow.

  F. [If] he suffers a death [in his family], he does not follow the bier.

  G. "But when [the bearers of the bier] are not visible, he is visible; when they are visible, he is not.

  H. "And he goes with them to the city gate," the words of R. Meir.

  I. R. Judah says, "He never leaves the sanctuary,

  J. "since it says, *'Nor shall he go out of the sanctuary'* (Lev. 21:12)."

K. And when he gives comfort to others

L. the accepted practice is for all the people to pass one after another, and the appointed [prefect of the priests] stands between him and the people.

M. And when he receives consolation from others,

N. all the people say to him, "Let us be your atonement."

O. And he says to them, "May you be blessed by Heaven."

P. And when they provide him with the funeral meal,

Q. all the people sit on the ground, while he sits on a stool.

M. 2:1

A. The king does not judge, and [others] do not judge him;

B. does not give testimony, and [others] do not give testimony about him;

C. does not perform the rite of removing the shoe, and others do not perform the rite of removing the shoe with his wife;

D. does not enter into levirate marriage, nor [do his brother] enter levirate marriage with his wife.

E. R. Judah says, "If he wanted to perform the rite of removing the shoe or to enter into levirate marriage, his memory is a blessing."

F. They said to him, "They pay no attention to him [if he expressed the wish to do so]."

G. [Others] do not marry his widow.

H. R. Judah says, "A king may marry the widow of a king.

I. "For so we find in the case of David, that he married the widow of Saul,

J. "For it is said, *'And I gave you your master's house and your master's wives into your embrace'* (II Sam. 12:8)."

M. 2:2

2:3

A. [If] [the king] suffers a death in his family, he does not leave the gate of his palace.

B. R. Judah says, "If he wants to go out after the bier, he goes out,

C. "for thus we find in the case of David, that he went out after the bier of Abner,

D. "since it is said, *'And King David followed the bier'* (2 Sam. 3:31)."

E. They said to him, "This action was only to appease the people."

F. And when they provide him with the funeral meal, all the people sit on the ground, while he sits on a couch.

2:4A-D

A. [The king] calls out [the army to wage] a war fought by choice on the instructions of a court of seventy-one.

B. He [may exercise the right to] open a road for himself, and [others] may not stop him.

C. The royal road has no required measure.

D. All the people plunder and lay before him [what they have grabbed], and he takes the first portion.

2:4E-I

E. *"He should not multiply wives to himself"* (Deut. 17:17) – only eighteen.

F. R Judah says, "He may have as many as he wants, so long as they *do not entice him* [to abandon the Lord (Deut. 7:4)]."

G. R. Simeon says, "Even if there is only one who entices him [to abandon the Lord] – lo, this one should not marry her."

H. If so, why is it said, "He should not multiply wives to himself"?

I. Even though they should be like Abigail [1 Sam. 25:3].

2:4J-N

J. *"He should not multiply horses to himself"* (Deut. 17:16) – only enough for his chariot.

K. *"Neither shall he greatly multiply to himself silver and gold"* (Deut. 17:16) – only enough to pay his army.

L. *"And he writes out a scroll of the Torah for himself"* (Deut. 17:17).

M. When he goes to war, he takes it out with him; when he comes back, he brings it back with him; when he is in session in court, it is with him; when he is reclining, it is before him,

N. as it is said, *"And it shall be with him, and he shall read in it all the days of his life"* (Deut. 17:19).

2:5

A. [Others may] not ride on his horse, sit on his throne, handle his sceptre.

B. And [others may] not watch him while he is getting a haircut, or while he is nude, or in the bath-house,

C. since it is said, *"You shall surely set him as king over you"* .(Deut. 17:15) – that reverence for him will be upon you.

2. TRACTATE AVOT

Torah from Our Sages: Pirke Avot. A New American Translation and Explanation. Chappaqua, 1983: Rossel.

Chapter One

1. Moses received Torah at Sinai and handed it on to Joshua, Joshua to elders, and elders to prophets. And prophets handed it on to the men of the great assembly. They said three things: Be prudent in judgment. Raise up many disciples. Make a fence for the Torah.

2. Simeon the Righteous was one of the last survivors of the great assembly. He would say: On three things does the world stand: On the Torah, and on the Temple service, and on deeds of loving-kindness.

3. Antigonus of Sokho received [the Torah] from Simeon the Righteous. He would say: Do not be like servants who serve the master on condition of receiving a reward, but [be] like servants who serve the master not on condition of receiving a reward. And let the fear of Heaven be upon you.

4. Yosé ben Yoezer of Zeredah and Yosé ben Yohanan of Jerusalem received [the Torah] from them. Yosé ben Yoezer says: Let your house be a gathering place for sages. And wallow in the dust of their feet, and drink in their words with gusto.

5. Yosé ben Yohanan of Jerusalem says: Let your house be open wide. And seat the poor at your table ["make the poor members of your household"]. And don't talk too much with women. (He referred to a man's wife, all the more so is the rule to be applied to the wife of one's fellow. In this regard did sages say: So long as a man talks too much with a woman, he brings trouble on himself, wastes time better spent on studying Torah, and ends up an heir of Gehenna.)

6. Joshua ben Perahyah and Nittai the Arbelite received [the Torah] from them. Joshua ben Perahyah says: Set up a master for yourself. And get yourself a companion-disciple. And give everybody the benefit of the doubt.

7. Nittai the Arbelite says: Keep away from a bad neighbor. And don't get involved with a bad person. And don't give up hope of retribution.

8. Judah ben Tabbai and Simeon ben Shetah received [the Torah] from them. Judah ben Tabbai says: Don't make yourself like one of those who advocate before judges [while you yourself are judging a case]. And when the litigants stand before you, regard them as guilty. But when they leave you, regard them as acquitted (when they have accepted your judgment).

9. Simeon ben Shetah says: Examine the witnesses with great care. And watch what you say, lest they learn from what you say how to lie.

10. Shemaiah and Avtalyon received [the Torah] from them. Shemaiah says: Love work. Hate authority. Don't get friendly with the government.

11. Avtalyon says: Sages, watch what you say, lest you become liable to the punishment of exile, and go into exile to a place of bad water, and disciples who follow you drink bad water and die, and the name of Heaven be thereby profaned.

12. Hillel and Shammai received [the Torah] from them. Hillel says: Be disciples of Aaron, loving peace and pursuing grace, loving people and drawing them near to the Torah.

13. He would say [in Aramaic]: A name made great is a name destroyed, and one who does not add, subtracts.
And who does not learn is liable to death. And the one who uses the crown, passes away.

14. He would say: If I am not for myself, who is for me? And when I am for myself, what am I? And if not now, when?

15. Shammai says: Make your learning of Torah a fixed obligation. Say little and do much. Greet everybody cheerfully.

16. Rabban Gamaliel says: Set up a master for yourself. Avoid doubt. Don't tithe by too much guesswork.

17. Simeon his son says: All my life I grew up among the sages, and I found nothing better for a person [the body] than silence. And not the learning is the thing, but the doing. And whoever talks too much causes sin.

18. Rabban Simeon ben Gamaliel says: On three things does the world stand: on justice, on truth, and on peace. As it is said, *Execute the judgment of truth and peace in your gates* (Zech 8:16).

Chapter Two

1. Rabbi says: What is the straight path which a person should choose for himself? Whatever is an ornament to the one who follows it, and an

ornament in the view of others. Be meticulous in a small religious duty as in a large one, for you do not know what sort of reward is coming for any of the various religious duties. And reckon with the loss [required] in carrying our a religious duty against the reward for doing it; and the reward for committing a transgression against the loss for doing it. And keep your eye on three things, so you will not come into the clutches of transgression. Know what is above you. An eye which sees, and an ear which hears, and all your actions are written down in a book.

2. Rabban Gamaliel, a son of Rabbi Judah the Patriarch, says: Fitting is learning in Torah along with a craft, for the labor put into the two of them makes one forget sin. And all learning of Torah which is not joined with labor is destined to be null and causes sin. And all who work with the community – let them work with them [the community] for the sake of Heaven. For the merit of the fathers strengthens them, and the righteousness which they do stands forever. And, as for you, I credit you with a great reward, as if you had done [all the work required by the community].

3. Be wary of the government, for they get friendly with a person only for their own convenience. They look like friends when it is to their benefit, but they do not stand by a person when he is in need.

4. He would say: Make His wishes into your own wishes, so that He will make your wishes into His wishes. Put aside your wishes on account of His wishes, so that He will put aside the wishes of other people in favor of your wishes. Hillel says: Do not walk out on the community. And do not have confidence in yourself until the day you die. And do not judge your companion until you are in his place. And do not say anything which cannot be heard, for in the end it will be heard. And do not say: When I have time, I shall study, for you may never have time.

5. He would say: A coarse person will never fear sin, nor will an *am ha-Aretz* ever be pious, nor will a shy person learn, nor will an ignorant person teach, nor will anyone too occupied in business get wise. In a place where there are no individuals, try to be in individual.

6. Also, he saw a skull floating on the water and said to it [in Aramaic]: Because you drowned others, they drowned you, and in the end those who drowned you will be drowned.

7. He would say: Lots of meat, lots of worms; lots of property, lots of worries; lots of women, lots of witchcraft; lots of slave girls, lots of lust; lots of slave boys, lots of robbery. Lots of Torah, lots of life; lots of discipleship, lots of wisdom; lots of counsel, lots of understanding; lots of righteousness, lots of peace. [If] one has gotten a good name, he has gotten it for himself. [If] he has gotten teachings of Torah, he has gotten himself life eternal.

8. Rabban Yohanan ben Zakkai received [the Torah] from Hillel and Shammai. He would say: If you have learned much Torah, do not puff yourself up on that account, for it was for that purpose that you were created. He had five disciples, and these are they: Rabbi Eliezer ben Hyrcanus, Rabbi Joshua ben Hananiah, Rabbi Yosé the Priest, Rabbi Simeon ben Nethanel, and Rabbi Eleazar ben Arakh.
He would list their good qualities: Rabbi Eliezer ben Hyrcanus – a plastered well, which does not lose a drop of water. Rabbi Joshua – happy is the one who gave birth to him. Rabbi Yosé – a pious man.

Rabbi Simeon ben Nethanel – a man who fears sin, and Rabbi Eleazar ben Arakh – a surging spring.

He would say: If all the sages of Israel were on one side of the scale, and Rabbi Eliezer ben Hyrcanus were on the other, he would outweigh all of them.

Abba Saul says in his name: If all of the sages of Israel were on one side of the scale, and Rabbi Eliezer ben Hyrcanus was also with them, and Rabbi Eleazar [ben Arakh] were on the other side, he would outweigh all of them.

9. He said to them: Go and see what is the straight path to which someone should stick.

Rabbi Eliezer says: A generous spirit. Rabbi Joshua says: A good friend. Rabbi Yosé says: A good neighbor. Rabbi Simeon says: Foresight. Rabbi Eleazar says: Good will.

He said to them: I prefer the opinion of Rabbi Eleazar ben Arakh, because in what he says is included everything you say.

He said to them: Go out and see what is the bad road, which someone should avoid. Rabbi Eliezer says: Envy. Rabbi Joshua says: A bad friend. Rabbi Yosé says: A bad neighbor. Rabbi Simeon says: A loan. (All the same is a loan owed to a human being and a loan owed to the Omnipresent, the blessed, as it is said, *The wicked borrows and does not pay back, but the righteous person deals graciously and hands over [what is* owed] (Ps. 37:21).)

Rabbi Eleazar says: Ill will.

He said to them: I prefer the opinion of Rabbi Eleazar been Arakh, because in what he says is included everything you say.

10. They [each] said three things.

Rabbi Eliezer says: Let the respect owing to your companion be as precious to you as the respect owing to yourself. And don't be easy to anger. And repent one day before you die. And warm yourself by the fire of the sages, but be careful of their coals, so you don't get burned – for their bite is the bite of a fox, and their sting is the sting of a scorpion, and their hiss is like the hiss of a snake, and everything they say is like fiery coals.

11. Rabbi Joshua says: Envy, desire of bad things, and hatred for people push a person out of the world.

12. Rabbi Yosé says: Let your companion's money be as precious to you as your own. And get yourself ready to learn Torah, for it does not come as an inheritance to you. And may everything you do be for the sake of Heaven.

13. Rabbi Simeon says: Be meticulous about the recitation of the *Shema* and the Prayer. And when you pray, don't treat your praying as a matter of routine; but let it be a [plea for] mercy and supplication before the Omnipresent, the blessed, as it is said, *For He is gracious and full of compassion, slow to anger and full of mercy, and repents of the evil.* And never be evil in your own eyes (Joel 2:13).

14. Rabbi Eleazar says: Be constant in learning of Torah; And know what to reply to an Epicurean; And know before whom you work, for your employer can be depended upon to pay your wages for what you do.

15. Rabbi Tarfon says: The day is short, the work formidable, the workers lazy, the wages high, the employer impatient.

16. He would say: It's not your job to finish the work, but you are not free to walk away from it. If you have learned much Torah, they will give you a good reward. And your employer can be depended upon to pay your wages for what you do. And know what sort of reward is going to be given to the righteous in the coming time.

3. THE TOSEFTA

The Tosefta. Translated from the Hebrew. N.Y., 1977-1980: Ktav. II-VI.

II. *The Tosefta. Translated from the Hebrew. Second Division. Moed.*

III. *The Tosefta. Translated from the Hebrew. Third Division. Nashim.*

IV. *The Tosefta. Translated from the Hebrew. Fourth Division. Neziqin.*

V. *The Tosefta. Translated from the Hebrew. Fifth Division. Qodoshim.*

VI. *The Tosefta. Translated from the Hebrew. Sixth Division. Tohorot.*

Edited: *The Tosefta. Translated from the Hebrew. I. The First Division (Zeraim).* N.Y., 1985: Ktav.

4:1

A. A high priest who committed homicide –

B. [if he did so] deliberately, he is executed; if he did so, inadvertently, he goes into exile to the cities of refuge [Num. 35:9ff.].

C. [If] he transgressed a positive or negative commandment or indeed any of the commandments, lo, he is treated like an ordinary person in every respect.

D. He does not perform the rite of removing the shoe [Deut. 25:7 9], and others do not perform the rite of removing the shoe with his wife [vs. M. San. 2:1C].

E. He does not enter into levirate marriage, and [others] do not enter into levirate marriage with his wife [cf. M. San. 2:1C-E].

F. [When] he stands in the line [to receive comfort as a mourner], the prefect of the priests is at his right hand, and the head of the father's houses [the priestly courses] at his left hand.

G. **And all the people say to him, "Let us be your atonement."**

H. **And he says to them. "May you be blessed by Heaven" [M. San. 2:1N-O].**

I. [And when] he stands in the line to give comfort to others, the prefect of the priests and the [high] priest who has now passed out of his position of grandeur are at his right hand, and the mourner is at his left.

J. **[People may] not watch him while he is getting a haircut, [or while he is nude] or in the bathhouse [M. San. 2:5B],**

K. since it is said, *And he who is high priest among his brothers* (Lev. 21:10) – that his brethren should treat him with grandeur.

L. But if he wanted to permit others to wash with him, the right is his.

M. R. Judah says, "[If] he wanted to disgrace himself, they do not pay attention to him,

N. "as it is said, *And you will keep him holy* (Lev. 21:8) – even against his will."

O. They said to R. Judah, "To be sure [Scripture] says, *From the Temple he shall not go forth* (Lev. 21:12), [but this is referring] only to the time of the Temple service" [M. San. 2:1I-J].

P. He goes out to provide a funeral meal for others, and others come to provide a funeral meal for him.

4.2

A. An Israelite king does not stand in line to receive comfort [in the time of bereavement],

B. nor does he stand in line to give comfort to others.

C. And he does not go to provide a funeral meal for others.

D. But others come to him to give a funeral meal [M. San. 2:3F],

E. as it is said, *And the people went to provide a funeral meal for David* (II Sam. 3:35).

F. And if he transgressed a positive or a negative commandment or indeed any of the commandments, lo, he is treated like an ordinary person in every respect.

G. He does not perform the rite of removing the shoe, and others do not perform the rite of removing the shoe with his wife.;

H. he does not enter into levirate marriage, nor [do his brothers] enter into levirate marriage with his wife [M. San. 2:2C-D].

I. R. Judah says, "If he wanted to perform the rite of removing the shoe, he has the right to do so" [M. San. 2:9].

J. They said to him, "You turn out to do damage to the glory owing to a king."

K. *And [others] do not marry his widow* [M. San. 2:3G], as it is said, *So they were shut up to the day of their death, living in widowhood* (II Sam. 20:3).

L. And he has the right to choose wives for himself from any source he wants, whether daughters of priests, Levites, or Israelites.

M. *And they do not ride on his horse, sit on his throne, handle his crown or scepter or any of his regalia* [M. San. 2:5].

N. [When] he dies, all of them are burned along with him, as it is said, *You shall die in peace and with the burnings of your fathers, the former kings* (Jer. 34:5).

4.3

A. Just as they make a burning for kings [who die], so they make a burning for patriarchs [who die].

B. But they do not do so for ordinary people.

C. What do they burn on their account?

D. Their bed and other regalia.

4.4

A. Everybody stands, while he sits.

B. And sitting was [permitted] in the Temple courtyard only for kings of the house of David.

C. All the people keep silent, when he is talking.

D. He would call them, "My brothers" and "My people," as it is said, *Hear you, my brothers and my people* (I Chron. 28:2).

E. And they call him, "Our Lord and our master,"

F. as it is said, *But our Lord David, the King, has made Solomon king* (I Kings 1:43).

4.5

A. *"He should not multiply wives for himself* (Deut. 17:17) – like Jezebel. But [if the wives are like] Abigail, it is permitted," the words of R. Judah [*vs.* M. San. 2:4H-I].

B. *He should not multiply horses for himself* (Deut. 17:16) – if the horses are left idle, even one [he may not keep],

C. as it is said, *Lest he multiply horses.*

D. R. Judah says, "Lo, it says, *And Solomon had forty thousand stalls of horses* (I Kings 4:26) – yet he did well,

E. "for it is written, *And Judah and Israel were as many as the sand that is on the seashore for multitude* (I Kings 4:20).

F. "And since it is written, *Twelve thousand horsemen* (I Kings 4:26), one has to conclude that the rest of the horses were left idle."

G. But an ordinary person is permitted [to do] all of these things.

H. R. Yosé says, "Everything that is spelled out in the pericope of the king (Deut. 17:14) is [an ordinary person] permitted to do."

I. R. Judah says, "That pericope is written only to make the people revere him [cf. M. San 2:5C],

J. "for it is written, *You will surely set a king over you* (Deut. 17:14)."

K. And so did R. Judah say, "Three commandments were imposed upon the Israelites when they came into the land.

L. "They were commanded to appoint a king, to build the chosen house, and to cut off the descendants of Amalek.

M. "If so, why were they punished in the days of Samuel [for wanting a king]? Because they acted too soon."

N. R. Nehorai says, "This pericope was written only because of [future] complaints [with the king].

O. "For it is said, *And you will say, I will set a king over me* (Deut. 17:14)."

P. R. Eleazar b. R. Yosé says, "The elders asked in the proper way, as it is said, *"Give us a king to judge us* (I Sam. 8:6).

Q. "But the ordinary folk went and spoiled matters, as it is said, *That we also may be like all the nations, and our king will judge us and go before us to fight our battles (I Sam. 8:20)."*

4.6

A. "Those put to death by the court – their property goes to their heirs.

B. "But those put to death by the king – their property goes to the king," [the words of R. Judah].

C. And sages say, "Those put to death by their king – their property goes to their heirs."

D. Said R. Judah to them, "It says, *Behold, he [Ahab] is in the vineyard of Naboth, where he has gone down to take posession* (I Kings 21:18)."

E. They said to him, "It was because he was the son of his father's brother [and] it was appropriate [to come] to him as in inheritance."

F. They said to him, "And did [Naboth] have no children?"

G. They said to him, "And did he not kill both him and his children,

H. "as it is said, *Surely I have seen yesterday the blood of Naboth and the blood of his sons, says the Lord; and I will requite you in this plot, says the Lord* (II Kings 9:26)?"

4.7

A. *And he writes for himself a scroll of the Torah* (Deut. 17:17) –

B. for his own use, that he not have to make use of the one of his fathers, but rather of his own,

C. as it is said, *And he will write for himself* –

D. that the very writing of the scroll should be for him [in particular].

E. And an ordinary person has no right to read in it,

F. as it is said, *And he will read in it* –

G. he, and no one else.

H. And they examine [his scroll] in the court of the priests, in the court of the Levites, and in the court of the Israelites who are of suitable genealogical character to marry into the priesthood.

I. [When] he goes to war, it is with him, when he comes back, it is with him [cf. M. San. 2:4M]; when he goes to court it is with him; when he goes to the urinal, it waits for him [outside] at the door,

J. and so does David say, *I have set God always before me [and he is on my right hand]* (Ps. 16:8).

K. R. Judah says, "A scroll of the Torah as at his right hand, and tefillin are on his arm."

L. R. Yosé said, "Ezra was worthy for the Torah to have been given by him, had not Moses come before him.

M. "Concerning Moses *going up* is stated, and concerning Ezra *going up* is stated.

N. "Concerning Moses *going up* is stated, as it is said, *And Moses went up to God* (Ex. 19:3).

O. "And concerning Ezra going up is stated, as it is written, And *he, Ezra, went up from Babylonia (Ezra 7:6).*

P. "Just as, in the case of *going up* mentioned in connection with Moses, he taught Torah to Israel, as it is stated, *And the Lord commanded me at that time to teach you statutes and judgments* (Deut. 4:14),

Q. "so, in the case of *going up* mentioned in connection with Ezra, he taught Torah to Israel, as it is said, *For Ezra had prepared his heart to expound the law of the Lord and to do it and to teach in Israel statutes and judgments* (Ezra 7:0)."

R. Also through him were given [both] a form of writing and language, as it is said, *And the writing of the letter was written in the Aramaic character and interpreted in the Aramaic tongue* (Ezra 4:7).

S. Just as its interpretation was in Aramaic, so its writing was in Aramaic.

T. And it says, *"But they could not read the writing, nor make known to the king the interpretation thereof* (Dan. 5:8) –

U. this teaches that on that very day it was given.

V. And it ways, *And he shall write a copy of this law* (Deut. 17:18) – A Torah which is destined to be changed.

W. And why was [the language] called Assyrian? Because it came up with them from Assyria.

X. Rabbi says, "In Assyrian writing was the Torah given to Israel, and when they sinned, it was changed to *Ro'as.*

Y. "But when they attained merit in the time of Ezra, Assyrian returned to them, as it is said, *Turn you to the stronghold, you prisoners of hope, even today do I declare that I will bring back – the change unto you* (Zech. 9:12).

4.8

A. R. Simeon b. Eleazar says in the name of R. Eleazar b. Parta who said it in the name of R. Eleazar of Modin, "In the present kind of writing the Torah was given to Israel, as it says, *The hooks (vavs) of the pillars* (Ex. 27:10) – *vavs* that are written like pillars.

B. "And it says, *And unto the Jews according to their writing and language* (Est. 8:9) – Just as their language has not changed, so their writing has not changed.

C. "And why is it called Assyrian *(ashur)*? Because they are upright *(me'usharim)* in their manner of shaping letters."

D. If so, why is it said, *And he shall write for himself a copy of this law* (Deut. 17:17)?

E. This teaches that he writes for himself two Torahs, one which comes in with him and goes out with him, and one which he leaves home.

F. This one which goes out and comes in with him should not go in with him to the bathhouse or the urinal, as it is said, *And it shall be with him and he shall read in it all the days of his life* – that is to say, in a place in which it is appropriate for reading [M. San. 2:4M-N].

G. And does this not produce an argument *a fortiori:*

H. Now if of an Israelite king, who is busy only with his public duties, it is said, *And it shall be with him and he shall read therein all the days of his life,*

I. the rest of the people, all the more so [should they have and read Torah-scrolls].

4.9

A. Similarly you say: *And Joshua the son of Nun was full of the spirit of wisdom, for Moses had laid his hund upon him* (Deut. 34:9).

B. And so it says, *And his minister, Joshua, the son of Nun, a young man, stirred not from the midst of the tent* (Ex. 33:11).

C. And so it says [*even to him*], *This book of the Torah shall not depart out of your mouth* (Josh. 1:8) –

D. the rest of the people, all the more so [should they have and read Torah-scrolls].

4.10

A. They do not appoint a king outside of the Land.
B. They appoint a king only if he was married into the priesthood.
C. And they anoint kings only over a spring,
D. as it is said, *And he said to them, Take with you the servants of your lord and mount Solomon, my son, upon my own mule, and bring him down to Gihon* (I Kings 1:33).

4.11

A. They anoint kings only on account of civil strife.
B. Why did they anoint Solomon? Because of the strife of Adonijah.
C. And Jehu? Because of Joram.
D. And Joash? Because of Athaliah.
E. And Jehoahaz? Because of Jehoiakim his brother, who was two years older than he.
F. A king requires anointing, [but] a son of a king does not require anointing.
G. A high priest, son of a high priest, even up to the tenth generation, [nonetheless] requires anointing.
H. And they anoint kings only from a horn.
I. Saul and Jehu were anointed from a flask, because their rule was destined to be broken.
J. David and Solomon were anointed from a horn, because their dominion is an eternal dominion.

4. THE YERUSHALMI

The Talmud of the Land of Israel. A Preliminary Translation and Explanation. Chicago: The University of Chicago Press: 1982-1989. IX-XII, XIV-XV, XVII-XXXV.

XXXIV.   *Horayot. Niddah.* 1982.

XXXIII. *Abodah Zarah.* 1982.

XXXII.   *Shebuot.* 1983.

XXXI.   *Sanhedrin. Makkot.* 1984.

XXX.   *Baba Batra.* 1984.

XXIX.   *Baba Mesia.* 1984.

XXVIII. *Baba Qamma.* 1984.

XXVII.   *Sotah.* 1984.

XXVI.   *Qiddushin.* 1984.

XXV.   *Gittin.* 1985

XXIV.   *Nazir.* 1985.

XXIII.   *Nedarim* 1985.

XXII.   *Ketubot.* 1985.

XXI.   *Yebamot.* 1986.

XX.   *Hagigah. Moed Qatan* . 1986.
XIX.   *Megillah.* 1987.
XVIII.   *Besah. Taanit.* 1987.
XVII.   *Sukkah.* 1987.
XV.   *Sheqalim.* 1987.
XIV.   *Yoma.* 1988.
XII.   *Erubin.* 1988.
XI.   *Shabbat.* 1988.
X.   *Orlah. Bikkurim.* 1988.
IX.   *Hallah.* 1989.

Edited: *In the Margins of the Yerushalmi. Notes on the English Translation.* Chico, 1983: Scholars Press for Brown Judaic Studies.

The Talmud of the Land of Israel. A Preliminary Translation and Explanation. Chicago: The University of Chicago Press: 1983.

XXXV.   *Introduction. Taxonomy.*

Judaism in Society: The Evidence of the Yerushalmi. Toward the Natural History of a Religion. Chicago, 1983: The University of Chicago Press. *Choice* , "Outstanding Academic Book List, 1984-1985."

Our Sages, God, and Israel. An Anthology of the Yerushalmi. Chappaqua, 1984: Rossel.

2.1

A.   A high priest judges, and [others] judge him;
B.   gives testimony, and [others] give testimony about him;
C.   performs the rite of removing the shoe [Deut. 25:7-9], and [others] perform the rite of removing the shoe with his wife.
D.   [Others] enter levirate marriage with his wife, but he does not enter into levirate marriage,
E.   because he is prohibited to marry a widow.
F.   [If] he suffers a death [in his family], he does not follow the bier.
G.   "But when [the bearers of the bier] are not visible, he is visible; when they are visible, he is not.
H.   "And he goes with them to the city gate," the words of R. Meir.
I.   R. Judah says, "He never leaves the sanctuary,
J.   "since it says, 'Nor shall he go out of the sanctuary' (Lev. 21:12)."

I

A.   It is understandable that he judges others.

B. But as to others judging him, [it is appropriate to his station?]
C. Let him appoint a mandatory.
D. Now take note: What if he has to take an oath?
E. Can the mandatory take an oath for his client?
F. Property cases involving [a high priest] – in how large a court is the trial conducted?
G. With a court of twenty-three judges.
H. Let us demonstrate that fact from the following:
I. **A king does not sit in the sanhedrin, nor do a king and a high priest join in the court session for intercalation [T. San. 2:15].**
J. [In this regard,] R. Haninah and R. Mana – one of them said, "The king does not take a seat on the Sanhedrin, on account of suspicion [of influencing the other judges].
K. "Nor does he take a seat in a session for intercalation, because of suspicion [that it is in the government's interest to intercalate the year].
L. "And a king and a high priest do not take a seat for intercalation, for it is not appropriate to the station of the king [or the high priest] to take a seat with seven judges."
M. Now look here:
N. If it is not appropriate to his station to take a seat with seven judges, is it not an argument *a fortiori* that he should not [be judged] by three?
O. That is why one must say, Property cases involving him are tried in a court of twenty-three.

II

A. [What follows is verbatim at M. Hor. 3:1:] Said R. Eleazar, "A high priest who sinned – they administer lashes to him, but they do not remove him from his high office."
B. Said R. Mana, "It is written, 'For the consecration of the anointing oil of his God is upon him: I am the Lord' (Lev. 21:12).
C. [Here omitted:] ("That is as if to say: 'Just as I [stand firm] in my high office, so Aaron [stands firm] in his high office,'")
D. [Here omitted:] (Said R. Abun, "'*He shall be holy to you [for I the Lord who sanctify you am holy]*' (Lev. 21:8).)
E. "That is as if to say, 'Just as I [stand firm] in my consecration, so Aaron [stands firm] in his consecration.'"
F. R. Haninah Ketobah, R. Aha in the name of R. Simeon b. Laqish: "An anointed priest who sinned – they administer lashes to him [by the judgment of a court of three judges].
G. "If you rule that it is by the decision of a court of twenty-three judges [that the lashes are administered], it turns out that his ascension [to high office] is descent [to public humiliation, since if he sins he is publicly humiliated by a sizable court]."

III

A. R. Simeon b. Laqish said, "A ruler who sinned – they administer lashes to him by the decision of a court of three judges."
B. What is the law as to restoring him to office?

C. Said R. Haggai, "By Moses! If we put him back into office, he will kill us!"

D. R. Judah the Patriarch heard this ruling [of R. Simeon b. Laqish's] and was outraged. He sent a troop of Goths to arrest R. Simeon b. Laqish. [R. Simeon b. Laqish] fled to the Tower, and, some say, it was to Kefar Hittayya.

E. The next day R. Yohanan went up to the meetinghouse, and R. Judah the Patriarch went up to the meetinghouse. He said to him, "Why does my master not state a teaching of Torah?"

F. [Yohanan] began to clap with one [20a] hand [only].

G. [Judah the Patriarch] said to him, "Now do people clap with only one hand?"

H. He said to him, "No, nor is Ben Laqish here [and just as one cannot clap with one hand only, so I cannot teach Torah if my colleague, Simeon b. Laqish, is absent]."

I. [Judah] said to him, "Then where is he hidden?"

J. He said to him, "In a certain tower."

K. He said to him, "You and I shall go out to greet him tomorrow."

L. R. Yohanan sent word to R. Simeon b. Laqish, "Get a teaching of Torah ready, because the patriarch is coming over to see you."

M. [Simeon b. Laqish] came forth to receive them and said, "The example which you [Judah] set is to be compared to the paradigm of your Creator. For when the All-Merciful came forth to redeem Israel [from Egypt], he did not send a messenger or an angel, but the Holy One, blessed be He, himself came forth, as it is said, *'For I will pass through the Land of Egypt that night'* (Ex. 12:12) – and not only so, but he and his entire retinue.

N. [Here omitted:] ([*'"What other people on earth is like thy people Israel, whom God went to redeem to be his people'* (2 Sam. 7:23).] 'Whom God went' (sing.) is not written here, but 'Whom God went' (plural) [–meaning, he and all his retinue].")

O. [Judah the Patriarch] said to him, "Now why in the world did you see fit to teach this particular statement [that a ruler who sinned is subject to lashes]?"

P. He said to him, "Now did you really think that because I was afraid of you, I would hold back the teaching of the All-Merciful? [And lo, citing 1 Sam. 2:23f.,] R. Samuel b. R. Isaac said, '[*Why do you do such things? For I hear of your evil dealings from all the people.]* No, my sons, it is no good report [that I hear the people of the Lord spreading abroad]. [Here omitted:] (If a man sins against a man, God will mediate for him; but if a man sins against the Lord, who can intercede for him? But they would not listen to the voice of their father, for it was the will of the Lord to slay them'* (1 Sam. 2:23-25.) [When] the people of the Lord spread about [an evil report about a man], they remove him [even though he is the patriarch].")

IV

A. [The reference to tearing above in M. Hor. 3:3A is at issue: *A high priest tears his garment [on the death of a close relative] below [at the bottom hem], and an ordinary one, above [at the hem of his garment nearest his shoulder].]* R. Eleazar in the name of Kahana: "'Above' means above the binding [therefore separating the binding], and 'below' means below the binding [therefore not separating the binding]."

B.   R. Yohanan said, "'Below' means what it says, literally [near the ground]."

C.   R. Yohanan went up to visit R. Hanina. When he was yet on the road, he heard that he had died. He sent word and said to send to him his best Sabbath garment, and [he went and] tore it [in mourning on account of this news]. [Thus he holds that one tears a garment at the demise of someone who is not a close relative.]

D.   R. Yohanan differs from R. Yudan in two matters. [First, that he maintains one has to tear the garment as a sign of mourning for any master who has died, not merely for the one from whom one learned most; second, that one does the tear above the binding.]

E.   The teaching of R. Eleazar in the name of Kahana is in accord with R. Judah [who does not distinguish among relationships to the deceased].

F.   And if he is in accord with R. Judah, [the high priest] should not perform the act of tearing at all [since R. Judah holds that "any tear which does not separate the binding ... is a worthless act of tearing" (I), and R. Eleazar holds that "'below' means below the binding" (A)].

G.   This [Mishnah] deals with the [death of] his father or mother and follows the view of R. Meir, for it has ... been taught in a Tannaitic teaching:

H.   "For no dead does he undo the binding, except for his father and his mother," the words of R. Meir.

I.   R. Judah says, "Any tear which does not separate the binding, lo, this is a worthless act of tearing."

J.   What is the rule [for the high priest]?

K.   It is a more strict ruling in the case of the high priest, that he should not undo the binding, [but he rips through the fabric].

V

A.   *A high priest makes an offering while he is in the status of one who has yet to bury a close relative, but he does not eat* [the priestly portion]," the words of R. Meir (M. Hor. 3:3B; T. Zeb. 11:3].

B.   R. Judah says, "That entire day."

C.   R. Simeon says, "He completes all the act of sacrifice which is his responsibility and then he goes along [and leaves the altar]."

D.   The difference between the view of R. Meir and R. Simeon is one point, [specifically: in Simeon's view, when the priest hears the news, while he is performing the rite, that a close relative has died, he completes the entire rite for which he is responsible. But if he has not begun the rite, he should not do so. And after he has completed the rite, he should not begin another. In Meir's view, he may carry on an act of service, without condition.]

E.   The difference between the view of R. Judah and R. Simeon is one point, [specifically: in Judah's view, the priest makes offerings that entire day, while in Simeon's, once he has completed the rite in which he is involved, he leaves the alter.]

F. The difference between the view of R. Meir and R. Judah is [whether or not the priest who has not yet buried his close relative] enters [the Temple at all. Meir maintains that if he has not gone out of the sanctuary, he is permitted to make an offering. But if he has gone out, he does not enter the sanctuary. Judah maintains that that entire day the priest is permitted even to enter the sanctuary and to undertake offerings.]

G. R. Jacob bar Disai [says, "Whether or not the priest at the altar] interrupts [his act of service] is what is at issue between [Meir and Simeon]."

H. R. Meir says, "[If, when the priest heard the news], he was inside, he would go out [of the sanctuary]. [If] he was outside [the sanctuary], he would [not] go back in."

I. R. Judah says, "[If, when he heard the news, the priest] was inside, he would go in [and, for the entire day on which he heard], carry out an act of service, as is his right], but if he was outside, he would not go in [to perform an act of service]."

J. **R. Simeon says, "He completes all the act of service which is his responsibility and then he goes along."**

VI

A. R. Yosé b. R. Bun in the name of R. Huna: "The following Mishnah saying [belongs] to R. Simeon: *"'And from the sanctuary he will not go forth'* (Lev. 21:12) – with [the bearers of the bier] he does not go forth, but he does go forth after them."

B. *"When [the bearers of the bier] are not visible, he is visible, when they are visible, he is not. And he goes with them to the city gate,"* the words of R. Meir.

C. *R. Judah says, "He never leaves the sanctuary, since it says, 'Nor shall he go out of the sanctuary' (Lev. 21:12)"* [M. San. 2:1G-J].

D. If he did go out, he should not come back.

E. R. Abbahu in the name of R. Eleazar: "The word 'mourning' applies only to the corpse alone, as it is written, *'And her gates shall lament and mourn'* (Is. 3:26)."

F. Hiyya bar Adda replied, "And is it not written, 'The fishermen shall mourn and lament' (Is. 19:8)?"

VII

A. Said R. Hanina, "So does the Mishnah [teach, that] the consideration of uncleanness by reason of mourning applies only on the account of the corpse [and not on account of hearing of the death. The day of the death, along with the night, imposes the status of the one who has yet to bury his close relative]."

B. It has been taught in a Tannaitic tradition: At what point does the status of the one who has yet to bury his close relative apply?

C. "It applies from the moment of death to the moment of burial," the words of Rabbi.

D. And sages say, "It applies for that entire day [on which the deceased dies]."

E. You may then discern both a lenient and a strict side to the ruling of Rabbi, and a lenient and a strict side to the ruling of rabbis.

F. What is the difference between their two positions [for strict and lenient rulings]?

G. If one dies and is buried at the proper time –

H. in accord with the position of rabbis the mourner [in such a case] is subject to prohibitions applying to mourning for that entire day. In accord with the position of Rabbi the mourner is subject to prohibitions only in the period of the day down to that hour [of burial] alone.

I. If one dies and is buried three days later –

J. in accord with the opinion of rabbis, the prohibitions applying to the mourner are valid throughout that entire day [but not for the next two].

K. In accord with the position of Rabbi, the prohibitions applying to the mourners pertain for all three days.

L. R. Abbahu came [to teach] in the name of R. Yohanan, [and] R. Hisda – both of them teach: "Rabbi concurs with sages [in the case of I] that the prohibition applies only to that day alone." [The dispute concerns only M-N.]

M. That is in accord with the following teaching on Tannaitic authority: Rabbi says, "You should know that the status of first-day mourning by the authority of the Torah does not apply to the night, for lo, they have said, 'A first-day mourner may immerse and eat his Passover offering in the evening [of the fifteenth of Nisan, having suffered a bereavement on the fourteenth.].'"

N. And lo, they have said that the laws of first-day mourning do apply by the authority of the Torah!

O. R. Yosé b. R. Bun in the name of R. Huna, "You may solve the contradiction by referring [Rabbi's ruling, M] to the case in which the [death was during the day and] burial took place in the last rays of sunlight [and Rabbi, M, holds that to that following night the status of first-day mourning does not apply by the authority of the Torah]."

2.2

A. And when he gives comfort to others –

B. the accepted practice is for all the people to pass one after another, and the appointed [perfect of the priests] stands between him and the people.

C. And when he receives consolation from others,

D. all the people say to him, "Let us be your atonement."

E. And he says to them, "May you be blessed by Heaven."

F. And when they provide him with the funeral meal,

G. all the people sit on the ground, while he sits on a stool.

I

A. [The statement at M. San. 2:2G] implies: A stool is not subject to the law of mourners' overturning the bed.

B. [But that is not necessarily so. For] the high priest [to begin with] is subject to that requirement of overturning the bed [and, it follows, no conclusion can be drawn from M.].

II

A. It was taught: They do not bring out the deceased [for burial] at a time near the hour of reciting the *Shema*, unless they did so an hour earlier or an hour later, so that people may recite the *Shema* and say the Prayer.

B. And have we not learned: *When they have buried the dead and returned, [If they can begin the Shema and finish it before reaching the row of mourners, they begin it; but if they cannot, they do not begin it] [M. Ber. 3:2]*. [Thus they do bring out the deceased for burial at a time quite close to that for reciting the *Shema*.]

C. Interpret [the cited pericope of Mishnah] to deal with a case in which the people thought that they had ample time for burying the corpse but turned out not to have ample time for that purpose [prior to the time for reciting the *Shema*].

D. It is taught: **The person who states the eulogy and all who are involved in the eulogy interrupt [their labor] for the purpose of reciting the Shema, but do not do so for saying the Prayer. M'SH W: Our rabbis interrupted for the purposes of reciting the Shema and saying the Prayer (T. Ber. 2:11).**

E. Now have we not learned, *If they can begin and finish ...?* [As above, B. Now here we have them interrupt the eulogy!]

F. The Mishnah refers to the first day [of the death, on which they are exempt from saying the *Shema*], and the Tosefta pericope to the second [day after death, on which they are liable to say the *Shema*].

G. Said R. Samuel bar Abedoma, "This one who entered the synagogue and found the people standing [and saying] the prayer, if he knows that he can complete the Prayer before the messenger of the congregation [who repeats the whole in behalf of the congregation] will begin to answer, 'Amen,' [to the Prayer of the community], he may say the Prayer, and if not, he should not say the Prayer."

H. To which "Amen" is reference made?

I. Two Amoras differ in this regard.

J. One said, "To the *Amen* which follows, 'The Holy God.'"

K. And the other said, "to the *Amen* which follows, 'Who hears prayer' on an ordinary day."

III

A. It was taught: **R. Judah says, "If there is only a single row [of mourners], those who are standing as a gesture of respect are liable o say the Shema], and those who are standing as a gesture of mourning are exempt [from the obligation to say the Shema]. If they proceed to the eulogy, those who see the face [of the mourners] are exempt [from having to say the Shema,] and those who do not see their face are liable [T. Ber. 2:11].**

B. Note that which we have learned: *When he gives comfort to others, the accepted practice is for all the people to pass after one another, and the appointed [prefect of the priests] stands between him and the people [M. San. 3:3A-B].*

C. This is in accord with the earlier practice [Mishnah] [to be cited below].

D.   And as to that which we have learned: *[Of those who stand in the row of mourners], the ones on the inner line are exempt from reciting the Shema, and the ones on the outer row are liable [M. Ber. 3:2]* –

E.   this is in accord with the later Mishnah [to be cited below].

F.   Said R. Haninah, "At first [the former mishnah = B], the families would stand and the mourners would pass before them. R. Yosé ordained that the families would pass and the mourners would stand still [the later Mishnah = D].

G.   **Said R. Samuel of Sofafta, "The matters were restored to their original condition."**

2.3

A.   **The king does not judge, and [others] do not judge him;**

B.   **does not give testimony, and [others] do not give testimony about him;**

C.   **does not perform the rite of removing the shoe, and others do not perform the rite of removing the shoe with his wife;**

D.   **does not enter into levirate marriage, not [do his brothers] enter levirate marriage with his wife.**

E.   **R. Judah says, "If he wanted to perform the rite of removing the shoe or to enter into levirate marriage, his memory is a blessing."**

F.   **They said to him, "They pay no attention to him if he expressed the wish to do so."**

G.   **[Others] do not marry his widow.**

H.   **R. Judah says, "A king may marry the widow of a king.**

I.   **"For so we find in the case of David, that he married the widow of Saul,**

J.   **"For it is said, 'And I gave you your master's house and your master's wives into your embrace' (2 Sam. 12:8)."**

I

A.   *[The king] does not judge [M. San. 2:3A].* And has it not been written: *"[So David reigned over all Israel;] and David administered justice and equity to all his people"* (2 Sam. 8:15).

B.   And yet do you say [that the king does not judge]?

C.   [From this verse of Scripture, we draw the following picture:] He would indeed judge a case, declaring the innocent party to be innocent, the guilty party to be guilty. But if the guilty party was poor, he would give him [the funds needed for his penalty] out of his own property. Thus he turned out doing justice for this one [who won the case] and doing charity for that one [who had lost it].

D.   Rabbi says, "[If] a judge judged a case, declaring the innocent party to be innocent, and the guilty party to be guilty, [the cited verse of Scripture indicates that] the Omnipresent credits it to him as if he had done an act of charity with the guilty party, for he has taken out of the possession of the guilty party that which he has stolen."

II

A. And [others] do not judge him [M. San. 2:3A]. This is in line with the verse [in the Psalm of David], *"From thee [alone] let my vindication come!"* (Ps. 17:2).

B. R. Isaac in the name of rabbi: "King and people are judged before Him every day, as it is said, '... and may he do justice for his servant and justice for his people Israel, as each day requires' (1 King 8:59)."

III

A. R. Judah says, "If he wanted to perform the rite of removing the shoe or to enter into levirate marriage, his memory is a blessing" [M. San. 2:3E].

B. They said to him, "If you rule in this way, you turn out to diminish the honor owing to the king."

IV

A. Others do not marry the widow of [M. San. 2:3G] or the woman divorced by a king.

B. This is by reason of that which is said: "So [David's concubines] were shut up until the day of their death, living as if in widowhood" (2 Sam. 20:3).

C. R. Yudah bar Pazzi in the name of R. Pazzi in the name of R. Yohanan: "This teaches that David [treating them as forbidden though in law they were not] would have them dressed and adorned and brought before him every day, and he would say to his libido, 'Do you lust after something forbidden to you?' By your life! I shall now make you lust for something which is permitted to you."

D. Rabbis of Caesarea say, "They were in fact forbidden [20b] to hand [and it was not merely that he treated the women whom Absalom had raped as forbidden to him, but the law deemed them prohibited].

E. "For if a utensil belonging to an ordinary man used by an ordinary man is prohibited for use of a king, a utensil belonging to a king which was used by an ordinary man – is not an argument a fortiori that the king should be forbidden to make use of it?"

V

A. R. Judah says, "The king may marry the widow of a king. For we find in the case of David that he married widows of Saul, for it is said, *'And I gave you your master's house and your master's wives into your embrace'* (2 Sam. 12:8)" [M. San. 2:3H-J].

B. This refers to Rispah, Abigail, and Bath Sheba.

C. [The reference to Abigail, 1 Sam. 25, calls to mind Nabal and his origins:] Hezron had three sons, as it is written, *"The sons of Hezron that were born to him: Yerahmeel, Ram, and Keluba*i" (1 Chron. 2:9)

D. The first [son] was Yerahmeel, but he married a gentile woman to be crowned through her [royal ancestry], as it is written, *"Yerahmeel also had another wife, whose name was Atarah [crown]"* (1 Chron. 2:26).

E. *"She was the mother of Onam"* (1 Chron. 2:26), for she brought mourning *(aninah)* into his household.

F.   *"Ram was the father of Amminadab, and Amminadab was the father of Nahshon, [prince of the sons of Judah]. Nahshon was the father of Salma, Salma of Boaz, [Boaz of Obed, Obed of Jesse]"* (1 Chron. 2:10-12). And Boaz married Ruth.

G.   Lo, Nabal came from Kelubai.

H.   Nabal said, "In all Israel there is no son better than I."

I.   This is in line with that which is written, *"And there was a man in Maon, whose business was in Carmel. The man was very rich"* (1 Sam. 25:2).

J.   *Now he was a Kelubaite* (1 Sam. 25:3), for he came from Kelubai.

K.   *"David heard in the wilderness that Nabal was shearing [his sheep. So David sent ten young men; and david said to the young men, 'Go up to Carmel, and go to Nabal, and greet him in my name]. And thus shall you salute the living one: 'Peace be to you, [and peace be to your house, and peace be to all that you have'"* (1 Sam. 25:4-6)].

L.   Said R. Yusta bar Shunam, "They became a whole camp."

M.   *"And Nabal answered David's servants, ['Who is David?']"* (1 Sam. 25:10).

N.   How do we know that *in capital cases they begin from the side* [the youngest members of the court] [M. San. 4:2]?

O.   Samuel the Elder taught before R. Aha: *"'And David said to him men, [Gird every man his sword, and every man girded on his sword, and David also girded on his sword'* (1 Sam. 25:13)." David thus is the last to express his opinion.]

P.   *"'And he railed at them'* (1 Sam. 25:14) – what is the meaning of 'And he railed at them/?

Q.   "He incited them with words" [but see QH].

R.   *"Now therefore know this and consider what you should do; [for evil is determined against our master and against all his house, and he is so ill-natured that one cannot speak to him"]* (1 Sam. 25:17).

S.   *"[And as she rode on the ass ... behold, David and his men came down toward her;] and she met them"* (1 Sam. 25:20).

T.   She showed her thigh, and they followed out of desire for her.

U.   *"'... she met them'* – all of them had [involuntary] ejaculations" (PM).

V.   *"Now David said, 'Surely in vain have I guarded [all that this fellow has in the wilderness ... and he has returned me evil for good. God do so to the enemies of David ... if by morning I leave so much as] one who pisses against the wall of all who belong to him'"* (1 Sam. 25:21-22).

W.   [This reference to one who pisses on a wall is to a dog.] Now what place is therefore referring to a dog, who pisses on the wall? The meaning is that even a dog will get no pity.

X.   *"When Abigail saw David, [she made haste, and alighted from the ass, and fell before David on her face, and bowed to the ground]"* (1 Sam. 25:23).

Y.   She said to him, "My lord, David, as to me, what have I done? And my children – what have they done? My cattle – what have they done?"

Z.   He said to her, "It is because [Nabal] has cursed the kingdom of David."

AA. He said to him, "And are you [now] a king?"

BB. He said to her, "And has not Samuel anointed me as king?"

CC. She said to him, "Our lord Saul's coinage still is in circulation."

DD. *"But I your handmaid ..."* (1 Sam. 25:25) – this teaches that he demanded to have sexual relations with her.

EE. Forthwith she removed her stained [sanitary napkin] and showed it to me [indicating that she was in her menses and forbidden to have sexual relations on that account].

FF. He said to her, "Can one examine stains at night?"

GG. They said to him, "And let your ears hear what your mouth speaks. They do not examine sanitary napkins by night – and do they judge capital cases by night [as David was judging Nabal]!"

HH. He said to her, "The trial concerning him was complete while it was still day."

II. She said to him, *"'[And when the Lord was done to my lord according to all the good that he has spoken concerning you ...] my lord shall have no causes of grief, [for pangs of conscience, for having shed blood without cause]'"* (1 Sam. 25:30-31).

JJ. Said R. Eliezer, "There were indeed doubts [riddles] there."

KK. R. Levi was reviewing this pericope. R. Zeira told the associates, "Go and listen to R. Zeira, for it is not possible that he will lay out the pericope without saying something fresh about it."

LL. Someone went in and told them that that was not so.

MM. R. Zeira heard and said, "Even in matters of biblical stores there is the possibility of saying something fresh:

NN. "'... have no doubts ...' – that is, there were indeed causes [riddles] there."

OO. [Continuing Abigail's speech to David:] *"When word of your cause of grief goes forth, people will say about you, 'You are a murderer'* (1 Sam. 25:31), and you are destined to fall *(ibid.)* into sin, specifically to err through the wife of a man. It is better that there should be but one such case, and not two.

PP. "A much greater sin is going to come against you than this one. Do not bring this one along with the one which is coming."

QQ. *"For having shed blood"* (1 Sam. 25:31) – "You are going to rule over all Israel, and people will say about you, 'He was a murderer.'

RR. "And that which you say, 'Whoever curses the dominion of the house of David is subject to the death penalty,'

SS. "but you still have no throne."

TT. *"[And when the Lord has dealt well with my lord], then remember your handmaid"* (1 Sam. 25:31).

UU. This indicates that she treated herself as available [to David by referring to herself as his handmaid], and since she treated herself as available, Scripture itself treated her as diminished.

VV. For in every other passage you read, *"Abigail,"* but in this one: *"And David said to Abigail"* (1 Sam. 25:32).

WW. *"And David said ..., 'Blessed be your discretion, and blessed be you, who have kept me this day from bloodguilt'"* (1 Sam. 25:33) – in two senses, in the sense of the blood of menstruation, and in the sense of bloodshed [for she kept him from both kinds of bloodguilt].

2.4

A. [If the king] suffers a death in his family, he does not leave the gate of his palace.

B. R. Judah says, "If he wants to go out after the bier, he goes out,

C. "for thus we find in the case of David, that he went out after the bier of Abner,

D. "since it is said, *'And King David followed the bier'* (2 Sam. 3:31)."

E. They said to him, "This action was only to appease the people."

F. And when they provide him with the funeral meal, all the people sit on the ground, while he sits on a couch.

I

A. There is a Tanna who teaches that the women go first [in the mourning procession], and the men after them.

B. And there is a Tanna who teaches that the men go first, and the women afterward.

C. The one who said that the women go first invokes as the reason that they caused death to come into the world.

D. The one who said that men go first invokes the reason that it is to preserve the honor of Israelite women, so that people should not stare at them.

E. Now is it not written, *"And King David followed the bier"* (2 Sam. 3:31)? They said to him, "This action was only to appease the people" (M. San. 2:4D-E).

F. Once he appeased the women, he went and appeased the men [in the view of A.].

G. Or: Once he appeased the men, he went and appeased the women [in the view of B].

III

A. *"And David returned [to bless his household. But Michal the daughter of Saul came out to meet David, and said, 'How the king of Israel honored himself today, uncovering himself today before the eyes of his servants' maids, as one of the vulgar fellows shamelessly uncovers himself!']"* (2 Sam. 6:20).

B. What is the meaning of "one of the vulgar fellows?"

C. Said R. Ba bar Kahana, "The most vulgar of them all – this is a dancer!"

D. She said to him, "Today the glory of father's house was revealed."

E. They said about Saul's house that [they were so modest] that their heel and their toe never saw [their privy parts].

F. This is in line with that which is written, *"And he came to the sheepfolds [by the way, where there was a cave; and Saul went in to relieve himself]"* (1 Sam. 24:3).

G. R. Bun bar R. Eleazar: "It was a sheepfold within yet another sheepfold."

H. *And Saul went in to relieve himself ["cover his feet"]: [David] saw him lower his garments slightly and excrete slightly [as needed].*

I. *[David] said, "Cursed be anyone who lays a hand on such modesty."*

J. This is in line with that which he said to him, *"Lo, this day your eyes have seen [how the Lord gave you today into my hand in the cave; and some bade me kill you, but it spared you]"* (1 Sam. 24:10).

K. It is not written, *"I* spared you," but *"it* spared you" – that is, "Your own modesty is what spared you."

L. And David said to Michal, *"But by the* maids of whom you have spoken, by them I shall be held in honor" (2 Sam. 6:22).

M. For they are not handmaidens ('amahot), but mothers ('immahot).

N. And how was Michal punished? *"And Michal the daughter of Saul had no child to the day of her death"* (2 Sam. 6:23).

O. And is it now not written, *"... and the sixth was Ithream of Eglah, David's wife"* (2 Sam. 3:5)?

P. She lowed like a cow (Eglah) and expired [giving birth on the day of her death].

Q. You have no Israelite who so lowered himself in order to do religious deeds more than did David.

R. On what account did he lower himself for the sake of religious deeds?

S. For the people were staring at the ark and dying, as it is written, *"And he slew some of the men of Beth Shemesh, [because they looked into the ark of the Lord; he slew seventy men, and fifty thousand men, of them, and the people mourned because the Lord had made a great slaughter among the people]"* (1 Sam. 6:19).

T. R. Haninah and R. Mana: one said, *"'And he smote of the people seventy men'* – this refers to the Sanhedrin.

U. *"'And fifty thousand men'* – for they were comparable in worth to fifty thousand men."

V. And one of them said, *"'He smote of the people seventy men'* – this is the Sanhedrin.

W. *"'And fifty thousand'* – of the ordinary people as well."

X. It is written, *"A song of ascents of David: O Lord, my heart is not lifted up"* (Ps. 131:1) – "when Samuel anointed me."

Y. *"My eyes are not raised too high"* (Ps. 131:1) – "when I slew Goliath."

Z. *"And I do not occupy myself with things too great or too marvelous for me]"* (Ps. 131:1) – "when I brought the ark up."

AA. "Or too wondrous for me" – " when they put me back on my throne."

BB. *"But I have calmed and quieted my soul, like a child quieted at its mother's breast"* (Ps. 1131:2) – "Like a child which gives up goes down from its mother's belly, so my soul is humbled for me."

2.5

A. [The king] calls out [the army to wage] an optional war [fought by choice on the instructions of a court of seventy-one].

B. He [may exercise the right of eminent domain in order to] open a road for himself, and [others] may not stop him.

C. The royal road has no required measure.

D. all the people plunder and lay before him [what they have grabbed], and he takes the first portion.

I

A. [The rule of M. San. 2:5A is in line with] that which is written, "At his word they shall go out, and at his word they shall come in, [both he and all the people of Israel with him, the whole congregation]" (Num. 27:21).

II

A. *He [may exercise the right of eminent domain in order to] open a road for himself and others may not stop him [... and he takes the first portion] (M. San. 2:5B-D).*

B. This is in line with that which is written, *"And the people drove those cattle before him, and said, 'This is David's spoil'"* (1 Sam. 30:20).

III

A. *"He was with David at Pas-dammim, [when the Philistines were gathered there for battle. There was a plot of ground full of barley, and the men fled from the Philistines. But he took his stand in the midst of the plot and defended it, and slew the Philistines; and the Lord saved them by a great victory]"* (1 Chron. 11:13-14). [Note also 2 Sam. 23:11f.: *"And next to him was Shamah, the son of Agee the Hararite. The Philistines gathered together at Lehi, where there was a plot of ground full of lentils; and the men fled from the Philistines. But he took his stand in the midst of the plot and defended it, and slew the Philistines; and the Lord wrought a great victory."*]

B. R. Yohanan said, "It was a field as red as blood [so the place name is taken literally]."

C. And R. Samuel said, "[It was so called] for from that place the penalties ceased [as will be explained below]."

D. *"When the Philistines were gathered [there for battle, there was a plot of ground full of barley."* R. Jacob of Kepar Hanan said, "They were lentils, but their buds were as fine as those of barley [which accounts for the divergence between 1 Chron. 11:12 and 2 Sam. 23:11]."

E. Said R. Levi, "This refers to the Philistines, who came standing up straight like barley, but retreated bent over like lentils."

F. One Scripture says, *"There was a plot of ground full of barley"* (1 Chron. 11:13), and it is written, *"... full of lentils"* (2 Sam. 23:11).

G. [20c] R. Samuel bar Nahman said, "The event took place in a single year, and there were two fields there, one of barley, the other of lentils."

H. [To understand the following, we must refer to 2 Sam. 23:15-16: *"And David longed and said, 'O that someone would give me water to drink from the well of Bethlehem which is by the gate!' And the three mighty men broke through the host of the Philistines and drew water out of the well of Bethlehem that was by the gate."* Now "water" here is understood to mean "learning," "gate," the rabbinical court, and David is thus understood to require instruction. At issue is the battlefield in which the Philistines had hidden themselves, that is, as at Pas-dammim. What troubled David now is at issue.] David found it quite obvious that he might destroy the field of grain and pay its cost (DMYM).

I. Could it be obvious to him that he might destroy the field and *not* pay its cost to its Israelite owners]? [It is not permissible to rescue oneself by destroying someone else's property, unless one pays compensation. So that cannot be at issue at all.]

J.   [If he did have to pay, as he realized, then what he wanted to know "at the gate" was] which of them to destroy, and for which of the two to pay compensation [since he did not wish to destroy both fields such as, at G, Samuel posits were there].

K.   [These are then the choices] between the one of lentils and the one of barley.

L.   The one of lentils is food for man, and the one of barley is food for beast. The one of lentils is not liable, when turned into flour, for a dough-offering, and the one of barley is liable, when turned into flour, for dough-offering. As to lentils, the *omer* is not taken therefrom; as to barley the *omer* is taken therefrom. [So these are the three choices before David, and since there were two fields, he wanted to know which to burn and for which to pay compensation.]

M.   [This entire picture of the character of the battlefield is rejected by rabbis,] for rabbis say there was one field, but the incident took place [twice, in a period of] two years [and hence, in one year, it was planted with one crop, in the other year, the other].

N.   David then should have learned from the rule prevailing in the preceding year. But they do not derive a rule from one year to the next.

O.   One verse states, *"They took their stand in the midst of the plot and defended it"* (1 Chron. 11:14).

P.   And the other Scripture states, *"... and he defended it"* (2 Sam. 23:12).

Q.   What this teaches is that he restored the field to its owner, and it was as precious to him as a field planted with saffron.

IV

A.   It is written, *"And David said longingly, 'O that some one would give me water to drink from the well of Bethlehem [which is by the gate']"* (1 Chron. 11:17).

B.   R. Hiyya bar Ba said, "He required a teaching of law."

C.   *"Then the three mighty men broke through [the camp of the Philistines]"* (1 Chron. 11:18).

D.   Why three? Because the law is not decisively laid down by fewer than three.

E.   *"But David would not drink of it; [he poured it out to the Lord, and said, 'Far be it from me before my God that I should do this. Shall I drink the lifeblood of these men? For at the risk of their lives they brought it']"* (1 Chron. 11:18-19).

F.   David did not want the law to be laid down in his own name.

G.   "He poured it out to the Lord" – establishing [the decision] as [an unattributed] teaching for the generations [so that the law should be authoritative and so be cited anonymously].

H.   [Delete:] *He may exercise the right of eminent domain in order to open a road for himself, and others may not stop him.*

I.   Bar Qappara said, "It was the festival of Sukkot, and the occasion was the water offering on the altar, and it was a time in which high places were permitted [before the centralization of the cult in Jerusalem]. [So the view that David required a legal teaching is not accepted; it was literally water which David wanted and got.]"

J.   *"And three mighty men broke through ..."* – Why three? One was to
      kill [the Philistines]; the second was to clear away the bodies; and the
      third [avoiding the corpse-uncleanness] was to bring the flask for water
      in a state of cultic cleanness.

K.   One version of the story states, *"... He poured it out to the Lord ..."* (1
      Chron. 11:18).

L.   And the other version of the story states, *"He spilled it ..."* (2 Sam.
      23:16).

M.   The one which states "spilled" supports the view of R. Hiyya bar Ba
      [who treats the story as figurative], and the one which stated, "poured it
      out to the Lord" supports the picture of Bar Qappara [who treats it as a
      literal account].

N.   Huna in the name of R. Yosé: "David required information on the laws
      covering captives."

O.   R. Simeon b. Rabbi says, "What he thirsted after was the building of
      the house for the sanctuary [the Temple]."

2.6

A.   "He should not multiply wives to himself" (Deut. 17:17)
      – only eighteen.

B.   R. Judah says, "He may have as many as he wants, so
      long as they do not entice him [to abandon the Lord]
      (Deut. 17:17)."

C.   R. Simeon says, "Even if there is only one who entices
      him [to abandon the Lord] – lo, this one should not
      marry her."

D.   If so, why is it said, *"He should not multiply wives to
      himself"*?

E.   Even though they should be like Abigail [1 Sam. 25:3].

F.   *"He should not multiply horses to himself"* (Deut. 17:16)
      – only enough for his chariot.

G.   *"Neither shall he greatly multiply to himself silver and
      gold"* (Deut. 17:17) – only enough to pay his army.

H.   *"And he writes out a scroll of the Torah for himself"*
      (Deut. 17:18) –

I.   When he goes to war, he takes it out with him; when he
      comes back, he brings it back with him; when he is in
      session in court, it is with him; when he is reclining, it
      is before him,

J.   as it is said, *"And it shall be with him, and he shall read
      in it all the days of his life"* (Deut. 17:19).

K.   [Others may] not (1) ride on his horse, (2) sit on his
      throne, (3) handle his scepter.

L.   And [others may] (4) not watch him while he is getting a
      haircut, or (5) while he is nude, or (6) in the bathhouse,

M.   since it is said, *"You shall surely set him as king over
      you"* (Deut. 17:15) – that reverence for him will be upon
      you.

I

A. R. Kahana: "[The limitation to eighteen wives] is be reason of the following: *'And the sixth, Ithream, of Eglah, David's wife. These were born to David in Hebron'* (2 Sam. 3:5). And what is stated further on? *'... I would add to you as much more ...'* (2 Sam. 12:8). [This indicates that there would be yet two more groups of six wives, eighteen in all.]"

B. *"He should not multiply horses to himself"* (Deut. 17:16), only enough for his chariot" (M. san. 2:6F).

C. This is in line with the following: *"And David hamstrung all the chariot horses, but left enough for a hundred chariots"* (2 Sam. 8:4).

D. *"Neither shall he greatly multiply to himself silver and gold"* (Deut. 17:17) – only enough to pay his army (M. San. 2:6G).

E. R. Joshua b. Levi said, "But that provides solely for the wages for a given year alone [and not wages for several consecutive years]."

II

A. Said R. Aha, *"Said Solomon, '[I said of laughter, it is mad'* (Qoh. 2:2)]. Three things the attribute of justice ridiculed and I profaned:

B. *"'He should not multiply wives to himself"* (Deut. 17:17).

C. "And it is written, *'Now King Solomon loved many foreign women'* (1 Kings 11:1)." [This pericope resumes below, I.]

D. R. Simeon b. Yohai said, "He loved them literally, that is, he fornicated with them."

E. Hananiah, nephew of R. Joshua, says, "[He actually married them and violated the precept,] *"You shall not marry with them'* (Deut. 7:3)."

F. R. Yosé says, "It was to draw them to the teachings of Torah and to bring them under the wings of the Indwelling Presence of God."

G. R. Eliezer says, "It was by reason of the following verse: *'Did not Solomon king of Israel sin on account of such women? ... nevertheless foreign women made even him to sin'* (Neh. 13:26)."

H. It turns out that R. Simeon b. Yohai, Hananiah, and R. Eliezer maintain one viewpoint, and R. Yosé differs from all three of them.

I. *"'He should not multiply horses to himself'* (Deut. 17:16).

J. "And it is written, *'Solomon had forty thousand stalls of horses for his chariots and twelve thousand horsemen'* (1 Kings 4:26).

K. "They were unemployed, [there being peace in Solomon's days].

L. "But one who is not a king is permitted in these [that is, having many wives and horses, and much gold and silver].

M. "And it is written, *'And the king made silver to be in Jerusalem as stones'* (1 Kings 10:27)."

N. Was none of them stolen?

O. Said R. Yosé b. Haninah, "They were stones of a measure of ten cubits or eight cubits, and so they were [too large to be so stolen]."

P. R. Simeon b. Yohai taught, "Even the weights in the time of Solomon were not of silver but of gold."

Q. What is the Scriptural basis for this statement? *"None was of silver; it was accounted as nothing in the days of Solomon"* (1 Kings 10:21).

R. It is written, *"I said of laughter, 'It is mad'* (Qoh. 2:2)."

S. Said the Holy One, blessed be He, to Solomon, "What is this crown [doing] on your head? Get off my throne."

T.   R. Yosé b. Hanina said, "At that moment an angel came down and took the appearance of Solomon and removed Solomon from his throne and took the seat in his stead."

U.   Solomon went around the synagogues and schoolhouses, saying, *"I, Qohelet, have been king over Israel in Jerusalem"* (Qoh. 1:12).

V.   But they showed him the king sitting in his basilica, and [said to him,] "Do you say, 'I Qohelet'?" And they beat him with reeds and placed before him a dish of grits.

W.   At that moment he wept and said, *"This was my portion from all my labor"* (Qoh. 2:10).

X.   There are those who say they eat him with a staff, and there are those who say they beat him with a reed, and some say that they beat him with a belt of knotted rope.

Y.   Now who caused Solomon's downfall [= was his adversary]?

Z.   Said R. Joshua b. Levi, "It was the *yud* in the word, 'increase' (YRBH) which served as his adversary."

AA. R. Simeon b. Yohai taught, "The book of Deuteronomy went up and spread itself out before the Holy one, blessed be He.

BB. "It said before him, 'Lord of the world! You have written in your Torah that any convenant part of which is null is wholly nullified.'

CC. "Now lo, Solomon wishes to uproot a *yud* [as above] of mine,'

DD. "Said to him the Holy One, blessed be He, 'Solomon and a thousand like him will be null, but not one word of yours will be nullified.'

EE. R. Huna in the name of R. Aha: "The *yud* which the Holy One, blessed be He, removed from our matriarch, Sarah, [when her name was changed from Sarai,] half of it was given to Sarah, and half of it was given to Abraham.

FF. R. Hoshaiah taught, "The *yud* went up and prostrated itself before the Holy One, blessed be He, and said, 'Lord of the world! You have uprooted me from the name of that righteous woman!'

GG. "The Holy One, blessed be he, said to him, 'Go forth. In the past you were set in the name of a woman, and at the end of the name [Sarai]. By your life, I am going to put you in the name of a male, and at the beginning of the name.'"

HH. This is in line with that which is written, *"And Moses called Hoshea b. Nun, 'Joshua'"* (Num. 13:16).

III

A.   *And he writes for himself a scroll of the Torah (Deut. 17:18)* –

B.   **for his own use, that he not have to make use of the one of his fathers, but rather of his own [T. San. 4:7].**

C.   And they correct his scroll by comparing it to the scroll of the Temple courtyard, on the authority of the Sanhedrin of seventy-one members.

D.   *When he goes forth to war, it goes with him,* as it is said, *"And it shall be with him, and he shall read in it all the days of his life"* (Deut. 17:19) [cf. M. San. 2:6I-J].

E.   **Lo, it is a matter of an argument *a fortiori*: Now if a king of Israel, who is taken up with the needs of Israel, is told, *"And he shall read in it all the days of his life,"* an ordinary person, how much the more so [must he read in the Torah all the days of his life].**

F. Along these same lines, concerning Joshua it is written, *"This book of the law shall not depart out of your mouth, but you shall meditate on it day and night"* (Joshua 1:8).

G. Lo, it is a matter of an argument *a fortiori*: Now if Joshua, who is taken up with the needs of Israel, is told, "You shall meditate in it day and night," an ordinary person, how much more so [must he meditate in the Torah all the days of his life] [T. San. 4:8-9].

IV

A. A king of Israel: *Others may not ride on his horse, sit on his throne, or handle his crown, scepter (M. San. 2:6K)*, or any other of his possessions.

B. And when he does, all of them are to be burned in the presence of his corpse, as it is said, *"You shall die in peace. And as spices were burned for your fathers, the former kings who were before you, so men shall burn spices for you and lament for you"* (Jer. 34:5).

C. And others may not see him while he is nude, or when he is getting a haircut, or in the bathhouse (M. San. 2:6L).

D. This is in line with the following verse: *"Your eyes will see the king in his beauty"* (Is. 33:17).

E. R. Haninah went up to R. Yudan the Patriarch. He came out to greet him, dressed in his undershirt.

F. He said to him, "Go and put on your woolen cloak, on the grounds of *'Your eyes will see the king in his beauty'* (Is. 33:17)."

G. R. Yohanan went up to call on R. Yudan the Patriarch. He came forth to receive him in a shirt made of cotton.

H. He said to him, "Go back and put on your cloak of wool, on the grounds of: 'Your eyes will see the king in his beauty.'"

I. When R. Yohanan was leaving, [R. Yudan the Patriarch] said to him, "Bring refreshment for the mourner [bring good cheer]."

J. He said to him, "Send and get Menahem, the cake baker, for it is written, *'The teaching of kindness is on her tongue'* (Prov. 31:26)."

K. As he was leaving, [Yohanan] saw R. Haninah bar Sisi chopping wood.

L. He said to him, "Rabbi, this occupation is not consonant with your status."

M. He said to him, "And what shall I do? For I have no one who serves me as a disciple."

N. He said to him, "If you have no one to serve you as a disciple, you should not accept upon yourself appointment [to a court]."

V

A. Yosé Meoni interpreted the following verse in the synagogue in Tiberias: *"'Hear this, o priests!'* (Hos. 5:1): Why do you not labor in the Torah? Have not the twenty-four priestly gifts been given to you?

B. "They said to him, 'Nothing at all has been given to us.'

C. [20d] *"'And give heed, O House of Israel!'* (Hos. 5:1).

D. "'Why do you not give the priests the twenty-four gifts concerning which you have been commanded at Sinai?'

E. "They said to him, 'The king takes them all.'

F.   *"'Hearken, O house of the king!   For the judgment pertains to you'*
     (Hos. 5:1).

G.   "To you have I said, 'And this shall be the priests' due from the people,
     from those offering a sacrifice ...:   *they shall give to the priest the
     shoulder, the two cheeks, and the stomach'* (Deut. 18:3).

H.   "I am going to take my seat with them in court and to make a decision
     concerning them and blot them [the kings] out of the world."

I.   R. Yudan the Patriarch heard [about this attack on the rulers] and was
     angry.

J.   [Yosé] feared and fled.

K.   R. Yohanan and R. Simeon b. Laqish went up to make peace with [the
     Patriarch].

L.   They said to him, "Rabbi, he is a great man."

M.   He said to them, "Is it possible that everything which I ask of him, he
     will give to me?"

N.   They said to him, "Yes." [So Yosé was called back.]

O.   [The Patriarch] said to [Yosé], "What is the meaning of that which is
     written: *'For their mother has played the harlot'* (Hos. 2:5)?

P.   "Is it possible that our matriarch, Sarah, was a whore?"

Q.   He said to him, "As is the daughter, so is her mother.

R.   "As is the mother, so is the daughter.

S.   "As is the generation, so is the patriarch.

T.   "As is the patriarch, so is the generation.

U.   "As is the altar, so are its priests."

V.   Kahana said likewise: "As is the garden, so is the gardener."

W.   He said to them, "It is not enough for him that he dishonors me one
     time not in my presence, but also in my presence he does so these three
     times [Q-T]!"

X.   He said to him, "What is the meaning of that which is written, *'Behold,
     everyone who uses proverbs will use this proverb about you, 'Like
     mother, like daughter'* (Ez. 16:44).

Y.   "Now was our matriarch, Leah, a whore?

Z.   "As it is written, *'And Dinah went out'* (Gen. 34:1) [like a whore, thus
     reflecting on her mother]."

AA. He said to him, 'It is in accord with that which is written, *'And Leah
     went out to meet him'* (Gen. 30:16).

BB. "They compared one going out to the other [and Leah went out to meet
     her husband, and Dinah learned from this that it was all right to go out,
     so she went out to meet the daughters of the land, but got raped]."
     [This was an acceptable reply to Yudan.]

VI

A.   R. Hezekiah was going along the way. A Samaritan met him. He said
     to him, "Rabbi, are you the rabbi of the Jews?"

B.   He said to him, "Yes."

C.   He said to him, "Note what is written, *'You will surely set a king over
     you'* (Deut. 17:15).

D.   "It is not written 'I shall set ...,' but *'You* shall set ...,' for you yourself
     set him over you."

5. SIFRA

Sifra. The Judaic Commentary on Leviticus. A New Translation. The Leper. Leviticus 13:1-14:57. Chico, 1985: Scholars Press for Brown Judaic Studies. Based on the translation of *Sifra Parashiyyot Negaim* and *Mesora* in *A History of the Mishnaic Law of Purities. VI. Negaim. Sifra.* [With a section by Roger Brooks.]

Parashat Negaim

Pereq 1

A. *And the Lord spoke to Moses and to Aaron saying, A man (Adam) when there will be on the skin of his body* (Lev. 13:1-2) –

B. Why does Scripture say so [speaking of Adam + will be]?

C. Because it is said, *And a man or a woman, when there will be on the skin of his flesh bright spots [the priest shall make an examination, and if the spots on the skin of his body are of a dull white, it is tetter that has broken out in the skin; he is clean]* (Lev. 13:38-9) –

D. [This refers to] clean bright spots.

E. It is hardly necessary to speak [in Lev. 13:2] of [GRA: I know only about] bright spots which do not exhibit the colors of plagues and which have not come into the category [of uncleanness, for Lev. 13:38-9 includes them].

F. But [there are, in accord with Lev. 13:2, clean] bright spots which do [nonetheless] exhibit the colors of plagues [namely]:

G. Which were on him and he converted –
on the infant and he was born –
on the crease [of the flesh] and it was unfolded –
on the head and on the beard –
on the festering boil and burning and blister –

H. Their [those items in G] colors changed, whether to produce a lenient or a stringent ruling –
R. Eleazar b. Azarah declares clean.
R. Eleazar b. Hisma says, To produce a lenient ruling – it is clean, and to produce a stringent ruling – let it be examined afresh.
R. Aqiva says, Whether to produce a lenient or a stringent ruling, it is examined afresh [M. Neg. 7:1].

I. Therefore it is said, *A man (Adam) – when there will be* (Lev. 13:1).

N1:1

A. *When there will be* (Lev. 12:2) –

B. From the [time at which this law is] proclaimed [namely, Sinai] onward.

C. And is it not logical?

D. It [Scripture] has declared unclean with reference to Zabim and has declared unclean with reference to plagues.

E. Just as in the case of Zabim, it declared clear [such appearances of uncleanness as occurred] before the pronouncement [of the Torah], so in reference to plagues, it declared clear [such appearances of uncleanness as occurred] on them before the pronouncement.

N1:2

F. It [moreover] is an argument *a fortiori*:
    If in the case of Zabim, whose uncleanness and uncleanness may be
    determined by anyone, it [Scripture] has declared free before the
    declaration, plagues, the uncleanness or cleanness of which may be
    declared only by a priest, is it not logical that it should declare them
    clear before the declaration?

G. No. If you have so stated concerning Zabim, whom it [Scripture] did not
    declare unclean when [the flux is] accidental, will you say so concerning
    plague, which is declared unclean [even when the uncleanness is]
    accidental?

H. Since is declared unclean [even when the uncleanness is] accidental, will
    it declare them clear before the pronouncement [of the Scriptural law]?

I. Therefore Scripture says, *When it will be,* meaning, from the
    pronouncement [at Sinai] and onward.

N1:3

A. *On the skin of his flesh* (Lev. 13:2).

B. What does Scripture mean to say?

C. Because it is said, *And hair in the diseased spot has turned white,* (Lev.
    13:3), might one say I have reference only to a place which is suitable
    to grow white hair? But a place which is not suitable to grow white hair
    – how do we know [that it is susceptible]?

D. Scripture says, *On the skin of his flesh* – as an inclusionary clause.

[E. *A swelling or an eruption or a spot* (Lev. 13:2).]

F. *A swelling* – this is a swelling.

G. *A spot* – this is a spot.

H. *An eruption (SPHT)* – this is secondary [in color] to the bright spot.

I. *And its shade is deep [Lev. 13:3: And the shade of the plague is deep]* –
    [the color of the SPHT is] secondary to that of the swelling.

J. What is the meaning of the word eruption (ST)? Prominent (MWBHQT)
    (GRA: MWGBHT).

K. **Like the shades of the shadow, which are higher than the
    appearance of the sun.**

L. What is the meaning of the word deep (MWQ)?

M. **Deep as the shades of the sun, which are deeper than the
    shadow.**

N. What is the meaning of the word eruption (SPHT)? Secondary (TPYLH).

O. As it is said, *Put me (SPHYNY), I pray you, in one of the priest's
    places...* (I Sam. 2:36).

P. *And it will be* (Lev. 13:2) – teaches that **they [the colors] join
    together with one another to declare clear and to certify
    and to shut up.**

Q. *On the skin of his flesh* (Lev. 13:2) – on the skin of that flesh which
    can be seen [or: in accord with its appearance].

R. On this basis have they said:
    **A bright spot appears dim on a German and the dim one on
    the Ethiopian appears bright.**

N1:4

S.   R. Ishmael says, The house of Israel – lo, I am atonement for them – lo, they are like box-wood, not black and not white but intermediate.

T.   R. Aqiva says, The artists have pigments with which they color skin black, white, and intermediate. One brings the intermediate pigment and surrounds it [the bright spot] on the outer perimeter, and it will appear like the intermediate.

U.   R. Yose says, One Scripture says, *On the skin of the flesh* (Lev. 13:2), and another Scripture says, *On the skin of the flesh* (Lev. 13:2).

V.   We therefore find that the specification of colors of plagues are meant to produce a lenient ruling, but not to produce a strict ruling. One therefore examines the German in accord with his skin-tone to produce a lenient ruling.

W.   It comes out that [thereby] one carries out, On the skin of his flesh.

X.   And the Ethiopian is adjudged in accord with the intermediate pigment to produce a lenient ruling.

Y.   It comes out that [thereby] one carries out, *On the skin of the flesh.*

Z.   And sages say, This [and this are adjudged in accord with] the intermediate [M. Neg. 2:1].

N1:5

A.   *And it will be on the skin of his flesh [for a plague]* (Lev. 13:2).

B.   This teaches that he is pained by it.

C.   And how do we know that also others are pained by it?

D.   They see him, that he is pained by it.

E.   Scripture says, *For a plague* (Lev. 13:2).

F.   *A leprosy [sign]* (Lev. 13:2) – the size of a split bean.

G.   And is it not logical?

H.   It has declared unclean here [where there is white hair], and it has declared unclean in reference to quick flesh.

I.   Just as quick flesh is the size of a split bean, so also here [we require] a sign the size of a split bean.

N1:6

J.   No. If you have said so concerning quick flesh, which must be the size of a lentil, will you say so concerning [a leprosy sign, marked as unclean by] white hair, for the space of white hair requires nothing [no specific area].

K.   Scripture says, *Leprosy* (Lev. 13:2) – a sign the size of a split bean.

N1:7

A.   *And he will be brought to Aaron [the priest or to one of his sons the priests]* (Lev. 13:2).

B.   I know only about Aaron himself.

C.   How do we know to include another priest?

D.   Scripture says, *The priest* (Lev. 13:2).

E.   How do we know to include [as suitable examining priests] those [priests who are] injured?

F.   Scripture says, *Among his sons* (Lev. 13:2).

G. Then perhaps should I also include profaned [disqualified priests, HLLYM]?
H. Scripture says, *The priests* (Lev. 13:2) – the disqualified priests are excluded.
I. And how do we know to include any Israelite [qualified to examine the plague]?
J. Scripture says, *Or to one.*

N1:8

K. If our end is to include every Israelite, why does Scripture say, *Or to one of his sons the priests?*
L. But to teach that the actual declaration of uncleanness or cleanness is only by a priest.
M. How so?
N. A sage who is an Israelite examines the plagues **and says to the priest, even though he is an idiot, Say, Unclean, and he says, Unclean. Say, Clean, and he says, Clean [M. Neg. 3:1].**
O. Another matter:
P. Why does Scripture say, *Or to one of his sons the priests* (Lev. 13:2).
Q. Since it is said, *In accord with their instructions will be every dispute and every plague* (Deut. 21:5), controversies are linked to plagues. Just as plagues must be decided by day, so controversies must be judged by day.

N1:9

R. **Just as controversies may not be settled by relatives, so plagues may not be examined relatives [M. Neg. 2:5].**
S. If [we should now attempt to continue]: Just as controversies must be with three [judges] so plagues must be examined by three [priests] – it is an argument a fortiori.
T. If his property [dispute] is settled by a decision of three judges, should his body not be examined by three?
U. Scripture says, *Or to one of his sons the priests* (Lev. 13:2).
V. This teaches that a single priest examines the plagues.

N1:10

Parashat Negaim

Pereq 2

A. *And the priest shall see the diseased spot* (Lev. 13:3) –
His eyes should be upon it when he sees it.
B. *[And the priest shall examine the diseased spot] on the skin [of the flesh]* (Lev. 13:3) –
C. **On skin of the flesh of an intermediate [color].**
D. *On the skin of the flesh* (Lev. 13:3) –
E. That he should see all of the flesh with it in one glance.
F. R. Yose b. R. Judah says, Why does Scripture say, *On the skin of the flesh* (Lev. 13:3)?
G. That all which is outside it be **near the skin of the flesh and suitable for spreading.**

H. For if it was near the head or the beard or the boil or the burning or the blister which are festering, it is not unclean [M. Neg. 2:12].

N2:1

A. *[And if the hair (in the diseased spot [plague]) [has turned white and the disease appears to be deeper than the skin of his body, it is a leprous disease (Lev. 13:3)].*

B. *And hair* (Lev. 13:3) – the smallest quantity of hair is two hairs.

C. *On the plague –*

D. to include what is inside it and lies outside it,

E. excluding that which is outside it and lying inside it.

F. *In the diseased spot has turned white* (Lev. 13:3) –

G. not that which was there before.

H. On this basis they have said:

I. If the bright spot preceded the white hair, it is unclean, and if white hair preceded the bright spot, it is clean, and if there is doubt [as to which came first], it is unclean.

J. R. Joshua says, It is doubtful [M. Neg. 4:11].

N2:2

A. *And [if] the hair in the diseased spot has turned white* (Lev. 13:3).

B. On this basis have they said:

C. Two hairs, their root is black and their head is white – it is clean.

D. Their root is white and their head is black – unclean.

E. And how much must be in the whiteness?

F. R. Meir says, Any amount at all [M. Neg. 4:4].

G. And sages say, About [the length of] the hair.

H. R. Meir says, That people should not imagine that they are judged by ignoramuses.
But [if] the tip (HWD) of the hair is white, it is unclean. But [if] it is not (a) white (hair), it is clean (QM) [Neg. 2:2].

N2:3 (b. Nid. 52b)

A. *White* (Lev. 13:3) –

B. Not red, and not green, and not black.

C. I shall exclude all of them, but I shall not exclude golden hair.

D. And is it not logical? If white hair, which is not a token of uncleanness in a scall, lo, it is a token of uncleanness in a plague-spot, golden hair, which is a token of uncleanness in a scall, will it not logically serve as a token of uncleanness in a plague-spot?

E. Scripture says, *A white hair* – and not a golden one.

N2:4

A. *And the plague appears to be deeper [than the skin of his body]* (Lev. 13:3) –

B. Touching it does not make it deeper [Hillel].

C. *The color of the plague is deeper* (Lev. 13:3) – the color of the white hair is not deep.

D. *The color of the plague* – [mentioning color is] to include for it [as a sign of uncleanness] the fourth shade.

E. *It* – it has no fifth shade.

N2:5

A. *And the disease appears to be deeper than the skin of his body – it is a leprous disease* (Lev. 13:3) –

B. Why does Scripture say this?

C. Because it is said, *[When the priest has examined him], he shall declare him unclean, he shall not shut him up* (Lev. 13:11) –

D. We learned that:

E. they do not shut up one who has been certified unclean [M. Neg. 3:1].

N2:6

A. How do we know that: they do not certify as unclean one who has been shut up, and they do not shut up one who has been shut up, and they do not certify one who has been certified? [M. Neg. 3:1]?

B. Scripture says, *And he will not shut him up, because he is unclean* (Lev. 13:11).

C. Whoever is called unclean is not subject on its [another spot's] account.

N2:7

A. Might one say, One should not say, Lo, you are shut up on account of this one and certified on account of this one, certified on account of this one and shut up on account of this one, and certified on account of this and on account of that?

B. Scripture says, *It is a diseased spot* (Lev. 13:3). *And he will see it* (Lev. 13:3).

C. *It is a leprous disease and he will see it* (Lev. 13:3) –

D. 1. all at once.

    2. That if it was on the tip of his nose, protruding this way and that, on the tip of his finger, protruding this way and that, he is not unclean [M. Neg. 2:12].

N2:8

E. On this basis they have said: Twenty four tips of limbs are in man which are not made unclean because of quick flesh:
the tips of the fingers of the hands, and toes of the feet, and the tips of the ears, and the tip of the nose, and the tip of the penis, and the tips of the breasts in the woman.
R. Judah says, Also of the man.
R. Eleazar says, The wens and the warts and warts are not made unclean because of quick flesh [M. Neg. 6:7].

N2:9

A. *And he will declare him unclean* (Lev. 13:3).

B. Him [whose tokens of uncleanness he has seen] does he declare unclean, and he does not declare unclean him who uproots the tokens of uncleanness from the midst of his diseased spot before he came to the priest.

C. Said R. Aqiva, I asked R. Ishmael and R. Joshua while they were going to Nidbat:

D. [If he does so] during his quarantine, what is the law?

E. They said to him, We have not heard, but we have heard, Before he came to the priest, he is clean; after he is certified unclean, he is unclean.

F. I began to bring proofs for them.

G. On what account is he clean if he does so before he came to the priest? Is it not because the priest has not actually seen the tokens of uncleanness?

H. So if this happens while he is shut up, he is clean until the priest will declare him unclean.

I. Another version:

J. If he is standing before the priest –

K. It is all the same whether he is standing before the priest or whether he is standing during his quarantine, he is clean until the priest will declare him unclean.

L. They said to him, Well have you spoken.

M. When is his purification?

N. R. Eliezer says, When another diseased spot will appear in him, and he will be declared clean on its account.

O. And sages say, Until it breaks forth over his entire body, or until his [original] bright spot will diminish to less than the size of a split bean [M. Neg. 7:4, T. 3:4].

N2:10

Parashat Negaim

Parashah II

A. A white spot (Lev. 13:4: But if the spot is white in the skin of his body and appears no deeper than the skin...) –

B. I know only the white spot.

C. How do we know that we should include the swelling [that it too is white (Hillel)]?

D. Scripture says below, A white swelling (Lev. 13:9: And if there is a white swelling in the skin...).

E. And how do we know that we should include the other shades?

F. Scripture says, And if a bright spot.

NII:3

G. Might one say that just as it is third in Scripture [1. swelling, 2. eruption, 3. spot], so it should be third in the shades [of white] [that is, it need not be so white as the others]?

H. Scripture says, White (Lev. 13:4), white (Lev. 13:9).

I. It is white, and there is no brighter than it.

J. And how white must it be?

K. Like snow, as it is said, And lo, Miriam was leprous like snow (Num. 12:10).

NII:2

L. Might one say that on account of every shade of snow they should be unclean, but [if they are as white as] all other shades [of white, except for the range of snow], they should be clean?

M. Scripture says, *It is a tetter* (Lev. 13:38).

N. [That which is as dull as] a tetter is unclean. From it [a tetter] and brighter, it is unclean.

NII:3

O. On this basis have they said:

P. The shades of plagues are two which are four.
A bright spot is as bright as snow. Secondary to it is [white] as the plaster of the Temple.
The rising is as white as the skin of an egg.
Secondary to it is a shade of white like wool, the words of R. Meir.
And sages say, The rising is [white] as wool, and secondary to it is [white] as the skin of an egg.

NII:4

Q. The variegation of the snow is like mixed wine.
The variegation of the lime is like blood mixed in water, the words of R. Ishmael.

R. R. Aqiva says, The reddishness which is in this and in that is like wine mixed in water.
But that of snow is bright, and that of plaster is duller than it.

NII:5

R. R. Hanina Prefect of the Priests says, The shades of plagues are sixteen.
R. Dosa b. Harkinas says, Thirty-six.
Aqavya b. Mehallel: Seventy-two.

S. Said R. Yose, R. Joshua the son of R. Aqiva asked R. Aqiva, saying to him, Why have they said, The shades of plagues are two which are four?
He said to him, If not, what should they say?
He said to him, Let them say, From the white of the skin of an egg and brighter it is unclean, and they join together with one another.

T. Said R. Yose, R. Joshua the son of R. Aqiva asked R. Aqiva, saying to him, Why have they said, The shades of plagues are two which are four?

U. He said to him, If not, what should they say?

V. He said to him, Let them say, From the shade of white like the skin of the egg and brighter is unclean.

W. He said to him, To teach you that they join together with one another.

X. He said to him, Let them say, Anything which is as white as the skin of an egg or brighter is unclean, and they [the colors] join together with one another.

Y. He said to him, It teaches that if one is not an expert in them and in their names, he should not examine plagues [M. Neg. 1:14, T. Neg. 1:1].

NII:6

A. *And its hair [has not turned white]* (Lev. 31:4) –
B. Not the hair of its quick flesh.
C. How so?
D. A bright spot the size of a split bean, and in it is quick flesh the size of a lentil –
   and white hair is in the midst of the quick flesh –
E. the quick flesh went away – it is unclean because of the white hair.
F. The white hair went away – it is unclean because of the quick flesh.
G. R. Simeon declares clean, because the bright spot did not turn it [the hair white].
H. He [Hillel: They] said to him, And has it not already been said, *And hair in the plague has turned white* (Lev. 13:4)?
I. This [quick flesh] is a plague in any event.

NII:7

G. *And its hair has not turned white* (Lev. 13:4).
H. And not hair of part of it.
I. How so?
J. A bright spot –
K. it [and] its quick flesh are the size of a split bean –
L. and white hair is in the midst of the bright spot –
M. the quick flesh went away –
N. it is unclean because of the white hair.
O. The white hair went away –
P. it is unclean because of the quick flesh.
Q. R. Simeon declares clean, because the bright spot the size of a split bean did not turn it [white].
R. And they agree [better: He (Simeon) agrees] that if there is in the place of white hair an area the size of a split bean, it is clean.

NII:8

S. *And its hair has not turned white, and he will shut up* (Lev. 13:4).
T. Lo, if there is in it black hair, it does not diminish it.
U. The disciples asked R. Yose, A bright spot and in it is black hair: do we take account of the possibility that its place has diminished the bright spot to a size less than a split bean?
V. He said to them, A bright spot, and [supply: in it is] white hair – do we take account of the possibility that its place has diminished the bright spot to less than a split bean?
W. They said to him, No. If you have said so concerning white hair, which is a sign of uncleanness [itself], will

you say so concerning black hair, which is not a sign of uncleanness?

X. He said to them, Lo, if there are in it ten white hairs, in any event are more than two of them tokens of uncleanness? Do we take account of the possibility that the excess has diminished the place of the bright spot to less than a split bean?

Y. They said to him, No. If you have said so concerning white hair, which is a kind of uncleanness, will you say so concerning black hair, which in any event is not a variety of uncleanness?

Z. He said to them, Also black hair turns and becomes a kind of uncleanness [M. Neg. 4:6, T. Neg. 2:3].

AA. But it says, *And its hair has not turned white, and he shuts up* – lo, if there is in it black hair, it does not diminish [the area of the spot].

BB. *And the priest shall shut up the diseased spot seven days* (Lev. 13:5) – first [this is the first of two quarantines].

NII:9

6. SIFRE TO NUMBERS

Sifré to Numbers. An American Translation. I. *1-58* Atlanta, 1986: Scholars Press for Brown Judaic Studies.

Sifré to Numbers. An American Translation. II. *59-115*. Atlanta, 1986: Scholars Press for Brown Judaic Studies. [III. *116-161*: William Scott Green].

Numbers 5:1-4

I:I

1. A. *"The Lord said to Moses, 'Command the people of Israel that they put out of the camp [every leper and every one having a discharge, and every one that is unclean through contact with the dead]'"* (Num. 5:1-2).
   B. For what purpose is this passage presented?
   C. Because it is said, *"But the man who is unclean and does not cleanse himself, [that person shall be cut off from the midst of the assembly, since he has defiled the sanctuary of the Lord, because the water for impurity has not been thrown upon him, he is unclean]"* (Num. 19:20).
   D. Consequently, we are informed of the penalty [for contaminating the sanctuary]. But where are we informed of the admonition not to do so?
   E. Scripture accordingly states, *"Command the people of Israel that they put out of the camp every leper and every one having a discharge, and every one that is unclean through contact with the dead"* (Num. 5:1-2).
   F. Lo, here is an admonition that unclean persons not come into the sanctuary ["out of the camp"] in a state of uncleanness. [Consequently, the entire transaction – admonition, then penalty – is laid forth.]

I:II

1. A. *"Command"* (Num. 5:2):

B. The commandment at hand is meant both to be put into effect immediately and also to apply for generations to come.

C. You maintain that the commandment at hand is meant both to be put into effect immediately and also to apply for generations to come.

D. But perhaps the commandment is meant to apply only after a time [but not right away, at the moment at which it was given].

E. [We shall now prove that the formulation encompasses both generations to come and also the generation to whom the commandment is entrusted.] Scripture states, *"The Lord said to Moses, 'Command the people of Israel that they put out [of the camp every leper and every one having a discharge, and every one that is unclean through contact with the dead. You shall put out both male and female, putting them outside the camp, that they may not defile their camp, in the midst of which I dwell.'] And the people of Israel did so and drove them outside the camp, as the Lord said to Moses, so the people of Israel did"* (Num. 5:1-4). [The verse itself makes explicit the fact that the requirement applied forthwith, not only later on.]

F. Lo, we have learned that the commandment at hand is meant to be put into effect immediately.

G. How then do we derive from Scripture the fact that it applies also for generations to come? [We shall now show that the same word used here, *command*, pertains to generations to come and not only to the generation at hand.]

H. Scripture states, *"Command the children of Israel to bring you pure oil from beaten olives [for the lamp, that a light may be kept burning continually outside the veil of the testimony in the tent of meeting, Aaron shall keep it in order from evening to morning before the Lord continually; it shall be a statute for ever throughout your generations]"* (Lev. 24:2).

I. Lo, we here derive evidence that the commandment at hand is meant both to be put into effect immediately and also to apply for generations to come, [based on the framing of the present commandment].

J. How, then, do we derive evidence that all of the commandments that are contained in the Torah [apply in the same way]? [We wish now to prove that the language, *command*, always bears the meaning imputed to it here.]

K. R. Ishmael maintained, "Since the bulk of the commandments stated in the Torah are presented without further amplification, while in the case of one of them [namely, the one at hand], Scripture has given explicit details, that commandment [that has been singled out] is meant both to be put into effect immediately and also to apply for generations to come. Accordingly, I apply to all of the other commandments in the Torah the same detail, so that in all cases the commandment is meant both to be put into effect immediately and also to apply for generations to come."

I.III

1. A. R. Judah b. Beterah says, "The effect of a commandment stated in any context serves only [1] to lend encouragement.

B. "For it is said, *'But command Joshua and encourage and strengthen him'* (Deut. 3:28).

C. "Accordingly, we derive the lesson that strength is granted only to the strong, and encouragement only to the stout of heart."

D. R. Simeon b. Yohai says, "The purpose of a commandment in any context is only [2] to deal with the expenditure of money, as it is said, *'Command the children of Israel to bring you pure oil from beaten olives for the lamp, that a light may be kept burning continually outside the veil of the testimony in the tent of meeting, Aaron shall keep it in order from evening to morning before the Lord continually; it shall be a statute for ever throughout your generations'* (Lev. 24:2). *'Command the people of Israel that they put out of the camp every leper and every one having a discharge, and every one that is unclean through contact with the dead'* (Num. 5:1-2). *'Command the children of Israel that they give to the Levites from the inheritance of their possession cities to dwell in, and you shall give to the Levites pasture lands round about the cities'* (Num. 35:2). *'Command the people of Israel and say to them, "My offering, my food for my offerings by fire, my pleasing odor you shall take heed to offer to me in its due season"'* (Num. 28:2). Lo, we see in all these cases that the purpose of a commandment is solely to bring about the expenditure of money.

E. "There is one exception, and what is that? It is this verse: *'Command the people of Israel and say to them, "When you enter the land of Canaan, this is the land that shall fall to you for an inheritance, the land of Canaan in its full extent"'* (Num. 34:2).

F. "You must give encouragement to them in the matter of the correct division of the land."

G. And Rabbi [Judah the Patriarch] says, "The use of the word, 'commandment' in all passages serves only for the purpose of [3] imparting an admonition [not to do a given action], along the lines of the following: *'And the Lord God commanded the man, saying, "You may freely eat of every tree of the garden, but of the tree of the knowledge of good and evil you shall not eat"'* (Gen. 2:16)."

I:IV

1. A. "[The Lord said to Moses, 'Command the people of Israel that] they put out of the camp [every leper and every one having a discharge, and every one that is unclean through contact with the dead']" (Num. 5:1-2).

B. Is it from the [innermost] camp, of the Presence of God, or should I infer that it is only from the camp of the Levites?

C. Scripture states, "...they put out them of the camp." [The sense is that they are to be put outside of the camp of the Presence.]

D. Now even if Scripture had not made the matter explicit, I could have proposed the same proposition on the basis of reasoning [that they should be put outside of the camp of the Presence]:

E. If unclean people are driven out of the camp that contains the ark, which is of lesser sanctity, all the more so should they be driven out of the camp of the Presence of God, which is of greater sanctuary.

F. But if you had proposed reasoning on that basis, you would have found yourself in the position of imposing a penalty merely on the basis of reason [and not on the basis of an explicit statement of Scripture, and one does not impose a penalty merely on the basis of reason].

G. Then why is it stated: "...they put out of the camp"?

H. Making that matter explicit in Scripture serves to teach you that penalties are not to be imposed merely on the basis of logic [but require explicit specification in Scripture]. [That is, Scripture made a point that reason could have reached, but Scripture made the matter explicit so as to articulate a penalty applicable for violating the rule.]

I. [Rejecting that principle,] Rabbi says, "It is not necessary for Scripture to make the matter explicit, since it is a matter of an argument *a fortiori*:

J. "If the unclean people are driven out of the camp that contains the ark, which is of lesser sanctity, all the more so should they be driven out of the camp of the Presence of God, which is of greater sanctity.

K. "Then why is it stated: '*...they put out of the camp every leper and every one having a discharge, and every one that is unclean through contact with the dead*'?

L. "[By specifying that all three are put out of the camp,] Scripture thereby served to assign to them levels or gradations [of uncleanness, with diverse rules affecting those levels, as will now be spelled out. Since we know that that rule applies to the ostracism of the leper, the specification that the others also are to be put out of the camp indicates that a singular rule applies to each of the category. If one rule applied in common, then the specification with respect to the leper alone would have sufficed to indicate the rule for all others.]"

M. [We review the distinctions among several gradations of uncleanness affecting human beings, inclusive of the three at hand: the leper, the one having a discharge, and the one unclean through contact with the dead.] *'The Lord said to Moses, 'Command the people of Israel that they put out of the camp every leper and every one having a discharge, and every one that is unclean through contact with the dead'"* (Num. 5:1-2).

N. Shall I then draw the conclusion that all three of those listed [the leper, the one affected by a discharge, the one unclean with corpse-uncleanness] are to remain in the same locale [in relationship to the Temple]?

O. With respect to the leper, Scripture states explicitly, "He shall dwell by himself; outside of the camp shall be his dwelling" (Lev. 13:46).

P. Now the leper fell into the same category as the others, and he has been singled out from the general category, thereby serving to impose a single rule on the category from which he has been singled out.

Q. [And this is the rule applicable to the leper and hence to the others from among whom he has been singled out:] Just as in the case of the leper, who is subject to a most severe form of uncleanness, and who also is subjected to a more severe rule governing ostracism than that applying to his fellow, so all who are subject to a more severe form of uncleanness likewise are subject to a more severe rule of ostracism than that applying to his fellow.

R. On this basis sages listed distinctions that apply to those that are unclean [since a different rule applies to each of them, in descending order of severity, as is now spelled out]:

S. To any object that one affected by a flux imparts uncleanness, a leper imparts uncleanness. A leper is subject to a more severe rule, however, in that a leper imparts uncleanness through an act of sexual relations.

T. To any object that one unclean with corpse-uncleanness imparts uncleanness, one affected by a flux imparts uncleanness. But a more severe rule affects one affected by a flux, in that he imparts uncleanness to an object located far beneath a rock in the deep [imparting uncleanness to that deeply-buried object merely by the application of the pressure of his weight, while one unclean with corpse-uncleanness does not impart uncleanness merely by pressure of his weight alone].

U. To any object that one unclean by reason of waiting for sunset after immersion imparts uncleanness one unclean by corpse-uncleanness imparts uncleanness. A more severe rule applies to one unclean by corpse-uncleanness, for he imparts uncleanness to a human being [which is not the case of one who is unclean by reason of waiting for sunset after his immersion].

V. What is made unfit by one who has not yet completed his rites of atonement following uncleanness and purification is made unfit by one who awaits for sunset to complete his process of purification. A more strict rule applies to one awaiting sunset for the completion of his rite of purification, for he imparts unfitness to food designated for priestly rations [while the one who has completed his rites of purification but not yet offered the atonement-sacrifice on account of his uncleanness does not impart unfitness to priestly rations that he may touch].

I:V

1. A. "[The Lord said to Moses, 'Command the people of Israel] that they put out of the camp every leper and every one having a discharge, and every one that is unclean through contact with the dead'" (Num. 5:1-2).

    B. Why is the matter stated as it is? I know only that these three, that are enumerated, are subject to the law. How do I know that ostracism applies to all other unclean persons?

    C. R. Josiah would say, "You may construct an argument *a fortiori*. If unclean people are driven out of the camp that contains the ark, which is of lesser sanctity, all the more so should they be driven out of the camp of the Presence of God, which is of greater sanctity.

    D. "But if you were to propose reasoning on that basis, you would find yourself imposing a penalty merely on the basis of reason [and not on the basis of an explicit statement of Scripture, and one does not impose a penalty merely on the basis of reason].

    E. "That is why it is stated: '...they put out of the camp.'

    F. "Making that matter explicit in Scripture serves to teach you that penalties are not to be imposed merely on the basis of logic [but require explicit specification in Scripture]. [That is, Scripture made a point that reason could have reached, but Scripture made the matter explicit so as to articulate a penalty applicable for violating the rule.]"

I:VI

1. A. ["The Lord said to Moses, 'Command the people of Israel that they put out of the camp every leper and every one having a discharge, and] every one [that is unclean through contact with the dead]'" (Num. 5:1-2).

    B. Concerning everyone Scripture speaks.

    C. Or is it possible that Scripture speaks only of the Levites, who bear the ark?

    D. Scripture states, "[You shall put out] both male and female, putting them outside the camp."

E. [Referring both to male and to female means that not only Levites are subject to the commandment at hand, since women do not carry the ark. Accordingly,] it is with reference to everyone that Scripture here speaks.

2. A. All the same are adults and minors.

B. You maintain that all the same are adults and minors.

C. But perhaps in the present case the rule is the same as that is made explicit in connection with the penalty for violating the law at hand. Specifically, just as in the case of one who imparts uncleanness to the sanctuary, in which instance the penalty applies only to adults, as it is said, *"But the man [not the minor] who is unclean and does not cleanse himself, that person shall be cut off from the midst of the assembly, since he has defiled the sanctuary of the Lord"* (Num. 19:20), so here too, the admonition applies only to adults. [Accordingly, one can construct an argument to show that the rule is not the same for both adults and minors.]

D. Scripture states, *"...You shall put out both male and female, putting them outside the camp."*

E. Encompassed within the statement are both adults and minors.

3. A. R. Jonathan says, *"'...You shall put out both male and female, putting them outside the camp.'* Why is that statement spelled out?

B. "Because it is said, '...that they put out of the camp every leper and every one having a discharge, and every one that is unclean through contact with the dead,' I know only that these three that are specified are encompassed within the statement.

C. "How do I know that the rule applies to others who are unclean?

D. "You may construct an argument *a fortiori.* If unclean people are driven out of the camp that contains the ark, which is of lesser sanctity, all the more so should they be driven out of the camp of the Presence of God, which is of greater sanctity.

E. "But if you had proposed reasoning on that basis, you would have found yourself in the position of imposing a penalty merely on the basis of reason [and not on the basis of an explicit statement of Scripture, and one does not impose a penalty merely on the basis of reason].

F. "That is why it is stated: *'...they put out of the camp.'*

G. "Making that matter explicit in Scripture serves to teach you that penalties are not to be imposed merely on the basis of logic [but require explicit specification in Scripture]. [That is, Scripture made a point that reason could have reached, but Scripture made the matter explicit so as to articulate a penalty applicable for violating the rule.]"

I:VII

1. A. "[The Lord said to Moses, 'Command the people of Israel that they put out of the camp every leper and every one having a discharge, and every one that is unclean through contact with the dead.] You shall put out both male and female, putting them outside the camp, that they may not defile their camp, in the midst of which I dwell'"* (Num 5:1-4).

B. I know, on the basis of the stated verse, that the law applies only to male and female [persons who are suffering from the specified forms of cultic uncleanness]. How do I know that the law pertains also to one lacking clearly defined sexual traits or to one possessed of the sexual traits of both genders?

C. Scripture states, *"...putting them outside the camp."* [This is taken to
    constitute an encompassing formulation, extending beyond the male and
    female of the prior clause.]

D. I know, on the basis of the stated verse, that the law applies only to
    those who can be sent forth. How do I know that the law pertains also
    to those who cannot be sent forth?

E. Scripture states, *"...putting them outside the camp."* [This is taken to
    constitute an encompassing formulation, as before.]

F. I know on the basis of the stated verse that the law applies only to
    persons. How do I know that the law pertains also to utensils?

G. Scripture states, *"...putting them outside the camp."* [This is taken to
    constitute an encompassing formulation.]

2. A. [Dealing with the same question as at 1.F,] R. Aqiba says, *"'You shall
        put out both male and female, putting them outside the camp.'* Both
        persons and utensils are implied."

    B. R. Ishmael says, "You may construct a logical argument, as follows:

    C. "Since man is subject to uncleanness on account of *negaim* ["plagues"],
        and clothing [thus: utensils] are subject to uncleanness on the same
        count, just as man is subject to being sent forth [ostracism], likewise
        utensils are subject to being sent forth."

    D. No, such an argument is not valid [and hence exegesis of the actual
        language of Scripture, as at A, is the sole correct route]. If you have
        stated the rule in the case of man, who imparts uncleanness when he
        exerts pressure on an object used for either sitting or lying, and, on
        which account, he is subject to ostracism, will you say the same rule of
        utensils, which do not impart uncleanness when they exert pressure on an
        object used for sitting and lying? [Clearly there is a difference between
        the uncleanness brought about by a human being from that brought about
        by an inanimate object, and therefore the rule that applies to the one will
        not necessarily apply to the other. Logic by itself will not suffice, and,
        it must follow, the proof of a verse of Scripture alone will suffice to
        prove the point.]

    E. [No, that objection is not valid, because we can show that the same rule
        does apply to both an inanimate object and to man, namely] lo, there is
        the case of the stone affected with a *nega*, which will prove the point.
        For it does not impart uncleanness when it exerts pressure on an object
        used for sitting or lying, but it does require ostracism [being sent forth
        from the camp, a rule that Scripture itself makes explicit].

    F. Therefore do not find it surprising that utensils, even though they in
        general do not impart uncleanness when they exert pressure on an object
        used for sitting or lying, are to be sent forth from the camp. [Ishmael's
        logical proof stands.]

3. A. R. Yose the Galilean says, *"'You shall put out both male and female,
        putting them outside the camp, that they may not defile their camp, in
        the midst of which I dwell.'*

    B. "What marks as singular male and female is that they can be turned into a
        generative source of uncleanness [when they die and are corpses], and, it
        follows, they are to be sent forth from the camp when they become
        unclean [even while alive], so anything which can become a generative
        source of uncleanness will be subject to being sent forth from the camp.

C. "What is excluded is a piece of cloth less than three by three fingerbreadths, which in the entire Torah is never subject to becoming a generative source of uncleanness."

4. A. R. Isaac says, "Lo, Scripture states, '*[And every person that eats what dies of itself or what is to torn by beasts, whether he is a native or a sojourner, shall wash his clothes and bathe himself in water and be unclean until the evening; they he shall be clean.] But if he does not wash them or bathe his flesh, he shall bear his iniquity'* (Lev. 17:15-16).

B. "It is on account of failure to wash one's body that Scripture has imposed the penalty of extirpation.

C. "You maintain that it is on account of failure to wash one's body that Scripture has imposed the penalty of extirpation. But perhaps Scripture has imposed a penalty of extirpation only on account of the failure to launder one's garments.

D. "Thus you may construct the argument to the contrary [*su eipas*]: if in the case of one who has become unclean on account of corpse-uncleanness, which is a severe source of uncleanness, Scripture has not imposed a penalty merely because of failure to launder one's garments, as to one who eats meat of a beast that has died of itself, which is a minor source of uncleanness, it is a matter of reason that Scripture should not impose a penalty on the account of having failed to launder the garments."

I:VIII

1. A. "*['You shall put out both male and female,] putting them outside the camp, [that they may not defile their camp, in the midst of which I dwell.' And the people of Israel did so and drove them outside the camp, as the Lord said to Moses, so the people of Israel did*" (Num. 5:3-4).

B. Why is this statement made?

C. Since it says, "And the people of Israel did so and drove them outside the camp," I might derive the view that such persons also should not lay hands on the ark or on those who bear the ark, but a place entirely apart should be designated for them.

D. Accordingly, Scripture makes explicit the rule: "...putting them outside the camp," [meaning that ostracism involves the camp, but not the holy objects when they are carried outside of the camp. These the ones affected by uncleanness may nonetheless touch, and so the unclean persons are not totally excluded from the people.]

I:IX

1. A. "*[You shall put out both male and female, putting them outside the camp,] that they may not defile their camp, [in the midst of which I dwell]*":

B. On the basis of this verse, the rule has been formulated:

C. **There are three camps, the camp of Israel, the camp of the Levitical priests, and the camp of the Presence of God. From the gate of Jerusalem to the Temple mount is the camp of Israel, from the gate of the Temple mount to the Temple courtyard is the camp of the Levitical priesthood, and from the gate of the courtyard and inward is the camp of the Presence of God [T. Kelim 1:12].**

I:X

1. A. *"[You shall put out both male and female, putting them outside the camp, that they may not defile their camp,] in the midst of which I dwell.' [And the people of Israel did so and drove them outside the camp, as the Lord said to Moses, so the people of Israel did]"* (Num. 5:3-4).

   B. So beloved is Israel that even though they may become unclean, the Presence of God remains among them.

   C. And so Scripture states, *"...who dwells with them in the midst of their uncleanness"* (Lev. 16:16).

   D. And further: *"...by making my sanctuary unclean, which [nonetheless] is in their midst"* (Lev. 15:31).

   E. And it further says: *"...that they may not defile their camp, in the midst of which I dwell"* (Num. 5:3-4).

   F. And it further says, *"You shall not defile the land in which you live, in the midst of which I dwell, for I the Lord dwell in the midst of the people of Israel"* (Num. 35:34).

2. A. R. Yose the Galilean says, "Come and take note of how great is the power of sin. For before the people had laid hands on transgression, people afflicted with flux and lepers were not located among them, but after they had laid hands on transgression, people afflicted with flux and lepers did find a place among them.

   B. "Accordingly, we learn that these three events took place on one and the same day: [transgression, the presence of those afflicted with flux, the development of leprosy among the people]."

3. A. R. Simeon b. Yohai says, "Come and take note of how great is the power of sin. For before the people had laid hands on transgression, what is stated in their regard?

   B. *"'Now the appearance of the glory of the Lord was like a devouring fire on the top of the mountain in the sight of the people of Israel'* (Ex. 24:17).

   C. "Nonetheless, the people did not fear nor were they afraid.

   D. "But once they had laid hands on transgression, what is said in their regard?

   E. *"'And when Aaron and all the people of Israel saw Moses, behold, the skin of his face shone, and they were afraid to come near him'* (Ex. 34:30)."

I:XI

1. A. *"[You shall put out both male and female, putting them outside the camp, that they may not defile their camp, in the midst of which I dwell.' And the people of Israel did so and drove them outside the camp, as the Lord said to Moses,] so the people of Israel did"* (Num. 5:3-4):

   B. This statement, *["...And the people of Israel did so,"]* serves to recount praise for the Israelites, for just as Moses instructed them, so did they do.

2. A. Scripture states, *"...as the Lord said to Moses, so the people of Israel did."*

   B. What this teaches is that even the unclean people did not register opposition [but accepted the decree without complaint].

7. GENESIS RABBAH

Genesis Rabbah. The Judaic Commentary on Genesis. A New American Translation. Atlanta, 1985: Scholars Press for Brown Judaic Studies.

I. *Genesis Rabbah. The Judaic Commentary on Genesis. A New American Translation. Parashiyyot One through Thirty-Three. Genesis 1:1-8:14.*

II. *Genesis Rabbah. The Judaic Commentary on Genesis. A New American Translation. Parashiyyot Thirty-Four through Sixty-Seven. Genesis 8:15-28:9.*

III. *Genesis Rabbah. The Judaic Commentary on Genesis. A New American Translation. Parashiyyot Sixty-Eight through One Hundred. Genesis 28:10-50:26.*

Reading Scriptures: An Introduction to Rabbinic Midrash. With special reference to Genesis Rabbah. Chappaqua, 1986: Rossel.

Genesis and Judaism: The Perspective of Genesis Rabbah. An Analytical Anthology. Atlanta, 1986: Scholars Press for Brown Judaic Studies.

I follow the numbering and order of Theodor-Albeck, hence we continue I:I with I:V.1.A.

Parashah One

Genesis 1:1

I:I

1. A. *"In the beginning God created"* (Gen. 1:1):
    B. R. Oshaia commenced [discourse by citing the following verse:] *"Then I was beside him like a little child, and I was daily his delight [rejoicing before him always, rejoicing in his inhabited world, and delighting in the sons of men]'* (Prov. 8:30-31).
    C. "The word for 'child' uses consonants that may also stand for 'teacher,' 'covered over,' and 'hidden away.'
    D. "Some hold that the word also means 'great.'
    E. "The word means 'teacher,' in line with the following: *'As a teacher carries the suckling child'* (Num. 11:12).
    F. "The word means 'covered over,' as in the following: 'Those who were covered over in scarlet' (Lam. 4:5).
    G. "The word means 'hidden,' as in the verse, *'And he hid Hadassah'* (Est. 2:7).
    H. "The word means 'great,' in line with the verse, *'Are you better than No-Ammon?'* (Nah. 3:8). This we translate, 'Are you better than Alexandria the Great, which is located between rivers.'"
2. A. Another matter:
    B. The word means "workman."
    C. [In the cited verse] the Torah speaks, "I was the work-plan of the Holy One, blessed be He."

D. In the accepted practice of the world, when a mortal king builds a palace, he does not build it out of his own head, but he follows a work-plan.

E. And [the one who supplies] the work-plan does not build out of his own head, but he has designs and diagrams, so as to know how to situate the rooms and the doorways.

F. Thus the Holy One, blessed be He, consulted the Torah when he created the world.

G. So the Torah stated, "By means of 'the beginning' [that is to say, the Torah] did God create..." (Gen. 1:1).

H. And the word for "beginning" refers only to the Torah, as Scripture says, *"The Lord made me as the beginning of his way"* (Prov. 8:22).

I:V

1. A. R. Huna in the name of Bar Qappara commenced [discourse by citing the following verse]: *"'Let the lying lips be made dumb [which arrogantly speak matters kept secret against the righteous]'* (Ps. 31:19).

B. "[Translating the Hebrew word for dumb into Aramaic one may use words meaning] 'bound,' 'made dumb,' or ' silenced.'

C. "Let [the lying lips] be bound,' as in the following verse: *'For behold, we were binding sheaves'* (Gen. 37:7).

D. "'Let the lying lips be made dumb,' as in the usage in this verse: *'Or who made a man dumb '* (Ex. 4:11).

E. "'Let them be silenced' bears the obvious meaning of the word."

F. *"Which arrogantly speak matters kept secret against the righteous"* (Ps. 31:19):

G. "...which speak against the Righteous," the Life of the Ages, matters that he kept secret from his creatures [Freedman: the mysteries of creation].

H. *"With pride"* (Ps. 31:19):

I. That is so as to take pride, saying, "I shall expound the work of creation."

J. *"And contempt"* (Ps. 31:19): Such a one treats with contempt the honor owing to me.

K. For R. Yose b. R. Hanina said, "Whoever gains honor through the humiliation of his fellow gains no share in the world to come.

L. "For one does so through the honor owing to the Holy One, blessed be He, how much the more so!"

M. And what is written after the cited verse [Ps. 31:19]?

N. *"How abundant is your goodness, which you have stored away for those who revere you"* (Ps. 31:20).

O. Rab said, "Let one [who reveals the mysteries of creation] not have any share in your abundant goodness.

P. "Under ordinary circumstances, if a mortal king builds a palace in a place where there had been sewers, garbage, and junk, will not whoever may come and say, 'This palace is built on a place where there were sewers, garbage and junk,' give offense? So too, will not whoever comes and says, 'This world was created out of chaos, emptiness, and darkness' give offense?"

Q. R. Huna in the name of Bar Qappara: "Were the matter not explicitly written in Scripture, it would not be possible to state it at all: *'God created heaven and earth'* (Gen. 1:1) – from what? From the following: *'And the earth was chaos'* (Gen. 1:2). [Freedman: God first created chaos and emptiness, and out of these he created the world, but this is not to be taught publicly.]"

I.VI

1. A. R. Judah bar Simon commenced discourse [by citing the following verse:] *"'And he reveals deep and secret things'* (Dan.2:22).

   B. "The word for deep things refers to Gehenna, as it is written, *'But he does not know that the shades are there, that in the depths of the nether world are her guests'* (Prov. 9:18).

   C. "And the word for 'secret things' speaks of the Garden of Eden, as it is written, *'And for a refuge and for a hiding place'* (Is. 4:6). [This hiding place, using the same word, is taken to mean the Garden of Eden]."

2. A. Another matter:

   B. *"And he reveals deep and secret things"* (Dan. 2:22):

   C. This refers to deeds performed by the wicked [which God brings out into the open], as it is said, *"Woe to the ones who try to hide their plans from the Lord"* (Is. 29:15).

   D. *"He knows what is in the darkness"* (Dan. 2:22):

   E. This refers to deeds performed by the wicked, as it is written, *"And their works are in the darkness"* (Is. 4:6).

   F. *"But the light dwells with him"* (Dan. 2:22):

   G. This refers to deeds performed by the righteous, as it is said, *"Light is sown for the righteous"* (Ps. 97:11).

3. A. Said R. Abba of Sarangayya, *"'Light dwells with him'* (Dan. 2:22) refers to the messiah-king."

4. A. Said R. Judah bar Simon, "To begin with, when the world was being created, 'He reveals deep and secret things,' for it is written, *'In the beginning God created the heaven'* (Gen. 1:1). But the matter was not spelled out.

   B. "Where then was it spelled out?

   C. "Elsewhere: *'Who stretches out the heaven as a curtain'* (Is. 40:22).

   D. *"'...and the earth'* (Gen. 1:1). But this matter, too, was not then spelled out.

   E. "Where then was it spelled out?

   F. "Elsewhere: 'For he says to the snow, *"Fall on the earth"'* (Job 37:6).

   G. "And God said, *'Let there be light'* (Gen. 1:3).

   H. "And this too was not spelled out.

   I. "Where then was it spelled out?

   J. "Elsewhere: *'Who covers yourself with light as with a garment'* (Ps. 104:2)."

I.VII

1. A. R. Isaac commenced [discourse by citing the following verse]: *"'The beginning of your word is truth [and all your righteous ordinance endures forever]'* (Ps. 119:16)."

   B. Said R. Isaac [about the cited verse], "From the beginning of the creation of the world, 'The beginning of your word was truth.'

   C. *"'In the beginning God created'* (Gen. 1:1).

D. "'*And the Lord God is truth'* (Jer. 10:9).

E. "Therefore: '*And all your righteous ordinance endures forever'* (Ps. 119:16).

F. "For as to every single decree which you lay down for your creatures, they accept that degree as righteous and receive it in good faith, so that no creature may differ, saying, 'Two powers gave the Torah, two powers created the world.'

G "[Why not?]' Because here it is not written, 'And gods spoke,' but rather, '*And God spoke'* (Ex. 20:1).

H. "'In the beginning [gods] created is not written, but rather, '*in the beginning [God] created'* [in the singular]."

I.II

1. A. R. Joshua of Sikhnin in the name of R. Levi commenced [discourse by citing the following verse]: "'*He has declared to his people the power of his works, in giving them the heritage of the nations'* (Ps. 111:6).

B. "What is the reason that the Holy One, blessed be He, revealed to Israel what was created on the first day and what on the second?

C. "It was on account of the nations of the world. It was so that they should not ridicule the Israelites, saying to them, 'Are you not a nation of robbers [having stolen the land from the Canaanites]?'

D. "It allows the Israelites to answer them, 'And as to you, is there no spoil in your hands? For surely: "*The Caphtorim, who came forth out of Caphtor, destroyed them and dwelled in their place"* (Deut. 2:23)!

E. "'The world and everything in it belongs to the Holy One, blessed be he. When he wanted, he gave it to you, and when he wanted, he took it from you and gave it to us.'

F. "That is in line with what is written, '*....in giving them the heritage of the nations, he has declared to his people the power of his works'* (Ps. 111:6). [So as to give them the land, he established his right to do so by informing them that he had created it.]

G. "He told them about the beginning: '*In the beginning God created...'* (Gen. 1:1)."

I.III

1. A. R. Tanhum commenced discourse, "*For you are great and do wonderful things, you alone are God"* (Ps. 86:10).

B. Said R. Tanhum b. R. Hiyya, "As to a skin, if it has a hole as small as the eye of a needle, all of the air will escape from it.

C. "But as to a human being, a person is made with many apertures and holes, but the spirit does not go forth through them.

D. "Who has done it in such a way? '*You alone are God'* (Ps. 86:10)."

2. A. When were the angels created?

B. R. Yohanan said, "On the second day of creation [Monday] were they created.

C. "That is in line with this verse of Scripture: '*Who lays the beams of your upper chambers in the waters'* (Ps. 104:3), after which it is written, '*Who makes the spirits of your angels'* (Ps. 104:4). [The waters were divided into upper and lower parts, and on that same day the angels were created.]"

D. R. Hanina said, "They were created on the fifth day of creation [Thursday]. For it is written, *'Let fowl   fly above the earth'* (Gen. 1:20), and it is written, *'And with two did the angel fly'* (Is. 6:21). [Freedman, p. 5, n. 3: Thus angels too fall within the category of beings that fly and were created on the same day as all flying creatures.]"

E. R. Luliani b. R. Tabari in the name of R. Isaac: "Both from the viewpoint of R. Hanina and from that of R. Yohanan, there is agreement that nothing at all was created on the first day.

F. "That is so that you will not reach the false conclusion that Michael was there, stretching out the heaven at the south, with Gabriel at the north, and the Holy One, blessed be He, measuring from the middle.

G. "Rather: *'I the Lord do everything by myself, stretching out the heaven on my own and spreading forth the earth by myself'* (Is. 44:24).

H. "'By myself' is written [in Scripture, as if to mean, 'who is with me?'] [That is, God asks, 'Who was my partner in creating the world?'

I. "In ordinary affairs when a mortal king is honored by a province the nobles of the province are honored with him. Why? Because they bear the burden with him.

J. "But that is not how it is with the Holy One, blessed be He.

K. "But he on his own created his world, so he on his own is glorified in his world."

3. A. Said R. Tanhuma, "'*For you are great and do wonderful things'* (Ps. 86:10).

B. "Why so? Because: *'You alone are God'* (Ps. 86:10).

C. "You by yourself created the world.

D. "'*In the beginning God created'* (Gen. 1:1)."

I:IV

1. A. [*"In the beginning God created"* (Gen. 1:1):] Six things came before the creation of the world, some created, some at least considered as candidates for creation.

B. The Torah and the throne of glory were created [before the creation of the world].

C. The Torah, as it is written, *"The Lord made me as the beginning of his way, prior to his works of old"* (Prov. 8:22).

D. The throne of glory, as it is written, *"Your throne is established of old"* (Ps. 93:2).

E. The patriarchs were considered as candidates for creation, as it is written, *"I saw your fathers as the first-ripe in the fig tree at her first season"* (Hos. 9:10).

F. Israel was considered [as a candidate for creation], as it is written, *"Remember your congregation, which you got aforetime"* (Ps. 74:2).

G. The Temple was considered as a candidate for creation], as it is written, *"You, throne of glory, on high from the beginning, the place of our sanctuary"* (Jer. 17:12).

H. The name of the Messiah was kept in mind, as it is written, *"His name exists before the sun"* (Ps. 72:17).

I. R. Ahbah bar Zeira said, "Also [the power of] repentance.

J. "That is in line with the following verse of Scripture: *'Before the mountains were brought forth'* (Ps. 90:2). From that hour: *'You turn man to contrition and say, Repent, you children of men'* (Ps. 90:3)."

K. Nonetheless, I do not know which of these came first, that is, whether the Torah was prior to the throne of glory, or the throne of glory to the Torah.

L. Said R. Abba bar Kahana, "The Torah came first, prior to the throne of glory.

M. "For it is said, *'The Lord made me as the beginning of his way, before his works of old'* (Prov. 8:22).

N. "It came prior to that concerning which it is written, *'For your throne is established of old'* (Ps. 93:2)."

2. A. R. Huna, R. Jeremiah in the name of R. Samuel b. R. Isaac: "Intention concerning the creation of Israel came before all else.

B. "The matter may be compared to the case of a king who married a noble lady but had no son with her. One time the king turned up in the market place, saying, 'Buy this ink, inkwell, and pen on account of my son.'

C. "People said, 'He has no son. Why does he need ink, inkwell, and pen?'

D. "But then people went and said, 'The king is an astrologer, so he sees into the future and he therefore is expecting to produce a son!'

E. "Along these same lines, if the Holy One, blessed be He, had not foreseen that, after twenty-six generations, the Israelites would be destined to accept the Torah, he would would never have written in it, 'Command the children of Israel.' [This proves that God foresaw Israel and created the world on that account.]"

3. A. Said. R. Benaiah, "The world and everything in it were created only on account of the merit of the Torah.

B. *"'The Lord for the sake of wisdom [Torah] founded the earth'* (Prov. 3:19)."

C. R. Berekiah said, "It was for the merit of Moses.

D. *"'And he saw the beginning for himself, for there a portion of a ruler [Moses] was reserved'* (Deut. 33:21)."

4. A. R. Huna in the name of Rab repeated [the following]: "For the merit of three things was the world created, for the merit of dough-offerings, tithes, and first fruits.

B. "For it is said, *'On account of [the merit of] what is first, God created...'* (Gen. 1:1).

C. "And the word 'first' refers only to dough-offering, for it is written, *'Of the first of your dough'* (Num. 15:20).

D. "The same word refers to tithes, as it is written, *The first fruits of your grain'* (Deut. 18:4).

E. "And the word 'first' refers to first fruits, for it is written, *'The choicest of your land's first fruit'* (Ex. 23:19)."

I:VIII

1. A. R. Menahem and R. Joshua b. Levi in the name of R. Levi: "One who builds requires six things: water, dust, wood, stones, canes, and iron. And should you say that [since God] is rich, he will not need canes [which are used only in hovels], lo, he requires a cane for measuring, for it is written, *'And a measuring reed in his hand'* (Ez. 40:3).

B.   "The Torah came before those six things [as indicated by Prov. 8:22]."
[Freedman: The idea is that six expressions of precedence are employed
in reference to the Torah]: 'the first,' 'of old,' 'from everlasting,' 'from the
beginning,' and 'or ever,' which stands for two such usages as at Prov.
8:22: 'The Lord made me...the first of his works of old, I was set up from
everlasting, from the beginning or ever the earth was' [Freedman, p. 8,
n. 3].

I:IX

1. A.   A philosopher asked Rabban Gamaliel, saying to him, "Your God was
indeed a great artist, but he had good materials to help him."

   B.   He said to him, "What are they?"

   C.   He said to him, "Unformed [space], void, darkness, water, wind, and the
deep."

   D.   He said to him, "May the spirit of that man [you] burst! All of them are
explicitly described as having been created by him [and not as pre-
existent]."

   E.   "Unformed space and void: *'I make peace and create evil'* (Is. 45:7).

   F.   "Darkness: *'I form light and create darkness'* (Is. 45:7).

   G.   "Water: *'Praise him, you heavens of heavens, and you waters that are
above the heavens'* (Ps. 148:4). Why? *'For he commanded and they were
created'* (Ps. 148:5).

   H.   "Wind: *'for lo, he who forms the mountains creates the wind'* (Amos
4:13).

   I.   "The depths: *'When there were no depths, I was brought forth'* (Prov.
8:24)."

I:X

1. A.   *["In the beginning God created" (Gen. 1:1):]* R. Jonah in the name of R.
Levi: "Why was the world created with [a word beginning with the letter]
B?

   B.   "Just as [in Hebrew] the letter B is closed [at the back and sides but]
open in front, so you have no right to expound concerning what is
above or below, before or afterward."

   C.   Bar Qappara said, *"'For ask now of the days past which were before you,
since the day that God created man upon the earth'* (Deut. 4:32).

   D.   "Concerning the day *after* which days were created, you may expound,
but you may not make an exposition concerning what lies before then.'

   E.   *"'And from one end of the heaven to the other'* (Deut. 4:32).

   F.   "[Concerning that space] you may conduct an investigation, but you may
not conduct an investigation concerning what lies beyond those points."

   G.   R. Judah b. Pazzi gave his exposition concerning the story of creation in
accord with this rule of Bar Qappara.

2. A.   Why with a B?

   B.   To tell you that there are two ages [this age and the age to come, for the
letter B bears the numerical value of two].

3. A.   Another matter: Why was the world created [with a word beginning with
the letter] B?

   B.   Because that is the letter that begins the word for blessing.

   C.   And why not with an A?

D. Because that is the first letter of the Hebrew word for curse.

4. A. Another matter: Why not with an A?

   B. So as not to give an opening to the *minim* to claim, "How can the world endure, when it has been created with a word meaning curse!"

   C. Rather, said the Holy One, blessed be He, "Lo, I shall write it with a letter standing for the word 'blessing,' and may the world endure!"

5. A. Another matter: Why with a B?

   B. Because the letter B has two points, one pointing upward, the other backward, so that [if] people say to it, "Who created you?" it will point upward.

   C. It is as if to say, "This one who is above has created me."

   D. "And what is his name?" And it points for them with its point backward: "The Lord is his name," [pointing to the first letter in the alphabet, backward from the second, which is the A, standing for the One].

6. A. R. Eleazar bar Abinah in the name of R. Aha: "For twenty-six generations the letter A made complaint before the Holy One, blessed be He, saying to him, 'Lord of the world! I am the first among all the letters of the alphabet, yet you did not create your world by starting with me!'

   B. "Said the Holy One, blessed be He, to the A, 'The world and everything in it has been created only through the merit of the Torah. Tomorrow I am going to come and give my Torah at Sinai, and I shall begin only with you: *"I [beginning with the A] am the Lord your God"* (Ex. 20:1).'"

7. A. Bar Hutah said, "Why is it called *'alef*? Because that is the word for a thousand: *The word which he commanded for a thousand [elef] generations'* (Ps. 105:8)."

I:XI

1. A. R. Simon in the name of R. Joshua b. Levi: "[The fact that the letters] M, N, S, P, and K [when appearing at the end of the word have a form different from that used when they appear at the beginning or the middle of a word] is a law revealed to Moses at Sinai."

   B. R. Jeremiah in the name of R. Hiyya bar Abba: "It is that which seers ordained."

2. A. Once on an overcast day, on which sages did not come into the assembly house, there were children there. They said, "Let's take up [the topic of the final form of the letters as these have been ordained by] the seers."

   B. They said, "What is the reason that there are two forms for the writing of the letters M, N, S, P, and K?

   C. "From Word to word [the word at hand begins with M], from Faithful to faithful [the word begins with N], from Righteous one to righteous one [with an S], from Mouth to mouth [with a P], from Hand to hand [with a K].

   D. "From the hand of the Holy One, blessed be He, to the hand of Moses."

   E. Sages took note of who these children were, and great sages in Israel emerged from that group.

   F. There are those who hold that these were R. Eliezer, R. Joshua, and R. Aqiba.

   G. They recited in their regard the following verse: *"Even a child is known by his doings"* (Prov. 20:11).

I:XII

1. A. *["In the beginning God created..."* (Gen. 1:1):] R. Yudan in the name of Aqilas: *"This* one it is appropriate to call God. [Why so?]

   B. "Under ordinary circumstances a mortal king is praised in province even before he has built public baths for the population or given them private ones. [God by contrast created the world before he had received the praise of humanity, so it was not for the sake of human adulation that he created the world.]"

2. A. Simeon b. Azzai says, *"'And your modesty has made me great'* (2 Sam. 22:36). A mortal person mentions his name and afterward his title, for example, 'Mr. So-and-so, the prefect,' 'Mr. Such-and-such, and whatever title he gets.' But the Holy One, blessed be He, is not that way.

   B. "Rather, only after he had created what was needed in his world did he make mention of his name, thus, 'In the beginning, created...,' and only afterward: 'God.'"

I:XIII

1. A. R. Simeon b. Yohai taught, "How [on the basis of Scripture] do we know that one should not say, 'For the Lord, a burnt-offering,' 'For the Lord, a meal-offering,' 'For the Lord, a peace-offering.'

   B. "Rather one should say, 'A burnt-offering for the Lord,' 'A meal-offering for the Lord,' 'A peace-offering for the Lord'?

   C. "Scripture says, *'An offering for the Lord'* (Lev. 1:2).

   D. "And lo, this produces an argument *a fortiori* :

   E. "If in the case of one who is planning to declare something sanctified, the Torah has said that one should make use of the name of Heaven only in connection with an offering [that has already been sanctified by being designated],

   F. "those who blaspheme, curse, and worship idols, all the more so that they should be blotted out of the world."

2. A. *["...the heaven and the earth"* (Gen. 1:1):] Rabbis said, "When a mortal builds a building, if the building goes as planned, he may continue to broaden the structure as it rises, but if not, he has to make it broad at the bottom but narrow at the top.

   B. "But that is not how things are for the Holy One, blessed be He. But: '...the heaven' meaning that very form of heaven as it had come to mind, first, and then: '...and the earth...,' as it had originally been planned."

3. A. R. Huna in the name of R. Eliezer, son of R. Yose the Galilean: "Even those concerning which Scripture states, *'For behold, I create a new heaven'* (Is. 65:17) were in fact created from the six days of creation.

   B. "This is in line with the following verse: *'For as the new heaven remains before me'* (Is. 66:22), not 'new,' but *'the new.'*" [Freedman, p. 12, n. 5: The definite article implies the specific new heavens, those created aforetime.]

I:XIV

1. A. *["...the heaven and the earth"* (Gen. 1:1):] R. Ishmael asked R. Aqiba, saying to him, "Because you served Nahum of Gimzo as disciple for twenty-two years, [learning from him the exegetical principles that] the words 'except' and 'only' are to be interpreted as exclusionary, and the

accusative particle *'eth'* and 'also' serve as inclusionary words [indicating that more is covered by the statement at hand than that which is explicitly mentioned in it], as to the accusative particle in the verse before us [Gen. 1:1], what is the exegesis that that usage applies?"

B. [Ishmael] said to [Aqiba], "If it were stated, 'In the beginning created God [without the accusative particle], heaven, and earth,' we might have taken the view that heaven and earth are divine. [Without the accusative particle, we might have understood the words 'heaven' and 'earth' to be subjects of the verb 'create,' along with God. Thus we might have thought that the world was made by three: God, heaven, and earth. So the accusative particle is not inclusionary but has its own purpose.]"

C. [Aqiba] said to [Ishmael], "'For it is no empty thing from you,' (Deut. 32:46) means that if the Torah seems empty, it is from you [and your own fault], specifically because you do not know how to expound Scripture.

D. "Rather, the accusative particle prior to the word 'heaven' serves to include the sun, moon, stars, and planets, and the accusative particle prior to the word 'earth' serves to encompass trees, grass, and the Garden of Eden."

I:XV

1. A. ["...the heaven and the earth" (Gen. 1:1):] The House of Shammai say, "The heaven was created first."

    B. The House of Hillel say, "The earth was created first."

    C. In the view of the House of Shammai the matter may be compared to the case of a king who first made a throne for himself and afterward the footstool for the throne, as it is said, "The heaven is my throne, and the earth the dust of my feet" (Is. 66:1).

    D. In the view of the House of Hillel the matter is to be compared to the case of a king who built a first palace for himself. Only after he had built the bottom floor did he build the upper floor, for so it is written, "On the day on which the Lord God made earth and [only then] heaven" (Gen. 2:4).

    E. Said R. Judah bar Ilai, "The following verse of Scripture supports the view of the House of Hillel: 'Of old you laid out the foundations of the earth..., ' and afterward, '...and the heavens are the work of your hands' (Ps. 102:25)."

    F. Said R. Hanin, "On the basis of the verse of Scripture that supports the position of the House of Shammai the House of Hillel find evidence to reject that same view: 'The earth was...' (Gen. 1:2), meaning that it had already come into being."

    G. R. Yohanan [said] in the name of sages, "As to the act of creation, heaven came first. As to the process of finishing off creation, the earth came first."

    H. Said. R. Tanhuma, "I shall supply a verse of Scripture to support that statement. As to creation, the heaven came first: 'In the beginning God created [the heaven, then the earth]' (Gen. 1:1). But as to the process of finishing off creation, the earth came first: 'On the day on which the Lord God made heaven and earth' (Gen. 2:4)."

    I. Said R. Simeon, "I should be surprised if the fathers of the world disputed concerning this matter. For both of them were created only as are the pot and its lid [which is to say, in a single act]. In this regard I recite the following verse of Scripture: '*[My hand established the earth, and my right hand spread out the heaven.] When I call them, they stand up together*' (Is. 48:13)."

J.   Said R. Eleazar b. R. Simeon, "According to this opinion of my father, why is it that sometimes heaven comes before earth, sometimes earth comes before heaven. But what it teaches is that the two of them are equal [having been created at the same instant]."

2.   A.   [T. Ker. 4:14 adds: R. Simeon says,] "In every place Scripture gives precedence to Abraham over Isaac, and to Isaac over Jacob. But in one passage Scripture says, '*And I remembered my covenant with Jacob [...Isaac and Abraham...]*' (Lev. 26:42).

B.   "This teaches that the three of them are equivalent to one another.

C.   "In every passage Scripture accords precedence to Moses over Aaron, but in one place Scripture states, '*That is Aaron and Moses*' (Ex. 6:26).

D.   "This teaches that the two of them are equivalent to one another.

E.   "In every passage Scripture gives precedence to Joshua over Caleb, but in one passage it says, '*except for Caleb, the son of Jephunneh the Kenizzite, and Joshua, the son of Nun*' (Num. 32:12).

F.   "This teaches that the two of them are equivalent to one another.

G.   "And in every passage Scripture gives precedence to the honor owing to the father over the honor owing to the mother, while in one place it says, '*A man must fear his mother and his father*' (Lev. 19:3), teaching that the two of them are equal to one another."

8. LEVITICUS RABBAH

Judaism and Scripture: The Evidence of Leviticus Rabbah.   Chicago, 1985: The University of Chicago Press.

The Integrity of Leviticus Rabbah. The Problem of the Autonomy of a Rabbinic Document.   Chico, 1985: Scholars Press for Brown Judaic Studies.

Comparative Midrash: The Plan and Program of Genesis Rabbah and Leviticus Rabbah.   Atlanta, 1986: Scholars Press for Brown Judaic Studies.

V:I

1.   A.   "*If it is the anointed priest who sins, [thus bringing guilt on the people, then let him offer to the Lord for the sin which he has committed a young bull without blemish]*" (Lev. 4:3).

B.   "*When he is quiet, who can condemn? When he hides his face, who can set him right [RSV: behold him] [whether it be a nation or a man? that a godless man should not reign, that he should not ensnare the people]*" (Job 34:29-30).

C.   R. Meir interpreted [the matter] (Gen. R. 36:1), "'*When he is quiet*' – in his world, '*when he hides his face*' – in his world.

D.   "The matter may be compared to the case of a judge who draws a veil inside and so does not see what goes on outside.

E.   "So the people of the generation of the flood thought: *The thick clouds cover him, so he will not see [what we do]*'" (Job 22:14).

F.   They said to him, "That's enough from you, Meir."

2. A. Another interpretation: *"When he is quiet, who can condemn? When he hides his face, who can set him right?"* (Job 34:29)

     B. When he gave tranquility to the generation of the flood, who could come and condemn them?

     C. What sort of tranquility did he give them? *"Their children are established in their presence, and their offspring before their eyes. [Their houses are safe from fear, and no rod of God is upon them]"* (Job 21:8).

     D. R. Levi and rabbis:

     E. R. Levi said, "A woman would get pregnant and give birth in three days. [How do we know it?] Here, the word 'established' is used, and elsewhere: *'Be established in three days'* [Ex. 19:15]. Just as the word 'established' used there involves a span of three days, so the word 'established' used here means three days."

     F. Rabbis say, "In a single day a woman would get pregnant and give birth.

     G. "Here, the word 'established' is used, and elsewhere: *'And be established in the morning'* [Ex. 34:2]. Just as the word 'established' stated there involves a single day, so the word 'established' used here involves a single day."

3. A. *"And their offspring before their eyes"* – for they saw children and grandchildren.

     B. *"They send forth their little ones like a flock, [and their children dance]"* (Job 21:11).

     C. [The word for "children" means] "their young."

     D. Said R. Levi, "In Arabia for children they use the word 'the young.'"

4. A. *"And their children dance"* (Job 21:11) –

     B. ["they dance"] like devils.

     C. That is in line with the following verse of Scripture: *"And satyrs will dance there"* (Is. 13:21).

5. A. They say: When one of them would give birth by day, she would say to her son, "Go and bring me a flint, so I can cut your umbilical cord."

     B. If she gave birth by night, she would say to her son, "Go and light a lamp for me, so I can cut your umbilical cord."

     C. M'SH B: A woman gave birth by night and said to her son, "Go and light a lamp for me, so I can cut your umbilical cord."

     D. [In Aramaic:] When he went out to fetch it, a devil, Ashmadon [Asmodeus], head of the spirits, met him. While the two were wrestling with one another, the cock crowed. [Ashmadon] said to him, "Go, boast to your mother that my time has run out, for if my time had not run out, I could have killed you."

     E. He said to him, "Go, boast to your mother's mother that my mother had not cut my umbilical cord, for if my mother had cut my umbilical cord, I would have beaten you."

     F. This illustrates that which is said: *"Their houses are safe from fear"* (Job 21:9) – from destroying spirits.

6. A. *"And no rod of God is upon them"* – [for their houses are free from suffering.

     B. [And this further] illustrates that which is said: *"When he is quiet, who can condemn,] when he hides his face, who can put him right"* (Job 34:30).

C. When [God] hides his face from them, who can come and say to him, "You have not done right."

D. And how, indeed, did he hide his face from them? When he brought the flood on them.

E. That is in line with the following verse of Scripture: *"And he blotted out every living substance which was upon the face of the earth"* (Gen. 7:23).

7. A. *"Whether it be to a nation [or a man together]"* (Job 34:29) – this refers to the generation of the flood.

B. *"Or to a man"* – this refers to Noah.

C. *"Together"* – he had to rebuild his world from one man, he had to rebuild his world from one nation.

V:II

1. A. Another interpretation: *"When he is quiet, who can condemn"* (Job 34:29).

B. When he gave tranquillity to the Sodomites, who could come and condemn them?

C. What sort of tranquillity did he give them?

D. *"As for the earth, out of it comes bread, but underneath it is turned up as by fire. Its stones are the place of sapphires, and it has dust of gold"* (Job 28:5-6).

2. A. *"That path no bird of prey knows, and the falcon's eye has not seen it"* (Job 28:7).

B. R. Levi in the name of R. Yohanan bar Shahina: "The falcon [bar hadayya-bird] spots its prey at a distance of eighteen mils."

C. And how much is its portion [of food]?

D. R. Meir said, "[A mere] two handbreadths."

E. R. Judah said, "One handbreadth."

F. R. Yosé said, "Two or three fingerbreadths."

G. [In Aramaic:] And when it stood on the trees of Sodom, it could not see the ground because of the density of [the foliage of] the trees.

3. A. *"When he hides his face, who can put him right?"* –

B. When he hid his face from them, who comes to say to him, "You did not do rightly"?

C. And when did he hide his face from them?

D. When he made brimstone and fire rain down on them.

E. That is in line with the following verse of Scripture: *"Then the Lord made brimstone and fire rain on Sodom and Gomorrah"* (Gen. 19:24).

V:III

1. A. Another interpretation of *"When he is quiet, who can condemn? When he hides his face, who can set him right?"* (Job 34:29).

B. When he gave tranquillity to the ten tribes, who could come and condemn them?

C. What sort of tranquillity did he give them? *"Woe to those who are at ease in Zion, and to those who feel secure on the mountain of Samaria, the notable men of the first of the nations, to whom the house of Israel to come"* (Amos 6:1).

2. A. *"Woe to those who are at ease in Zion"* refers to the tribe of Judah and Benjamin.

   B. *"Those who feel secure on the mountain of Samaria"* refers to the ten tribes.

   C. *"The notable men of the first of the nations"* who derive from the two noteworthy names, Shem and Eber.

   D. When the nations of the world eat and drink, they pass the time in nonsense talk, saying, "Who is a sage, like Balaam! Who is a hero, like Goliath! Who is rich, like Haman!"

   E. And the Israelites come after them and say to them, "Was not Ahitophel a sage, Samson a hero, Korah rich?"

3. A. *"Pass over to Calneh and see, [and thence go to Hamath the great, then go down to Gath of the Philistines. Are they better than these kingdoms? Or is their territory greater than your territory?]"* (Amos 6:2).

   B. [Calneh] refers to Ctesiphon.

   C. "Hamath the great" refers to Hamath of Antioch.

   D. *"And go down to Gath of the Philistines"* refers to the mounds of the Philistines.

   E. "Are they better than these kingdoms? Or is their territory greater than your territory?"

   F. *"O you who put far away the evil day"* (Amos 6:3) [refers to] the day on which they would go into exile.

4. A. *"And bring near the seat of violence?"* (Amos 6:3). This refers to Esau.

   B. *"Did you bring yourselves near to sit next to violence"* – this refers to Esau.

   C. That is in line with the following verse of Scripture: *"For the violence done to your brother Jacob, [shame shall cover you]"* (Obad. 1:40).

5. A. *"[Woe to] those who lie upon beds of ivory"* (Amos 6:4) – on beds made of the elephant's tusk.

   B. *"And stink on their couches"* (Amos 6:4) – who do stinking transgressions on their beds.

   C. *"Who eat lambs from the flock [and calves from the midst of the stall]"* (Amos 6:4).

   D. They say: When one of them wanted to eat a kid of the flock, he would have the whole flock brought before him, and he would stand over it and slaughter it.

   E. When he wanted to eat a calf, he would bring the entire herd of calves before him and stand over it and slaughter it.

6. A. *"Who sing idle songs to the sound of the harp [and like David invent for themselves instruments of music]"* (Amos 6:5).

   B. [They would say that] David provided them with musical instruments.

7. A. *"Who drink wine in bowls"* (Amos 6:6).

   B. Rab, R. Yohanan, and rabbis:

   C. Rab said, "It is a very large bowl" [using the Greek].

   D. R. Yohanan said, "It was in small cups."

   E. Rabbis say, "It was in cups with saucers attached."

   F. Whence did the wine they drink come?

   G. R. Aibu in the name of R. Hanina said, "It was wine from Pelugta, for the wine would entice (PTH) the body."

H. And rabbis in the name of R. Hanina said, "It was from Pelugta's [separation], since, because of their wine drinking, the ten tribes were enticed [from God] and consequently sent into exile."

8. A. "And anoint themselves with the finest oils" (Amos 6:6).

B. R. Judah b. R. Ezekial said, "This refers to oil of unripe olives, which removes hair and smooths the body."

C. R. Haninah said, "This refers to oil of myrrh and cinnamon."

9. A. And [in spite of] all this glory: "They are not grieved over the ruin of Joseph" (Amos 6:6).

B. "Therefore they shall now be the first of those to go into exile, [and the revelry of those who stretch themselves shall pass away]" (Amos 6:7).

C. What is the meaning of "the revelry of those who stretch themselves"?

D. Said R. Aibu, "They had thirteen public baths, one for each of the tribes, and one additional one for all of them together.

E. "And all of them were destroyed, and only this one [that had served all of them] survived.

F. "This shows how much lewdness was done with them."

10. A. "When he hides his face, who can set him right?" (Job 34:29).

B. When he hid his face from them, who then could come and say to him, "You did not do right"?

C. How did he hide his face from them?   By bringing against them Sennacherib, the king of Assyria.

D. That is in line with the following verse of Scripture: "In the fourteenth year of King Hezekiah, Sennacherib, king of Assyria, came up [against all the fortified cities of Judah and took them]."

11. A. What is the meaning of, "and took them"?

B. Said R. Abba b. R. Kahana, "Three divine decrees were sealed on that day.

C. "The decree against the ten tribes was sealed, for them to fall into the hand of Sennacherib; the decree against Sennacherib was sealed, for him to fall into the hand of Hezekiah; and the decree of Shebna was sealed, to be smitten with leprosy."

12. A. "Whether it be a nation [or a man]" (Job 34:29) – this refers to Sennacherib, as it is said, "For a nation has come up upon my land" (Joel 1:6).

B. "...or a man" (Job 34:29) – this refers to Israel: "For you, my sheep, the sheep of my pasture, are a man" (Ez. 34:31).

C. "Together" (Job 34:29) – this refers to King Uzziah, who was smitten with leprosy.

D. That is in line with the following verse of Scripture: "And Uzziah the King was a leper until the day he died" (2 Chron. 26:21).

13. A. [Margulies: What follows treats "...whether it be a nation or a man together" (Job 34:29):] Now the justice of the Holy One, blessed be He, is not like man's justice.

B. A mortal judge may show favor to a community, but he will never show favor to an individual.

C. But the Holy One, blessed be He, is not so.   Rather: "If it is the anointed priest who sins, [thus bringing guilt on the people,] then let him offer [for the sin which he has committed] a young bull [without blemish to the Lord as a sin offering]" (Lev. 4:3-4).

D. "*[If the whole congregation of Israel commits a sin unwittingly, and the thing is hidden from the eyes of the assembly, and they do any one of the things which the Lord has commanded not to be done and are guilty, when the sin which they have committed becomes known,] the assembly shall offer a young bull for a sin offering*" (Lev. 4:13-14). [God exacts the same penalty from an individual and from the community and does not distinguish the one from the other. The anointed priest and the community both become subject to liability for the same offering, a young bull.]

V:IV

1. A. Said R. Abbahu, "It is written, *'Take heed that you do not forsake the Levite [as long as you live in your land]'* [Deut. 12:19]. What follows thereafter? *'When the Lord your God enlarges your territory [as he has promised you]'* [Deut. 12:20].

   B. "What has one thing got to do with the other?

   C. "Said the Holy One, blessed be He, 'In accord with your gifts will they enlarge your [place].'"

   D. R. Huna in the name of R. Aha, "If a slave brings as his offering a young bull, while his master brings a lamb, the slave takes precedence over his master.

   E. "This is in accord with what we have learned in the Mishnah: **'If the young bull of the anointed priest and the young bull of the community are waiting [sacrifice], the young bull of the anointed priest takes precedence over the young bull of the community in all aspects of the sacrificial rite'**" (M. Hor. 3:6).

2. A. "*A man's gift makes room for him and brings him before great men*" (Prov. 18:16).

   B. M'SH B: R. Eliezer, R. Joshua, and R. Aqiba went to the harborside of Antioch to collect funds for the support of sages.

   C. [In Aramaic:] A certain Abba Yudan lived there.

   D. He would carry out his religious duty [of philanthropy] in a liberal spirit, but had lost his money. When he saw our masters, he went home with a sad face. His wife said to him, "What's wrong with you, that you look so sad?"

   E. He repeated the tale to her: "Our masters are here, and I don't know what I shall be able to do for them."

   F. His wife, who was a truly philanthropic woman – what did she say to him? "You only have one field left. Go, sell half of it and give them the proceeds."

   G. He went and did just that. When he was giving them the money, they said to him, "May the Omnipresent make up all your losses."

   H. Our masters went their way.

   I. He went out to plough. While he was ploughing the half of the field that he had left, the Holy One, blessed be he, opened his eyes. The earth broke open before him, and his cow fell in and broke her leg. He went down to raise her up, and found a treasure beneath her. He said, "It was for my gain that my cow broke her leg."

   J. When our masters came back, [in Aramaic:] they asked about a certain Abba Yudan and how he was doing. They said, "Who can gaze on the face of Abba Yudan [which glows with prosperity] – Abba Yudan, the owner of flocks of goats, Abba Yudan, the owner of herds of asses, Abba Yudan, the owner of herds of camels."

K. He came to them and said to them, "Your prayer in my favor has produced returns and returns on the returns."

L. They said to him, "Even though someone else gave more than you did, we wrote your name at the head of the list."

M. Then they took him and sat him next to themselves and recited in his regard the following verse of Scripture: *"A man's gift makes room for him and brings him before great men"* (Prov. 18:16).

3. A. R. Hiyya bar Abba called for charity contributions in support of a school in Tiberias. A member of the household of Siloni got up and pledged a litra of gold.

B. R. Hiyya bar Abba took him and sat him next to himself and recited in his regard the following verse of Scripture: *"A man's gift makes room for him and brings him before great men"* (Prov. 18:16).

4. A. [In Aramaic:] R. Simeon b. Laqish went to Bosrah. A certain Abba [Lieberman deletes: Yudan], "the Deceiver," lived there. It was not – Heaven forfend – that he really was a deceiver. Rather, he would practice [holy] deception in doing the religious duty [of philanthropy].

B. [In Aramaic:] He would see what the rest of the community would pledge, and he would then pledge to take upon himself [a gift equivalent to that of the rest of the] community.

C. R. Simeon b. Laqish took him and sat him next to himself and recited in his regard the following verse of Scripture: *"A man's gift makes room for him and brings him before great men"* (Prov. 18:16).

V:V

1. A. Reverting to the base text (GWPH): *"If it is the anointed priest who sins"* (Lev. 4:3).

B. This refers to Shebna.

2. A. *"[Thus says the Lord, God of hosts,] 'Come, go to this steward (SKN), to Shebna, who is over the household, [and say to him, 'What have you to do here and whom have you here, that you have hewn here a tomb for yourself, you who hew a tomb on the height and carve a habitation for yourself in the rock? Behold, the Lord will hurl you away violently, O you strong young man! He will seize firm hold on you, and whirl you round and round and throw you like a ball into a wide land; there you shall die, and there shall be your splendid chariots, you shame of your master's house. I will thrust you from your office and you will be cast down from your station]"* (Is. 22:15-19).

B. R. Eliezer said, "He was a high priest."

C. R. Judah b. Rabbi said, "He was steward."

D. In the view of R. Eliezer, who said he was a high priest, [we may bring evidence from Scripture,] for it is written, *"And I will clothe him with your robe [and will bind your girdle on him and will commit your authority into his hand]"* (Is. 22:21).

E. In the view of R. Judah b. Rabbi, who said he was steward, [we may bring evidence from Scripture,] for it is written, *"And I will commit your authority to his hand"* (Is. 22:21).

F.   R. Berekiah said, "What is a 'steward' (SWKN)? It is one who comes from Sikhni."

3. A.   And he went up and was appointed *komes opsarion* [the Greek for chief cook] in Jerusalem.

B.   That is in line with the prophet's condemnation, saying to him, *"What have you to do here, and whom have you here"* (Is. 22:16).

C.   "You exile, son of an exile! What wall have you built here, what pillar have you put up here, and what nail have you hammered in here?!"

D.   R. Eleazar said, "A person has to have a nail or a peg firmly set in a synagogue so as to have the right to be buried in that place [in which he is living]."

E.   *"And have you hewn here a tomb for yourself?"* (Is. 22:16). He made himself a kind of a dovecot and put his tomb on top of it.

F.   *"You who hew a tomb on the height"* (Is. 22:16) –

G.   R. Ishmael in the name of Mar Uqba, "On the height the decree was hewn out concerning him, indicating that he should not have a burial place in the land of Israel."

H.   *"You who carve a habitation for yourself in the rock"* (Is. 22:16) – a stone coffin.

I.   *"Behold, the Lord will hurl you away violently"* (Is. 22:17) – one rejection after another.

J.   *"...hurl away violently (GBR)"* – [since the word GBR also means cock:] said R. Samuel b. R. Nahman, "[In Aramaic:], it may be compared to a cock which is driven and goes from place to place."

K.   *"He will seize a firm hold on you"* (Is. 22:17), [since the words for "firm hold" may also be translated, "wrap around," thus: "And he will wrap you around"] the meaning is that he was smitten with saraat, in line with that which you find in Scripture, "And he will wrap his lip around" (Lev. 13:45).

L.   *"And whirl you round and round [and throw you like a ball]"* (Is. 22:18) – exile after exile.

M.   *"Like a ball"* – just as a ball is caught from hand to hand and does not fall to the ground, so [will it be for him].

N.   *"Into a wide land"* – this means Casiphia (Ezra 8:17).

O.   *"There you shall die and there shall be your splendid chariots"* (Is. 22:18):

4. A.   In accord with the position of R. Eliezer, who said that Shebna had been a high priest, [the reference to the splendid chariots implies] that he had been deriving personal benefit from the offerings.

B.   In accord with the view of R. Judah b. Rabbi, who said that he had been steward, [the reference to the splendid chariots implies] that he had derived personal benefit from things that had been consecrated for use in the upkeep of the sanctuary.

C.   *"You shame of your master's house"* (Is. 22:18).

D.   In accord with the position of R. Eliezer, who said that Shebna had been a high priest, [the shame was] that he had treated the offerings in a disgraceful way.

E.   In accord with the view of R. Judah b. Rabbi, who said that he had been steward, [the shame was] that he had treated both of his masters disgracefully, that is Hezekiah, on the one side, Isaiah on the other.

5. A. R. Berekhiah in the name of R. Abba b. R. Kahana: "What did Shebna and Joahaz [2 Kgs. 18:18] do? They wrote a message and attached it to an arrow and shot it to Sennacherib through the window. In the message was written the following: 'We and everyone in Jerusalem want you, but Hezekiah and Isaiah don't want you.'"

B. Now this is just what David had said [would happen]: *"For lo, the wicked bend the bow, they have fitted their arrow to the string"* (Ps. 11:2).

C. *"For lo, the wicked bend the bow"* – this refers to Shebna and Joahaz.

D. *"They have fitted their arrow to the string"* – on the bowstring.

E. *"To shoot in the dark at the upright in heart"* (Ps. 11:2) – at two upright in heart, Hezekiah and Isaiah.

V:VI

1. A. *"If it is the anointed priest who sins"* (Lev. 4:3).

B. [What follows occurs at T. Hor. 2:4, explaining M. Hor. 3:4, cited above at V:IV.1.E:] [If] the anointed high priest must atone [for a sin] and the community [SBWR for SRYK] must be atoned for [in line with Lev. 4:13], it is better that the one who [has the power to] make atonement take precedence over the one for whom atonement is made,

C. as it is written, *"And he will atone for himself and for his house"* (Lev. 16:17).

D. ["His house"] refers to his wife.

2. A. *"If it is the anointed priest who sins"* (Lev. 4:3) –

B. Will an anointed priest commit a sin!

C. Said R. Levi, "Pity the town whose physician has gout [and cannot walk to visit the sick], whose governor has one eye, and whose public defender plays the prosecutor in capital cases."

3. A. *"[If it is the anointed priest who sins,] thus bringing guilt (L'SMT) [on the people, then let him offer for the sin which he has committed a young bull ...]"* (Lev. 4:3).

B. Said R. Isaac, "It is a case of death (MWT) by burning ('S) [inflicted on one who commits sacrilege by consuming offerings from the altar]."

C. "The matter may be compared to the keeper of a bear, who ate up the rations of the bear. The king said, 'Since he went and ate up the bear's rations, let the bear eat him.'

D. "So does the Holy One, blessed be He, say, 'Since Shebna enjoyed benefit from things that had been consecrated to the altar [for burning], let fire consume him.'"

4. A. Said R. Aibu (Y. Ter. 8:3, A.Z. 2:3), "M'SH B: Once there was a butcher in Sepphoris, who fed Israelites carrion and torn meat. On the eve of the Day of Atonement he went out drinking and got drunk. He climbed up to the roof of his house and fell off and died. The dogs began to lick him.

B. "[In Aramaic.] They came and asked R. Hanina the law about moving his corpse away from the dogs [on the Day of Atonement].

C. "He said to him, 'You will be holy people to me, therefore you shall not eat any meat that is torn of beasts in the field, you shall cast it to the dogs' (Ex. 22:30).

D. "This man robbed from the dogs and fed carrion and torn meat to Israelites. Leave him to them. They are eating what belongs to them.'"

5. A. *"He shall bring the bull to the door of the tent of meeting before the Lord, [and lay his hand on the head of the bull and kill the bull before the Lord]"* (Lev. 4:4).

   B. Said R. Isaac, "The matter may be compared to the case of a king, one of whose admirers paid him honor by giving him a handsome gift and by offering him lovely words of praise. The king then said, 'Set this gift at the gate of the palace, so that everyone who comes and goes may see [and admire] it,'

   C. "as it is said, *'And he shall bring the bull [to the door of the tent of meeting].'"*

V:VII

1. A. *"[If the whole congregation of Israel commits a sin unwittingly and the thing is hidden from the eyes of the assembly, and they do any one of the things which the Lord has commanded not to be done and are guilty, when the sin which they have committed becomes known, the assembly shall offer a young bull for a sin offering and bring it before the tent of meeting;] and the elders of the congregation shall lay their hands [upon the head of the bull before the Lord]"* (Lev. 4:13-15).

   B. [Since, in laying their hands (SMK) on the head of the bull, the elders sustain (SMK) the community by adding to it the merit they enjoy,] said R. Isaac, "The nations of the world have none to sustain them, for it is written, *'And those who sustain Egypt will fall'* (Ez. 30:6).

   C. "But Israel has those who sustain it, as it is written: *'And the elders of the congregation shall lay their hands [and so sustain Israel]'"* (Lev. 4:15).

2. A. Said R. Eleazar, "The nations of the world are called a congregation, and Israel is called a congregation.

   B. "The nations of the world are called a congregation: *'For the congregation of the godless shall be desolate'* [Job 15:34].

   C. "And Israel is called a congregation: *'And the elders of the congregation shall lay their hands'* [Lev. 4:15].

   D. "The nations of the world are called sturdy bulls and Israel is called sturdy bulls.

   E. "The nations of the world are called sturdy bulls: *'The congregation of [sturdy] bulls with the calves of the peoples'* [Ps. 68:31].

   F. "Israel is called sturdy bulls, as it is said, *'Listen to me, you sturdy [bullish] of heart'* [Is. 46:13].

   G. "The nations of the world are called excellent, and Israel is called excellent.

   H. "The nations of the world are called excellent: *'You and the daughters of excellent nations'* [Ex. 32:18].

   I. "Israel is called excellent: *'They are the excellent, in whom is all my delight'* [Ps. 16:4].

   J. "The nations of the world are called sages, and Israel is called sages.

   K. "The nations of the world are called sages: *'And I shall wipe out sages from Edom'* [Ob. 1:8].

   L. "And Israel is called sages: *'Sages store up knowledge'* [Prov. 10:14].

   M. "The nations of the world are called unblemished, and Israel is called unblemished.

N. "The nations of the world are called unblemished: *'Unblemished as are those that go down to the pit'* [Prov. 1:12].

O. "And Israel is called unblemished: *'The unblemished will inherit goodness'* [Prov. 28:10].

P. "The nations of the world are called men, and Israel is called men.

Q. "The nations of the world are called men: *'And you men who work iniquity'* [Ps. 141:4].

R. "And Israel is called men: *'To you who are men I call'* [Prov. 8:4].

S. "The nations of the world are called righteous, and Israel is called righteous.

T. "The nations of the world are called righteous: *'And righteous men shall judge them'* [Ez. 23:45].

U. "And Israel is called righteous: *'And your people – all of them are righteous'* [Is. 60:21].

V. "The nations of the world are called mighty, and Israel is called mighty.

W. "The nations of the world are called mighty: *'Why do you boast of evil, O mighty man'* [Ps. 52:3].

X. "And Israel is called mighty: *'Mighty in power, those who do his word'* [Ps. 103:20].

V:VIII

1. A. R. Simeon b. Yohai taught, "How masterful are the Israelites, for they know how to find favor with their creator."

   B. Said R. Yudan, [in Aramaic:], "It is like the case of Samaritan [beggars]. The Samaritan [beggars] are clever at begging. One of them goes to a housewife, saying to her, 'Do you have an onion? Give it to me.' After she gives it to him, he says to her, 'Is there such a thing as an onion without bread?' After she gives him [bread], he says to her, 'Is there such a thing as food without drink?' So, all in all, he gets to eat and drink."

   C. Said R. Aha [in Aramaic:], "There is a woman who knows how to borrow things, and there is a woman who does not. The one who knows how to borrow goes over to her neighbor. The door is open, but she knocks [anyhow]. Then she says to her neighbor, 'Greetings, good neighbor. How're you doing? How's your husband doing? How're your kids doing? Can I come in? [By the way], would you have such-and-such a utensil? Would you lend it to me?' [The neighboring housewife] says to her, 'Yes, of course.'

   D. "But the one who does not know how to borrow goes over to her neighbor. The door is closed, so she just opens it. She says [to the neighboring housewife], 'Do you have such-and-such a utensil? Would you lend it to me?' [The neighboring housewife] says to her, 'No.'"

   E. Said R. Hunia [in Aramaic:], "There is a tenant farmer who knows how to borrow things, and there is a tenant farmer who does not know how to borrow. The one who knows how to borrow combs his hair, brushes off his clothes, puts on a good face, and then goes over to the overseer of his work to borrow from him. [The overseer] says to him, 'How's the land doing?' He says to him, 'May you have the merit of being fully satisfied with its [wonderful] produce.' 'How are the oxen doing?' He says to him, 'May you have the merit of being fully satisfied with their fat.' 'How are the goats doing?' 'May you have the merit of being fully satisfied with their young.' 'And what would you like?' Then he says,

'Now if you might have an extra ten denars, would you give them to me?' The overseer replies, 'If you want, take twenty.'

F. "But the one who does not know how to borrow leaves his hair a mess, his clothes filthy, his face gloomy. He too goes over to the overseer to borrow from him. The overseer says to him, 'How's the land doing?' He replies, 'I hope it will produce at least what [in seed] we put into it.' 'How are the oxen doing?' 'They're scrawny.' 'How are the goats doing?' 'They're scrawny too.' 'And what do you want?' 'Now if you might have an extra ten denars, would you give them to me?' The overseer replies, 'Go, pay me back what you already owe me!'"

G. Said R. Hunia, "David was one of the good tenant farmers. To begin with, he starts a psalm with praise [of God], saying, *The heavens declare the glory of God, and the firmament shows his handiwork'* [Ps. 19:2]. The Heaven says to him, 'Perhaps you need something?' 'The firmament shows his handiwork.' The firmament says to him, 'Perhaps you need something?'

H. "And so he would continue to sing: *'Day unto day utters speech, and night to night reveals knowledge'* [Ps. 19:3].

I. "Said to him the Holy One, blessed be He, 'What do you want?'

J. "He said before him, *'Who can discern errors?'* [Ps. 19:13].

K. "'What sort of unwitting sin have I done before you!'

L. "[God] said to him, 'Lo, this one is remitted, and that one is forgiven you.'

M. *"'And cleanse me of hidden sins'* [Ps. 19:13]. '...from the secret sins that I have done before you.'

N. "He said to him, 'Lo, this one is remitted, and that one is forgiven to you.'

O. *"'Keep back your servant also from deliberate ones.'* This refers to transgressions done in full knowledge.

P. *"'That they may not have dominion over me. Then I shall be faultless'* [Ps. 19:14]. This refers to the most powerful of transgressions.

Q. *"'And I shall be clear of great transgression'"* (Ps. 19:14).

R. Said R. Levi, "David said before the Holy One, blessed be he, 'Lord of the age[s], you are a great God, and, as for me, my sins are great too. It will take a great God to remit and forgive great sins: *"For your name's sake, O Lord, pardon my sin, for [your name] is great""* (Ps. 25:11).

9. THE BAVLI

Editor: *The Formation of the Babylonian Talmud. Studies on the Achievements of Late Nineteenth and Twentieth Century Historical and Literary-Critical Research.* Leiden, 1970: Brill.

The Talmud of Babylonia. An American Translation. Chico, 1984-1985: Scholars Press for Brown Judaic Studies.

XXIII.C.   *Sanhedrin IX-XI.*

XXXII.   *Arakhin.*

Judaism: The Classical Statement. The Evidence of the Bavli.   Chicago, 1986:
University of Chicago Press.

Bavli Sanhedrin

Chapter Two

2:1-2

A.   [18A] A high priest judges, and [others] judge him;

B.   gives testimony, and [others] give testimony about him;

C.   performs the rite of removing the shoe [Deut. 25:7-9], and [others] perform the rite of removing the shoe with his wife.

D.   [Others] enter levirate marriage with his wife, but he does not enter into levirate marriage,

E.   because he is prohibited to marry a widow.

F.   [If] he suffers a death [in his family], he does not follow the bier.

G.   "But when [the bearers of the bier] are not visible, he is visible; when they are visible, he is not.

H.   "And he goes with them to the city gate," the words of R. Meir.

I.   R. Judah says, "He never leaves the sanctuary,

J.   "since it says, *'Nor shall he go out of the sanctuary'* (Lev. 21:12)."

K.   And when he gives comfort to others

L.   the accepted practice is for all the people to pass one after another, and the appointed [prefect of the priests] stands between him and the people.

M.   And when he receives consolation from others,

N.   all the people say to him, "Let us be your atonement."

O.   And he says to them, "May you be blessed by Heaven."

P.   And when they provide him with the funeral meal,

Q.   all the people sit on the ground, while he sits on a stool.

M. 2:1

A.   The king does not judge, and [others] do not judge him;

B.   does not give testimony, and [others] do not give testimony about him;

C.   does not perform the rite of removing the shoe, and others do not perform the rite of removing the shoe with his wife;

D.   does not enter into levirate marriage, nor [do his brother] enter levirate marriage with his wife.

E.   R. Judah says, "If he wanted to perform the rite of removing the shoe or to enter into levirate marriage, his memory is a blessing."

F. They said to him, "They pay no attention to him [if he expressed the wish to do so]."

G. [Others] do not marry his widow.

H. R. Judah says, "A king may marry the widow of a king.

I. "For so we find in the case of David, that he married the widow of Saul,

J. "For it is said, 'And I gave you your master's house and your master's wives into your embrace' (II Sam. 12:8)."

M. 2:2

I

A. A high priest judges [M. 2:1A]:

B. That is self-evident.

C. It was necessary to make that point in the context of the statement that others judge him.

D. That too is self-evident. If others do not judge him, how can he serve as a judge?

E. For has it not been written, "Gather yourselves together, yes, gather together" (Zeph. 2:1), on which R. Simeon b. Laqish said, "[The word for gather together bears the meaning of adorn, in consequence of which:] Adorn yourself and afterward adorn others."

F. Rather, since the framer of the passage wished to make reference to the king, who does not judge others and is not judged by others, he made reference in his clause on the high priest to the fact that he does judge and is judged by others.

G. And if you wish, I shall propose that what the framer of the passage teaches is in line with that which has been taught on Tannaite authority:

H. A high priest who committed homicide

I. [if he did so] deliberately, he is executed; [if he did so] inadvertently, he goes into exile to the cities of refuge [Num. 35:9ff.].

J. [If] he transgressed a positive or negative commandment, [T: or, indeed, and of the commandments,] lo, he is treated like an ordinary person in every respect. [T. San. 4:1A-C].

K. [Proceeding to the exegesis of the passage of Tosefta just now cited;] If he did so deliberately, he is executed:

L. That is self-evident.

M. It was included because of the other part of the statement, If he did so inadvertently, he goes into exile to the cities of refuge.

N. But that fact also is self-evident.

O. It was necessary to make it explicit. It might have entered your mind to claim that since it is written, "And he shall dwell thererin until the death of the high priest" (Num. 35:25), only one who is subject to the remedy of return [at the death of the high priest] is subject to the rule [of taking refuge in the city to begin with].

P. But someone who is not subject to the remedy of return [at the death of the high priest] should not go into exile at all.

Q. For we have learned in the Mishnah:

R. [18B] He who kills a high priest and a high priest who commited involuntary manslaughter never leaves [the city of refuge] [M. 2:7B-D].

S. I might then have concluded that such a one should not go into exile at all.

T. [The framer of the passage] tells us that that is not the case.

U. But might I say that it is indeed the case?

V. Scripture has said, "*Every man slayer may flee there*" (Deut. 19:3) – including even a high priest.

W If he transgressed a positive or negative commandment, or indeed any of the commandments, lo, he is treated like an ordinary person in every respect [T. San. 4:1C].

X. Is it not possible that he will not transgress?

Y. This is the sense of the passage: If he transgressed a positive or negative commandment, lo, he is treated like an ordinary person in every respect.

Z. That is self-evident.

AA. It might have entered our mind to say that, since we have learned in the Mishnah, A tribe, a false prophet, and a high priest, are judged only by a court of seventy-one judges [M. 1:6], in which connection R. Ada bar Ahbah said, "*Every great matter they shall bring to you*" (Ex. 18:22), meaning matters involving a great [important] man, [such as the high priest], one should reach the conclusion that any and every matter affecting a great man [must come to such a court].

BB. So we are informed [that that is not the case].

CC. But perhaps that indeed is the case?

DD. Is it written, "Matters affecting a great man"? What is written is, "A great matter," meaning, something that is quite literally a matter of importance.

II

A. Gives testimony and others give testimony about him [M. 2:1B]:

B. He gives testimony:

C. And has it not been taught on Tannaite authority:

D. "*And hide yourself from them*" (Deut. 22:4)–

E. There are times in which you do hide yourself, and there are times that you do not hide yourself.

F. How so?

G. In the case of a priest, if [the man who needs help] is in a graveyard [where a priest may not go, for fear of contracting corpse uncleanness], or if it is an elder and the work involved is not in accord with the honor owing to him, or if it is a case in which his own work is greater in value than that of his fellow, for such a case it is written, "And you shall hide yourself. [Shachter, p. 94, n. 7: In the same way the duty of bearing testimony should be abrogated in favor of a high priest, since it is not in keeping with his exalted office.]

H. Said R. Joseph, "He gives testimony for the king."

I.   But have we not learned in the Mishnah: **The king does not judge
     and others do not judge him [M.** 2:2A], **he does not give
     testimony and others do not give testimony about him [M.
     2A:2B]?**

J.   Rather, said R. Zera, "He gives testimony for the son of the king."

K.   But the son of a king falls into the category of an ordinary person!

L.   Rather: He gives testimony before the king.

M.   **And lo, the king does not join in the session of a
     sanhedrin [T. San.** 2:15A]!

N.   On account of the honor owing to the high priest, the king will come
     and join in the session of the sanhedrin. The court then will take the
     testimony of the high priest. Then the king will go his way, and the
     rest of us [the rabbis] will then look into the case [on which the high
     priest has testified].

III

A.   Reverting to the body of the text just now cited:

B.   **The king does not join in the session of a sanhedrin,**

C.   **and neither the king nor the high priest joins in the
     session called for intercalating the year. [T. San.** 2:15A-
     B].

D.   As to a king in the sanhedrin, it is written, "*You shall not speak in a
     case*" (Ex. 23:2), [reading the consonants differently, it is] "You shall
     not speak against the head [of the judges]." [Shachter, p. 94, n. 13: If
     the king were a member of the sanhedrin, other members would be
     inclined to suppress their opinions in deference to him.]

E.   **And neither the king nor the high priest joins in the
     session called for intercalating the year:**

F.   **The king, on account of the army's wages [for he would
     have a special interest in whether or not the year gets an
     extra month, if he is paying the army by the year],**

G.   **and the high priest, because of the cold in the fall [he
     would oppose adding an extra month, which places the Day
     of Atonement late in autumn].**

H.   Said R. Pappa, "The latter statement bears the implication that the year's
     seasons fall [Shachter:] with the normal lunar months. [Shachter, p. 95,
     n. 4: When the year is intercalated, the weather in Tishri (ordinarily:
     September) is the equivalent of that of Marcheshvan (ordinarily:
     October) in an ordinary year]."

I.   Is this the case? And lo, there were three cowboys, who were standing
     [and talking], and rabbis overheard them speaking.

J.   One of them said, "If the early and late sowing [wheat, barley] sprout
     together, it is Adar, and if not, it is not Adar."

K.   The second said, "If the morning frost is harsh enough to kill an ox, but
     at mid-day the ox lies in the shade of a fig-tree and scratches its hide
     [because of heat], it is Adar, and if not, it is not Adar."

L.   The third said, "When your breath can blow against a strong east wind, it
     is Adar, and if it is not, it is not Adar."

M.   The rabbis forthwith intercalated the year [Shachter, p. 95, n. 9: Thus
     we see that the purpose of intercalation is to readjust the seasons, and

the second Adar then has the climate of the first Adar in normal years, therefore Tishri will have its usual degree of heat in an intercalated year.]

N. But do you thing that rabbis would intercalate the year depending on cowboys?

O. They depended on their own calculations and the views of the cowboys supported their decision. [Shachter, p. 95, n. 10: In case, therefore, intercalation has been prompted by a reason other than the readjusting of the seasons, the weather will vary according to the months.]

IV

A. **He performs the rite of removing the shoe, and others perform the rite of removing the shoe with his wife [M. 2:1C]:**

B. Does the Tannaite authority at hand take the view that there is no difference whether the widow was merely betrothed or was partner to a fully consummated marriage?

C. Now in the case of a widow of a fully consummated marriage, you have a case of an affirmative religious duty and a prohibition *["A virgin of his people he shall take to wife"* (Lev. 21:14) as against *"A widow he shall not take"* (Lev. 21:14)]. [So the high priest does not marry the widow at hand.]

D. [19A] And a positive religious duty cannot set aside a negative one and a positive one.

E. But as to doing so when the relationship is merely one of betrothal why should he not [marry her, rather than going through the rite of removing the shoe]?

F. Let a positive religious duty come and set aside a negative religious duty. [The positive religious duty is to take the deceased childless brother's widow as his wife, so Deut. 25:5ff. The negative religious duty is not to marry a non-virgin, as indicated].

G. It is a decree against his having sexual relations [to effect the levirate marriage] on account of later acts of sexual relations [which are not subject to a religious duty. He will have carried out his duty only by the first act of sexual relations.]

H. It has been taught on Tannaite authority along these same lines;

I. If [the high priest] went ahead and had sexual relations with the widow of his deceased childless brother, the first act of sexual relations has effected acquisition. But he is forbidden to go ahead and have further sexual relations with her, [but has to divorce her].

V

A. **If he suffers a death in his family, he does not follow the bier [M. 2:1F]:**

B. Our rabbis have taught on Tannaite authority:

C. *"Neither shall he go out of the sanctuary"* (Lev. 21:12):

D. He should not go out with them, but he may go out after them. How so?

E. **When the bearers of the bier are not visible, he is visible, and when they are visible, he is not [M. 2:1G].**

VI

A. "And he goes with them to the city gate," the words of R. Meir. R. Judah says, "He never leaves the sanctuary, since it says ..." [M. 2:1H-J]:

B. Has R. Judah given a good argument?

C. R. Meir may say to you, "If that is the sense of the verse at hand [as Judah explains] it, then he should also not go to his own home.

D. "But this is the sense of the matter: 'From the sanctuary he shall not go forth' means he should not go forth from his status as sanctified. But since in the present matter there is provision for giving full recognition to that status, he will not come to have contact [with corpse-matter]."

E. And R. Judah?

F. On account of his bitter mourning, it might happen that [unknowingly] he will come into contact with corpse-matter.

VII

A. When he gives comfort to others [M. 2:1K]:

B. Our rabbis have taught on Tannaite authority:

C. [And when] he stands in the line to give comfort to others, the prefect of the priests and the anointed [high] priests who has now passed out [of his position of grandeur] are at his right hand, and the head of his father's house, the mourners, and all the people are at his left.

D. [When] he stands in the line to receive comfort from others [as a mourner], the prefect of the priests is at his right hand, and the head of the father's houses [the priestly courses] and all the people are at his left hand [T. San. 4:1 I, F].

E. But [in the latter case] the anointed high priest who has left office does not come to him.

F. Why not?

G. [The present high priest] might be upset at his presence, thinking, "[My predecessor] is happy at my misfortune."

H. Said R. Pappa, "The present teaching on Tannaite authority yields three points:

I. "First, the prefect is the same as the one called in the Mishnah's version 'the one who is appointed.'

J. "Second, the mourners stand and the people pass by them.

K. "Third, the mourners are to the left of those who come to give comfort."

L. Our rabbis have taught on Tannaite authority:

M. The original practice was for the mourners to stand still and all the people to pass by them. There were two families in Jerusalem who competed with one another.

N. This one said, "I shall pass first," and that one said, "I shall pass first."

O. Sages ordained that the people should stand still and the mourners should pass by.

P. Said R. Ammi bar Abba, "In Sepphoris R. Yose restored the original practice, so that the mourners would stand still and all the people would pass by."

Q. And said R. Ammi bar Abba, "In Sepphoris R. Yose ordained that a woman should not walk through the market place with her children behind her, on account of an incident that took place."

R. And said R. Ammi bar Abba, "In Sepphoris R. Yose ordained that women should talk aloud in the privy, so as to preserve privacy [since men would know not to come in]."

S. Said R. Menassia bar Avat, "I asked R. Josiah, the elder, in the cemetery of Husal, and he said to me, 'There can be no line of comforters less than ten people, not counting the mourners,

T. "'and that is the case whether the mourners are standing and all the people passing by them, or whether the mourners pass by and all the people are standing still.'"

VIII

A. **And when he receives consolation from others [M. 2:1M]:**

B. The question was raised: When he comforts others, what does he say to them?

C. Come and take note: And he says, "May you be comforted."

D. Now to what circumstances would such a statement pertain?

E. If one should propose that it is when others comfort him, could he say to them, "Be comforted"? That would represent some sort of enchantment that he set against them!

F. Rather it is that, when he comforts others, he says to them, "Be comforted."

G. That indeed is definitive proof.

IX

A. **The king does not judge, and others do not judge him [M. 2:2A]:**

B. Said R. Joseph, "That law applies only to Israelite kings. But as to the kings of the house of David, such a king judges and others judge them.

C. "For it is written, *'House of David, thus says the Lord, execute justice in the morning'* (Jer. 21:12).

D. "Now if others do not judge him, how can they judge others? And has it not been written, *'Ornament yourselves and be ornamented'* (Zeph. 2:1), interpreted by R. Simeon b. Laqish to mean, 'Adorn yourself and then adorn others'?"

E. What then is the reason that Israelite kings are not judged and do not judge?

F. It is because of a case that actually took place.

G. King Yannai's agent killed someone. Simeon b. Shetah said to sages, "Set your eyes against him and let us judge him."

H. They sent a message to him, "Your agent has killed someone."

I. He sent back to them, "Send him to me."

J. They replied to him, "You come too. *'If a warning has been given to its owners'* (Ex. 21:29) is what the Torah has said, so let the owner of the ox come and take responsibility for his ox."

K. The king came and took his seat.

L. Simeon b. Shetah said to him, "King Yannai, stand on your feet, so that people can give evidence against you. And it is not before us that you stand, but before Him who spoke and brought the world into being that you stand, as it is said, *'Then both the men between whom the controversy is shall stand'* (Deut. 19:17)."

M. He said to him, "It is not as you say, but as your fellows will say."

N. [19B] [Simeon] looked to his right, and the sages looked to the ground. He looked to the left, and they looked to the ground.

O. Said Simeon b. Shetah to them, "You are lost in thought? Let the Master of thought come and exact a penalty from you."

P. Forthwith Gabriel came and knocked them to the ground, and they all died.

Q. At that moment they ruled: **The king does not judge and others do not judge him, he does not give testimony and others do not give testimony about him [M. 2:2A-B].**

X

A. **He does not perform the rite of removing the shoe, and others do not perform the rite of removing the shoe with his wife...   [R. Judah says, "If he wanted to perform the rite of removing the shoe or to enter into levirate marriage, his memory is a blessing"] [M. 2:2C-E]:**

B. [Is what R. Judah says] true?

C. And has not R. Ashi said, "As to a patriarch who was willing to forego the honor owing to him, the honor is foregone, but as to a king who was willing to forego the honor owing to him, the honor owing to him is not foregone, for it is said, *'You shall in any way set him as a king over you'* (Deut. 17:15), meaning that fear of him should remain over you"?

D. A matter involving a religious duty is different [in Judah's view].

XI

A. **Others do not marry his widow [M. 2:2G]:**

B. It has been taught on Tannaite authority:

C. They said to R. Judah, "[David] married women of the royal family who were permitted to him, Merab and Michal, [but these were not his widows]."

D. **His disciples asked R. Yose, "How did David marry two sisters while both were yet alive"?**

E. **He said to them, "He married Michal after the death of Merab."**

F. **R. Joshua b. Qorha says, "His act of betrothal of Merab was made in error, as it is said, 'Give me my wife, Michal, whom I betrothed at a price of a hundred foreskins of the Philistines' (2 Sam. 3:14).   [T. adds: Just as his act of betrothal was not a completely valid one, so his marriage was not a completely valid one]" [T. Sot. 11:18-19].**

G. What sort of proof is derived?

H. Said R. Pappa, "Michal is my wife, and Merab is not my wife."

I. And what sort of error in the betrothal was there?

J. It is as it is written, *"And it shall be that the man who kills him the king will enrich him with great riches and will give him his daughter"* (1 Sam. 17:25).

K. David went and killed him. [Saul] said to him, "You have a debt with me [which I owe to you], and one who betrothes a woman by forgiving a debt does not accomplish the woman's betrothal."

L. [Saul] went and gave her instead to Adriel, as it is written, *"But it came to pass at the time when Merab, Saul's daughter, should have been given to David, that she was given to Adriel the Meholathite to wife"* (1 Sam. 18:19).

M. [Saul] said to [David], "If you want me to give you Michal, go and bring me a hundred foreskins of Philistines."

N. He went and brought him a hundred foreskins of Philistines.

O. He said to him, "Now you have with me an unpaid debt [which I owe you], and also a perutah [coin]."

P. Saul had the notion that, where there is a loan and a small coin, [the creditor] is thinking about the loan [in any transaction or exchange with the debtor, hence David will be thinking about the loan and his act of betrothal once more would be null]. But David was thinking that where there is a loan and a coin, one's thought is about the coin.

Q. And if you wish, I shall propose that all parties concurred that where there is a loan and a coin owing, one's thought is on the coin. But Saul took the view that [the foreskins] were worthless anyhow, while David took the view that they were fit for dog- or cat-food.

R. And how does R. Yose interpret the language, *"Give me my wife, Michal"* (2 Sam. 3:14)?

S. R. Yose interprets it in a way consistent with his reasoning.

T. For it has been taught on Tannaite authority:

U. **R. Yose would interpret confused verses of Scripture: "It is written, '*But the king took the two sons of Rizpah the daughter of Ayah whom she bore to Saul, Armoni and Mephibosheth, and the five sons of Michal, the daughter of Saul, whom she bore to Adriel the son of Barzillai the Meholathite* (2 Sam. 21:8).**

V. **"Now where do we find that Michal was given to Adriel the son of Barzillai the Meholathite?   Was she not given only to Palti the son of Laish who was of Gallim, as it is said, '*And Saul had given Michal, his daughter, David's wife, to Palti, the son of Laish, who was of Gallim*' (1 Sam. 25:44).**

W. **"But Scripture thereby links the marriage of Merab to the marriage of Michal.   Just as the marriage of Michal to Palti the son of Laish was in transgression, so the marriage of Merab to Adriel was in transgression"** [T. Sot. 11:17A-C].

X. And as to R. Joshua b. Qorhah, is it not written, *"And the five sons of Michal, the daughter of Saul, whom she bore to Adriel"* (2 Sam. 21:8)?

Y. R. Joshua can say to you: But did Michal produce them?   And is it not so that Merab produced them?   But Merab gave birth to them and Michal raised them, so they were called by Michal's name, [T. adds: as it is said, '*And the women of the neighborhood gave him a name, saying, A son has been born to Naomi*' (Ruth 4:17)] [T. Sot. 11:20].

Z.   [T. lacks:]   "This serves to teach you that whoever raises an orphan in his house is regarded by Scripture as if he had given birth to him.

XII

A.   R. Hanina says, "Proof [of the proposition just now cited] derives from the following verse of Scripture: *'And the women of the neighborhood gave him a name, saying, A son has been born to Naomi'* (Ruth 4:17)."

B.   "Now did Naomi give birth to the child? Was it not Ruth? But Ruth gave birth to the child, and Naomi raised him, so he bore Naomi's name."

C.   R. Yohanan said, "Proof [of the same proposition] derives from here: *'And his wife, the Judaite [Bithia, the daughter of Pharaoh] bore Yered, father of Gedor [and Heber, father of Soco, the child, and Naomi raised him, so he bore Naomi's name].'"*

C.   R. Yohanan said, "Proof [of the same proposition] derives from here: *'And his wife, the Judaite [Bithia, the daughter of Pharaoh] bore Yered, father of Gedor [and Heber, father of Soco, and Jekuthiel, father of Zanoah], and these are the sons of Bithia, daughter of Pharaoh, whom Mered took'* (1 Chr. 4:18).

D.   ("Mered was Caleb, and why was he called Mered? Because he rebelled (MRD) against the counsel of the spies.)

E.   "And did Bithia give birth [to Moses], and did not Jochebed do so?

F.   "But while Jochebed gave birth to him, Bithia raised him, therefore he bore her name."

G.   R. Eleazar said, "Proof derives from here: *'You have with your arm redeemed your people, the sons of Jacob and Joseph, Selah'* (Ps. 77:16). Did Joseph beget [the people]? Was it not Jacob? But Jacob begot them and Joseph kept them alive, therefore they bore his name."

H.   Said R. Samuel bar Nahmani said R. Jonathan, "Whoever teaches Torah to his fellow's son is credited by Scripture as if he begat him,

I.   "as it is said, *'Now these are the generations of Aaron and Moses'* (Num. 3:1), and later, *'These are the names of the sons of Aaron'* (Num. 3:1), so teaching the lesson that Aaron begat them and Moses taught them [Torah], and therefore they bore his [Moses'] name."

J.   "Therefore *thus says the Lord to the house of Jacob, who redeemed Abraham"* (Is. 29:22):

K.   Now where in Scripture do we find that Jacob redeemed Abraham?

L.   Said R. Judah, "He redeemed him from the trouble of raising children [because Abraham had few children, while Jacob had many]. That is in line with what is written, *'Jacob shall not now be ashamed, neither shall his face now wax pale'* (Is. 29:22).

M.   "'He shall not now be ashamed' – of his father.

N.   "'Neither shall his face now become pale' – because of his grandfather."

XIII

A.   It is written "Palti" (at I Sam. 25:44), and it is written "Paltiel" (2 Sam. 3:15) [so the second husband of David's undivorced wife had two names].

B.   Said R. Yohanan, "He was really called Palti, and why was he later called Paltiel? Because God (el) saved him from transgression [namely, marrying an already-married woman].

C. "What did [God] do? He put a sword between him and her [so they did not have sexual relations], saying, 'Whoever gets involved in this matter will be pierced by this sword.'"

D. But is it not written, *"And her husband Palti went with her"* (2 Sam. 3:16)?

E. That he became like her husband [but he was not in fact ever he husband].

F. But is it not written, *"He went weeping"* (2 Sam. 3:16)?

G. It was on account of the loss of the religious duty [Shachter: of self-restraint]."

H. *"He followed her to Bahurim"* (2 Sam. 3:16): Both of them [Palti and his wife] were like youths [bahurim], who had not tasted the flavor of sexual relations [having remained celibate for their marriage].

I. Said R. Yohanan, "The strong desire affecting Joseph [Gen. 39:7-13] was modest for Boaz, and the strong desire affecting Boaz [Ruth 3:8-15] was modest for Palti ben Laish.

J. "The strong desire affecting Joseph was modest for Boaz, in line with that which is written, *'And it came to pass at midnight, and the man was startled'* (Ruth 3:8)."

K. What is the meaning of "was startled"?

L. Said Rab, "His penis became as hard as a turnip top. [A play on the consonants for 'was startled' which are shared with the word for turnip.]"

M. [20A] [Yohanan continues], "And the strong desire affecting Boaz was modest for Palti ben Laish," – as we have said.

N. Said R. Yohanan, "What is the meaning of the verse of Scripture, *'Many daughters have done valiantly, but you excel them all'* (Prov. 31:29)?

O. "'Many daughters have done valiantly' refers to Joseph and Boaz.

P. "'And you excel them all' speaks of Palti, son of Laish."

Q. Said R. Samuel bar Nahman said R. Jonathan, "What is the meaning of the verse of Scripture: *'Grace is deceitful and beauty is vain, but a woman who fears the Lord shall be praised'* (Prov. 31:30)?

R. "'Grace is deceitful' speaks of Joseph.

S. "'Beauty is vain' speaks of Boaz.

T. "'A woman who fears the Lord shall be praised' speaks of Palti ben Laish.

U. "Another interpretation: 'Grace is deceitful' speaks of the generation of Moses.

V. "'Beauty is vain' speaks of the generation of Joshua.

W. "'A woman who fears the Lord shall be praised' speaks of the generation of Hezekiah.

X. "Another interpretation: 'Grace is deceitful' speaks of the generation of Moses and Joshua.

Y. "'Beauty is vain' speaks of the generation of Hezekiah.

Z. "'A woman who fears the Lord shall be praised' speaks of the generation of R. Judah b. R. Ilai.

AA "They said concerning R. Judah b. R. Ilai that six disciples [in his time] would cover themselves with a single cloak but [nonetheless] would spend their time studying Torah [despite gross want]."

2:3

A. [If] [the king] suffers a death in his family, he does not leave the gate of his palace.
B. R. Judah says, "If he wants to go out after the bier, he goes out,
C. "for thus we find in the case of David, that he went out after the bier of Abner,
D. "since it is said, 'And King David followed the bier' (2 Sam. 3:31)."
E. They said to him, "This action was only to appease the people."
F. And when they provide him with the funeral meal, all the people sit on the ground, while he sits on a couch.

I

A. Our rabbis have taught on Tannaite authority:
B. In a place in which women are accustomed to go forth after the bier, they go forth in that way. If they are accustomed to go forth before the bier, they go forth in that manner.
C. R. Judah says, "Women always go forth in front of the bier.
D. "For so we find in the case of David that he went forth after the bier of Abner.
E. "For it is said, 'And King David followed the bier' (2 Sam. 3:31)."
F. They said to him, "That was only to appease the people [M. 2:3D-E].
G. "They were appeased, for David would go forth among the men and come in among the women, go forth among the women and come in among the men,
H. "as it is said, 'So all the people and all Israel understood that it was not of the king to slay Abner' (2 Sam. 3:37)."

II

A. Raba expounded, "What is the meaning of that which is written, 'And all the people came to cause David to eat bread' (2 Sam. 3:35)?
B. "It was written, 'to pierce David' [with a K], but we read, 'to cause him to eat bread' [with a B].
C. "To begin with they came to pierce him but in the end to cause him to eat bread."

III

A. Said R. Judah said Rab, "On what account was Abner punished? Because he could have prevented Saul but did not prevent him [from killing the priest of Nob, 1 Sam. 22:18]."
B. R. Isaac said, "He did try to prevent him, but he got no response."
C. And both of them interpret the same verse of Scripture: "And the king lamented for Abner and said, Should Abner die as a churl dies, your hands were not bound or your feet put into fetters" (2 Sam. 2:33).
D. He who maintains that he did not try to stop Saul interprets the verse in this way: "Your hands were not bound nor were your feet put into

fetters" − so why did you not try to stop him? *"As a man falls before the children of iniquity so did you fall"* (2 Sam. 3:33).

E. He who maintains that he did try to stop Saul but got no response interprets the verse as an expression of amazement: "Should he have died as a churl dies?   Your hands were not bound and your feet were not put into fetters."

F. Since he did protest, why "As a man falls before the children of iniquity, so did you fall"?

G. In the view of him who has said that he did protest, why was he punished?

H. Said R. Nahman bar Isaac, "Because he held up the coming of the house of David by two and a half years."

IV

A. **And when they provide him with the funeral meal, [all the people sit on the ground, while he sits on a couch] [M. 2:3F]:**

B. What is the couch?

C. Said Ulla, "It is a small couch [Shachter, p. 106, n. 3: not used for rest but placed in the home merely as an omen of good fortune]."

D. Said rabbis to Ulla, "Now is there something on which, up to that time, he had never sat, and now we seat him on that object?"

E. Raba objected to this argument, "What sort of problem is this?   Perhaps it may be compared to the matter of eating and drinking, for up to this point we gave him nothing to eat or drink, while now we bring him food and drink.

F. "But if there is a question, this is the question: As to a couch [of the present sort], it is not necessary to lower it but it is stood up.   Now if you think that the couch under discussion is a small couch [such as was described above], why is it not necessary to lower it?

G. "Has it not been taught on Tannaite authority:

H. "He who lowers beds [in the house of mourning] does not lower the mourner's bed alone but all of the beds in the house.' [So why not lower the one under discussion?]"

I. But what is the problem?   Perhaps it falls into the category of a bed set aside for the storage of utensils, concerning which it has been taught on Tannaite authority:

J. If it was a bed set aside for storing utensils, it is not necessary to lower it.

K. Rather, if there is a problem, this is the problem:

L. R. Simeon b. Gamaliel says, "As to a small couch, one loosens the loops, and it will fall on its own."

M. Now if you maintain that it is a small couch [such as was described above], are there any loops?

N. Rather, when Rabin came, he said, "One of the rabbis told me, and it was R. Tahalipa by name, that he would frequent the leather-workers market, and he asked one of them, 'What is a couch?'   And he was told, 'It is the name of a bed of skins.' [Shachter, p. 107, n. 2: Its strapping consisted of leather instead of ropes.   Not being supported by long legs, it stood very low, and therefore on practical grounds, the first Tanna maintains that is must not be undone and lowered, as the leather will be spoiled through the damp earth, while Rabban Simeon b. Gamaliel holds that there is no fear of this.]"

O. Said R. Jeremiah said R. Yohanan, "A couch [20B] has its webbing affixed on the inside, while a bed has its webbing affixed on the outside."

P. An objection was raised: At what point in the process of manufacture do wooden objects become susceptible to uncleanness [as useful objects]?

Q. **As to a bed and a cradle, it is when they have been sanded with a fish-skin [M. Kel. 16:1] [which polishes the surface].**

R. Now if a bed has its webbing on the outside of the frame, what need is there to smooth the wood with a fish-skin? [The webbing covers the wood anyhow].

S. But both sorts have the webbing on the inside, and the webbing of a bed is inserted through slits, while the webbing of a couch is inserted through loops.

T. Said R. Jacob said R. Joshua b. Levi, "The decided law accords with the opinion of Rabban Simeon b. Gamaliel."

U. Said R. Jacob bar Ammi, "In the case of a bed the poles of which protrude, it is enough to set it up [on one side] [Shachter, p. 107, n. 8: because if actually lowered, it may appear to be standing in its usual position, since then the poles protrude upwards]."

2:4A-D

A. **[The king] calls out [the army to wage] a war fought by choice on the instructions of a court of seventy-one.**

B. **He [may exercise the right to] open a road for himself, and [others] may not stop him.**

C. **The royal road has no required measure.**

D. **All the people plunder and lay before him [what they have grabbed], and he takes the first portion.**

I

A. But has not the point [of M. 2:4A] already been made on Tannaite authority: **They bring forth the army to wage a war fought by choice only on the instructions of a court of seventy-one [M. 1:5B]?**

B. Since the Tannaite framer of the passage dealt with all sorts of matters pertaining to the king, he included also a reference to his bringing forth the army to wage war by choice.

II

A. Said R. Judah said Samuel, "Everything included in the chapter [1 Sam. 8] on the king the king is permitted to do."

B. Rab said, "What is stated in that chapter is included only to make the people fear [having a king], as it is said, *You shall in any manner set him as king over you'* (Deut. 17:15) meaning that fear of him should be upon you."

C. The foregoing dispute follows along the lines of a dispute among Tannaite authorities, as follows:

D. R. Yose says, "Everything that is spelled out in the pericope of the king the king is permitted to do."

E. R. Judah says, "That pericope is written only to make the people revere him [cf. M. San. 2:5C],

F. "for it is written, *'You will surely set a king over you'* (Deut. 17:14), so that fear of him will be upon you."

G. And so did R. Judah say, "Three commandments were imposed upon the Israelites when they came into the land.

H. "[They were commanded] to appoint a king, to cut off the descendents of Amalek and to build the chosen House.

I. [T. adds:] "If so, why were they punished in the days of Samuel [for wanting a king]? Because they acted too soon."

J. R. Nehorai says, "This pericope was written only because of [future] complaints [with the king],

K. "For it is said, *'And you will say, I will set a king over me'* (Deut. 17:14)."

L. It has been taught on Tannaite authority: R. Eleazar [b. R. Yose] says, "The elders asked in the proper way, as it is said, *'Give us a king to judge us'* (1 Sam. 8:6).

M. "But the ordinary folk went and spoiled matters, as it is said, *'That we also may be like all the nations, and our king will judge us and go before us to fight our battles'* (1 Sam. 8:20)" [T. San. 4:5H-Q].

III

A. It has been taught on Tannaite authority:

B. R. Yose says, "Three commandments were imposed upon the Israelites when they came into the land. They were commanded to appoint a king, to cut off the descendents of Amalek, and to build the chosen House" [T. San. 4:5K-L].

C. Now I do not know which of them comes first.

D. When Scripture says, *"The hand upon the throne of the Lord, the Lord will have war with Amalek from generation to generation"* (Ex. 17:16), one must conclude that first of all they are set up a king.

E. For "throne" refers only to the king, as it is said, *"Then Solomon sat on the throne of the Lord as king"* (1 Chr. 29:23).

F. Still, I do not know whether they are to build the chosen House first, or to cut off the seed of Amalek first.

G. When Scripture says, *"And when he gives you rest from all your enemies round about,"* then it goes on, *"Then it shall come to pass that the place which the Lord your God shall choose"* (Deut. 12:10), we reach the conclusion that first of all comes cutting off the seed of Amalek.

H. So too in the case of David it says, *"And it came to pass when the king dwelt in his house, and the Lord had given him rest from his enemies round about,"* and then it goes on, *"that the king said to Nathan the prophet, See, now, I dwell in a house of cedars"* (2 Sam. 7:1-2).

IV

A. Said R. Simeon b. Laqish, "At first Solomon ruled over the creatures of the upper world, as it is said, *Then Solomon sat on the throne of the Lord as king'* (1 Chr. 29:23). Then he reigned over the creatures of the lower world, as it is written, *'For he had dominion over all the region on this side of the river, From Tifsah even to Gaza'* (1 Kgs. 5:4)."

B. Rab and Samuel:

C. One said, "Tifsah is at one end of the world, Gaza at the other."

D. The other said, "Tifsah and Gaza were next to one another. And just as he ruled over Tifsah and Gaza, so he ruled over the entire world."

E. But in the end he ruled only over Israel, as it is said, *"I, Qohelet, have been king over Israel"* (Qoh. 1:12).

F. Then he ruled over Jerusalem alone, as it is written, *"The words of Qohelet, son of David, king of Jerusalem"* (Qoh. 1:12).

G. In the end, he ruled only over his own bed, as it is written, *"Behold it is the bed of Solomon, three score mighty men are about it"* (Song 3:7).

H. In the end he ruled only over his staff, as it is written, *"This was my portion from all my labor"* (Qoh. 2:10).

I. Rab and Samuel:

J. One said, "[All he had at the end] was his staff." The other said, "He had his pitcher."

K. Did he or did he not recover [his glory]?

L. Rab and Samuel:

M. One said, "He did." The other said, "He did not."

N. The one who said that he did not return to his high position says that he first was king and then an ordinary person, and the one who said that he reverted to his glory holds that first he was king, then an ordinary person and finally king again.

V

A. He may open a road for himself, [and others may not stop him] [M. 2:4B]:

B. [With reference to M. 2:4D: All the people plunder... and he takes the first portion], our rabbis have taught on Tannaite authority:

C. The royal treasuries [of a defeated foe] belong to the king, and as to the rest of the spoil that the army takes, half is for the king and the other half is for the people.

D. Said Abayye to R. Dimi, and some say to R. Aha, "Now there is no difficulty in understanding that the royal treasuries should go to the king. That is as things should be.

E. "But how on the basis of Scripture do we learn that as to the rest of the spoil, half goes to the king and half to the people?"

F. [The reply:] "As it is written, [21A], *'And anointed [Solomon] unto the Lord to be prince and Sadok to be priest'* (1 Chr. 29:22).

G. "An analogy is drawn between the prince and Sadok.

H. "Just as, in the case of Sadok, half belonged to him and half to his brothers [the other priests], so in the case of the prince, half belongs to him and half to his brothers."

I. And how do we know that that was the fact with Sadok himself?

J. As it has been taught on Tannaite authority:

K. Rabbi says, *"And [the showbread] shall be for Aaron and his sons'* (Lev. 24:9) – half to Aaron, half to the sons."

2:4E-I

E. "He should not multiply wives to himself" (Deut. 17:17) – only eighteen.

F. R Judah says, "He may have as many as he wants, so long as they do not entice him [to abandon the Lord (Deut. 7:4)]."

G. R. Simeon says, "Even if there is only one who entices him [to abandon the Lord] – lo, this one should not marry her."

H. If so, why is it said, "He should not multiply wives to himself"?

I. Even though they should be like Abigail [1 Sam. 25:3].

I

A. Does the dispute [at M. 2:4F, G] bear the implication that R. Judah seeks out the reasoning behind a verse of Scripture, and R. Simeon does not seek out the reasoning behind a verse of Scripture?

B. But do we not find just the opposite?

C. For it has been taught on Tannaite authority:

D. "As to a widow, whether she is poor or rich, people do not exact a pledge from her, for it is said, *'You shall not take the widow's raiment as a pledge'* (Deut. 24:17)," the words of R. Judah.

E. R. Simeon says, "If she is rich, they do exact a pledge from her. If she is poor they do not exact a pledge from her, because one is liable to return it to her, and so may give her a bad name among her neighbors [by constant visitations]."

F. In that connection we raised the question, What is the sense of that statement?

G. This is the sense of that statement: Because you take a pledge from her, you are liable to return the object to her, and so you give her a bad name among neighbors [so Simeon].

H. What follows is that R. Judah does not take account of the reasoning behind a verse of Scripture, and R. Simeon does take account of the reasoning behind a verse of Scripture.

I. In general R. Judah does not take account of the reasoning behind a verse of Scripture, but the present case is different, for he spells out the reason given in the Scripture itself.

J. What is the reason that *"he shall not multiply wives to himself"*? It is because *"his heart should not be turned aside."*

K. And R. Simeon? He may reply to you that in general, we do interpret the reason behind a verse of Scripture. In the present case, therefore, the Scripture should have stated, *"He should not multiply wives to himself"* and then fallen silent. I should then have stated on my own then, "What is the reason that *he should not multiply them?* So that his heart should not turn away."

L. Why make "not turning away" explicit therefore?

M.   To indicate, Even if there is only one who entices him to abandon the Lord, lo, this one should not marry her [M. 3:4H].

N.   Then how shall I explain the sense of "He should not multiply"?

O.   *Even one like Abigail [M. 2:4I].*

II

A.   As to the number of eighteen [specified at M. 2:4E], what is the source for that number?

B.   It is from the following verse of Scripture: *"And unto David were sons born in Hebron, and his first-born son was Amnon, of Ahinoam the Jezreelites, the second, Chileab, of Abigail, the wife of Nabal the Carmelite, the third Absalom, son of Maacah; the fourth, Adonijah, son of Haggith; and the fifth, Shefatiah, son of Abital, and the sixth, Ithream, of Eglah, David's wife. These were born to David in Hebron"* (2 Sam. 3:2-5).

C.   And the prophet said to him, *"And if that were too little, then would I add to you the like of these and the like of these"* (2 Sam. 12:8).

D.   Each "like of these" means six more [since the referent is the original six], so eighteen in all.

E.   Rabina objected, "Might I say that 'Like of these' stands for twelve, and the second such reference means twenty-four [Shachter, p. 113, n. 3: He increased the number in geometrical progression, 6, 12, 24]?"

F.   So it has been taught on Tannaite authority:

G.   *"He should not multiply wives to himself"* (Deut. 17:17) – more than twenty-four.

H.   In the view of him who interprets the "and," the number is forty-eight.

I.   It has been taught on Tannaite authority along these very lines:

J.   *"He should not multiply wives to himself"* (Deut. 17:17) – more than forty-eight.

K.   And what is the reason for the view of the Tannaite authority who framed the Mishnah-passage at hand?

L.   Said R. Kahana, "He draws an analogy between the first 'and the like' and the second 'and the like.' Just as the former refers to six, so the latter refers to the six."

M.   But there was Michal [beyond the six wives who are listed]?

N.   Rab said, "Eglah is Michal, and why was she called Eglah? Because she was as beloved of him as a calf [eglah] is of its mother.

O.   "And so it is said, *'If you had not ploughed with my heifer'* (Jud. 14:18)."

P.   But did Michal have children? And is it not written, *"And Michal, daughter of Saul, had no child to the day of her death"* (2 Sam. 6:23)?

Q.   Said R. Hisda, "To the day of her death she had none, but on the day of her death she had one."

R.   Now where, in point of fact, is the number of sons reckoned? It is in Hebron. But the case involving Michal took place in Jerusalem, for it is written, *"Michal, daughter of Saul, looked out at the window and saw King David leaping and dancing before the Lord, and she despised him in her heart"* (2 Sam. 6:16).

S.   And R. Judah, and some say R. Joseph, said, "Michal took her due punishment, which was childlessness."

T.   Rather, one might propose, prior to that event she had children, but afterward she had none.

U.   [Referring to the issue of the number of eighteen specified in the Mishnah-paragraph], is it not stated, *"And David took concubines and wives out of Jerusalem"* (2 Sam. 5:13)?

V.   It was to reach the number of eighteen [wives].

W.   What is the difference between wives and concubines?

X.   Said R. Judah said Rab, "Wives are with a marriage contract and a rite of betrothal, concubines are without a marriage contract and without a rite of betrothal."

III

A.   Said R. Judah said Rab, "David had four hundred sons, all of them born of beautiful captive women. All grew long locks plaited down the back. All of them were seated in golden chariots.

B.   "And they went forth at the head of troops, and they were the powerful figures in the house of David."

C.   And R. Judah said Rab said, "Tamar was the daughter of a beautiful captive woman.

D.   "For it is said, *'Now, therefore, I pray you, speak to the king, for he will not withhold me from you'* (2 Sam. 13:13).

E.   "Now if you hold that she was the daughter of a valid marriage, would the king ever have permitted [Amnon] to marry his sister?

F.   "But, it follows, she was the daughter of a beautiful captive woman."

G.   *"And Amnon had a friend, whose name was Jonadab, son of Shimeah, David's brother, and Jonadab was a very subtle man"* (2 Sam. 13:3): Said R. Judah said Rab, "He was subtle about doing evil."

H.   *"And he said to him, Why, son of the king, are you thus becoming leaner... And Jonadab said to him, Lay down on your bed and pretend to be sick... and she will prepare the food in my sight... and she took the pan and poured [the cakes] out before him"* (2 Sam. 13:4ff.): Said R. Judah said Rab, "They were some sort of pancakes."

I.   *"Then Amnon hated her with a very great hatred"* (2 Sam. 13:15): What was the reason?

J.   Said R. Isaac, "One of his hairs got caught [around his penis and cut it off] making him one whose penis had been cut off."

K.   But was she the one who had tied the hair around his penis? What had she done?

L.   Rather, I should say, she had tied a hair around his penis and made him into one whose penis had been cut off.

M.   Is this true? And did not Raba explain, "What is the sense of the verse, *'And your renown went forth among the nations for your beauty'* (Ez. 16:14)? It is that Israelite women do not have armpit or pubic hair."

N.   Tamar was different, because she was the daughter of a beautiful captive woman.

O.   *"And Tamar put ashes on her head and tore her garment of many colors"* (2 Sam. 13:19):

P.   It was taught on Tannaite authority in the name of R. Joshua b. Qorhah, "Tamar established a high wall at that time [protecting chastity]. People said, 'If such could happen to princesses, all the more so can it happen to ordinary women.' If such could happen to virtuous women, all the more so can it happen to wanton ones!"

Q. Said R. Judah said Rab, "At that time they made a decree [21B] against a man's being alone with any woman [married or] unmarried."

R. But the rule against a man's being along with [a married woman] derives from the authority of the Torah [and not from the authority of rabbis later on].

S. For R. Yohanan said in the name of R. Simeon b. Yehosedeq, "Whence in the Torah do we find an indication against a man's being alone [with a married woman]? As it is said, 'If your brother, of your mother, entice you' (Deut. 13:7).

T. "And is it the fact that the son of one's mother can entice, but the son of the father cannot entice? Rather, it is to tell you that a son may be alone with his mother, and no one else may be alone with any of the consanguineous female relations listed in the Torah."

U. Rather, they made a decree against a man's being alone with an unmarried woman.

V. "And Adonijah, son of Haggith, exalts himself, saying, I will be king" (1 Kgs. 1:5):

W. Said R. Judah said Rab, "This teaches that he tried to fit [the crown on his head], but it would not fit."

X. "And he prepares chariots and horses and fifty men to run before him" (1 Kgs. 1:5):

Y. So what was new [about princes' having retinues]?

Z. Said R. Judah said Rab, "All of them had had their spleen removed [believed to make them faster runners] and the flesh of the soles of their feet cut off [Shachter, p. 115, n. 12: so that they might be fleet of foot and impervious to briars and thorns]."

2:4J-N

J. "He should not multiply horses to himself" (Deut. 17:16) – only enough for his chariot.

K. "Neither shall he greatly multiply to himself silver and gold" (Deut. 17:16) – only enough to pay his army.

L. "And he writes out a scroll of the Torah for himself" (Deut. 17:17)

M. When he goes to war, he takes it out with him; when he comes back, he brings it back with him; when he is in session in court, it is with him; when he is reclining, it is before him,

N. as it is said, "And it shall be with him, and he shall read in it all the days of his life" (Deut. 17:19).

I

A. Our rabbis have taught on Tannaite authority:

B. "He shall not multiply horses to himself" (Deut. 17:16).

C. Is it possible to suppose that [he may not possess] even sufficient animals for his chariots and horsemen?

D. Scripture says, "To himself," meaning, for his own use he does not multiply them, but he does have a multitude for his chariots and horsemen.

E. How shall I explain the use of the words "horses" [rather than his horses]?

F. This refers to horses that remain idle.

G. How do we know that even a single horse that remains idle violates the commandment not to multiply horses?

H. Scripture states, *"That he should multiply a horse"* (Deut. 17:16).

I. But if the rule is that even a single horse that is idle falls under the prohibition against not multiplying horses, why does Scripture speak of horses in the plural as well?

J. It is to indicate that should one violate the rule, he is liable for violating a negative commandment on account of each horse.

K. [To review:] The basic consideration, then, is the fact that the All-Merciful has written the word "for himself." Had it not done so, might we have supposed that even the number sufficient for his chariots and horsemen he may not possess? [Surely not, since the king has to have an army.]

L. No, it was necessary to make that specification ["to himself"] to allow the king to have a large number [of horses in his army].

II

A. *"Neither shall he greatly multiply to himself silver and gold"* (Deut. 17:16) – only enough to pay his army [M. 2:4K]:

B. Our rabbis have taught on Tannaite authority:

C. *"Neither shall he greatly multiply to himself silver and gold"* (Deut. 17:16):

D. Might one suppose that the prohibition covers even enough to pay his army?

E. Scripture says, "To himself" – to himself he may not multiply silver and gold, but he may multiply silver and gold sufficient to pay his army.

F. [To review:] The reason therefore appears to be that the All-Merciful has written "to himself." Had it not written "to himself," should I have supposed that even sufficient funds to pay his army he may not collect?

G. No, it was necessary to include the exclusionary reference, to allow for a large budget.

H. Now if you maintain that the word "to himself" serves an exegetical purpose, how will you explain the equivalent usage in *"He shall not multiply wives to himself"* (Deut. 17:16)? It serves to exclude from the rule ordinary people, [who may have any number of wives].

III

A. R. Judah contrasted verses as follows: "It is written, *'And Solomon had forty thousand stalls of horses for his chariots'* (1 Kgs. 5:6), and elsewhere, *'And Solomon had four thousand stalls for horses and chariots'* (2 Chr. 9:25).

B. "How so? If he had forty thousand stables, each one of them had four thousand horse stalls, and if he had four thousand stables, each one of them had forty thousand horse stalls."

C. R. Isaac contrasted verses as follows: "It is written, *'Silver was nothing accounted for in the days of Solomon'* (1 Kgs. 10:21), and it is written,

'And the king made silver to be in Jerusalem as plentiful as stones' (1 Kgs. 27:3), [so silver did have some value].

D.   "There is no contradiction. The former verse refers to the time before Solomon married the daughter of Pharaoh, the latter verse refers to the time after he married the daughter of Pharaoh."

E.   Said R. Isaac, "When Solomon married the daughter of Pharaoh, Gabriel came down and stuck a reed in the sea, and a sandbank gathered around it, on which the great city of Rome was built."

F.   And said R. Isaac, "On what account were the reasons behind rules of the Torah not revealed? Because two verses of Scripture contain an account of the reasons [behind them], and the greatest one in the world [Solomon] stumbled in them.

G.   "It is written, 'He shall not multiply wives to himself' (Deut. 17:17: 'That his heart not turn away'), and Solomon said, 'I shall have many wives, but my heart will not turn away.'

H.   "And it is written, 'When Solomon was old, his wives turned away his heart' (1 Kgs. 11:4).

I.   "And it is written, 'He shall not multiply to himself horses' (Deut. 17:17: 'so as not to bring the people back to Egypt') and Solomon said, 'I will have many horses, but I will not bring the Israelites back to Egypt.'

J.   "And it is written, 'And a chariot came up and went out of Egypt for six hundred shekels of silver' (1 Kgs. 10:29)."

IV

A.   "And he writes out a scroll of the Torah for himself" (Deut. 17:17) [M. 2:4L]:

B.   It has been taught on Tannaite authority:

C.   But that is one the condition that he not take credit for one made by his ancestors.

D.   Said Rabbah, "Even though one's fathers have left him a scroll of the Torah, it is his religious duty to write one for himself, as it is said, 'Now therefore write you this song for yourself' (Deut. 31:19)."

E.   Abayye objected [citing a Tannaite teaching], "And the king writes a scroll of the Torah for himself, so that he should not take credit for one made by his ancestors. That applies to a king, not to an ordinary person."

F.   No, it was necessary to indicate that he should have two scrolls of the Torah.

G.   So it has been taught on Tannaite authority:

H.   "And he shall write for himself the repetition of this Torah" (Deut. 17:18):

I.   He writes for himself two scrolls of the Torah, one that goes out and comes in with him, and one that remains in his treasury.

J.   The one that goes out and comes in with him does not, in point of fact, go in with him to the bath house or to the privy, for it is said, "And it shall be with him and he shall read in it" (Deut. 17:19) – thus referring to places in which it is proper to read in it [T. San. 4:8F, cf. 4:7I].

V

A. Said Mar Zutra, and some say Mar Uqba, "In the beginning the Torah was given to Israel in Hebrew writing and in the Holy Language [of Hebrew]. Then it was given to them in the time of Ezra in Assyrian writing and in the Aramaic language. The Israelites chose for themselves Assyrian letters and the Holy Language and they left for common folk Hebrew letters and the Aramaic language."

B. Who are the common folk?

C. Said R. Hisda, "The Samaritans."

D. What is "the Hebrew writing"?

E. Said R. Hisda, "The Libunaah-script."

VI

A. It has been taught on Tannaite authority:

B. R. Yose says, "Ezra was worthy for the Torah to have been given by him, had not Moses come before him.

C. "Concerning Moses 'going up' is stated, and concerning Ezra 'going up' is stated.

D. "Concerning Moses 'going up' is stated, as it is said, 'And Moses went up to God' (Ex. 19:3).

E. "And concerning Ezra, 'going up' is stated, as it is written, 'And he, Ezra, went up from Babylonia' (Ezra 7:6).

F. "Just as in the case of 'going up' mentioned in connection with Moses, he taught Torah to Israel, as it is said, 'And the Lord commanded me at that time to teach you statutes and judgments' (Deut. 4:14),

G. "[so in the case of 'going up' mentioned in connection with Ezra, he taught Torah to Israel,] as it is said, 'For Ezra had prepared his heart to expound the law of the Lord and to do it and to teach in Israel statutes and judgments' (Ezra 7:10)"

H. And even though the Torah was not given through [Ezra], the script was changed through him.

I. For it is said, [22A] "And the writing of the letter was written in the Aramaic character and interpreted in the Aramaic tongue" (Ezra 4:7).

J. [T. adds:] Just as its interpretation was in Aramaic, so its writing was in Aramaic.

K. And it says, "But they could not read the writing, nor make known to the king the interpretation thereof" (Dan. 5:8) –

L. [T. adds:] this teaches that on that day it was given [and not before].

M. And it says, "And he shall write a copy of this law" (Deut. 17:18) – a Torah which is destined to be changed.

N. And why was [the language] called Assyrian? Because it came up with them from Assyria.

O. It has been taught on Tannaite authority:

Rabbi says, "In Assyrian writing the Torah was first given to Israel, and when they sinned, it was changed to Roas.

P. "But when they repented [T: attained merit in the time of Ezra], Assyrian returned to them, as it is said, *'Turn you to the stronghold, you prisoners of hope, even today do I declare that I will bring back the change unto you'* (Zech. 9:12)" [T. San. 4:7L-Y].

Q. Why is it called "Assyrian"? Because its script is upright [a play on the consonants shared by the words 'Assyrian' and 'upright'].

R. R. Simeon b. Eleazar says in the name of R. Eleazar b. Parta, who spoke in the name of R. Eleazar of Modim, "In the present kind of writing [the Torah] never changed in any way, it says, *'The hooks (vavs) of the pillars'* (Ex. 27:10) – 'vavs' that are written like pillars. Just as pillars do not change, so 'vavs' do not change.

S. "And it says, *'And unto the Jews according to their writing and language'* (Est. 8:9) – Just as their language has not changed, so their writing has not changed.

T. [T. inserts here:]   "And why is it called Assyrian (ashur)? Because they are upright (meusharim) in their manner of shaping letters."]

U. If so, how shall I interpret, *"And he shall write for himself a copy of this law"* (Deut. 17:17)?

V. [This teaches that he writes for himself] two Torahs, one which comes in with him and goes out with him, and one which he leaves in his treasury [T. San. 4:8A-E].

W. As to the one that is to go out and come in with him, he makes it in the form of an amulet and ties it on to his arm, as it is said, *"I have set God always before me"* (Ps. 16:8).

X. As to the other [who does not think the writing was changed by deducing that fact from the use of the word "a copy of this Torah"], how does he treat the verse, "I have set God always before me"?

Y. He interprets that verse in accord with what R. Hannah bar Bizna said.

Z. For R. Hannah bar Bizna said R. Simeon the Pious said, "He who prays has to see himself as if the Presence of God is before him, as it is said, *'I have set God always before me'* (Ps. 16:8)."

AA. Now, from the viewpoint of R. Simeon, who takes the view that the script did not change, what is the meaning of the statement, *"They could not read the writing nor make known to the king the interpretation thereof"* (Dan. 5:8)?

BB. Said Rab, "The passage was written in Gematria [Shachter, p. 121, n. 4: either a cryptograph which gives, instead of the intended words, its numerical value, or a cipher produced by the permutation of letters, as in this case]: YTT YTT ADK PWGHMT. How did he interpret it to them? [Shachter, p. 121, n. 6: By interchanging the letters of the alphabet, the first with the last, the second with the one before the last, the Hebrew then reads:] Mene, Mene, Tekel, Upharsin: *'Mene, God has numbered your kingdom and brought it to an end. Tekel, you are weighed in the balances and are found wanting. Peres, your kingdom is divided and given to the Medes and the Persians'* (Dan. 5:8ff.)."

CC. Samuel said, [Shachter, p. 121, n. 7: The original words were written vertically, not horizontally, thus:] MMTWS, NNKPY, AALRN."

DD. R. Yohanan said, "[From left to right, thus] ANM ANM LKT NYSRPW."

EE. R. Ashi says, "It was written in such a way that [Shachter, p. 122, n. 2: Daniel shifted the second letter of each word to the beginning:] NMA NMA KTL PWRSYN."

2:5

A. [Others may] not ride on his horse, sit on his throne, handle his sceptre.

B. And [others may] not watch him while he is getting a haircut, or while he is nude, or in the bath-house,

C. since it is said, *"You shall surely set him as king over you"* (Deut. 17:15) – that reverence for him will be upon you.

I

A. Said R. Jacob said R. Yohanan, "Abishag would have been permitted to be married to Solomon, but was forbidden to be married to Adonijah.

B. "She would have been permitted to Solomon, because he was king, and the king is permitted to make use of the sceptre of [a former] king.

C. "But she was forbidden to Adonijah, for he was an ordinary person."

II

A. And what is the story of Abishag?

B. It is written, *"King David was old, stricken in years... His servants said to him, Let there be sought..."* And it is written, *"They sought for him a pretty girl..."* and it is written, *"And the girl was very fair, and she became a companion to the king and ministered to him"* (1 Kgs. 1:1-5).

C. She said to him, "Let's get married."

D. He said to her, "You are forbidden to me."

E. She said to him, "When the thief fears for his life, he seizes virtue. You make an excuse to hide your impotence."

F. He said to them, "Call Bath Sheba to me."

G. And it is written, *"And Bath Sheba went into the king to the chamber"* (1 Kgs. 1:15).

H. Said R. Judah said Rab, "At that time [having had sexual relations with David] Bath Sheba wiped herself with thirteen cloths [to show that he was hardly impotent, contrary to Abishag's accusation]."

I. Said R. Shemen bar Abba, "Come and take note of how difficult is an act of divorce.

J. "For lo, they permitted King David to be alone [with the woman], but they did not permit him to divorce [one of his other wives]."

III

A. Said R. Eliezer, "Whoever divorces his first wife – even the altar weeps tears on that account, for it is said, *'And this further did you do, you cover the altar of the Lord with tears, with weeping and with sighing, in so much that he regards not the offering any more, nor receives it with good will at your hand'* (Mal. 2:13). And it is written, *'Yet you say,*

Why? Because the Lord has been witness between you and the wife of your youth, against whom you have dealt treacherously, though she is your companion and the wife of your covenant' (Mal. 2:14)."

IV

A. Said R. Yohanan, and some say, R. Eleazar, "A man's wife dies only if people ask for money from him and he does not have it, as it is said, *'If you have not wherewith to pay, why should he take away the bed from under you'* (Prov. 22:27)."

B. And R. Yohanan said, "Any man whose first wife dies is as if the Temple was destroyed in his day.

C. "For it is said, *'Son of man, behold I take away from you the desire of your eyes with a stroke, yet you shall not make lamentation nor weep, neither shall your tears run down.'* And it is written, *'And I spoke to the people in the morning, and at evening my wife died.'* And it is written, *'Behold I will profane my sanctuary, the pride of your power, the desire of your eyes'* (Ez. 24:16-18)."

D. Said R. Alexandri, "For every man whose wife dies in his life time the world grows dark, as it is said, *'The light shall be dark because of his tent and his lamp over him shall be put out'* (Job 18:6)."

E. R. Yose bar Hanina said, "His steps grew short, as it is said, *'The steps of his strength shall be straightened'* (Job 18:7)."

F. R. Abbahu said, "His good sense fails, as it is said, *'And his own counsel shall cast him down'* (Job 18:7)."

V

A. Said Rabbah bar bar Hannah said R. Yohanan, "And it is as difficult to match people up as it is to split the Red Sea, as it is said, *'God sets the solitary in families, he brings prisoners into prosperity'* (Ps. 68:7)."

B. Is that really the accepted view? And did not Rab Judah say Rab said, "Forty days prior to the formation of the foetus, an echo goes forth and proclaims, 'The daughter of Mr. So-and-so is assigned to Mr. Such-and-such, [the house of Mr. So-and-so is assigned to Mr. Such-and-such, the field of Mr. So-and-so is assigned to Mr. Such-and-such.'"]

C. There is no contradiction between the implications of the cited views. The former refers to the first marriage, the latter to the second.

VI

A. Said R. Samuel bar Nahman, "Everything can be replaced except for the wife of one's youth,

B. "as it is said, *'And a wife of one's youth, can she be rejected?'* (Is. 54:6)."

VII

A. R. Judah repeated on Tannaite authority to his son, R. Isaac, "A man finds true serenity only with his first wife, as it is said, *'Let your fountain be blessed and have joy of the wife of [22B] your youth'* (Prov. 5:18)."

B. He said to him, "Such as whom?"

C. He said to him, "Such as your mother."

D. Is this so? And did not R. Judah recite for R. Isaac, his son, the verse of Scripture, *"And I find more bitter than death the woman whose heart is snares and nets"* (Qoh. 7:26)?

E. And he said to him, "Such as whom?"

F. He said to him, "Such as your mother."

G. She was easy to anger but easy to appease with a good word.

VIII

A. Said R. Samuel bar Onia in the name of Rab, "A woman is unformed, and she makes a covenant only with him who turns her into a utensil,

B. "as it is said, *'For your maker is your husband, the Lord of hosts is his name'* (Is. 54:5)."

C. It has been taught on Tannaite authority:

D. A man dies only for his wife, and a woman dies only for her husband.

E. A man dies only for his wife, as it is said, *"And Elimelech, Naomi's husband, died"* (Ruth 1:3).

F. And a woman dies only for her husband, as it is said, *"And as for me, when I came from Padan, Rachel died for me"* (Gen. 48:7).

IX

A. *And others may not watch him [while he is getting a haircut] [M. 2:5B]:*

B. Our rabbis have taught on Tannaite authority:

C. A king gets a haircut every day, a high priest on Fridays, an ordinary priest once in thirty days.

D. "A king gets a haircut every day," as it is said, *"Your eyes shall see the king in his beauty"* (Is. 33:17).

E. "A high priest on Fridays:" Said R. Samuel bar Nahman said R. Yohanan, "Since the priestly watches change [each Friday]."

F. "An ordinary priest once in thirty days:" because it is written, *"Neither shall they shave their heads nor allow their locks to grow, they shall only poll their heads"* (Ez. 44:20).

G. We establish an analogy on the basis of the use of the word "allow their locks to grow" both here and in regard to the Nazirite.

H. Here it is written, *"They shall not let their locks grow"* (Ez. 44:20) and there it is said, *"He shall let the locks of the hair of his head grow long"* (Num. 6:5).

I. Just as in the latter context, it is a matter of thirty days, so here it is a matter of thirty days.

J. So too we have learned [M. Naz. 1:3A]:

K. *A pledge of Naziriteship not bearing a specified number of days lasts for thirty days.*

L. And how do we know it in that case?

M. Said R. Mattenah, "It is because Scripture has said, *'He will be holy'* (Num. 6:5), and the numerical value of the letters for the word 'will be' is thirty."

N. Said R. Pappa to Abayye, "May I propose that it means they should not let their hair grow long [for a full month] [so Shachter]?"

O. He said to him, "If it were written, 'They shall not let their hair grow long,' it would have been as you say. But now that it is written, *'They*

may not let their locks grow long,' the sense is, they may let it become
long, but not too long."

X

A. If that is the case, then the rule should apply now, just as does the rule governing excessive use of wine [by priests].

B. Just as in the case of wine, it was at the time that one came to the Temple that it was forbidden, but when one did not come to the Temple, it was permitted, so in the case of those who let the hair grow long, when one can come to the Temple it is forbidden, but when one cannot come to the Temple, it should be permitted.

C. But is it the case that wine is permitted [even now] when it is not possible to come to the Temple?

D. And has it not been taught on Tannaite authority:

E. Rabbi says, "I maintain that priests may not drink wine at any time, but what can I do? For the calamity that has overcome them [in the destruction of the Temple] also is their remedy [since they can drink wine until the Temple is rebuilt]."

F. And Abayye said, "In accord with whose view do priests drink wine these days? It is in accord with the view of Rabbi."

G. That leaves the inferences that, from the viewpoint of rabbis, they are forbidden to drink wine.

H. What is the reason in that special case? It is because of the hope that the Temple will be rebuilt quickly, so that we shall require a priest who is in shape to participate in the Temple cult, and [if priests are drinking wine routinely] such a one will not be available.

I. But can not the same consideration apply here too, namely, we should require a priest who is in shape to participate in the Temple cult [and if the priests let their hair grow long, such a one will not be available]?

J. In this case it is possible that the priest can quickly get a haircut and go into the Temple.

K. But in the other case it is possible that the priest will take a snooze and be ready to go into the Temple.

L. That is in line with R. Aha's statement, "A short walk or a little sleep take away the effects of wine."

M. But in that regard has it not been stated, Said R. Nahman said Rabbah bar Abbuha, "That statement applies to one who has drunk no more than a quarter-log of wine, but if someone has drunk more than a quarter-log, a walk makes him all the more tired, and sleep will cause all the more drunkenness."

N. R. Ashi said, "Those priests who are drunk defile the sacred service, so the rabbis made a decree against priests' drinking wine.

O. "Those whose hair is too long do not defile the service, so the rabbis made no decree against that condition."

P. An objection was raised:

Q. **The following priests are subject to the death-penalty [if they participate in the cult]: those who have excessively long hair and those who are drunk [T. Ker. 1:5C].**

R. Now as to the drunk ones, that is in line with the verse of Scripture, *"Drink no wine or strong drink, you or your sons with you, so that you do not die"* (Lev. 10:9).

S. But what is the proof text for those with excessively long hair?

T. The ones who are drunk are comparable to the ones with long hair.

U. It is written, *"Neither shall they shave their heads nor let their locks grow long,"* followed by, *"Neither shall they drink wine"* (Lev. 10:9).

V. Just as drunkenness [during the sacred service] is subject to the death-penalty, so participating in the rite with excessively long hair likewise is subject to the death-penalty.

W. And on the same basis: Just as priests who are drunk desecrate the sacred service, so priests with excessively long hair desecrate the sacred service.

X. That is indeed a question.

XI

A. Said Rabina to R. Ashi, "As to this teaching [that priests whose hair is too long should not officiate and are subject to the death-penalty if they do], before Ezekiel came along, who stated it?"

B. [The reply of Ashi:] "And in accord with your reasoning [that there should have been a source prior to Ezekiel], what do you make of what R. Hisda said?

C. "[R. Hisda said] This matter we did not learn from the Torah of Moses, until Ezekiel came along and taught it to us:

D. *""No alien, uncircumcised in heart and uncircumcised in flesh shall enter my sanctuary to serve me"* (Ez. 44:9).

E. "'Now, before Ezekiel came along, who taught it?'

F. "But it was learned as a tradition, and Ezekiel came along and supplied scriptural support for the tradition, and here too, it was a tradition, and Ezekiel came along and supplied a scriptural basis for it."

G. What is the sense of the statement, *"They shall only poll their heads"* (Ez. 44:20)?

H. It was taught by a Tannaite authority: "Hair cut in the Julian style."

I. And what is that style?

J. Said R. Judah said Samuel, "An unusual hair cut."

K. What is it like?

L. Said R. Ashi, "[Shachter, p. 128:]   The ends of one row of hair lie alongside the roots of the next."

M. They asked Rabbi, "What sort of haircut did the high priest get?"

N. He said to them, "Go and look at the haircut of [my son-in-law,] the son of Eleasa."

O. It has been taught along these lines on Tannaite authority:

P. Rabbi says, "It is not for nothing that the son of Eleasa spent so much money for a haircut, but so that he may show what sort of haircut a high priest got."

Index

Harkinas 232

hermeneutics 4, 7, 9, 11, 28, 33, 147, 148, 151, 158

Herr 36, 53, 91

Hezekiah 175, 187, 224, 257, 260, 261, 275

Hillel 161-169, 171-173, 177-179, 181-183, 185, 188, 196, 197, 229, 231, 233, 252

Hisda 51, 187, 210, 282, 287, 293

history 7, 9, 13, 15, 20, 22-28, 38, 80, 86, 88, 89, 91, 102, 104, 112, 135, 136, 140, 157, 191-193, 205, 225

Hiyya 169, 170, 175, 177, 178, 180, 186, 188, 189, 209, 219, 220, 246, 250, 259

Huna 170, 172, 174, 178, 182, 183, 186, 189, 209, 210, 220, 222, 244, 248, 251, 258

imitation 148, 152, 153

integrity 56-58, 70, 74, 75, 80-82, 84, 104, 105, 147, 253

interlocking 9, 11, 28, 39, 40, 55, 56, 60, 75, 79, 80, 84, 90, 91, 118, 121, 143, 149, 157

intersection 5, 8, 27, 31, 41, 43, 47, 56, 98, 104, 149

intertextuality 4, 5, 8, 11, 20, 31, 55, 143, 147, 150-155, 157, 159

intrinsic 3-6, 12, 22, 40, 85-88, 90, 98, 104, 105, 143, 148, 149, 152, 153, 155, 157-159

Isaac 89, 170, 171, 184, 189, 207, 213, 241, 245, 247, 248, 253, 261, 262, 276, 277, 283, 285, 286, 290, 291

Ishmael 130, 178, 227, 231, 232, 235, 240, 251, 252, 260

Israelite 19, 41, 162, 164, 166, 175, 177, 184-186, 188, 200, 203, 216-218, 228, 271, 283

Jacob 53, 89, 91, 170, 174, 175, 209, 218, 253, 256, 274, 278, 289

John 13, 39

Joseph 51, 183, 257, 267, 271, 274, 275, 282

Joshua 50, 111, 112, 168, 170, 179, 195-198, 203, 221-223, 229, 231, 232, 235, 246, 248, 250, 253, 258, 272, 273, 275, 278, 283

Joshua b. Levi 50, 168, 170, 221, 222, 248, 250, 278

Joshua b. Qorha 272

Josiah 238, 271

Judah 51, 130, 163, 165, 168, 172, 173, 175, 176, 179, 180, 183, 185-187, 189, 193-197, 200-202, 205, 207-209, 211-214, 216, 220, 228, 230, 235, 236, 245, 249, 252, 255-257, 259, 260, 265, 266, 270, 272, 274-276, 278, 279, 281-285, 289-291, 293

Judah bar Simon 245

Judaism 5-9, 11-13, 15-20, 22-25, 28, 31, 53, 57, 59, 60, 74, 81, 83, 91, 99, 103-105, 118, 121, 134, 147, 148, 155-157, 159, 193, 205, 243, 253, 265

Kahana 18, 22, 50, 51, 53, 71, 72, 79, 80, 83, 84, 91, 170, 207, 208, 216, 221, 224, 248, 257, 261, 282

Kapstein 53, 79, 91

Kings 13, 26, 200-202, 204, 221, 223, 224, 271

Leviticus 17, 18, 22, 27, 55-62, 64, 66, 68, 70-75, 78-85, 90, 91, 103, 105, 113, 115-118, 121, 131-137, 140-143, 148, 152, 189, 225, 253

Leviticus Rabbah 17, 18, 22, 27, 55-62, 66, 68, 70-75, 78-85, 90, 91, 103, 105, 115, 117, 118, 121, 131-137, 140-143, 148, 152, 253

library 5, 15, 57, 91, 98, 104, 143, 155, 156

Lieberman 162-166, 259

logic 3, 4, 8, 12, 25, 53, 69, 84-88, 90, 91, 97, 102-104, 121-125, 127, 128, 130, 133, 135, 147, 158, 237-240

Luke 31, 33, 36, 37, 39, 43, 96

Mar Zutra 188, 287

Mark 11, 23, 31-33, 35, 36, 39, 41, 43, 80, 96, 116, 148, 151, 157

Matthew 11, 31-33, 35-37, 39, 41, 43, 96

Meir 169, 171, 179, 183, 193, 205, 208, 209, 229, 232, 253, 255, 265, 270

Melammed 53, 91

Merab 272, 273

metaphor 9, 10, 15, 24-28, 31-35, 38, 57, 96, 98, 143, 149

metatextuality 151

Michael 247

Michal 51, 216, 217, 272, 273, 282

miscellany 57, 59, 64, 75, 82

Mishnah 6, 13, 15-19, 22, 24, 26-28, 33-50, 52, 53, 56-58, 60, 70, 71, 85, 86, 91, 95, 99, 102, 103, 108-114, 116-118, 121, 123,

125-130, 132, 133, 135-142, 148, 151, 152, 156, 161, 162, 164, 166, 167, 169, 171, 172, 174, 177, 179, 191-193, 208, 209, 211, 212, 258

Morgan 150, 152

Nahman 184, 189, 218, 260, 275, 277, 290-292

Nehorai 189, 201, 279

Numbers 13, 17, 20, 35, 66, 84-91, 103, 113-118, 121, 124, 129, 130, 133, 135-137, 139, 141-143, 148, 234

Oral Torah 6, 8, 15, 107

originality 148, 152, 153

Oshaia 176-178, 182, 243

Pesiqta de R. Kahana 18, 22, 71, 72, 79, 80, 83, 84, 91

philology 157

piety 19, 154

proof-texts 5, 50-53, 63, 64, 71, 77, 78, 99, 108-114, 116, 117, 128, 138-140, 151

Q (Quelle) 11, 13, 31-33, 35-39, 41-43, 48, 50-53, 71, 72, 79-84, 149

Rab 51, 53, 91, 244, 248, 256, 275, 276, 278, 280, 282-284, 288-291

Raba 276, 277, 283

Rabbah 17, 18, 22, 27, 47, 55-62, 66, 68, 70-75, 78-85, 88-91, 103, 105, 114, 115, 117, 118, 121, 130-137, 139-143, 148, 152, 188, 189, 243, 253, 286, 290, 292

Rabbah bar Abbuha 292

Rabbi 6, 19-22, 58, 60, 91, 99, 101, 123, 126, 133, 156, 167, 170, 177, 178, 189, 196-198,

203, 209, 210, 212, 213, 220, 223, 224, 236, 237, 259, 260, 281, 288, 292, 293

Rabin 277

Rabina 51, 282, 293

Rava 183, 187

Resh Laqish 188

rhetoric 3, 4, 8, 25, 53, 57-59, 61, 69, 84, 85, 88, 96, 97, 102, 104, 121, 123-127, 133, 135, 147

Samaritan 43, 162, 166, 177, 224, 263

Samuel 168, 170, 173, 174, 176, 177, 189, 201, 207, 211, 212, 214, 217-219, 248, 260, 274, 275, 278-280, 289-291, 293

Sanhedrin 40-51, 108-112, 116, 117, 124-128, 132, 138, 140, 192, 193, 204, 206, 217, 222, 264, 265, 268

Saul 51, 194, 198, 204, 212, 213, 216, 217, 266, 273, 276, 277, 282

Schiffman 9-12, 28, 39, 55-57, 60, 71, 84, 96, 143, 147-149, 154, 157, 158

scrapbook 57, 75, 82, 90, 91

Scripture 2, 6-8, 11, 12, 15-19, 22, 27, 38-40, 43-46, 49, 50, 52, 53, 56, 59, 64, 71, 72, 78, 85-89, 99-102, 107-118, 121, 125, 126, 128-132, 134-136, 138-141, 143, 151-153, 158, 174, 178, 189, 193, 200, 212, 215, 218, 219, 225-232, 234-242, 244, 246-248, 251-257, 260, 273-276, 279-282, 291, 292

Shammai 161-169, 171-173, 177-183, 185, 187, 188, 196, 197, 252

Sheba 112, 138, 213, 289

Shebna 63, 64, 257, 259-261

Sifra 13, 17, 22, 27, 35, 36, 57, 71, 84, 85, 90, 91, 103, 113-118, 121, 129, 130, 133, 135-137, 139, 141-143, 148, 152, 191, 225

Sifré 13, 17, 85, 86, 88-91, 103, 113-118, 121, 129, 130, 133, 135-137, 139, 141-143, 148, 234

Simeon 130, 169, 171, 173, 175, 195-198, 203, 206-209, 220-222, 224, 233, 236, 242, 251-253, 259, 263, 266, 271, 272, 277, 278, 280, 281, 284, 288

Simeon b. Gamaliel 277, 278

Simeon b. Laqish 169, 175, 206, 207, 224, 259, 266, 271, 280

Simeon b. Shetah 271, 272

Simeon the Righteous 195

Simon 35, 175, 245, 250

Smith 32, 34-37, 41, 52, 53, 71, 82-84, 91

Stock 155, 156, 159

symmetrical 8

synoptic 9-11, 13, 24, 26, 28, 31-39, 41-45, 50, 52, 53, 55, 57, 58, 71, 79, 81-83, 96, 149

system 7, 9, 15, 16, 19, 23, 28, 33, 55, 82, 148-150, 153, 156-159, 192, 193

Talmud 15, 16, 19, 49, 53, 83, 91, 129, 134, 137, 159, 204, 205, 264

Tarfon 198

taxonomy 24-26, 58, 66, 96, 102, 104, 107, 117, 118, 129, 136, 137, 141, 159, 205 text 4, 5, 8-10, 13, 25, 26, 28, 31-33, 37-39, 41, 42, 47, 52, 55-57, 59, 60, 63, 70, 79, 80, 82, 85, 91, 95, 101, 102, 108, 123, 128, 129, 132, 136, 142, 143, 148-158, 259, 268, 293

textual community 4-7, 15, 91, 98, 143, 144, 153, 155-157

textuality 31, 55, 57, 90

theology 4, 13, 60, 101, 104, 135, 148, 157, 158

topic 3, 4, 8, 18, 25, 44, 50, 51, 53, 69, 84, 85, 88, 96, 97, 100-102, 104, 112, 113, 116, 126, 134, 135, 137, 138, 140, 250

Torah 5, 6, 8, 9, 12, 15-17, 19, 25, 32, 40, 60, 82, 87-89, 91, 95, 99, 103, 107, 111, 130, 133, 134, 143, 154, 156-158, 186, 193, 195-199, 202, 203, 207, 210, 220-223, 225, 235, 241, 243, 244, 246-252, 271, 274, 275, 284, 286-288, 293

Tosefta 13, 16, 18, 22, 24, 26-28, 33, 35-49, 52, 53, 56, 57, 86, 91, 95, 103, 110, 111, 116-118, 121, 127, 128, 133, 135, 137, 138, 140-142, 151-153, 161, 162, 164, 192, 193, 199, 211, 266

Ulla 187, 277

uncleanness 124, 169, 171, 180, 182, 192, 209, 225, 226, 228-231, 233, 234, 237-242, 267, 278

Written Torah 6, 15, 17, 32, 91, 107

Yannai 271

Yerushalmi 16, 18, 22, 24, 26-28, 34, 38, 39, 41-43, 45-50, 52, 53, 56, 57, 60, 71, 73, 75, 78-80, 83, 84, 95, 103, 112, 113, 116-118, 121, 124, 128-130, 133, 135, 137, 138, 140-143, 152, 153, 161, 166, 191, 204, 205

Yohanan 127, 168, 169, 174-177, 182, 183, 186, 188, 195-197, 207, 208, 210, 213, 218, 223, 224, 246, 247, 252, 255, 256, 274, 275, 278, 284, 289-291